W9-CCD-055

# Rebels and Mafiosi

# Rebels & Mafiosi

## Death in a Sicilian Landscape

## JAMES FENTRESS

*Cornell University Press*

ITHACA AND LONDON

First published 2000 by Cornell University Press

Printed in the United States of America

Library of Congress Cataloging-in-Publication
Data

Fentress, James
Rebels and mafiosi : death in a Sicilian landscape /
James Fentress.
p. cm.
ISBN 0-8014-3539-0 (cloth)
1. Mafia—Italy—Sicily—History.  2. Revolutions—Italy—Sicily—History—19th century.
3. Government, Resistance to—Italy—Sicily—
History—19th century.  4. Sicily (Italy)—Social
conditions.  5. Crime—Italy—Sicily—History.
HV6453.I83 M3415 2000
364.1'06'09458—dc21        99-055041

Cloth printing
10  9  8  7  6  5  4  3  2  1

# Contents

# Illustrations and Maps

# Acknowledgments

This book was an adventure that I could never have undertaken on my own. There is not enough room to thank all the friends who have helped me along the way or to acknowledge more than a fraction of my debts. Any rendering of accounts must start at Oxford, with John Campbell and Denis Mack Smith, who patiently withstood my enthusiasms while pointing out my many shortcomings. I am pleased that my friendship with both of them continued after I left the university, and I am particularly grateful to Denis Mack Smith, who has continued to help me and to play the role of an emeritus supervisor. I include him among those who had the patience and kindness to read and criticize earlier chapters and drafts. On this score, I especially thank Chris Wickham, Lisa Fentress, Jeremy Johns, and Henner Hess as well. I am well aware that they are all relieved that this book is finally seeing the light of day.

My greatest debts, however, are in Sicily. I wish to express my gratitude to the late Professor Gaetano Falzone, who kindly made available to me the collections of the Pitré Museum in Palermo. I also thank Professor Nino Buttita, Professor Virgilio Titone, Professor Massimo Ganci, Professor Francesco Renda, and Pompeo and Gigi Colajanni for taking time to answer my questions. I am particularly grateful to Professor Francesco Brancato, with whom I had a number of extremely rewarding discussions. Marisa Famà and Niel Walker were never-failing sources of friendship, hospitality, and cheer. I feel privileged to have known Marcello Cimino and his wife, Giuliana Saladino, and like so many others in Palermo, mourn his passing. There is a saying that "in Palermo, you need a baron." I can testify that the assistance of a baroness is even more valuable. So it is to my friend and sometime *compagna di ventura*, Renata Pucci di Benisichi, professor of Palermitology *honoris causa*, that I owe my final and greatest thanks.

The maps are reproduced from G. M. Trevelyan, *Garibaldi and the Thousand* (London: Longmans, 1909).

JAMES FENTRESS

Rome

# Rebels and Mafiosi

# Introduction

In the spring of 1865 the prefect of Palermo was growing alarmed. Five years earlier, Garibaldi and his Red Shirts had fought their way into Palermo, there to be welcomed as deliverers. In the plebiscite held in October of the same year, Sicilians had overwhelmingly voted to become part of the newly united Italian nation under the king of Piedmont. Yet now, in 1865, this jubilation had evaporated, and the prefect felt it his grave duty to inform his government that "public spirit" in Sicily's capital city was being gravely troubled by "a deep and prolonged misunderstanding between the Country and Authority." It was the sort of misunderstanding, he continued darkly, that "was helping to make it possible for the so-called Maffia or delinquent association to grow in audacity."[1]

Like most leading officials of the new Italian state, the prefect of Palermo, Count Gualterio, was Piedmontese. Sicily was unfamiliar territory for him. Its architecture, its food, and its politics were as exotic to him as its incomprehensible dialect. As for this "so-called Maffia," Gualterio plainly assumed that no one in the North had ever heard of such a thing before. The term was a new one, and Gualterio hastened to provide a gloss. Still, it is not clear that he knew any better himself; for his definition, "associazione malandrinesca," is not very helpful. On the one hand, he seems to have been thinking of a hooligan or disruptive element in the population in and around Palermo. Yet, on the other, he also seems to have imagined that this troublemaking element constituted a sort of natural-born brotherhood of the evilly disposed. It was a fraternity of the enemies to law and order, including not so much professional criminals as all those who, for whatever reason, were resisting the new state's efforts to impose peace and legitimate authority upon the troubled island.

Gualterio's report is the first official reference to the mafia—a surprise, for 1865 seems a late date. I had come to Sicily imagining that the mafia had originated in the island's distant past. I had been told by one eminent Sicilian historian that "mafia" represented no less than the Sicilian soul, and had read his admittedly ironic claim that by hurling rocks at Ulysses' ship and by sacrificing their children to Moloch, Cyclops and the ancient Carthaginians had shown that a "mafia spirit" had persisted in Sicily even in the time of legends. There is certainly no lack of violence in the history of the island; I was thus taken aback to discover that the earliest references to the mafia date only from the 1860s, and that they are all from the Palermo region.

This, however, is the mafia as we first meet it—in police reports and newspaper accounts, as well as in the writings of those contemporary to events. In the words of the Sicilian policeman-turned-criminologist Antonio Cutrera, writing at the end of the nineteenth century, "The true mafia, the legendary mafia, the mafia of the great criminal trials, the mafia whose great crimes aroused a terror such . . . as to give it first place in the history of Sicilian criminality," arose in the fertile garden suburbs around Palermo—the Conca d'Oro, or Golden Shell. Furthermore, it was a recent arrival. Cutrera regarded it as "indubitable" that the mafia had emerged early in the century among the small-holders and tenants of the Conca d'Oro who had prospered by planting orange and lemon groves for export.[2]

Was it any coincidence that the mafia grew in a time of violent revolution? Neither Gualterio nor Cutrera thought so. In his 1865 report, Gualterio went on to explain how the mafia had arisen during the 1848 and 1860 revolutions in Palermo. For nineteenth-century Sicilians, mafia and revolution went together.

Why should there be a relation between revolution and crime? Political revolutions are often violent upheavals. They are rents in the fabric of order, political breakdowns where criminality may flourish unchecked. Periods of revolution may thus be periods of lawlessness and crime. But is this the only way that revolution goes with crime?

According to a very old school of political thought, subjects simply do not have the right to rebel against their legitimate sovereigns. Sovereignty, according to this way of thinking, does not depend on the democratically expressed will of the people, but rather upon a natural or divine order. Sovereigns serve as the fountainhead of justice, as the source of law, and as the protector of the rights of their subjects. But among the rights that sovereigns may grant their people can never be the right of rebellion, for this would constitute a denial of the sovereigns' own sovereignty and thus be a contradiction in terms.

This was the view of the kings of Naples for most of the nineteenth century. They and their allies in Austria and (after 1848) papal Rome viewed Sicily's attempts to win its freedom through rebellion as nothing less than criminal acts. Their publicists and sympathizers painted Sicily's partisans as bandits and cutthroats intent only on looting and venting their blood lust. They represented the revolutionary leaders as political terrorists, and argued that Piedmont's intervention on the side of the revolution in 1860 was a thinly disguised land grab devoid of justification, either legal or moral.

This, however, is a very limited view. Over the course of the last two hundred years, the globe has been reshaped through revolutions. It is hard for a historian to regard all the republics and constitutional monarchies that resulted from them, along with their politics and their legal institutions, as nothing other than the fruits of crime. Few historians are disposed to support such a jaundiced and sterile view of the modern world, at least in a general way, and thus most accept revolution as a legitimate historical force. This is not to say that they accept each and every revolution, let alone every act that takes place during a revolution, as justified. These are quite different matters. More simply, it is to say that historians see change as a natural part of history and recognize revolution as a major force for change.

On the basis of this more tolerant view, there are at least two other ways of interpreting the outbreaks of internecine violence and crime that sometimes accompany revolution. The first way is to embrace them. Revolution, according to this view, is, or ought to be, a generalized social process. The real task of the revolution is not just to change the government at the top, but instead to change an entire social order. The wider the revolution spreads and the deeper it extends its roots into the population, the more thorough the revolution can become. A revolution that embraces an entire population from top to bottom has the opportunity to cleanse society of all its accumulated evils and injustices, and to set a new, more rational and just, order in its place.

On such a view, riots, brigandage, and acts of destructive vandalism such as crop burning are not necessarily criminal acts at all. They may instead appear as evidence that the revolution is evolving, changing, entering into a deeper phase. No longer a struggle with limited political aims, the revolution is now attaining that general social character that will permit it to pursue much wider social goals.

The second way of viewing the relation between revolution and violence is the opposite. On this view, crime and violence are neither desirable nor necessary in a revolution. Revolution is a temporary descent into illegality, a readjustment of the relations between governors and the governed often made necessary by the obstinacy, inflexibility, or sheer stupidity of certain governing classes. The aim of revolution, on this view, is to promulgate the necessary legal and political reforms and to install a new and forward-looking governing class as quickly as possible, before the revolution has a chance to transform itself into a generalized social upheaval in which lawlessness and destructive violence may flourish. Those who regard revolution in this manner regard outbreaks of popular violence in an unsympathetic light, seeing them as evidence that the revolution has indeed gotten out of hand, that criminality is spreading, and that therefore the period of revolutionary illegality must be closed as rapidly as possible by whatever means are available.

These various ways of looking at revolution and the relation between revolution and criminality are more than just abstractions. They delineate instead the contours of a real debate. For the Neapolitan government, the revolution in Sicily was, we saw, simply criminal. For the Piedmontese government, by contrast, revolution had provided the opportunity to annex Sicily and southern Italy in 1860. Piedmont was thus hardly in a position to argue that revolutions could never be justified. Nevertheless, the official Piedmontese line was still to deplore revolution in principle, only adding that, in the particular case of Sicily and southern Italy, continuing rebellion had revealed the kings of Naples as unfit rulers. In these circumstances, Piedmont claimed it had a moral duty to intervene in the south in order to prevent the revolution from spreading. When the subjects of the now defunct kingdom of Naples later voted to join the kingdom of Piedmont, now in the process of renaming itself the kingdom of Italy, the Piedmontese government could also claim that it had a further moral duty to accept the people's wishes.

In this way, Piedmont was able to profit by revolution while still claiming strict adherence to the principles of legitimacy and legality. One of the results of this somewhat convoluted foreign policy, however, was that Piedmont took a tough line with its newly acquired southern territories, moving quickly to suppress crime, brigandage, and popular violence. In one sense, this followed logically from Piedmont's claim that the persistence of rebellion and disorder in the south was what had forced it to intervene in the first place. Yet the tough line was also a consequence of a much less publicized fear. Whatever Piedmont may have ingenuously claimed to the contrary, it had for years been quietly working to foment political unrest in the kingdom of Naples. It had sown the seeds of rebellion; it had reaped the fruit; now it wanted desperately to pull the noxious plant up by its roots before it could poison its former master.

What about the people of Sicily itself? What did they think about the relation between revolution and crime? Sicilians' own views were more complex and ambiguous. Sicily was involved in a struggle for freedom during the entire first half of the nineteenth century. It had been a long, grueling, and, on occasion, very bloody struggle. It had also been, in the minds of many Sicilians, a heroic one. It was this that made it impossible for Sicilians to accept the doctrine of limited revolution quite in the way that the Piedmontese government was proposing. Sicily wanted to celebrate its revolutionary tradition, not sweep it under the rug.

This did not mean, however, that Sicilians ever wished to transform their revolution into a generalized social upheaval. Most Sicilians would have been appalled by the idea, and, indeed, the doctrine that revolution ought to have social rather than political goals was one that had very little resonance in Sicily before the 1890s. If Sicilians regarded their revolution as a generalized process at all, it was in the Mazzinian sense of a moral force that had united the island in a common political cause and provided it with a consciousness of a common political identity.

This more generous idea of revolution as a unifying moral force helping to create a collective political identity made Sicilians reluctant to view brigandage and collective violence as criminal acts. The burning of a town hall, the sacking of a rich landowner's house, the murder of police officials were all deplorable acts; but were they really criminal? Nineteenth-century Sicilians preferred to think of them rather as "revolutionary excesses," excusable expressions of the pent-up frustrations of a freedom-loving but uneducated people. Thus Sicily's more generous understanding of the notion of revolution resulted in a tolerance of public disorder far greater than that displayed by the Piedmontese government.

Nowhere were the consequences of these opposed notions of revolution clearer than in the opposed definitions of the mafia which they generated. Sicilians were aware that decades of revolutionary activity had left parts of their island in lawless turmoil. They were also aware that revolution might provide a cover under which family feuds and personal vendettas could be prosecuted. Still they were reluctant to abandon their image of revolution as a force that had unified Sicilians of all classes in a common moral enterprise. Thus Sicilians continued to assert that, whatever else he might have been, the mafioso was a true-born son of the Sicilian nation who had taken up arms against the foreign oppressor.

The Italian state took the opposite view: mafia, it argued, was simply another name for crime in Sicily. This did not mean that the state was unaware of the close connection between the revolution and the mafia. As we shall see, the new Italian state was obsessed by the fear that plotters were stirring up popular unrest in Sicily. Yet as frightened as the new state was by the specter of revolution in Sicily, it was determined never to air this fear publicly, and especially never to grant to the trouble-makers and plotters the slightest shred of political legitimacy. This meant treating the mafia and all those segments of Sicilian society that cooperated with the mafia simply as parts of an extensive criminal underworld.

Who was right? It is important to remember that the term "mafia" itself started out as Palermitan slang, where, as far as we can tell, it originally meant something like "flashy." All the other political and ideological meanings that the term later acquired were meanings that various authors and authorities assigned to it, inventing them as they went along, usually to support particular views about the relation between revolution and crime in Sicily. Thus by 1900 the word had acquired a vast range of conflicting meanings, none of which were originally there.

The real question is not about the meaning of the term but about the reality beneath this meaning. Who got that right? The answer is that for both approaches to the mafia, that of Sicily and that of the Italian state, a need for self-justification was obscuring this reality. Sicilians might well insist on associating the mafia with their sense of victimization, their struggle for freedom, and their traditions of resistance to tyranny, but this hides a fact evident to anyone who knows the island's earlier history: the mafia reflected social problems and patterns of criminal behavior far older than the particular struggle against Naples.

For the Italian state, by contrast, denying that the mafia was anything more than simple criminality became a convenient way of denying that there were segments of Sicilian society dissatisfied with the new order. This was an interpretation that avoided any number of embarrassing questions. By denying that political dissatisfaction existed, the state exempted itself from asking what its causes were. Why, if the mafia was simply criminality, were so many Sicilians willing to go along with it? A surprisingly large number of northern writers responded in terms of racial inferiority combined with historical backwardness. The mafia had been defined so as to preclude any other sort of explanation. Thus arose a doctrine of Sicilian backwardness that was used to justify martial law and the suspension of civil liberties for a people "not yet ready" for the liberties enjoyed by the North. Finally, a definition of the mafia that denied the reality of Sicilian resistance also denied to the new state any means of understanding the form that this resistance was taking. The state was thus never able to understand that the mafia was neither simply the criminal underworld nor a form of political subversion, but something quite different from either. It was rather, as later authors put it, a kingdom within the kingdom. It was a network of submerged power, an alternative structure that sometimes supplemented and sometimes substituted for the authorized and official channels of social mediation provided by the state.

Part of the intention of this book is to tell the story of the emergence of this alternative network of power in Sicily's struggle for freedom, and its development after the unification of Sicily with Piedmont in 1860. Yet even after this story has been told, even after the mysteries surrounding the origin of the mafia have been clarified as far as our sources will allow, the original problem still remains: What did crime have to do with the revolution in Sicily? What did the rebels and mafiosi have in common?

This might be taken as a moral question. Revolution, it might be argued, is, in general, a good thing, while crime is, in general, a bad thing. As long as Sicilians were struggling for their liberties, they were revolutionaries, and therefore good; when they continued this struggle after the revolution had ended, they became criminals and therefore bad. This, we shall see, was the interpretation advanced by Napoleone Colajanni at the end of the century. As attractive as it may be, it simply does not work. How could Sicilians be rebels at one point and criminals at another? Colajanni's interpretation seems to imply that the behavior of Sicilians that changed. But this is not true. Sicilians had not changed; it was rather the rules of the game that had. But who blew the whistle that ended the revolution? And—this is more important—who gave that someone the right to blow that whistle? Under the surface, Colajanni's interpretation is the same as that of the Italian state in 1860: Revolution is a good thing, but only where authorized and conducted under the supervision of the proper authorities. Revolution in any other form is simply criminality.

The real answer to the question of where the line that divided revolution from crime might lie was that, in Sicily, that line was never established. Revolution creates its own rules, and in nineteenth-century revolutionary Sicily there arose an ample space, a no-man's land in which all sorts of ambiguous social relations could develop—relations that were never precisely subversive, never precisely criminal, always somewhere in between the legal and illicit. This was the space in which the mafia grew and the space that the mafia came to dominate.

The story of the mafia cannot be understood except against the background of the revolution. We begin our own account with the four revolutions in Palermo: 1820, 1848, 1860, and 1866. We will find that the 1866 uprising marks a turning point—a point when the revolution, victorious in appearance, yet still frustrated and unsatisfied, turned in upon itself, transforming itself into the mafia.

Why did this transformation occur? Was it the fault of the new state, as Sicilians sometimes argued? Or had the struggle for liberty in Sicily been taken over by brutal and archaic forces, groups wishing to prolong the anarchy and disorder as long as they might, groups that, already by 1865, were organizing themselves to nullify the state's attempts to introduce the rule of law? The final chapters describe the mafia itself. The ground here is less familiar, and the story has had to be pieced together from police archives, trial records, contemporary journalism, and government reports. Most of these sources are obscure; many contradict one another; none of them is complete. We shall sometimes have to stop, in the manner of explorers into dark places, and shine our light into several dusky corridors before deciding which way to proceed.

The story of rebels and mafiosi is also the story of the people of Sicily. Like all stories, it must be repeated lest it be forgotten.

The historian G. M. Trevelyan describes how, in the days before the April 1860 uprising, Francesco Riso brought into Palermo "a little wooden cannon and a meager store of blunderbusses and muskets, hidden under cartloads of material for his own trade, and stored in the Terrasanta, a building annexed to the old Gancia convent." He adds: "That fine building, and the network of old, narrow and romantic streets surrounding it, remain to-day, like so much else in Palermo, exactly as they were when the Italian Revolution of 1860 began in their midst."[3] Not anymore. When Trevelyan wrote in 1907, a half-century after the events he describes took place, Sicily still seemed unchanged. Since then, change has come with a bang.

The prelude to the 1848 revolution in Palermo—the demonstration of November 1847—took place, appropriately enough, at the opera. At the time the opera house was called the Teatro Carolina, in honor of the Bourbon queen. After 1860 this name seemed inappropriate, and so it was changed to Teatro Bellini. (As such it remained in use until the 1940s, when the founder of the Sicilian Separatist Movement, Andrea Finocchiaro-Aprile, was still able to deliver his erudite views on the Sicilian constitution to the crowds from its balcony. During the 1960s, however, Teatro Bellini closed. It reopened as the Pizzeria Bellini, one of the few remaining restaurants in Palermo's increasingly dirty and degraded city center. In the 1980s, Pizzeria Bellini was closed by the health authorities.)

Palermo soon acquired new opera houses. One of the rebel redoubts in the 1866 rebellion was the large Convent of the Stigmata, located near the city's northern wall. After the revolution the convent was razed, together with the old medieval walls. The new open space was called Piazza Verdi. Where the old convent had stood, there arose one of the largest and most ornate structures in nineteenth-century Italy—the Teatro Massimo. Around its gilded frieze in massive letters was written the portentous motto "Art Renews the Peoples and Reveals Their Life: Vain Is the Pleasure of Scenes Which Do Not Aim to Prepare for the Future."[4]

The Teatro Massimo was closed for repairs in 1964. The repairs were supposed to last several months, but for over thirty years successive Palermo administrations managed to buy patronage and political support for themselves by sucking huge sums from the national government for the restoration.

The area to the north of the long-razed Porta Macqueda, the gate marking the old northern boundary of the city, is no less rich in history. It was the scene of Giovanni Corrao's entrance with his troops in 1860, of Domenico Corteggiani's hidden arsenal and munitions factory, of a rallying point for *squadre* in the 1866 uprising, and it was home to some of the most powerful mafia *cosche* in the 1870s. Today the whole zone is buried in concrete; some of the charming villas erected by the Palermitan aristocracy when the area was still parkland survive, though it is hard to make out their crumbling façades behind a half-century's grime and neglect.

There is hardly a block of stone, a street name, or an archway in the heart of this beautiful and mutilated old city that fails to hold its memories—memories of revolution and mafia. Yet like the façades themselves, crumbling with neglect, the memories are at risk of annihilation when the landscape that supports them is no longer legible. Telling the story of revolution and mafia is a step toward restoration of the landscape.

# The Setting: Sicily before the Mafia

On July 20, 1943, the first Allied convoys rolled down the Monreale road into Palermo. They were part of the force that had landed ten days earlier on Sicily's south coast in what was to remain until the Normandy invasions a year later the largest amphibious landing in military history. Eisenhower had wished to take no chances; even though the Italian army had caused him few problems in North Africa, he was worried that here, on "Italian soil," resistance might stiffen. Indeed, the Allied advance was, on occasion, resisted by northern Italian units, usually fighting alongside German battalions. Yet the bulk of the Italian forces in Sicily consisted of Sicilians, and few of them offered any sort of resistance at all. Instead, many threw down their arms and welcomed the Allies.[1]

Soon the Allied military police had their hands full just keeping order. In town after town, the population rose up, sacking government buildings, opening jails, and burning land and tax registers. Peasants broke into the abandoned army camps and military deposits, carting away whatever they could find. An estimated 150,000 refugees from Palermo had taken shelter from the Allied aerial bombardments by hiding in cellars, barracks, and grottos around Monreale in the hills southwest of the city. When the columns appeared, they were greeted rapturously by these refugees bearing oranges, lemons, melons, and flowers—the only foods available at the time. "I don't like it," General Patton remarked, perplexed at finding cheering crowds where he had expected to see barricades and snipers' nests. "These people are crazy."[2]

The crowd that welcomed the Anglo-American troops improvised banners, hand-painted Stars and Stripes and Union Jacks. Yet from the windows, yellow or yellow and white scarves also appeared. These were the colors of Sicily. Far from considering the Allies invaders of "Italian soil," the crowds were saluting them as the liberators of "terra Sicula." The Allies would be welcomed in Naples and Rome during the following year, but never in quite the same fashion. In July 1943, the Sicilians were not only demonstrating that they were tired of fascism, the war, and the German occupation; they were also showing that they were tired of being Italians.

A week later a newly formed Committee for the Independence of Sicily issued its first proclamation. The 1860 plebiscite, it said, in which Sicily had agreed to become part of a united Italy under Piedmont's House of Savoy, obliged the new state to recognize the island's right to autonomy. The Italian state, the proclamation continued, had never met this obligation; and so the committee demanded that a new plebiscite be held. Sicilians would be invited to declare the rights of the House of Savoy defunct on their island and to proclaim a sovereign Sicilian state in its stead.

Later, with the Movement for the Independence of Sicily now the largest party on the island, a group of Allied officers were invited by the acting mayor of Palermo, Lucio Tasca, to meet the leader of the "separatists," Andrea Finocchiaro-Aprile. A tall, elegant man, with slicked-back hair and a monocle in his left eye, Finocchiaro-Aprile explained to the guests that Sicily did not base its claim to independence solely on the 1860 plebiscite. In 1812 Sicily had written its own constitution, a constitution that had been inspired and guaranteed by the British government. What is more, Sicily's legal right to independence could be traced even further back than this. The foundations of the Sicilian nation lay in the eleventh century, in the Norman kingdom of Sicily. When the Neapolitans and Angevin French had tried to suppress Sicilian independence in the thirteenth century, the people of Sicily had risen in revolt—the Sicilian Vespers of 1282.

To the Allied military commanders, their minds concentrated on the business of fighting Germany, these dynastic and constitutional arguments seemed quaint and irrelevant. Yet Finocchiaro-Aprile was no irrelevant figure. He had served as a minister in the last liberal governments before the Fascist takeover. So had his father before him, for in Sicily it was by no means unusual for a son to inherit not only his father's parliamentary seat but his ministerial position as well. In fact, Andrea's father, Camillo Finocchiaro-Aprile, friend and disciple of the great Mazzini and Grand Master in Italian Freemasonry, was a leader of the generation who, as we shall see, were swept into power in the late 1870s. The Allied military commanders can be excused for not understanding the relevance of Andrea Finocchiaro-Aprile's historical references, for he spoke in the idiom of an earlier generation. Nevertheless they still recognized that this quaint old politician was speaking in the name of an aggrieved Sicilian nation.

History has not dealt kindly with the Movement for the Independence of Sicily. In a sense, this fate is no less than it deserves; the movement was quixotic, anachronistic, and riddled with contradictions from start to finish. The new Italy, the Italy that had salvaged its self-respect from the Fascist debacle, was the Italy of the partisans and of the parties that had supported them. These were northern parties, parties whose perspectives and political philosophies were far removed from those of most Sicilians. Postwar Sicilians were forced to to adapt themselves to the new climate, the so-called "wind from the North"; and so, without undue remorse, they consigned the project for an independent Sicily to the dustbin of history.

The new climate was more propitious to the discussion of reforms and projects for the future than to the claims of medieval history. There were initiatives for land reform, for industrialization, and for the modernization of Sicily's infrastructure. The government set up a number of quasi-autonomous agencies to oversee these initiatives. By the 1970s, however, it was becoming clear that, at least in terms of their original design, all were failures.

Sicily in the years after World War II bears a striking resemblance to that in the years following 1860. In both eras, a new, self-confident government inspired by reforming zeal took power. In both cases the new governments assumed that, given the right package of projects and initiatives, and given the political energy to pursue them vigorously, Sicily might soon be rescued from its secular marginality. In both cases, however, the engine of reform soon stalled, bogged down in Sicily's political quagmires. Reformers discovered to their dismay that most Sicilians were uninterested in their ideas; they were pleased when new projects meant a job or a government subsidy for them, but were disinclined to help the state in its campaign to transform Sicily by eradicating racketeering, corruption, crime, and political cronyism. There is one further resemblance: in both cases, blame for the failure of reform was laid at the feet of the mafia.

There is a great deal of truth in this final claim. Yet, given the remarkable similarity between the two chains of events, a suspicion must arise. Is there not some connection between mafia and reform? Sicily's leading crime fighter, the prosecutor Giovanni Falcone, assassinated by the mafia in 1993, saw such a connection. "We have a reached a point," he said, "where any sort of economic initiative on the part of the state only risks offering the mafia a new area of speculation."[3]

Most postwar studies treat the mafia from a socioeconomic perspective. These studies contain much valuable information. Nevertheless, they approach the mafia from the perspective of what ought to have happened, but did not, that is, from the premise that the reforms would have succeeded had the mafia not been there to thwart them. But this is a one-sided view; the mafia was, in equal measure, the creation of those reforms which it seemed bent on destroying or perverting. To understand this, one must drop the theoretical perspective and ask what really happened. This is all to the good, for the story of what happened is far more interesting, more bizarre and unexpected, than any sociological theory.

## A Tale of Two Cities

In 1743 political control of Sicily passed from the Spanish crown to the Neapolitan Bourbons, a cadet branch of the Hapsburgs the ruling dynasty of Spain. On paper it seemed a sensible arrangement. The two regions, Naples and Sicily, were culturally and economically similar; the aristocracy of each was linked to the other by ties of kinship and marriage. The Neapolitans, at least, were well satisfied. Although eighteenth-century Neapolitan political life was dominated by court intrigues and by legal and dynastic squabbles, the earlier Spanish viceroys in Naples had been able to curb somewhat the power of the kingdom's fractious nobility, creating a class of administrators loyal to the crown. This class was delighted when Naples became the capital of an independent kingdom. They were especially pleased that, with the addition of Sicily, the kingdom became an empire, just as it had been under the medieval Angevin kings and had remained until the Sicilians had thrown them out after the Vespers uprising in 1282.

Eighteenth-century Naples was a cosmopolitan city, where intellectuals were in touch with the political and economic doctrines of the Physiocrats in France, and influenced by Vico's new legal philosophy. Despite a notable lack of encouragement on the part of their own monarchs, these intellectuals were resolved to reform the Bourbon state along enlightened and absolutist lines. This meant reforming the province of Sicily as well.

To enlightened Neapolitans such as the marquis of Caracciolo or the prince of Caramanico, viceroys in Sicily from 1781 to 1795, Sicily was badly in need of reform. Public finances were in a shambles; tax exemptions and lack of a census made nonsense of any fiscal policy. Yet there was a logic behind this chaos: weak central government served the interests of the Sicilian barons.

No one could doubt where the real power in eighteenth-century Sicily lay. The dominion of the barons had spilled over the confines of their own estates to include the neighboring towns and villages with their communal lands. Barons held sway over freeholders and tenants in these areas, and individuals came under their control and influence whether they lived on feudal or on communal land, and whether they were tenants or freeholders. The barons also dominated the Sicilian courts, making it nearly impossible for towns or individuals to obtain judgments against them for encroachments and usurpations, or, if such judgments were obtained, to do much about enforcing them.[4]

It had not always been thus. In the comparatively prosperous fifteenth and sixteenth centuries, towns had defended their rights against the barons, often taking them to court. With the decline of Sicilian prosperity in the seventeenth century, however, an opposite tendency set in. Increasingly unable to bear the political and legal expenses of defending their liberties, the towns began to lose their rights and their lands to the barons. The Hapsburgs' shift of interest away from the Mediterranean and toward their colonies in the New World meant that crown rights were not well defended in Sicily either. Baronial power grew to fill the void; and, as it grew, the barons were able to usurp or encroach on the rights and lands of the commune wherever these were not vigilantly defended by local landowners and tenants or by the crown. By the seventeenth century, the structure of feudal power in Sicily had stabilized into recognizable geopolitical units, each of which was under its own baronial or ecclesiastical sovereign—the *contea* of Modica, the *principato* of Trabia, the *ducato* of Terranuova, the *vescovato* of Monreale.

The barons were not alone in their fight to escape Neapolitan jurisdiction. In contrast to the Neapolitan *foro*, or legal classes, the Sicilian *foro* took the side of the barons. Sicilian jurists defended the rights, acquisitions, and usurpations of the local baronage, elaborating each concession wrested, bought, or extorted from the crown into a general common law that served as the basis of Sicilian feudalism. In their hands, Sicilian legal culture grew into a system of moats, fosses, and chevaux-de-frise behind which the privileged classes might exercise their dominance undisturbed.

The barons could hardly have conducted their struggles without local allies, and it was in Palermo, where most barons kept houses, that the supporters and clients of baronial rule were naturally found. It was not only the nobility and church that enjoyed privileges and exemptions; the Palermo *foro* had amassed their own system of privileges and exemptions. The *maestranze*, or artisan guilds in Palermo, enjoyed legal protection as well; they could set prices and limit membership to their associations. They even had the right to bear arms and to hunt in the area around Palermo. They also acted as a local police force and civic guard—a tradition that had considerable importance in shaping the course of Palermitan rebellions.[5]

Nor were the *basso popolo* or common people of Palermo always enemies of baronial rule. Although they withheld their feudal dues and refused to invest in their estates, the barons threw spectacular parties. Reformers were outraged when money that should have been used on improving administration and agriculture was thrown away in lavish wedding feasts and fireworks displays to which half the population was invited. Bakers baked 365 different kinds of cakes—one for every saint in the calendar—and *feste* were incomplete without brass band concerts. Such display was all part of the Sicilian art of holding power; a hundred years later, civil servants from northern Italy were just as scandalized to discover Sicilian municipal councils squandering their meager resources in exactly the same manner.

Offering such entertainments was politic, however, for the people of Palermo were inclined to be restless. The nobility was riven by feuds and family rivalries which made coherent administration impossible. Order was kept by the *maestranze*; but if the urban poor rose up and the *maestranze* took their side, the nobility had to turn tail and run for their lives. The history of Palermo was punctuated by such uprisings; when they happened, the great barons simply fled to the safety of their country villas, leaving the urban plebs free to sack their palaces in the city. The barons knew how vulnerable they were, and saw that the urban plebs had to be kept contented. Not every day was a *festa*, even in Palermo; but even on workdays the poor benefited from a regime of subsidized bread and benefactions that they received from nuns working in the capital's hospitals and

*Perched on hills and stony outcroppings, overlooking the wheat-sown plains, the towns of the Sicilian highlands have a forbidding aspect.*

charitable foundations. The catch was that all the entertainments, privileges, and benefactions that kept Palermo happy had to be paid for, and so inevitably, as an eighteenth-century British consul remarked, "the welfare of the whole has been sacrificed to the capital."[6]

The population of Sicily might be roughly divided into two groups: those who, in some way or another, were allied to or beneficiaries of baronial rule, and those who were not. The people of Palermo and the surrounding villages mostly fell into the first group, while the peasants of the interior mostly fell into the second. This left the Palermitans and the coastal villagers to enjoy the advantages of living next to the barons, while their country cousins had to foot the bill. The pleasures of the town were paid for by the sweat of the countryside.

The life of eighteenth-century Sicilian peasants was primitive in the extreme. Perched on hills and stony outcroppings overlooking the wheat-sown plains, the towns of the Sicilian highlands have a forbidding aspect. The dwellings of the peasants seem to cling to the hillsides, looking up at the castle, fortress, or monastery crowning the summit. Yet the feudal overlords of these castles were rarely to be seen, for they preferred the life of the city or the comforts of their suburban villas, leaving their castles in the hands of agents charged with making sure that the rents were paid.

The peasants, who saw half their year's labors disappear on the backs of mule trains bound for the coast, had little love for the overlord, his bailiffs, or even their cousins in the coastal cities, who could buy the products of their labor at subsidized prices. Yet at least they were left to themselves. Barons and the crown took their religious duties seriously, and so churches were built and monasteries endowed—some of them masterpieces of baroque architecture. Yet the peasants were ministered to by a clergy scarcely less ignorant than themselves, and pastoral care was at best intermittent. This did not make the peasants indifferent to religion. Instead, they remodeled the rites and doctrines of the official religion into something that served their own needs and reflected their particular view of the world. Ferociously independent, they elaborated their own code of justice—a code that, needless to say, made no reference to statute law or legal procedures. And so, out of poverty and neglect, the peasants of Sicily forged one of the richest folk cultures in Europe.

The Neapolitan reformers also perceived this divide between the privileged cities and the neglected interior. For all their many shortcomings, the Bourbons of Naples regarded the succoring of the poor as a sacred duty. When intellectuals suggested reforms designed to improve the lot of the poor peasants, King Ferdinand of Naples was uncharacteristically willing to listen. The ambitions of the reformers, of course, ran deeper than this. Their aim was nothing less than to transform the entire kingdom of Naples into a modern state. This implied more than land reform; it implied a showdown with the Sicilian barons.

The Neapolitan viceroys Caracciolo and Caramanico wanted to force the Sicilian nobility to acknowledge their duties to the crown, and to make the two hundred or so leading families, in whose hands wealth and power lay, but who neither paid taxes nor improved their estates nor engaged in anything more onerous than ceremonial administrative duties, take their responsibilities more seriously. They introduced legal, administrative, and agrarian reforms; but, at the same time, they demanded that Sicilian feudatories submit the deeds and titles under which they exercised their authority to the scrutiny of the courts in Naples. Behind this demand lay the suspicion that many of the powers and exemptions that the barons claimed were bogus. It was a suspicion that was often justified; baronial authority often turned out to rest on lost charters and forged titles. Yet the barons refused to yield the powers they claimed belonged to them by right of tradition.

Attempts at reform were thus already setting Naples and Palermo on a collision course, a course that, had not the French Revolution intervened, might well have provoked a crisis sooner than it did.

## The 1812 Constitution

Tidings of revolution in France were first received in Sicily with foreboding: "The ideas [of the Revolution] are not discussed here," wrote a citizen of Trapani, "they are rather condemned without appeal as those of criminals and blasphemers."[7] Yet even if Sicily was too isolated to partake in the great contest of ideas, it could not avoid the political fallout of Napoleon's invasion of Italy.

In 1798, as Napoleon's armies poured into Naples, a badly shaken King Ferdinand arrived in Palermo aboard Nelson's flagship. At first the population cheered; this was the first royal visit in over forty years, and a reminder that Palermo was still a capital. Sicilian enthusiasm over the presence of the sovereign began to cool, however, when the people discovered that Ferdinand's main interest was in using the island as a tax base to finance his reconquest of Naples. When the return of Napoleon's armies forced him to flee to Sicily eight years later, in 1806, the welcome he received from the Sicilian nobility was distinctly less cordial.[8]

With Napoleon's armies firmly established in Naples, the rival British forces arrived to occupy Sicily. As political exiles in Palermo, King Ferdinand and his queen, Maria Carolina, lived under the protection of the British crown, which granted them a large subsidy. Supposedly this subsidy was to pay for recruiting an army and building a navy. Ferdinand, however, had little aptitude for such administration, preferring to spend his money on intrigues and on his own comforts and those of the members his court who had followed him into Sicilian exile. Despite his lack of administrative skills, Ferdinand displayed few qualms about using the new Napoleonic tax code, introduced in Naples, to collect taxes in Sicily.

The British were popular in Sicily. Their presence stimulated agriculture and commerce, and they began to overhaul public finance as well. They might have felt entitled to some say in how the island was being governed; after all, they were maintaining not only the Neapolitan court in exile, but also a garrison of seventeen thousand British soldiers. As the Bourbon court in exile grew increasingly unpopular in Palermo, peace was maintained by the political skills of William Bentinck, the British governor and effective ruler of the island. Sicilian jurists admired British methods and began to feel a curiosity about British political institutions. Was it not true, they asked, that it was to Parliament, and particularly the House of Commons, that British citizens owed the protection of their liberties?

Sicily had possessed its own parliament since 1296; it was divided into three houses or *brazos*—ecclesiastical, baronial, and communal. Unlike its British counterpart, however, the communal house in Sicily had not evolved into a House of Commons, as the towns had fallen under baronial domination. The Sicilian parliament had never governed the island or served as a political forum. Instead it had become a baronial syndicate. By the seventeenth century, in the words of Denis Mack Smith, parliament had degenerated into a place for the barons "to obtain titles, jobs and privileges for their families and clients."[9] This, however, could be changed, and, during the years of British occupation, barons and jurists began to see the British Parliament as a model for an institution that would guard Sicilian liberties against Naples.

In 1812 a new parliament met in Sicily. By now, the so-called "English school" was predominant. An English-style constitution was drafted by Paolo Balsamo and his associates and presented before parliament. The ecclesiastical and baronial houses were to be merged into a House of Peers, while royal and baronial towns joined together to form a House of Commons. The English-style jury system was to be adopted as well. Leading nobles, such as the princes of Belmonte and Castelnuovo, secured enough votes in the ecclesiastical and communal houses to override any objections from more conservative barons, and the new constitution quickly passed both houses.[10]

In 1815, however, Napoleon was defeated and the British withdrew their forces. This left Ferdinand and his ministers free to launch a countercoup. It was a maneuver that, despite his promises to the contrary, Ferdinand had undoubtedly been planning all along. In 1816, following a decision of the Congress of Vienna (in which Sicily was not represented), Ferdinand restyled himself "King of the Kingdom of the Two Sicilies," adopting a title last used in the 1440s. Sicily was no longer considered a separate state in a unified realm (for example, like Scotland in the United Kingdom) but rather a mere province. This was restoration with a vengeance; the Sicilian flag was promptly banned, and the civil liberties guaranteed by the 1812 constitution were suppressed. Neapolitan jurists, who had devised the change, exulted, for they had now fully reinstituted the Swabio-Norman kingdom that had been demolished by the Sicilian revolt of 1282.[11] In Palermo the mood was quite different. The relegation of the proud Sicilian "nation" to a mere province of Naples rankled in the breasts of Palermitans throughout the rest of the century.

In the short term, the 1812 constitution was a failure. It was designed as a defense against the demands of the state rather than as a blueprint for a working government; it was a Bill of Rights without a Constitution. It worked so long as real power remained the in the hands of the British. As soon as they left, there was nothing to force the Neapolitans to abide by its provisions. It had appealed to the Sicilian baronage precisely because it seemed to protect local liberties better than the constitutions of revolutionary France, which failed to pose any effective limit on the actions of the state. Appropriately, these were the very aspects of the British model which Neapolitan intellectuals objected to, preferring the constitution of revolutionary France as an instrument of radical social change. Yet radical social change was the last thing Sicilians had in mind in 1812. They wrote their constitution in order to keep things as they were. There was no revolutionary party in Sicily, no one eager to brand the nobility and the clergy as enemies of the people—an attitude that was to shape Sicily's subsequent struggles.

Nevertheless, the 1812 constitution was still a revolutionary document, for among its provisions it abolished feudalism in Sicily. Baronial privileges, primogeniture, and feudal dues and privileges were all swept away. In reality, these reforms were less radical than they seemed. Already by the 1790s certain nobles were responding to the reexamination of feudal charters by declaring that they had had enough of feudalism, renouncing their feudal rights, and with them, of course, their feudal obligations to the crown. Feudal law also prevented noble landholders from disposing of their lands; this was a real disadvantage at a time when the prosperity induced by the British occupation was making speculation in land highly profitable. Thus, the barons had adopted the 1812 constitution for a mixture of motives. On the one hand, they genuinely admired the British model and understood that protecting liberty meant protecting liberty for all citizens, not just defending the privileges of the nobility. Yet on the other, they were also astute enough to see that by abolishing feudalism, and with it their feudal obligations and restrictions, they were cutting themselves a good deal.[12]

## The Carboneria and the 1820 Revolt in Naples

Great changes had been occurring in Naples, too. Under Napoleon, a new law code had been introduced, legal practice had been reformed, and the civil service had been totally overhauled. These changes were popular among Neapolitan intellectuals and a large segment of the Neapolitan nobility. With the help of Metternich, they forced King Ferdinand to keep these reforms after his restoration. Thus, in 1816 Naples found itself in the curious position of having the most reactionary and obscurantist monarch as well as the most enlightened and progressive civil administration in all of Italy.

Administrative reform meant centralization. Magistrates and officials no longer inherited their positions or obtained them through friendship with the powerful; all appointments were now made by the government, or at least were subject to government approval. Although much was allowed to go on as it had always done, in theory the authority of the Neapolitan bureaucracy now replaced that of the barons and church in Sicily, reaching into every town and village on the island. Centralization created new opportunities for non-noble families without baronial connections to win magistracies and other official posts. These families were especially numerous in the eastern part of the island. Here were the great commercial cities Messina and Catania, rivals of the capital, whose merchants cared little for the grandees of Palermo, their palaces, their coats of arms, or their firework displays. True, these merchants cared just as little for King Ferdinand and the House of Bourbon in Naples; but they did appreciate the honest and businesslike demeanor of the new civil servants.

Yet these reforms also had a price tag attached to them. The Napoleonic Wars had drained Naples's treasury, and someone had to pay the bill. According to Naples, Sicily had unfairly prospered under British occupation; now it was time to make the island pay its share. The privileges and exemptions that Sicily had won appeared in the eyes of Naples as nothing more than schemes for avoiding taxes. Eliminating these anomalies would not only modernize the Sicilian economy; it would also greatly increase the government's tax revenues. Thus, along with new opportunities, reforms brought the tax collector to Sicily. This was enough to dampen the enthusiasm for reform, even among landowning and merchant families who, in other ways, were its chief beneficiaries.

Reform and centralization had a further, and totally unexpected, side effect as well: they helped introduce the Carboneria into Sicily.

The arrival of the armies of revolutionary France set off a flurry of conspiratorial activity throughout the whole of Italy. During the short-lived Roman Republic of 1798, there were reports of men meeting in the *campagna* to swear secret oaths. Some thought that the choice of the countryside was inspired by the need to keep the meetings secret; yet these men, described as Giacobini (Jacobins), seem, at this juncture at least, to have been anything but security-conscious. They sported *coccardes;* they denounced the Roman nobility; they formed parties to chisel off the noble insignia from the palazzi of Rome; they organized masques that celebrated the pure customs of the republican heroes of ancient Rome. When the majority of the Roman population failed to become electrified by these activities; the Giacobini denounced their fellow citizens for "crassness," "torpor," and "boorishness." As one Cardinal remarked ruefully, they seemed to stagger around drunk on Jean-Jacques Rousseau.[13]

In 1796 the conspirator and revolutionary leader Gracchus Babeuf had written in Paris, "The French Revolution is nothing but a forerunner of another revolution, very much bigger, very much more solemn, and which will be the last."[14] The early Italian sectarians embraced Babeuf's vision of the "final revolution." They were the first true "revolutionaries" in the modern sense; even the term *révolutionnaires* seems first to have been applied to them. The oaths that they swore were anything but pacific. According to a Napoleonic government report, the North Italian sectarians "were bound to one another by oaths; they each swore that all who uncovered their secrets or even abandoned the cause would fall under the points of their daggers." As early as 1799 there was a battle between the sectarians and the French army near the town of Alexandria when France moved to annex Piedmont. After the fight, blue *coccardes* and medallions with portraits of Marat and Lepelletier, the two Jacobin martyrs and victims of assassination, were found pinned on the chests of the fallen insurgents.[15]

These secret societies took their organizational blueprint from the Freemasons. Freemasonry had long been fashionable among the southern Italian nobility, and in part the leading southern sect, the Carboneria of Naples, developed from southern Italian Masonry. Nevertheless, its direct antecedent was the Charbonniers or the Bons Cousins, a small Masonic Société des Plaisirs in the Franche-Comté.[16]

The original Bons Cousins had been a nonpolitical group. During the 1790s, however, along with Nice, the Franche-Comté served as a refuge for Italian Jacobins. It also served as a staging post for the Napoleonic Armée d'Italie between 1796 and 1798. Among the Napoleonic officers who stayed here during these two years was a certain P. J. Briot du Doubs, an individual in trouble with the police under the Directoire for his Jacobin past and his participation in Babeuf's Conspiracy of Equals in 1796. According to his own testimony, Briot helped refashion the Charbonniers into a radical sect on the model of Babeuf's conspiracy. In 1798 Briot was part of the force invading Naples. Once in the South, he became active in founding new branches of the Charbonniers.

Leading magistrates in Naples had served during the Napoleonic period; officers in the Neapolitan army had had close ties to the French army. These men were drawn into the world of French revolutionary societies, becoming *carbonari*, the Italian version of *charbonniers*. Even after the return of the Bourbons, revolutionary ideas were far from spent, and branches of the Carboneria continued to be founded throughout the continental South. In the capital itself, membership in the Carboneria was highly fashionable, a way of demonstrating one's progressive and enlightened attitudes.

In truth, most of the high-ranking members of the Neapolitan Carboneria were neither Jacobins nor revolutionaries; they were rather supporters of reform and administrative centralization, policies that Neapolitan intellectuals had traditionally favored. Outside the capital, however, the situation was different: here the Carboneria remained true to its radical Jacobin origins. In Basilicata and Apulia, the Carboneria called for adoption of republicanism and the French constitution of 1791. This was the radical Jacobin constitution, and it long remained a point of reference for revolutionaries in all parts of Italy.

And not only in Italy: the 1791 constitution served as a model for Spain as well. In 1812 the revolutionary Spanish Cortes had voted for it. Two years later, however, the Spanish king, Ferdinand VII, was able to dissolve the Cortes, abrogate the new constitution, and restore absolutist government.

On the first of January 1820, Spanish troops massed at Cádiz for embarkation to Latin America rebelled. Many of their officers were members of a Spanish sect, the Comuneros, a secret society analogous to the Carboneria. The rebels at Cádiz demanded that the 1812 Spanish constitution be re-instated; and when troops sent to suppress the mutiny passed over to the rebel side, the king was forced to comply.

There was no direct connection between the Comuneros and the Carboneria. Still, the news from Cádiz electrified the southern Italian sectarians. In the six months that followed the Spanish revolt, there was feverish activity among *carbonari* throughout the South. On the night of July 1st, 1820, an uprising broke out in the town of Nola, near Naples. The *carbonari* of Nola, Avellino, and surrounding towns lit signal fires from the hills. These sparked off revolts in Basilicata and down through Molise and Apulia. As in Spain, the battalions that the commander of Neapolitan forces, the Austrian General Laval Nugent, sent to quell the outbreaks passed over to the rebel side. After several days the king gave way and promised to accept the Spanish constitution.

On the ninth of July, accompanied by the Neapolitan troops, the sectarians paraded into the capital. There they assembled their followers to administer a public oath, modeled on the great oath-taking ceremonies of revolutionary France. They even went so far as to rebaptize the ground upon which the oath was taken after the Champ de Mars in Paris. At the end of the ceremony, the Carboneria released the brothers from their oath of secrecy, and, handing out the black, blue, and red *coccardes* that distinguished the sect, began to march toward the royal palace. By now, many of the Neapolitan troops were also adorned with the *carbonara coccardes*. As they trooped by the royal palace, they could see that even the crown prince, Francis, was wearing the three-colored ribbon as he applauded the troops and sectarians from the royal balcony (his father, King Ferdinand, feigning an illness, was not present). In a description of this day's events we read that "after the ceremony . . . thousands triumphally marched through the populous city streets . . . to the royal palace amidst general jubilation."[17]

The Carboneria seemed about to become the party of the new regime, as was repeatedly to happen with revolutionary sects in South America. Yet the wily King Ferdinand, who certainly was not wearing a *coccarde* that night, hated the sect and all its liberal doctrines. He was no more inclined to honor his undertakings to his Neapolitan subjects in 1820 than his pledges to the Sicilians in 1815. As soon as he was sure of the backing of the Austrian army, he planned to betray his promise to grant the new constitution. Yet before he launched his counterstroke, he was content to wait and see how the new revolutionary government in Naples would deal with an unexpected development—a revolt in Sicily.

**The 1820 Revolt in Sicily**

Unlike the continental South, Sicily had never been occupied by French troops. Revolutionary sects were slow to spread here; when they arrived, moreover, they were often introduced by the Neapolitan army. Hence the Carboneria was at first strongest in the eastern part of the island, especially in Palermo's traditional rival, Messina.

The spread of the Carboneria was not entirely the work of Neapolitans, however. There were a number of Sicilian *carbonari* who had served in the armies of revolutionary France; some had even served in France itself.

These *carbonari* were less favorably disposed toward rule from Naples. In 1819 a new cell, or *vendita*, was discovered in Caltagirone. According to a police report:

> The sect of the *carbonari* consists in the union of a number of individuals, who, calling one another Good Cousins [Buoni Cugini], oblige themselves under oath not to reveal the secret, to respect the rules of the Carboneria, to help one another in case of need, and all this under pain of being cut into pieces and incinerated in a furnace. This sect, like all others that are covered by a mystery, has its grades, the first of which is called Apprentice, the second is Master, the third is called the First Symbolic, the fourth the Lofty Light, and so on.[18]

These were the standard grades of esoteric eighteenth-century Masonry. The reference to being cut into pieces and incinerated in a furnace is, in contrast, a new addition, and one whose echoes remain in mafia initiation ceremonies to the present day.

The Caltagirone *vendita* had, in fact, been founded in 1815 by a priest, Luigi Oddo. Oddo had lived in Calabria between 1810 and 1820, and it seems likely that he had been inducted into the more revolutionary French wing of the Carboneria during his stay.

Another Sicilian priest involved in the Carboneria was don Gaetano Abele from Siracusa. He is described in police reports as "a man of irregular conduct, who for thirteen years served France in civil and military employment, who was made a member of the sect of Masons in Calais, and who, finding himself in the French army with the rank of captain, took part in the occupation of Naples."[19] When the police raided don Gaetano's home, along with the usual Masonic literature, they found genealogical charts and papers on the kings of medieval Sicily among his effects.

Although the 1812 constitution had been a failure in the short term, in retrospect it came to be seen as the foundation of Sicilian liberties. After 1816, Sicilians jurists had argued that the decision of the Congress of Vienna was invalid. Sicilians, they said, were a free and autonomous people, and had been so since the Vespers uprising of 1282. Sicily was, to use the term that was now becoming so charged with meaning, a "nation."[20]

Don Gaetano's royal genealogies and medieval lore seem to indicate that he was thinking along similar lines. Already in the first years of the Restoration, Sicilians were beginning to refashion the instruments of revolutionary France into a Sicilian ideology that would serve as the basis of their own revolt against Naples.

Nor were these Sicilian revolutionaries the only point of diffusion for the sects. Upon its restoration, the Neapolitan government had arrested a number of Neapolitan revolutionaries, sectarians, and political malcontents; wishing to keep them as far away from the capital as possible, they transported them to Sicilian prisons. As a result, the police soon discovered that a *vendita* of the Carboneria had been founded in Palermo's central prison, the Vicaria, with branches in the fortress of Castellammare as well as the prisons in Trapani and the island of Favignana.

We are still in the age of sail, and the overwhelming majority of Sicilians, even in Palermo, knew little about the Continent. Even fewer knew of the Carboneria. Besides, Palermo had other things to think about. July was the month in which the *festa* of Santa Rosalia took place. Santa Rosalia was the beloved patron saint of Palermo; her *festa* was the biggest of the Palermitan's year. For the rich, it meant a string of masked balls; for the rest of the population, it meant solemn religious processions ending in dancing in the *piazze* and the inevitable fireworks and band concerts. Little work was done during *festa* time, and so, when a government brigantine sailed in from Naples on the morning of July 14, 1820, there were plenty of idlers in the city with nothing better to do than to go down to the port and meet it:

> When more than 180 Neapolitans and Sicilians stepped ashore decorated with tricolored ribbons, the Palermo crowd, influenced by the festive spirit prevailing during the popular celebrations and curious to know what had been happening in Naples, drew near the shoreline. Seeing the unfamiliar ribbons fluttering on the mast-stays and on the breasts of the travelers, the crowd became ever more curious. This was the electric spark that generated the flame in the combustible material that had been prepared. . . . Emissaries [*carbonari*] ran forth to greet the crowd; they told of events in Naples; they proclaimed liberty, *carbonaria* [brotherhood], and the extinction of tyrants. . . . Others set off to arm themselves in the name of their clubs [*vendite*].[21]

Overjoyed at the news of the fall of King Ferdinand, the crowd began to congratulate the Neapolitan soldiers, embracing them and inviting them to take part in the *festa*. In this way the first of Palermo's great revolts started with Neapolitan soldiers and Palermitans dancing together in honor of Santa Rosalia. On the next day, a Te Deum was celebrated in Palermo Cathedral. The crowd began to shout "Viva la costituzione di Spagna" (Long live the Spanish constitution) and "Viva l'indipendenza siciliana" (Long live Sicilian independence), failing, however, to respond when the lieutenant governor, Naselli, loyally shouted "Viva il re" (Long live the king). Despite this minor incident, the first few days of the 1820 uprising passed with neither bloodshed nor, indeed, disorders of any sort.

News of revolution in Naples brought the Bourbon military commandant in Sicily, the Irish General Richard Church, scurrying back to Palermo. Together with Lieutenant Governor Naselli, he went to the Quattro Cantoni, the center of Palermo. There he found festivities in full swing, his own officers celebrating with the crowd. "Go back to your quarters!" he commanded, and leaned forward to rip the *carbonaro* ribbons off the nearest man's chest. At this, a priest stepped up (tradition identifies him as a Calabrian priest sent by the *carbonari* the day before) and shouted, "Avenge the insult, O brave Palermitans, that the vile foreigner has made to the mark of liberty!" Threatened now by the crowd, General Church was forced to retreat back to his own quarters, protected by a circle of his officers. That night he fled the city for Trapani, where, abandoning his command, he took ship for Naples.

With Church gone, the crowd abandoned its restraint, lighting bonfires and looting government offices. The following morning, Naselli assembled the remaining loyal officers and nobles to try to restore order. He commissioned a new municipal governing council, or *giunta*, formed by eight representatives of the nobility and eight members of the *maestranze*. Giuseppe Bonanno, the prince of Cattolica, assumed command over an improvised police force of twenty-five companies of infantry and cavalry, whose officers were to be made up from the nobility and remaining officers of the Neapolitan army, and whose ranks were to be recruited by the *maestranze* and the clergy.

The Palermo aristocracy had their own sources of information, and had heard rumors of the revolt in Naples four or five days before it became known to the rest of the population. This had given the barons time to confer privately over the message that the Palermo *giunta* was to send the revolutionary government in Naples. Sicily, the message said, still considered its 1812 constitution to be valid. Sicilian prosperity, it continued, depended on the separation of Sicily from Naples, for the island was now suffering from a "grave and complicated bureaucratic regime of stamp duties, official papers, and forced labor [i.e., military conscription], the hard provisions of which all the Governments of Europe have just recently blamed on the French Emperor [i.e., Napoleon]."[22]

This was simply a demand that the Neapolitan countercoup of 1816 be annulled. If Naples would agree to Sicilian autonomy, the barons did not much care what regime happened to be sitting in Naples itself. To the young crown prince, Francis, this seemed a callous response. Still filled with romantic ardor, the prince asked the Sicilian barons why they would not accept the new Spanish constitution, which had, after all, all the glamour and prestige of the French Revolution behind it. At this the prince of Cassaro wrote to him, responding rather unkindly that "we would far prefer being subjects to the Bey of Tunis than to You."[23]

In truth, the barons were in a dilemma. They wanted to be free of Naples; but this was not exactly what the *carbonari* were demanding. What the sectarians wanted was that Naples be governed according to the 1791 constitution in its Spanish version. If they succeeded, however, Sicily would simply come under the authority of the new revolutionary government in Naples, a government that would feel no compunctions whatsoever about saddling the island with even more "stamp duties, official papers, and forced labor" than before.

The barons could see the implications of the 1791 constitution. The common people, however, saw only the promise of the Carboneria: freedom from tyranny, a universal republic, the reign of justice and equality. The *carbonari* were inviting them to take up arms and join the final revolution, a revolution which Babeuf had said would be very much bigger, very much more solemn than any before. The people responded enthusiastically. In the event, the barons decided to try and ride out the storm. They would support the revolution. They gambled that once the rebellion had delivered them from Naples, they would be able to step back in to resume control. They should have known better. Rebellions in Palermo had a habit of taking unpredictable turns. It was easy to start a riot; it was much harder to usher the angry plebs off the stage once their destructive might had been unleashed.

The barons made up only half of the new government in Palermo; the other half was made up of the *maestranze*, who were sympathetic to the *carbonari*. While the barons tried to restrain the revolution, the *maestranze* tried to push it forward. The two sides soon viewed each other with deepening suspicion.

Afraid that the Neapolitan forces might train their guns upon the city, the *maestranze* had demanded possession of the government fortress at the port—the Castellammare. The fortress was nearly impregnable, and, understandably, neither the barons nor the lieutenant governor wished to see it fall into popular hands. Yet the fortress was garrisoned by Neapolitan soldiers, often young conscripts who shared the *maestranze*'s sympathy toward the *carbonari*. While Naselli and the *giunta* were debating a solution, there was a mutiny inside the Castellammare itself, and the garrison sur-rendered the fortress to the *maestranze*.

With the Castellammare in their hands, the *maestranze* grew in confi-dence. Control was slipping from the *giunta*, and the nobility's position was becoming vulnerable. As the nobles desperately tried to come to a new agreement with Naselli, rioting spread to the city's streets.

At first there was no violence. The rioting was neither anarchic nor dis-orderly; rather it consisted of the systematic, regular, and almost punctil-ious destruction of everything to do with government administration. There were neither thefts nor sackings nor violence to persons, private houses, or shops; yet every piece of paper, every stick of government fur-niture that the insurgents seized was fed into the great bonfires, whose flames, writes Francesco Renda, assumed an emblematic significance. Neapolitan troops joined the holocaust; their regimental bands saluted the crowds with military marches.[24]

On the next day the festive atmosphere suddenly changed. According to Francesco Paternò-Castello, on the night of July 16, Naselli secretly or-dered loyal troops to attack the city at dawn. Fearing that Naselli might also have ordered their own arrest, several of the noble leaders of the *giunta* fled into hiding. Whatever their motives, the crowd interpreted their flight as admission of betrayal. The prince of Cattolica and the prince of Aci were dragged from their hiding places and murdered.[25]

This was not the only reason for the change. On the fourteenth and fif-teenth, the crowd had adorned themselves with the black, blue, and red *coccardes* of the Carboneria; on the sixteenth, however, they had begun to add a yellow stripe, symbolizing Sicilian independence. Soon they were wearing yellow and red *coccardes*, the colors of the Sicilian flag. This made fraternization between the Palermitans and the Neapolitan troops impossible.

On the morning of the seventeenth, the army launched an assault. At first it had the upper hand, as the people, unarmed and not expecting the attack, fell back in a confused fashion. Yet the *maestranze* soon began to organize a defense. What turned the tide in favor of the Palermo crowd was the timely arrival of a group of *contadini* from Monreale, led by Gioacchino Vaglica, a monk from a poor peasant family. Vaglica led his band of followers in an attack on the Vicaria prison, liberating the in-mates, who swelled the ranks of the insurgents. Gangs of peasants soon arrived from Bagheria and from other of the surrounding towns, trapping the garrison between the crowd within the city walls and the peasants without. With this, the Neapolitan commanders decided on retreat. The

*Prisoners released from the Vicaria prison in Palermo joining the plebs in their attack on the Bourbon police, September 1820.*

troops tried to force their way out of the city; yet even where they succeeded, they fared no better, for by now the villages in the Conca d'Oro had all risen as well. Gangs from these villages fell upon the Neapolitans, hacking them to pieces and despoiling them of their clothes and belongings. Sources speak of three hundred Neapolitan dead and four hundred wounded on the seventeenth.

The murder of the leading barons and the rout of the Neapolitan army left a vacuum. The head of the tanners' guild, Francesco Santoro, and the leader of the Monreale peasants, the monk Vaglica, became the de facto rulers of Palermo. They persuaded the venerable archbishop of Palermo, Cardinal Gravina, to assume titular authority. Yet the situation could only grow worse. On the eighteenth, there were murders in the open streets. On the nineteenth, sackings and lootings, which up to now had been carried out only against selected targets, became general. The bloodletting and pillaging lasted from the eighteenth to the twenty-third, and ended only with the return to Sicily of the prince of Villafranca, whom Cardinal Gravina nominated to serve as his prime minister.

Outside Palermo, all semblance of Neapolitan authority had collapsed in western Sicily. The released prisoners returned to their villages, setting off orgies of destruction:

It was these sorts of people that spread the seeds of popular license in the communities in which they arrived. And in fact, in some of the

towns in the abovementioned valley [between Palermo and Caltanis-
setta] they committed all manner of excesses, persecuting financial officials, devastating their houses, torching official papers, registers, and
everything else connected to their office as well as massacring the majority of excellent and good citizens for private vendetta.[26]

In the eastern part of the island, the revolution had taken a far different
course. Messina had staged a *carbonaro* revolt as early as the ninth of July;
this was quickly followed by revolts in Catania and Siracusa. There had
been a much stronger *carbonaro* presence in the eastern half of the island—
there seem to have been thirty-five revolutionary clubs in Messina alone—
and the revolts in eastern Sicily resembled those on the Continent. The
easterners made no demands for Sicilian independence; they simply demanded the Spanish constitution. In fact, the east was not particularly eager for a new edition of the 1812 constitution if this meant only a restoration of Palermitan dominance. As a result, peaceful relations were
maintained between the *carbonari* and the army. There were no riots. The
eastern revolts were all bloodless coups.

When the Palermo *giunta* sent its emissaries to the cities of the east,
they were rebuffed. Nor was the *giunta* any more successful with its emissaries in Naples. Encouraged by the resistance of eastern Sicily to
Palermo, the revolutionary government in Naples refused to negotiate
with the Palermo *giunta*, placing its delegation in prison. Naples in-

*Execution of eight prisoners, September 1820. Six of them were found guilty of killing Bourbon
soldiers, two of killing Bourbon policemen.*

structed its *intendenti* (local governors) in Sicily to arrest any representative from Palermo who arrived in their districts.

The Palermo *giunta* responded to this insult to its authority by organizing three *guerriglie*, or flying columns, with which to force the rest of the island into submission. In dispatching these columns, the prince of Villafranca may also have hoped to get the more violent elements out of Palermo. In the event, however, all he achieved was to export the murders, factional riots, and other disorders which had been gripping the Palermo area since the mid-July to the rest of Sicily. There followed a chain of local uprisings, often accompanied by factional bloodlettings, in which local landowning families assassinated their rivals. The Palermo *guerriglie* were beaten back from the walls of Catania and Siracusa. They managed to take Caltanissetta, however, sacking the town and laying waste to the countryside. In the west, the Palermo forces attacking Trapani were aided by forces from Trapani's rival Marsala. These helped liberate the inmates from Trapani's prison, who formed an independent guerrilla band, terrorizing the countryside.

Another guerrilla band was organized by the Palermitan ex-monk Salvatore Errante. His band, consisting of around two-hundred escaped convicts and laborers recruited in the region of Bagheria, Ficarazzi and Santa Flavia, marched east along the north coast road. When they reached the territories of Messina, they began to lay the countryside to waste; the town of Santo Stefano was able to buy them off with the sum of two thousand *onze*. Errante's band was eventually defeated by the *guerriglie* under the prince of San Cataldo.

Horrified at the havoc and carnage, the Villafranca *giunta* in Palermo turned to Naples and decided to sue for peace. The revolutionary government in Naples had dispatched General Florestano Pepe to subdue Sicily. Pepe was a leading member of the moderate, pro-constitution Carboneria of Naples, and in Messina he was welcomed as a liberator. Soon Pepe's Neapolitan troops, supplemented by a number of eastern Sicilian volunteers, were marching against Palermo. On the twenty-second of September, seeing the hopelessness of their situation, Villafranca and the *maestranze* leaders sneaked out of the city to meet Pepe in the town of Termini Imeresi to discuss the surrender of Palermo.

Yet surrender was no longer easy to achieve. Civil administration had collapsed; murder and looting remained rife; bands of peasants poured in from the countryside to loot the prostrate capital. The only force for order was the *maestranze*. Yet even they were growing increasingly truculent. There was nothing to restrain them from holding the Palermo *giunta* to ransom:

It was equally necessary [for the *giunta*] to find a way of meeting the daily expense of maintaining the horde of armed men, and especially the tanners, whose thirst for gold knew no limits. This armed horde presented itself en masse each morning to the chief city magistrate asking for money, and he, on the basis of the bills that a self-styled captain of the force presented him, had to pay the requested sum.[27]

The *maestranze* may well have wished to extort all they could get; they harbored no illusions about the *giunta*'s real attitude. Cardinal Gravina and the prince of Villafranca were certain to turn against them the moment Neapolitan troops arrived. When the crowd discovered that Villafranca had slipped off to Termini to negotiate a surrender with Pepe, they reacted violently. A new mob formed; the prisons were opened once again, and Villafranca's palazzo in Palermo and his two country villas were sacked. As Pepe's troops and the eastern Sicilian volunteers tightened their stranglehold around Palermo, bombarding the city from the sea, the rebels organized a last-ditch defense.

They had no hope of victory; yet fighting continued for several weeks, during which many of the empty palazzi were gutted and burned to the ground. Nor was even this the end of the suffering. Pepe had been empowered to offer Palermo some measure of autonomy in exchange for its surrender. Yet the government in Naples, enraged by Palermo's defiance, later repudiated all these concessions, dispatching another three thousand troops to Sicily under Pietro Colletta.

Not that the revolutionary government in Naples came to a much better end. The bulk of Naples's constitutional armed forces were now in Sicily, leaving the continental South unguarded. This was the moment King Ferdinand had been waiting for. In March 1821 he reappeared at the head of an Austrian expeditionary force. Soon the revolutionary government was dissolved, its leaders imprisoned. Absolutist government was restored to Naples. For its temerity, Sicily was forced to bear the cost and burden of ten thousand Austrian troops sent to make sure that Palermo would not rise again.

The 1820 revolution was duly celebrated by a later generation of Sicilian historians; yet, in retrospect, it seems a sorry affair. Palermo distrusted the barons. When the *maestranze* marched through Palermo with the head of the prince of Cattolica stuck on a pikestaff, it was clear that the revolution had failed. Arson and bloodshed could only follow.

Yet, for all their arrogance, the barons had read this situation correctly.

If the Neapolitan reforms succeeded, Sicily would become even more subordinate to Naples. That was not what they wanted and this is why they had embraced liberalism and free trade in the 1812 constitution. It is why they wrote to the revolutionary government in Naples in 1820 that the prosperity of Sicily depended on the complete economic separation of Sicily from Naples.

Nevertheless, the barons saw matters only from their own perspective. They were the traditional rulers of their island, rulers who, especially on their own estates, did pretty much as they pleased. Administrative centralization and legal reforms threatened to make all subjects of the Neapolitan crown, even the barons, answerable to the law. This was an unbearable affront.

What the barons had failed to see was that the people of the coastal villages had their own reasons for resisting the state. During the 1820 revolt, gangs of peasants, armed with axes and knives, fell upon the retreating Neapolitan troops with unparalleled ferocity. These villagers saw the state in the guise of tax collectors, recruiting officers and officials who arrived with incomprehensible documents proclaiming them even more indebted, even less free than before.

Such convergences of interests were frequent in Sicily's history. In a letter to Madrid dated November 3, 1577, the viceroy of Sicily, Marc'Antonio Colonna, wrote that the Holy Inquisition in Sicily already possessed 25,000 "familiars," that is, collaborators or agents. Now, he said, the Sicilian Inquisitors were proposing to raise the number to 39,000. Religious zeal? As agents of the Inquisition, familiars were outside the jurisdiction of crown courts. Among the familiars in Sicily, Colonna noted, were to be found the nobles, the rich, and all the leading criminals. It was an "alliance between the [Inquisitorial] tribunal and the influential and the dangerous classes."[28] After 1820 this alliance between the "influential and the dangerous classes" was soon to become the engine of revolution in Sicily. First, however, the appropriate instrument needed to be forged.

# 2

## The 1848 Revolt

Eighteen forty-eight was the year of the revolution, the year when, writing the *Communist Manifesto*, Marx and Engels loosed the specter of a communist revolution in the chancelleries of France, Germany, and Austria. It was the year of revolution for Italy as well, the year in which Italians tried to overthrow the edifice that Metternich had built. Yet it was not in France, Germany, or Austria that the cycle of revolt was initiated.

To northern Europeans before 1848, Sicily seemed as much a part of North Africa as of Europe. True, there were enthusiasts who might brave its lack of roads, its appalling accommodations, and the dangers of brigands to behold its ruined Greek cities and temples; beyond these, the island was seldom visited even by southern Italians. Nevertheless, it was in Palermo that, on the night of January 9, notices appeared proclaiming, in the name of a "Directive Committee," that the revolution would take place on the morning of the twelfth.

Palermo's ambition to become the capital of an independent Sicilian state was anything but quenched after 1820. Nevertheless, the nobility, whose lands and palaces had been devastated in the uprising, hardly relished the prospect of fresh tumults. Nor did the ideals that had inspired the *carbonari*—republicanism and universal brotherhood—precisely coincide with the political ambitions of Palermo's ruling classes. For the moment, the influential classes in Palermo were in no mood for revolt.

Still, the *carbonari* remained active. Inspired by the Paris uprising of 1830 and by the activities of plotters in central Italy, a small group of Palermo conspirators attempted to set off an uprising in 1831. It was a total failure: the city failed to ignite. Having forced one of the city's gates during the night, the little group of armed rebels was quickly rounded up by the police. They were placed in front of firing squads and shot.[1]

In 1837 there were fresh disturbances. These, however, were set off not by real plotters, but by imaginary ones. Nor were the phantom plotters political intriguers; instead, they were poisoners and plague-spreaders.[2]

According to tradition, epidemics were the work of plague-spreaders. When, in 1837, a cholera epidemic broke out in Sicily, university professors and even the archbishop of Palermo assumed that these plague-spreaders were once again at work.

Rumors about these poisoners soon began to take a more definite form. The poison, it was said, had been carried to Sicily by the Bourbon government. It was reported that the leader of the gang of poisoners, disguised as a Capuchin friar, was wandering through the streets of Palermo, surveying the effects of his handiwork and giving encouragement and supplies to his gang of villains. Who could this false friar be? A government packet had appeared in Palermo harbor on the fourth of July. This, it was whispered, was the boat that had brought the poisoners. What is more, the man who had stepped off the boat disguised as a Capuchin was none other than King Ferdinand himself.

Despite these fantastic rumors, Palermo remained relatively quiet; only one supposed poisoner was murdered in the streets. Not so the outlying districts. Members of the Minecci family had left their home in Villagrazia to go to the capital to buy some pills which, they were told, would protect them from the epidemic. When they came back, they were met by a suspicious crowd who insisted on searching through their belongings. The crowd found the pills and, convinced that they had found the poison itself, proceeded to club to death the elder Minecci along with his sixteen-year-old son, Francesco. After this, they hastily burned the bodies.

News from Villagrazia spread to the towns of Villabate and Parco (modern-day Altofonte), and to Bagheria along the coast. Excited mobs materialized and burst into the houses of other supposed poisoners. More mysterious substances were found, and more poor inhabitants were dragged out of their homes and murdered. Soon, a wave of killings was spreading throughout the entire province.

The disturbances did not stop with the killings of supposed poisoners. After sacking the houses of these poisoners and murdering the inhabitants, the mob turned their attention to police stations and tax offices. The police were overwhelmed, their weapons seized by the rioters. Tax offices were gutted, and all their records were removed and burned. Jails were opened and the prisoners set free to join in the carnage.

Murder, however, was always selective; the houses of only a few families were singled out. We do not know why these particular families were picked, but they all seem to have been landowners or merchants. We might suspect that these were the families that had done well out of the Bourbon reforms, obtaining for themselves land, offices, or tax concessions. Nor would it be surprising if it turned out that some of the rioters had owed money to the merchants they murdered.

From the *agro palermitano* the riots spread to towns in the interior of the province. Misilmeri was first to ignite; it became the scene of a bloody riot in which a number of other landowners were slain. From here the riots spread to Marineo and Prizzi. In all these cases the supposed poisoners were landowners and merchants.

After more than a week, government troops arrived. By then, however, the hysteria had vanished and the mobs had dissipated. Still, the troops set about arresting those who had been involved. The repression was severe. There were 156 arrests in Misilmeri alone, with 7 summary executions. In Palermo province, where the death toll from the riots was around 80 persons, there were 650 arrests and 90 summary executions, which were later followed by 140 judicial executions.

From Palermo province, the rioting had spread to the rest of the island—to Trapani and Agrigento in the west, and to the province of Syracuse in the east. As the riots spread, they became increasingly political in character, and by the time the Bourbon troops reached Catania, the city was flying the yellow flag of Sicilian independence.

The 1837 riots are curious; whatever set them off, their pattern resembled that of the provincial uprisings in 1820, and would be even closer to those of 1848 and 1860. Even the geography was the same: Misilmeri was to become a revolutionary center in both 1848 and 1860. Nor do the parallels end here, for in the late 1870s, Misilmeri was described as the home of one of the most powerful mafia groups in Sicily. These resemblances are too systematic to be dismissed as fortuitous. What, then, is the connecting thread?

If the rich in Palermo lived off the rest of the island, the Conca d'Oro lived by catering to Palermo. It was a good living, for the soil of the coastal valleys was exceptionally fertile. Crops grew well and could be sold in the city for a good price, and the smallholders and workers on the coast were far better off than the wheat-growing peasants in the interior. The British had recognized this, and saw the commercial possibilities in Sicily's coastal agriculture. They encouraged these coastal farmers to produce even more. The fruits of the vines and trees that grew so abundantly on Sicily's coasts would find a ready market in northern Europe, and British subjects arrived from nearby Malta to produce and export the wines of Marsala. Soon, oranges and tangerines from Sicily had become a part of the English Christmas dinner, while Marsala wines remained on the sideboard all year round.

The coastal economy had blossomed in response to demand from northern Europe. But few had foreseen this demand, and no one had planned its growth. In economic terms, this was an advantage. Trade was not hampered by regulations, nor were profits creamed off by bureaucrats. Socially, however, the situation was more ambiguous. The most prosperous and fast-growing sector of Sicily's economy was also its most violent and lawless. Profits were high, often exceeding those of the market gardens around Paris; but land and rental prices were correspondingly high as well. Small holders or tenants had to borrow money to buy or rent the land they farmed. Speculation was rife, and there were battles over rents, over usury, and over water rights. The low-lying pockets into which the groves and vineyards were tucked were crisscrossed by a network of meandering paths and surrounded by high walls, behind which thieves and assassins could lurk undetected. Competition between growers led to gang warfare. Smuggling was a traditional occupation. Smallholders hid stolen livestock on their property, which then reappeared in the clandestine meat markets of the capital.

This was the situation as it presented itself to Neapolitan officials in the first half of the nineteenth century. Besides administrative centralization, the Neapolitan reforms after 1816 aimed at attacking feudal privileges left untouched by Sicily's 1812 constitution. With these privileges were swept away a set of customary rights, like pasturage or the gathering of wood and stone, that Silician peasants had enjoyed for centuries. Reformers also recommended that the large tracts of demesnal land in the interior of Sicily be broken up and given to individual peasant families. King Ferdinand himself had expressed his sympathy for small- and medium-scale farmers oppressed by corrupt magistrates and by arrogant representatives of absentee landowners avid for rent.[3]

The sympathies of the Neapolitan state were focused on the wheat-growing peasants of the interior. This was a traditional attitude; bread was the staff of life, and the peasants who grew the wheat that made this bread were regarded as a downtrodden and put-upon class which the crown had a special duty to succor. Thus the reformers' main concern was to seek ways of easing the peasants' burdens.

The state's opinion of the prosperous but unruly populations in the tightly packed villages of the coastal plains was much less flattering. These villages were seen as coves of smugglers and racketeers, of men ready to pull out their knives for a *nonnulla* or to settle an affair of honor with a shotgun blast from behind a wall.

Inevitably, the policy of benevolence toward the peasants of the interior was counterbalanced by measures against the coastal populations. Although many of these measures might equally be described as much-needed reforms—measures to curb violence, to prevent smuggling and fraud, and to make sure that taxes were regularly paid—in the eyes of these populations they were all hostile acts.

The coastal dwellers had never liked government officials; they liked them even less now. Why should the coastal dwellers welcome reforms if these meant more taxes? Why should they welcome more customs officials if these meant they could no longer sell to whomever they pleased? Why should they welcome a more efficient police force if this meant that they were no longer free to regulate their own affairs? The state did not wish to succor them and they did not wish to be succored.

There was thus an enmity between state officials and the coastal populations. Officials regarded these populations as seditious, unruly, larcenous, violent, and truculent. This is an enmity that continues today. Here is a description from the 1880s by a police officer. Enter, one of the towns in the Palermo area on a public holiday, he writes, and you will see a uniformity in dress. Everyone shows off their costly clothing, their hats, their elegant little boots and gloves. Worse than that: a professional or a state functionary is put to shame by the peasant. For the peasant has always got a big gold chain to his watch and a pair of rings on his fingers. He has got two or more luxurious suits. His wife and children who on working days dress badly and work as hard as the head of the family, transform themselves on Sunday with silk dress and plumed bonnets that rival those of the ladies of the town.[4]

"And they wear vulgar clothes." We must add this to our list of things that officials disliked about these people. For a state functionary, with a uniform and a badge proclaiming him a Representative of Superior Authority (as it is put in official correspondence), the thought that these ghastly people might make more money than he did was more than an indignity; it was a subversion of the legitimate order. It could almost be counted an act of insurrection.

It is impossible to know exactly what was in the rioters' minds in 1837. Still, it was hard for the villagers of the Conca d'Oro to believe that a government in Naples could wish them anything but ill, and in 1837 these villagers may have concluded that Naples was trying to kill them off as well—handing out packets of poison to its clandestine agents, probably promising them a share of their victims' goods and chattels. This ill will not only helps explain why the 1837 mobs believed that the plague-spreaders were Bourbon agents; it also illuminates the dynamic that, in ten years, would transform Palermo and the surrounding towns and villages into dynamos of revolutionary energy.

This same dynamic also helped shape the mafia. Villagers avoided contact with state institutions, preferring to conduct their affairs and settle their disputes privately, through informal mediation. Affairs in a Sicilian town were managed between landowners or, since many of the landowners were absentees, between their tenants and agents. Parish priests were often at the center of such networks of informal power. Through centralization, and by opening up magisterial offices to the sons of the gentry, Naples hoped to break up these impenetrable thickets of power. This was a policy that had a measure of success in the eastern part of the island. Not in the west, however, and especially not in the Palermo region: here local hostility to the state was strongest; here, moreover, the barons were close at hand. Instead of eradicating the networks of informal power, reform merely drove them underground.

How was such a network of hidden power managed? In 1820 Palermo had embraced the Carboneria, and for the rest of the century its promise of republic, brotherhood, and freedom from tyrants would be the revolution's guiding star. Yet the Carboneria offered more than this. It could also serve as the instrument that linked the influential and the dangerous classes, as well as serving, in its own right, as an instrument of clandestine control.

We have a description of Sicilian secret societies during this period from Pietro Calà Ulloa, a high-ranking Neapolitan magistrate sent to report on conditions in Sicily.[5] Ulloa described these societies as "brotherhoods" or "sects." They were centered around a *capo*, "who is here a landowner and there a priest." They were also criminal organizations, not, as one might suppose, because they were involved in revolutionary plotting, but because they were involved in crimes such as cattle rustling. He also described them as "parties," for they were involved in deal-making and mediating. They had friends in the aristocracy and megistracy who, much to Ulloa's shock, intervened for them at official levels and acted as their protectors. Finally, they had contacts with other secret societies, those of neighboring towns and even those of other provinces. It was a veritable underground network of power which the magistrate described as "so many tiny governments within the Government."

There would be nothing surprising were this a description of a typical mafia *cosca* or political clientele from the 1890s or 1900s. It is surprising, however, to see clandestine revolutionary societies taking on these functions as early as the 1830s. Informal political control was already transmuting itself into clandestine political control, and the sects were providing the means by which clandestine political power was organized and articulated. Sicilians thus quickly discovered that the sects were not only a means to foment revolution, but served equally well as the instrument of, as it were, practical *omertà*, the Sicilian code of silence.

Such an instrument was, by its nature, radically ambiguous. Ulloa refers to "common funds," in the sense of both the treasury of particular societies and a common stock of funds that affiliated groups could draw on in time of need. Presumably these common funds were raised through membership dues or the proceeds of crime or both. Ulloa tells us nothing about this, however; he merely continues, "Many of the landowners, reasoning that it is better to be on the side of the oppressors than of the oppressed, join these *parties*." What are we to make of this? Although the mafia in its characteristic form does not appear until later, the crimes that it is associated with are very old: Sicilians certainly did not have to wait until the 1860s to learn what extortion was. Thus it is possible that some of the landowners who seemed to be siding with "the oppressors" were really their victims, paying protection money and keeping silent in the hope of being left alone. This is certainly what they would all claim if interrogated by the police. Yet not all of them were victims; someone had to be pocketing the money. There had to be real oppressors as well.

From the point of view of a state functionary like Ulloa, however, there was little ambiguity: these "parties" were inherently seditious and criminal, and landowners had no business cooperating with them.

## More Conspiracies

Revolution was a *carrière ouverte aux talents*, a career open to talents. The revolutionaries of nineteenth-century Italy were ambitious and romantic young men, sons of professionals or of landowners, who had often come to the larger cities such as Palermo or Naples to finish their education. Here they found themselves swept in a heady world of sects, conspiracies, and revolutionary politics, a world that absorbed much of the intellectual and political energies of young Italians at this time. On the Continent, the older nobility held themselves aloof from this world. They might share the romantic patriotism of the sectarians and endorse some of their projects for reform; yet revolution implied hostility to privilege and to legitimacy, and this was something that was hardly to the liking of hereditary peers. In western Sicily, however, the Sicilian nobility had chosen the side of revolution in 1820; it would do so again in 1848.

In theory, though rarely in fact, the sects were an international network, a secret web that disseminated news of conspiracies and new revolutionary projects. Thus, young Sicilians looked abroad for ideas and initiatives. These often arrived through those Sicilians who had left the island as political exiles or those who had left Sicily in search of better opportunities. By the 1840s, groups of Sicilian émigrés, both in Italy and abroad, were in contact with other conspiratorial groups interested in fomenting revolt. Through these groups, sectarians on the island were in contact with Nicola Fabrizi and the Legione italica in Malta, as well as with Giuseppe Mazzini in London.

By 1847, wrote Rosolino Pilo, "all the good citizens [of Palermo] had begun to organize themselves in Secret Societies."[6] This is a considerable exaggeration; still, Bourbon police records show that the subversive groups, few in number throughout the 1820s and 1830s, were now rapidly growing. No more than little brotherhoods or clubs, the groups held se-

cret meetings where the brothers would discuss politics or write mani-
festos, which they sometimes printed and distributed clandestinely as
leaflets or posters. Clubs kept in contact with other clubs, seeking news,
trading information, and entering into intricate and highly acrimonious
debates about the finer points of political doctrine.

Mostly, however, they waited. Revolutions were cataclysms; they were
supposed to start at the center and spread out to the provinces. This is
what happened in Paris in 1789 and 1830, and most revolutionaries assumed that this was what would happen again. Although they subscribed
to the ideals of liberty, equality, and brotherhood, Sicilian revolutionaries
still acted like provincials, country cousins who would wait deferentially
until the North gave them permission to join in.

Malta and London were not the only centers of plotting; Giuseppe La
Masa and Giuseppe La Farina were the Sicilian representatives of a revolutionary group in Florence. In October 1847 the British envoy in Florence, Lord Minto, received a petition that La Farina had written on behalf of certain "Sicilian notables." The letter was, in fact, a subtle attempt
to sound out the British government: Would it be prepared to lend its support in the event of a Sicilian rebellion? Since the British had "sponsored"
the 1812 constitution, many Sicilians hoped that Britain would feel itself
obliged to help Sicily in further attempts to gain independence. A well-
meaning but unimaginative diplomat, Minto missed the point entirely. It
never occurred to him that Her Majesty's government might feel such an
obligation; it did not even occur to him to wonder whether La Farina's letter indicated that revolution was brewing in Sicily. Minto simply mentioned La Farina's letter in his report to London as another example of
how bad Bourbon rule was becoming.[7]

Even in 1847 the sectarians were still a small minority. Without the support of the middle and upper classes, all the machinations of the Palermo
conspirators would have counted for little. This support, however, would
soon be forthcoming. In 1846, Pope Gregory XVI had died in Rome; Cardinal Mastai-Ferretti was elected and took the name of Pius IX. The new
pope became a focus of liberal and nationalist hopes, hopes that extended
far beyond the narrow bounds of the sectarian circles. Throughout the
peninsula, people looked to the new pope as a possible leader of a federation of Italian states. Enthusiasm for "Pio Nono" spread to Sicily as well,
where the idea of Italian federalism not only was popular but also proved
broad and vague enough to unite all segments of constitutional opinion. As
a result, by late 1847 the tide had begun to run in the conspirators' favor.

Of all the centers of conspiratorial activity, however, the most important to Sicily in 1848 was Naples itself.[8] Here a revolutionary central committee had been established with representatives from Naples, Calabria, and Sicily. The leader was the Neapolitan Carlo Poerio, one of the Carbonaria leaders in 1820. The most important representative from Sicily was the ambitious young lawyer Francesco Crispi. Although they were bitter rivals, there was a constant flow of traffic between Naples and Palermo, and it is probable that Crispi's group had a more intimate knowledge of subversive politics in Palermo than either Niccola Fabrizi in Malta or La Farina in Florence. In any case, it was in Naples that all the revolutionary currents began to converge in September 1847.

At the beginning of September there was an uprising in Messina and in Reggio Calabria on the mainland shore. This was another *carbonaro* conspiracy, and the police and army had no difficulty coping with it, though aftershocks in the wilder Aspromonte region persisted for some time thereafter. As always, news of an uprising, no matter how unsuccessful, reverberated throughout the sectarian world, exciting the hopes of revolutionaries everywhere. In Palermo the sectarians began feverish preparations. Rosolino Pilo sailed to Naples to confer with Crispi. He arrived in time to witness a large demonstration there. The demonstration was moderate and peaceful; indeed, considering the strength of the city's garrison, any other sort of demonstration would have been suicidal. Nonetheless, Pilo was indignant; he promised Crispi that when he got back to Palermo he would arrange a more impressive demonstration of popular will.

Although it was not part of Pilo's plans, the opera provided the scene for such a demonstration. Librettos based on contemporary subjects were expressly forbidden, as, of course, were plots that celebrated the deeds of ancient tyrannicides or even cast rulers in a bad light. Nevertheless, it was difficult for government censors to excise all references to brotherhood and love of fatherland on the part of morally unimpeachable characters in plots that were of a politically unexceptionable character. Yet, however innocuous the context in which such sentiments might be declaimed, in the politically electric atmosphere of 1847, their mere declaration was frequently enough to set off prolonged applause and stomping and shouts of "Viva Pio Nono e la Lega italiana!" or, more simply, "Viva l'Italia."

On the night of November 27, during a performance of Donizetti's *La Gemma di Vergy* in Palermo's Teatro Carolina, the faithful slave began an aria with the words, "You took from me heart and mind, Fatherland, Gods, and liberty." At these words, the audience burst out in cheers so overwhelming that the performance had to be interrupted. The tenor then improvised an Italian *tricolore* and stepped forward to intone a patriotic hymn. This sent the audience into further raptures. Revolutionary placards appeared in the balconies, leaflets rained down upon the stage, and the audience began to chant "Viva l'Italia." The next evening the company gave a repeat performance in the open air for the benefit of the poorer classes. The entire city seems to have attended in an unprecedented display of political solidarity, which showed that, by now, the city was prepared to take the side of the revolution. It was, as one of the leading conspirators, Vincenzo Fardella, the marquis of Torrearsa, later wrote, the "moral revolution."[9]

An incident taken from Rosolino Pilo's account sheds light on this "moral revolution." As the tenor began the patriotic hymn, the audience rose to their feet, joining in the song. In the boxes and in the loggias below, the ladies removed their scarves and, tying their scarf ends to those of their neighbors, formed a chain symbolizing unity and solidarity. The chain wound its way through the rows and from box to box. Only one box remained silent, however, refusing to stand, sing, or link itself to the chain of scarves. This was the box of the ex-president of the Sicilian supreme court, Francesco Franco, who sat there with his daughter and his wife, whom Pilo describes as an "old Bourbonic harpy." Next to theirs was the box of Romualdo Trigona, the prince of Sant'Elia. Insulted by the refusal of the Franco family to take part in the patriotic demonstration, the youngest of the prince's sons (Pilo describes him as *giovinetto*) picked up his seat cushion and threw it at them. It caught Signora Franco square in the face. She stood up and drowned out the singing with her screams and rantings.[10]

Pilo and the prince of Sant'Elia, from whose box the cushion was thrown, are two emblematic figures in the 1848 revolution. Pilo was the leader of the "democratic" faction, whereas Sant'Elia was a leading "moderate." Later, the two groups—"democrats" and "moderates"—were to become the two contending parties in the struggle for Italian unity, and eventually the nuclei of the two major parliamentary parties of united Italy. There is a temptation to look at them as ideological adversaries from the start. This would be a mistake. In Sicily in 1848, the distinction between the democrats and moderates was neither one of political outlook nor one of class; more than anything else, it was a difference of generation.

We see Pilo in a sketch from the early 1860s. He is dressed in what must be the red shirt of a Garibaldino, with a mountaineer's cap resting on his hip. He is wearing a tricolor scarf and a belt bearing the arms of Sicily. His sword hangs by his side. By then Pilo had militated in the ranks of the revolution for almost fifteen years; he had undergone exile, privations, and persecutions; yet what strikes the observer is not a look of grim resolution

*Rosolino Pilo with scarf in the Italian* tricolore *and belt buckle with the arms of Sicily. From Trevelyan 1947.*

but the youthfulness and serenity of his gaze. His beard and mustache seem those of twenty-year-old. His forehead is broad and domed. His large, dark eyes stare intensely out with the look typical of a romantic Sicilian intellectual. It is the face of a poet in arms.

Sant'Elia's photograph dates from roughly the same time. In it a grizzled

*Romualdo Trigona, prince of Sant'Elia. From Sciascia 1976.*

face, set off by ample white mustaches, stares defiantly out from the black background. It is the face of a corpulent man, and a powerful, brusque, and impatient man as well. The large lips are set in a frown, while the dark eyes shine forth from behind massive, arched brows. The observer is being stared down by a proud old Sicilian baron.

Active revolutionaries like Pilo were younger men, men with neither civic responsibilities nor domestic ties to encumber them. Participation in the demimonde of revolutionary politics was a full-time occupation for them. The moderates, by contrast, were of an older generation, nobles, senior magistrates, and professors. The prince of Sant'Elia, the duchino di Verdura, the marchese di Spedalloto, Ruggero Settimo, Francesco Ferrara, and Emerico Amari all had important offices and highly visible social positions that made romantic cloak-and-dagger activities inappropriate for them. They took little part in the revolutionary preparations: they neither plotted nor helped to assemble caches of arms and ammunition. Neither did they participate in the initial uprising. Yet they knew what was going on. Both Sant'Elia and Verdura were members of secret societies. On the night of November 27, together with the *pretore* (acting mayor) of Palermo, Spedalotto, they presented the Bourbon governor with a petition demanding that Sicily be allowed to form its own citizens' militia or National Guard. The governor knew that such a petition from such men boded more danger for the Bourbon government than all of the proclamations of Pilo and the young firebrands; he responded by temporarily imprisoning the three Sicilian nobles, together with eight other moderates.

Pilo was a romantic. The night of November 27 and the days immediately following were for him a "sublime moment." He assembled with his fellow democrats in the Palazzo Arcuri in the heart of the old city and debated what to do next. Below, the crowds were milling in the streets waiting to see what course events would take. The revolution was breaking cover, and Pilo spoke out for an immediate insurrection. The crowd was on their side, he proclaimed, and the government forces were not prepared for a coup. All the democrats needed to do was to descend from their headquarters and lead the crowd into battle. They could disarm the police and soldiers and make themselves masters of the city by dawn.

Yet the majority wavered. As they wavered, news of the goings-on at the Palazzo Arcuri reached the ears of the moderates. Sant'Elia and Verdura peremptorily ordered the young revolutionaries not merely to abandon their schemes for immediate uprising, but to leave the palazzo and try to disperse the crowd before serious trouble occurred. Pilo's later account seethes with indignation; Sant'Elia, Verdura, and Spedalotto, he wrote, had let a golden opportunity go to waste. They presented petitions when they should have called their followers to arms. Yet from his own account it is clear that most democrats agreed with the moderates. Revolution was serious business, and not everyone shared Pilo's faith in spontaneous gestures.

Launching an uprising, in fact, required more than a conspiratorial network and the moral support of the upper and middle classes of Palermo; it required the active participation of the urban populace and the peasants and villagers outside the city gates. Preparing these men for revolution had been the task of the Palermo sectarians. Like many of the leading democrats, Pilo was a noble, the younger brother of the count of Carini. Yet, by now, the young sectarians had recruited men from more humble social origins into their groups: Pilo mentions meetings with a pharmacist and a hairdresser, and in other accounts we find butchers, tanners, ex-soldiers, and municipal employees as well as "other men from the common people and the artisans."[11]

Pilo mentions meeting with both "capi-popolo" and "capi-maestra." The *maestranze* had taken part in the 1820 uprising and, as a consequence, had been disbanded by the restored Bourbon government. Yet it seems that the tradition of organization by trade (*di mestiere*) remained. At the end of November 1847, there was a meeting between the sectarian leaders and several hundred workers and artisans in the piazza in front of the Duomo of Palermo. It appears that the sectarians were recruiting these *capi-popolo* and *capi-maestra* as a revolutionary police force. This is the tenor of the oath that was administered during the meeting: the *capi-popolo* swore to "maintain perfect order and to depend in all things upon the advice of those of civil status."[12] The democrats of 1848 were political, not social, revolutionaries. They were Sicilian "patriots" who wished to avoid the looting and vandalism that had marred the 1820 uprising.

The sectarians also worked to ensure the participation of the rural *squadre*, parties of men from a particular locality. Some of the *squadre* were recruited by local liberal committees in contact with conspiratorial groups in Palermo. Sometimes it was members of conspiratorial groups in the capital itself who established contact. Pilo describes trips to meet leaders from Villabate, Santa Flavia, and Ciaculli. They told him that all had been in readiness for an uprising since September.

The police had heard rumors as well; there had been raids and police sweeps in the popular quarters of the city, and quantities of arms had been discovered. By now the entire population of Palermo and the Conca d'Oro seems to have been awaiting the signal to begin. In early December another émigré revolutionary, Giuseppe La Masa, traveled from Florence to Naples to learn of the situation in Palermo from Crispi. Crispi, who had recently conferred with Pilo, told him that the population of Palermo was ready to rise up. Giving him his calling card, Crispi told La Masa to travel to Palermo and make contact with Pilo.

Rumors that an "emissary" had been sent from the revolutionary central in Naples led Palermitans to believe that a "Directive Committee" had been formed in Sicily too. In reality no such committee existed. Still, on the night of January 9, a mysterious poster appeared summoning Sicilians to arms. The poster was signed by the "Directive Committee," and in the circumstances few doubted its authenticity. In fact, the author of the poster was a certain Francesco Bagnasco, a Palermo lawyer and veteran of the *carbonaro* uprising of 1820, who believed that by using the name of a fictitious committee he would lend weight to his call to arms.

Bagnasco even gave the date when the revolution was to begin, and this date, unlike his Directive Committee, was no invention. For at least a week the police had been receiving persistent tip-offs that the towns around Palermo were ready for robbery and bloodshed, and that both inside and outside the city, the seditious innovators and evil-doers had set the day when the revolution was to begin: January 12, King Ferdinand's official birthday.

Being the king's birthday, January 12 was a public holiday. The streets of Palermo began to fill at the crack of dawn. The crowd at first milled around idly, curious to see what would happen. The police were out in force, too, and if no less curious than the crowd, were probably more apprehensive. There were few soldiers present, however. Apart from the cavalry, whose barracks were outside the city gates, the city's garrisons were confined to their quarters.[13]

At the heart of old Palermo lies the Fieravecchia. A small, irregularly shaped piazza, the Fieravecchia was the scene of the "fiera di braccia." On working mornings, laborers from the city and the surrounding villages would trudge into the Fieravecchia and wait, curled up in their cloaks or stomping their feet in the pre-dawn chill, for the arrival of the employers' representatives. These came to assemble gangs and work crews for agricultural labors outside the city or for hauling and carrying in the city itself. In this way, the Fieravecchia came to symbolize these laborers, and thus, appropriately enough, it was in the Fieravecchia that the 1848 uprising began to take shape.

By 8:00 A.M., the first timid shouts of "Viva Pio Nono!" "Viva la Sicilia!" and "Viva l'Italia!" were heard. Armed men appeared shortly thereafter in the Fieravecchia. The moment they appeared, shopkeepers ran out to board up their shops, and from the balconies and windows above, people crowded out, applauding and waving their handkerchiefs. Below, Paolo Paternostro, a young lawyer from Misilmeri, began to harangue the crowds. Workmen brought muskets out of hiding and fired them in the air, shouting "All'armi! All'armi!" At Quattro Cantoni in the middle of the city a crowd had gathered to hear a priest preaching in favor of revolt.

Despite the shouting, haranguing, and shots fired in the air, the revolt had yet to commence. The crowd was waiting for a leader, the "emissary" from the "Directive Committee," to reveal himself and assume command. At about 10:30, Giuseppe La Masa appeared in the Fieravecchia. A small, dapper man with an immense gift for theatrics, La Masa had spent the three days since his arrival from Naples in hiding; he had adopted a continental accent to disguise his Sicilian identity. The ruse, intended to fool the police, fooled the crowd as well, for they took him to be the expected emissary from the Directive Committee. At his best when improvising in front of a crowd, La Masa seized a broomstick and, tying to it red, white, and green garments hastily snatched from the clotheslines above, he stepped forward and, waving his improvised *tricolore*, led the crowd into the church of the nearby Convent of Saint Ursula. Here he began to ring its large bells. When they were answered by the bells from the Convent of Gancia, the revolt had begun.

To understand what happened next, it is necessary to consider the urban topography of Palermo (see the city map in Chapter 3). In 1848 the layout of the city had changed little since the end of the cinquecento. From the Porta Nuova gate to the port, or *cala*, ran the via Toledo, known locally as the Cassaro; this was intersected by the via Macqueda, whose construction in the 1590s marked the final stage in the transformation of medieval Palermo during the Renaissance. The point at which these two roads met, ornamented with fountains and statues, was the Quattro Cantoni, the center of Palermo from the Renaissance to the end of the nineteenth century. Surrounded by walls and bastions, the city resembles in contemporary maps an elongated shield divided into four quarters by these two major thoroughfares.

The topography of each of the four quarters was determined by the noble palazzi and churches found there. In front of most there was, if not usually a full piazza, at least an open space, or *slargo*, which the original builders had carved into the medieval and Arab fabric of the city. There was thus no orderly gridwork of streets within the quarters, for the palazzi and churches were often linked to one another only by narrow twisting alleyways going off in unexpected directions. For the Bourbon generals, it

*Insurgents attacking the Episcopal Palace, January 1848. Note priest in foreground.*

was a terrain that offered few strategic points, and little that could be used for citadels or for command centers from which they could regroup their forces and deploy them in offenses against the rebels.

The Bourbon commandant, General Pietro Vial, was determined not to repeat the mistake of 1820, when the troops, charging recklessly into the labyrinthine network of streets in the popular quarters, had found themselves cut off and surrounded. This explains his decision to confine the city garrison to their barracks. These were grouped around the Palazzo Reale, next to the Porta Nuova, and in the Castellammare, at the northwestern tip of the port. Here, despite their overwhelming superiority in numbers and arms, the troops waited, largely inactive, for the first two days of the revolt, while Generals de Majo and Vial telegraphed urgent calls for reinforcement to Naples.

The decision not to engage the rebels at the outset of the uprising was a timid one. Neapolitan officials and functionaries, whose homes and offices were scattered throughout the city, were left unprotected. These men together with their families, now flooded into the Palazzo Reale, where the presence of a large number of noncombatants soon caused serious problems for the military authorities. Worse, the police were unprotected as well. Police stations, or *commissariati*, were scattered throughout the city, and were usually manned by no more than a handful of officials.

The strategy could not have suited the insurgents better. The city mob

*Crowd sacking a Bourbon police station, January 1848.*

hated the police and were delighted with the opportunity to pick off the police stations one by one. By the afternoon of the twelfth, the first bands began to lay siege to the police stations, starting with those farthest away from the troop concentrations. At first the rebels were dispersed either by police patrols issuing from police headquarters at Piazza Bologni, just north of Quattro Cantoni, or by cavalry patrols entering the city from Porta Sant'Antonino in the south. Yet the urban terrain was ideal for small bands who could pop up out of nowhere, surprising government patrols, then melt away into the confusion of alleyways, *cortili*, and *piazzette* to appear unexpectedly in some other spot.

Although the streets were filled with scurrying men, beggars, and swarms of shouting children, and the windows and balconies above were filled with onlookers, few were actually armed on January 12. Estimates differ, but La Farina's guess that during the first confused day the number of armed insurgents in the crowd numbered no more than forty is probably as good as any. These men skirmished throughout the afternoon of the twelfth; and by evening the number of casualties on the Bourbon side seems to have been about ten.

During the first night, however, the revolt was reinforced by a *squadra* arriving from Villabate, armed with muskets, hunting rifles, knives, and axes. Early the next morning, larger and better-organized *squadre* began arriving from Misilmeri and Bagheria. The Misilmeri *squadra* was led by Antonino Paternostro, the brother of the young lawyer who had first addressed the crowds on the morning of the rebellion. Someone among them had had the foresight to hold up the royal mail carriage from Caltanissetta, which was found to be carrying tax receipts. The rejoicing crowds dragged the carriage and its valuable baggage in from the Porta di Termini, the city gate closest to the Fieravecchia and the natural link between the city and the countryside during the first days of the rebellion.

Despite a week's foreknowledge that the rebellion had been recruiting fighters in the region around the city, the commandant had thought neither to bar the town gates nor to reinforce the troops in nearby Monreale and Bagheria. This was another costly error. Rising up immediately after the capital, these towns had little difficulty in subduing the local garrisons. Giuseppe Scordato, the brother of a notorious, though popular, brigand chieftain, Giambattista, led the *squadra* from Bagheria. Turi Miceli led the *squadra* from Monreale. Miceli and his men had captured a government cavalry unit outside the walls of Palermo on the thirteenth; the day afterward he attacked the garrison in his native Monreale. Both Scordato and Miceli arrived with prisoners and spoils of war; Scordato even brought with him a large cannon, which the people of Palermo baptized "Pio Nono." With these reinforcements, the number of armed rebels had by now grown to about three hundred.

On the afternoon of the fifteenth, five thousand troops arrived from Naples under the command of General Robert de Sauget. They were allowed to rest in their ships on the sixteenth, but on the next day they tried to force their way into the city from the Castellammare and from the northern gates in the area of the Convent of San Francesco di Paolo.

By now, the *squadre* had wiped out the police headquarters at Piazza Bologni. Except for the zones around the Palazzo Reale and the Castellammare, the entire city was in the hands of the rebels when the Bourbons launched their counterattack. Outside the walls, rural *squadre* had been organizing and pouring into the city, many arriving from the Colli and from San Lorenzo Colli districts to the north of the city. Thus, though they outnumbered and outgunned the insurgents, the Bourbon forces could, once again, be attacked from within and without the city gates. In Palermo itself, Scordato and his Bagheresi led the way. As in 1820, the Neapolitans let themselves be divided, surrounded, and cut off from one another. In this way, after heavy fighting the insurgents managed to repulse the Bourbon counterattack.

Much chagrined at this unexpected turn of events, the Neapolitans retired to their ships and began to bombard the city. It was over this incident that Ferdinand II earned the nickname "King Bomba." It was another tactic that played into the rebels' hands. An indiscriminate bombardment of a city containing a large number of foreign businessmen and representatives quickly caused protests to be lodged by the French, Sardinian, and, possibly, American consuls. Many British citizens escaped to the *HMS Bulldog*, a Royal Navy frigate which happened to be in Palermo harbor at the time. Among them was Lord Mount Edgcumbe, a peer whose health cure in Palermo's temperate Conca d'Oro had been rudely cut short. The *squadra* leaders persuaded Mount Edgcumbe to intervene on their behalf and request a cessation of hostilities. He consented, though he gave the rebels his frank opinion that without a military victory, diplomatic approaches would have no effect.

Mount Edgcumbe nevertheless wrote a private letter to Lord Minto in Rome. It would more reasonable, he said, to expect two wild cats to settle their differences by negotiations than to expect the same of the Sicilians and the Neapolitans. The Sicilians completely distrusted King Ferdinand, who, on his side, was too enraged at the temerity of his Sicilian subjects even to consider offering them concessions. Generals de Majo and Vial had both told Mount Edgcumbe privately that concessions were necessary; but they were too frightened to suggest this to their king. Thus, both sides continued to proclaim publicly that they would accept only the total surrender of the other. Sitting on the deck of the *Bulldog* as he wrote, Mount Edgcumbe could hear the sound of the rebels' brass bands above the gunfire. They were showing spunk, he thought, and for all the superiority in numbers and armaments, the Neapolitan soldiers were revealing themselves as nothing more than a pack of cowards.[14]

With international sympathy turning its way, the revolution hastened to put forward an acceptable face. La Masa had begun to organize a "Provisional Revolutionary Committee" as early as January 13, though its first functions were simply to write incendiary proclamations, send appeals for aid, and organize the building of barricades. On the next day the Provisional Revolutionary Committee was changed to a Provisional Committee made up four subcommittees. At a meeting in the Palermo city hall, Palazzo Pretorio, the moderates, under Mayor Spedalotto, agreed to form a provisional government. Leadership was first offered to Emanuele Requesens, prince of Pantelleria, a leader of the 1820 revolt. Yet Requesens was weak and ill, and so the choice passed to Ruggero Settimo. Spedalotto was reconfirmed as mayor of Palermo, and the provisional government reconfirmed La Masa as commander of military forces.

In this first provisional government the senior nobility predominated. Ruggero Settimo of the Princes of Fitalía, had taken part in both the 1812 parliament and the 1820 revolution and later had served as rear admiral in the Bourbon navy. Marxists later castigated La Masa, arguing that the democrats should have formed a government on their own. This is to miss the point: none of the democratic leaders wanted social revolution; instead, they wanted Sicilian independence based on a revised edition of the 1812 constitution.

This is clear in the government's first acts. On the eighteenth, in response to a government request for a temporary cease-fire, Spedalotto wrote that "having courageously arisen, the people will neither put down their arms nor cease hostilities until, reunited in a General Parliament in Palermo, Sicily will be able to readapt its Constitution which, sworn to by its kings and recognized by all powers, none has ever dared to openly abrogate for this island." As if this were not clear enough, Settimo's secretary, Mariano Stabile, amended the reference to "The Constitution . . . recognized by all powers" to read "the Constitution, which, under the influence of the English Nation, was reformed in 1812 and recognized by all powers."[15]

In any case, the revolutionaries had a pressing practical need to entrust the provisional government to respected aristocrats and moderates. A successful insurrection in Palermo could be only a first step; the simple fact remained that the Bourbons possessed a large standing army and the Sicilians possessed no army at all. Even if the aroused people were able to drive the Neapolitan garrisons out of Palermo and the other major cities, there was nothing to prevent them from coming back, just as they had done in 1820. Against a well-organized counterattack by the Bourbon army, the Sicilians could only mount a destructive and debilitating guerrilla war. Their only hope was for the intervention of a foreign or Italian power. The revolutionaries had foreseen this from the start: this was why La Farina had approached the British in October 1847, and why La Masa had got in touch with moderate liberal groups in central Italy at the same time. This was why Mariano Stabile now became so anxious to bring Lord Minto to Sicily.

The shelling of Palermo had meanwhile done nothing to diminish the ardor of the insurgents; and from the eighteenth, the *squadre* began the systematic reduction of the Palazzo Reale and the Castellammare. By now they possessed a number of cannons taken from the garrison at Termini Imeresi and the services of two Sicilian-born artillery officers who had deserted from the Neapolitan army. The urban *squadre* leveled the buildings surrounding the Palazzo Reale and began their attack. On the twenty-fourth, there was a halt when the Palermitans temporarily ran out of ammunition. The Neapolitans were now thoroughly demoralized; the palace was crowded with women and children; food, water, and ammunition was running low. Although no order seems to have been given, the Neapolitans took advantage of the lull to evacuate the building, carrying with them all their possessions.

With the abandoning of the Palazzo Reale, all that was left to the Neapolitans was to ask for a cessation of hostilities in order to evacuate their unprotected troops and civilians. Before this could be granted, however, the Provisional Committee in Palermo demanded that the Castellammare, still held by government troops, be evacuated and turned over to the Sicilians. While negotiations were going on, the troops, functionaries, and their families assembled at the port outside the city near the Ucciardone prison. They were without provisions, and many of their officers had disappeared. Some said that Generals de Majo and Vial had already escaped in women's clothing; others claimed that they had been driven out of the city hiding under bedclothes and mattresses. General de Sauget remained and tried to lead this mass toward Solunto, near Bagheria, where he expected to embark for Naples. On the coast road, however, they were attacked by Sicilian *squadre*, and many of the Neapolitans fled in panic toward the hills around Boccadifalco. Here, unfortunately, the attack turned into a massacre reminiscent of 1820 as peasants descended from their villages in the hills to kill the Neapolitans, despoiling them of whatever goods they carried or wore.

Although the Castellammare held out until February 5, the evacuation of the Palazzo Reale marked the end of the Palermo rebellion of 1848. On the second of February, the Provisional Committee renamed itself the provisional government, assuming power until a general parliament could meet to adapt the 1812 constitution to the needs of 1848. Settimo was reconfirmed as president with Stabile as his secretary—serving, in other words, as prime minister. The elderly Requesens was made the president of the committee for war, with Baron Riso as vice president; Francesco Crispi was appointed secretary. The marchese di Torrearsa was appointed president of the finance committee; Pasquale Calvi the president of the justice and public security committee; Pietro Lanza, prince of Scordia, president of the committee for civil administration.

Divided into a House of Peers and a Commons, the Sicilian parliament met in April 1848. Proceedings were dominated by the lower house, the majority of whose members were lawyers, and who took the drafting of an amended version of the 1812 constitution as their first priority. Parliament immediately set to work, and a new constitution was ready by early July. The clauses limiting the power of the executive and guaranteeing civil rights were strengthened, and clauses concerning political democracy were added as well. Sicily could be proud that its constitution offered far more guarantees of civil liberties than the constitution eventually granted by Ferdinand II to the revolutionary government in Naples. Yet before the new constitution could be put into effect, the government was forced to confront the anarchy that was rapidly spreading across the length and breadth of the island.

### The Island in Flames

The 1848 revolution was haunted by the failure of the Bourbon agrarian reform, a reform that suffered from conflicting aims from the very start. Certain of the reformers had foreseen that, with the creation of a free market in arable land, the abolition of older restrictions would favor the emergence of a class of new landowners with practical expertise and money to invest. For such reformers, the logical outcome of agrarian reform was thus the rise of a gentry. This hope, however, conflicted with an older strand of paternalistic charity which maintained that the crown had a special mission to act as the guardian of the poor and landless peasantry against the exactions of rapacious landowners—the very gentry, in other words, who might otherwise hope to benefit from the abolition of the older restrictions. The Bourbon government seems never to have realized how deeply incompatible its two aims were, or that the likely result of a policy aimed at satisfying the incompatible demands of different classes would be to set these classes at one another's throats.

Although the goals of the agrarian reforms were genuinely benevolent, the means by which the state pursued these goals were woefully inadequate if not counterproductive. In 1817 the restored government in Naples drew up lists of Sicilians eligible for public office. It specifically instructed its officials to show a preference for the landed nobility over the professional classes, as the government viewed the latter as "unstable"—that is, of having, liberal sympathies. Officials were especially cautioned against the legal classes in Palermo, for here there existed an overabundance of "poor and dubious" lawyers, who should in no circumstances be allowed to hold office.[16]

The government seems to have supposed that by relying on the older nobility in Sicily, a nobility which they imagined was sympathetic to the crown and its outlook, the unseemly scramble could be avoided and the "unstable" professional classes (especially the "poor and dubious" lawyers of Palermo) could be excluded. Nothing could have been further from the truth.

Sicilian agriculture was expanding throughout the nineteenth century. Given the dearth of liquid capital in the interior, landowners typically acquired new land not by buying it outright but by marrying into it or gaining it through political influence. Marriage and officeholding were the traditional ways in which Sicilian families climbed the social ladder. Both were political strategies, and it helped if, among his brothers, sons, sons-in-law, and nephews, a landowner could number an important lawyer, official, or local magistrate.

Agrarian reforms meant that communal lands, crown lands, and monastic estates would suddenly come up for grabs. The stakes were being raised, and an unseemly scramble would inevitably ensue. It was unrealistic to expect this scramble to be an entirely amicable affair. The best that could be hoped was that rival families might settle their matrimonial and political differences through lawyers and political friends rather than—as had often occurred in the past—with bands of armed retainers.

In theory, in the great land share-out it was the government that decided who got what. In reality, these were local bureaucratic decisions. Reform creates its own bureaucracy, and the Bourbon agrarian reforms entailed a good deal of clerical work: the drawing up of lists, surveying of boundaries, running of auctions and sales. Since there were few qualified Neapolitan officials in the Sicilian interior, the administration of agrarian reform was handed over to Sicilians. Theoretically, these Sicilians were all loyal servants of the Bourbon crown who executed their duties faithfully and impartially. In reality, they were all members of landowning families, and no one ever doubted where their true loyalties lay. Reform was thus handed over to the very classes that the government wished to exclude.

The result was that in every town of agrarian Sicily there arose a small group of families who dominated and profited from the agrarian reforms. These families constituted what, in 1848, was called the "Bourbon party" in the towns in which they lived. For the less favored families, the 1848 revolution was sometimes less about Sicilian liberties than about getting revenge.

The peasant, too, were out for revenge. They were the supposed beneficiaries of the reforms. Nevertheless, the breakup of the common lands had stripped them of innumerable communal rights—grazing, hunting, charcoal making, gathering building stone, clay, and wild plants. Activities that had once taken place on the old municipal commons now became privately owned and controlled. The government had foreseen that the peasants would lose these traditional rights and had passed laws requiring that they receive compensation for their losses. Few had benefited; though taxes were regularly increased, the promised compensation was rarely paid.

Property ownership also entailed expenses. Peasant families had few sources of liquid capital and, of course, no savings. Families who received lands during the share-out might suddenly be faced with new expenses. They were forced to borrow, becoming entrapped in an endless cycle of debt, in which bankruptcy and the forced sale of their newly allotted lands was the usual end. Few peasants prospered, and land reform became a story of blighted hopes, of promises made but never fulfilled.[17]

Within two weeks of the Palermo up rising, disturbances were erupting in cities and towns throughout the island. The rural disturbances started in the central and eastern parts of the interior. These were the areas most affected by land reform. In March and early April, the time of spring sowing, peasants began to occupy and cultivate the unassigned commons and by April had begun to occupy the lands of "usurper" proprietors as well. Revolutions in Sicily were tax holidays, while restorations meant the reinstitution of the registers that recorded the taxes paid on grain, on transactions (*carta bollata*), and even on windows and doors. Thus the peasants rarely stopped at the occupation of unassigned commons or lands in the hands of usurper landowners. Mobs destroyed government offices, burned the registers, and opened the prisons. Other landowning families sought to capitalize on the peasants' anger, leading them in attacks which gutted the palazzi of the "Bourbon" families. There were pitched battles in the streets and bloody ambushes as parties armed themselves with shotguns and set out to eliminate their rivals.[18]

The provisional government in Palermo at first turned a blind eye, insisting that the sacking of municipalities and the occupation of uncultivated lands were "patriotic" deeds. It applauded the peasants' actions, and when it received complaints from owners whose lands had been occupied, it issued pardons and amnesties to all involved. As the disturbances moved westward toward Palermo province, however, they grew increasingly violent. Peasants began to cut down the plants and burn the crops on cultivated land as well. When occupations and sackings began to transform themselves into robbery, arson, and homicide, the provisional government grew seriously alarmed.

The lawyers who dominated the Sicilian House of Commons had done a very creditable job of rewriting the 1812 constitution; nevertheless, they had little idea how to solve the agrarian crisis. In fact, the revolutionary government shared all of the Neapolitan government's misconceptions. The government also assumed a mission of succoring the peasants, whose poverty, the revolutionary deputies naturally claimed, was an effect of Bourbon misrule. They vowed to liberate them from the hated *macinato* tax, the tax paid by the peasants when they took their grain to be ground into flour. It was accepted that this was an iniquitous burden; yet the revolutionary government had few alternative sources of revenue. To those parliamentary deputies who proposed to "liberate" the peasants from the *macinato*, the secretary to the minister of finance, Michele Amari, pointed out that this would deprive the new state of approximately one third of its tax revenues. He observed that those who argued that the revolution had a duty to abolish the *macinato* had themselves a duty to find the state a new source of revenue. Since they were unable to do so, the Sicilian parliament was forced to decree that the peasants would temporarily have to "suffer" the *macinato* as a patriotic duty.[19]

Unable to come up with any solution, the provisional government was forced to treat the peasants' depredations as a public security matter. This meant repression. But repression by whom? Most police officials in Sicily were Neapolitans, and any Neapolitan policeman who had survived the first few months of 1848 in Sicily with his skin intact could count himself a lucky man.

One solution was to use the *squadre*. Preparation for the rebellion had been well under way from September 1847, and the *squadre* that had arrived in Palermo during the first week of the rebellion had been formed in advance by the secret societies. During the Battle of Palermo, these *squadre* maintained their discipline and fought bravely. They were from the same revolutionary clubs that had assumed power locally. In this way, towns such as Monreale and Misilmeri were able to maintain civil order during the 1848 revolution, sparing themselves the devastation that held other towns in its grip.

The most effective *squadra* leaders—Turi Miceli from Monreale, Vincenzo Pagano from Parco, Giuseppe Scordato from Bagheria—found themselves decked with medals and honors by a grateful government. These leaders were heroes, and they formed the nucleus of a projected revolutionary army. The leader of this army was Giuseppe La Masa, a little man with very big ideas. Bewitched by the vision of a final revolution that would free all peoples from the chains of tyranny, La Masa convinced himself that the rebellion he had started was the harbinger of this final revolution. Thus, taking Miceli, Pagano, Scordato and the other *squadra* leaders commissioned as officers in his new Sicilian army along with him, in the summer of 1848 he sailed off. Just when the island most needed the services of these men, they were marching fruitlessly through the wilds of Calabria.

This left the other *squadre*, the ones that had arrived later. Much less is known about these men. The safest thing to say is that, while some of them probably conducted themselves well, others were indistinguishable from the mob.

Responsibility for the *squadre* fell to Pasquale Calvi, who, as head of the justice and public security committee, was effectively both the minister of justice and the minister of the interior on the island. A fiery revolutionary from Castellammare in Trapani province, Calvi later wrote that the *squadre* were largely innocent of crime and violence. During the revolt in Palermo, he claimed, the *squadre* attacked only Bourbon institutions and symbols of Bourbon authority.[20]

Certainly some of the destruction was symbolic. The crowd pulled down and destroyed all the statues of foreign rulers—Philip IV, Charles III, and Maria Amalia of Saxony. Somewhat less symbolic was the looting of the royal palace and other royal building of all their fittings and furnishings. Still less symbolic was the felling of the trees lining public streets.

The destruction of the fish and meat markets was especially emblematic of the attitude of the crowd. Palermo benefited from subsidized bread. In economic terms, the hated *macinato* represented a transfer of wealth from the peasants in the interior to Palermo. This was one of the reasons why the plight of the interior peasantry was not an issue over which Palermo felt strongly. About other foodstuffs, however, their feelings were different. The decision to centralize the retailing of fish and meat through licenses and other controls and the construction of government-operated fish and meat markets were partially dictated by considerations of hygiene; yet the decision was equally dictated by a wish to ensure that taxes on these foodstuffs were regularly paid. Unlike the *macinato*, these were taxes that were paid by the consumers themselves. This helps explain why the crowd did not just attack the newly built butchery and fish markets, but razed them to the ground.

Finally, the sacking and burning of virtually every precinct station in the city and the murder of 340 policemen can hardly be called symbolic. The Neapolitan state had tried to cope with tax evasion, smuggling, and crime by issuing identification papers, licenses, stamped receipts, permissions, and good conduct certificates. The cost of these controls was borne by the local population in the form of new taxes. Administering them fell to the police, and the local population found themselves continually obliged to pay fees and wait upon the pleasure of unsympathetic Neapolitan police officials in order to obtain their necessary papers.

On the night of January 13, the rebels captured the military hospital of San Francesco Saverio. The soldiers they found there, as well as those brought in by Scordato and Miceli, were well treated. Not so the police. The Neapolitan police were capable of great brutality; there were rumors that they tortured prisoners to extract confessions. When the crowds broke into the precinct stations at San Domenico and elsewhere, they discovered gruesome human remains—bones, teeth, and mutilated bodies. This confirmed their worst fears; the police captured at San Domenico and at via del Celso were hacked to pieces by the crowd.

With this, the provisional government ordered the incarceration of all Bourbon police officers; it was a measure for their own protection. Yet on the twenty-first of February, the *squadre* burst open the prison of Santa Anna, where a large number of these police officers were being kept. They were summarily tried, one by one, and executed, all except a few who, as Calvi cynically remarked, were famous for their "corruption"—they worked hand in glove with racketeers and organized crime.[21]

In March and April many of the *squadristi* who had fought in Palermo or who had joined in the attack on the Neapolitan army as it had tried to retreat from the city, returned to their towns and villages to take a leading role in the municipal riots and the attacks on Bourbon sympathizers. Their ranks were swelled by released prisoners. Shortly before abandoning Palermo, the Neapolitan army had opened the doors of the Ucciardone prison, freeing between ten and twelve thousand convicts. Most of the prison records were burned; beyond knowing that a large proportion of these men were from the Continent, we know nothing about them except that they added their presence to the bands of brigands and parties of *tristi* or "rogues" infesting the countryside.[22]

The vast majority of landowners in Sicily supported independence from Naples, even if a few of them used the rebellion to wreak revenge on their rivals. Yet, whatever his political opinions, no landowner was going to sit idly by and watch his rents go up in smoke as bands of peasants burned his crops. As early as the twenty-eighth of January, a Sicilian National Guard had been instituted and placed under the command of Baron Riso, the vice president of the committee for war. This National Guard was supposed to be a citizens' militia; instead, it became a loosely coordinated group of vigilante units. These units were led by landowners, who picked and equipped their followers, either paying them from their own pockets or choosing them from among their own men. The units were armed and mounted, and, by the summer of 1848, they were ready to ride.

By then, the provisional government had had enough. Its leaders had turned a blind eye to the excesses of the mobs and peasants in the late spring and early summer; now they turned a blind eye to the excesses of the National Guard. In the Corleone area the National Guard consisted of seventy men under the command of the prince of Acicatena. The prince was accused of trampling on the rights of local administrators in his areas. Yet the Sicilian National Guard defended these rough-and-ready methods. The captain of the National Guard from nearby Roccapalumba wrote to Riso complaining that the government wished to restrain evildoers with "sweetness and persuasion." Not by these means, he argued, but only by "terrible examples" could peace be brought to the interior. "In the name of the entire National Guard," he beseeched the government to give him permission "to summarily shoot all evildoers."[23]

These were the sorts of sentiments that quickly brought the National Guard into conflict with Calvi and the democrats. The democrats still saw the *squadre* as a revolutionary army. On April 28, however, there had been a shoot-out in the Fieravecchia between the *squadra* of Teresa Testa di Lana and the National Guard. Even Calvi could not represent Testa di

Lana as the vanguard of the revolution. Instead, he described her as "a wrinkled little goatherd in men's dress, with a pistol and dagger in her belt, a saber in the sword belt across her chest, who was the *capo* of a *squadra* at the Fieravecchia which distinguished itself in its assaults on police barracks and in its persecution of police agents (*Sbirri*)."[24]

Calvi was criticized, first in the Peers and later in the Commons. There were public demonstrations against him (organized and paid for, he claimed, by his enemies), and at the end of May, Settimo published a pointed warning against those men who wished to bring anarchy down upon their country. There followed a ministerial crisis in which Calvi fell from office. He was replaced by Riso, who, as minister of justice and public security as well as commandant of the National Guard, held almost dictatorial powers.

## The Defeat

Still, the real threat to the Sicilian revolution was not internal but external: Sicily lacked an army, and there was nothing to prevent the Neapolitans from returning in force.

The January 12 uprising had shaken King Ferdinand II of Naples, leading him to fear for his throne. On the eighteenth of January he started granting concessions: he agreed to a limited autonomy for Sicily and to the release of all political prisoners in Neapolitan prisons. By the end of the month he had granted a new constitution for Naples itself, and began to form a new, liberal ministry. It is possible that behind this apparent change of heart Ferdinand was fighting for time, hoping to obtain a free hand with which to deal with the Sicilian rebellion. This at least was the opinion of the British chargé d'affaires in Naples, who commented that "the Neapolitan government has satisfied the liberals of Naples in order to revenge itself upon those of Sicily."[25] It was a cunning stratagem, for the 1848 Neapolitan liberals were no more sympathetic to Sicilian independence than those of 1820. Any hopes that Settimo and Stabile might have held out that the new constitutional government in Naples would come to terms with the Sicilian government were soon dashed.

Nevertheless, changes in Naples gave Sicily some breathing room; more than six months were to elapse before Naples attempted a reconquest. This was a lull that the Sicilian government might well have used to organize some sort of defense. Instead, the provisional government spent the time feverishly seeking a foreign patron. France was caught up in its own political turmoils. King Charles Albert of Piedmont refused to permit the duke of Genoa to accept the offer of the Sicilian crown. This left only Great Britain.

Late January saw a flurry of British diplomacy on Sicily's behalf. Lord Napier, the ambassador in Naples, advised Lord Palmerston, the foreign secretary, to press Ferdinand to grant concessions to Sicily—a suggestion that Palmerston supported. Palmerston and Prime Minister Lord John Russell exchanged informal notes on the subject. The Sicilians, they thought, were just like the Irish, a pugnacious and irascible little race. Unfortunately, the analogy ended here, for, unlike Her Majesty's government in London, the Bourbon government in Naples was an abomination. In Rome, Lord Minto was surprised to discover that even Pius IX thought that the Sicilians had a right to their 1812 constitution. Although the revolutionary leaders continued to insist publicly on total independence from Naples, privately they indicated that they would be happy to accept a negotiated settlement brokered by a foreign power.

In March and April 1848, Lord Minto, the British special envoy, strove to negotiate a settlement between Naples and Sicily. Stabile, who had been a proponent of a British solution from the beginning, saw the British as Sicily's only hope. He forced himself to believe that the well-meaning but obtuse Minto was offering more than he really was. Minto still failed to understand that many Sicilians regarded Britain as the sponsor of the 1812 constitution, and therefore morally obliged to intervene on Sicily's behalf. In a letter of April 6, he advised Stabile to try every means of "avoiding the calamity of a republican form of government." What was intended as a piece of avuncular advice was taken as a broad hint: if only the moderates were to purge the republicans from the government, Britain would be happy to send over some member of its royal family to rule as king of Sicily. The Sicilians were eager to oblige. Not only did Calvi fall from office but, shortly thereafter, Paolo Paternostro published a manifesto naming Calvi, Crispi, and others as the leaders of a republican faction. He suggested that the government ought to stand them against a wall and shoot them. It was not until November that Palmerston himself finally wrote the Sicilians that the British had no intention of intervening. By then it was too late, for the Neapolitan army was already back in Sicily.[26]

By September 1848 the Neapolitan commander, Carlo Filangieri, had retaken Messina. There now followed another lull, for in October the British and French consuls at Messina persuaded Filangieri to grant Sicily a six months' truce. The two governments hoped to use the time to mediate a settlement between Naples and Sicily; and in fact, in February 1849,

King Ferdinand issued a set of proposals from his fortress at Gaeta. Sicily was offered a constitution with a House of Commons, elected on a limited suffrage, and a House of Peers, nominated by the king. Sicily was to have its own government, though the Foreign Ministry and the army would remain in Neapolitan hands. On the surface, nothing could have seemed more reasonable; yet the proposals were nothing but a ruse. King Ferdinand was clever enough to see that all that was needed was an offer generous enough to satisfy the consciences of the British and the French. Once that was done, they would go away, leaving him free to deal with Sicily as he wished. There was thus nothing to guarantee that the king would abide by his promises, and every reason to believe that he would not. That was how his father and namesake had behaved in 1820.

This possibility became painfully real when, exactly two weeks later, the king suddenly abrogated the constitution that he had granted Naples and suppressed the Neapolitan parliament. It had sat for a mere forty days. He later imprisoned many of the ministers he himself had called into power.

King Ferdinand's offer placed the Sicilian government in a dilemma. The wording was that of an ultimatum, and acceptance would mean total capitulation. Yet a Bourbon army was in Messina, and Sicily had no armed forces. Resistance seemed futile. The government vacillated. Riso fell and was replaced by the marquis of Torrearsa, committed to continuing the struggle. Torrearsa soon resigned and was replaced by a new government headed by Pietro Lanza, prince of Scordia, and representatives of the older nobility. Lanza's ministry sued for peace. As in 1820, however, the Palermo populace would not hear of capitulation. There were popular demonstrations, and the Lanza government was forced to resign. Calvi and the democrats were called back to power and proceeded to reject the conditions set down at Gaeta. This was the break between the moderates and the democrats—not over social policy or world revolution, but over last-ditch resistance.

Calvi's rejection of the Gaeta proposals gave Naples the excuse it was looking for, and hostilities were reopened. The Neapolitan army marched out of Messina. At first, General Filangieri concentrated on the east coast of Sicily, where he encountered serious resistance only at Catania. After reimposing Bourbon rule on the east, Filangieri slowly turned to the west. The leisurely pace of his advance allowed panic to spread in the capital. Although surrender was inevitable, no one wished to take upon himself the opprobrium of signing Sicily's act of capitulation. Ruggero Settimo ceded all executive powers to the municipality of Palermo and, boarding an English ship with a number of other Sicilian ministers, escaped to Malta.

Calvi, Crispi, and La Farina took charge of the defense of Palermo. Peasants, priests, and titled ladies all pitched in, seizing shovels to dig trenches around the town walls. *Squadre* from the Conca d'Oro returned to the city. There was some looting, but a British naval officer reported that the city's underworld bosses had undertaken to ensure that order was maintained.[27] Baron Riso argued for surrender; yet Calvi had disbanded his National Guard, and he was without power. He was attacked by the Palermo mob and barely escaped with his life. Meanwhile, the *squadre* from Monreale and Bagheria had returned from Calabria, and Calvi tried to entice Miceli and Scordato into assuming command. Yet Miceli and Scordato were no romantics; they looked at the situation, saw its hopelessness, and declined. They secretly met with Riso, and the three of them escaped to Bagheria, where they met with Filangieri. Here, in an effort to avoid needless bloodshed and destruction, they agreed to accompany the Neapolitan army into the city.

The situation was familiar. Just as the prince of Villafranca had slipped out of Palermo to meet General Pepe in Termini Imeresi in 1820, defying a crowd determined on a suicidal defense, now Baron Riso was treating with General Filangieri in Bagheria. Yet the differences were even more important. The 1848 revolution had forged a Sicilian nation.

Hatred of Naples was strongest in Palermo province, and it was the Palermitans who initiated the struggle. Already by the festival of Santa Rosalia in September 1847, the population of Palermo was preparing for revolt. According to Pilo, the revolutionaries had the support of the laborers in the vineyards and groves and even of the inmates of the Ucciardone prison. Describing the night of September 3, Pilo wrote:

> The workers in the fields and in the city had left off their work that day, and, eager to act, awaited the signal to fight. It should also be noted that during these sublime days even the corrupted class of prison inmates were inspired by the principles of justice and virtue. They issued an order to their affiliates in which they declared that *he who dared commit thefts during the supreme days that were probably to follow was a traitor to the Fatherland.* Consequently, in those days no disturbances occurred.[28]

The story that the bosses of organized crime in Palermo's prison gave their blessing and support to the revolution was to shape Sicily's perception of these bosses for generations to come.

**3**

# The 1860 Revolution

There were four great uprisings in nineteenth-century Palermo; of these, 1860 stands out as the exception. A simple set of figures may explain why. In the 1820 and 1848 revolts, the Neapolitan garrison numbered between five and ten thousand men. By 1866, when a revolt in Palermo was the last thing the new government was expecting, the garrison numbered only about two thousand. Throughout the 1850s, however, there were usually around twenty thousand Bourbon troops stationed in Palermo.[1]

After 1848 the attitude of Naples hardened. The new lieutenant governor of Sicily, Carlo Filangieri, tried to initiate a policy of conciliation. His government, he proclaimed, never wished to suppress legitimate aspirations for reform and change; it intended only to repress the actions of those disruptive few who, exploiting discontent, had led Sicily down the path of violence and anarchy. He issued a general amnesty, excluding only forty-three individuals, almost all of whom had already escaped abroad.

Even those *popolani* (common people) captured with their arms and condemned to be shot as rebels were pardoned. This policy was supported neither by the king nor by his ministers, who showed themselves unwilling to countenance dissent of any variety.[2]

Among the losers under the new regime were Sicily's barons. The aristocracy had played a leading role in 1848; figures associated with the 1812 constitution had worked together with the bold and idealistic younger spirits who sat in the House of Commons. They had rallied to the provisional government, lending the revolution social legitimacy and a sense of historic continuity. After 1849, however, Naples was in no mood to flatter the historic sensibilities of Sicily's barons, men whom Naples regarded—with considerable justification—as irremediably tainted by separatist aspirations. The state dropped the fiction that the Kingdom of the Two Sicilies was a legitimate "restoration" state where the king in Naples ruled in partnership with Sicily's own nobility. After 1849, Naples ruled through the police.

The government in Naples had few illusions. After 1849, Palermo and the larger provincial towns were treated as enemy territory, cities whose population would jump at the chance to revolt if ever the state were careless enough to let down its guard. Not only did the Bourbon state increase its garrisons in Sicily, but it also brought in crack regiments of German mercenaries, who were less likely to fraternize with the local population or allow themselves to become drawn into liberal conspiracies.

We saw that shortly after the 1848 January revolt in Palermo, there had been a revolt in Monreale. The Bourbon garrison was overcome its soldiers led as prisoners to Palermo by the *squadra* leader Turi Miceli. Jails in Monreale were opened and the prisoners set free, their place taken by Bourbon officials. A new municipal council was created, its seats filled by occupational categories: there was a seat for the clergy, for the gentry, for the smallholders, for the artisans, and for the agricultural laborers. There was even a seat for the *calcarai*—meaning either "quarrymen" or "lime burners"—whose representative, in any case, was described as entirely illiterate. This new municipal council was simply a consultative body, however, with no effective power. Real authority rested in the hands of the archbishop of Monreale, as it had in previous centuries. In 1848 the archbishop was an enthusiastic supporter of the revolution; he followed events in Palermo closely and ordered the singing of a Te Deum to mark each of the revolution's victories. He was especially delighted with the 1812 constitution and the restoration of the House of Peers, as this allowed him to descend on the capital with his suite and take his seat as one of Sicily's leading ecclesiastical dignitaries.

In 1860, by contrast, there were six thousand Bourbon soldiers in the town of Monreale and another four thousand in the surrounding hills. Their numbers ruled out any local uprising. So numerous were the troops and police, in fact, that the government had been forced to seek new quarters for them. Parts of the old Benedictine convent, the abbey cloisters, and the communal theater were all commandeered as billets for the troops. The jails were also filled, though not by soldiers but by enemies of the regime. Already in May 1850, four men had been executed for revolutionary activities. The archbishop himself had been replaced by an appointee from Naples, so there was no thought of protesting this offense against Monreale's historic dignity or the abuse of its religious properties. Indeed, when, following the insurrection in Palermo in April 1860, there were skirmishes in the countryside surrounding Monreale, the new archbishop, together with the Monreale chief of police, hastened to send the new king of Naples Francis, a telegram congratulating him on his success in eradicating the *tristi*.[3]

## Piedmont

On the surface, 1848 had ended in a general failure in Italy. In the North, the Austrians, together with their protégés in Tuscany and the central Italian duchies, were all back in power. In the center, Pius IX had returned to Rome and had immediately set about eliminating all vestiges of Mazzini's Roman Republic; the Inquisition was reinstated and a harsh censorship reimposed. In Naples, the only conclusion that Ferdinand II had seemed to draw from recent events was that the power of his dynasty rested more on the police and on mercenary regiments than on the consent of the governed.

The only exception was Piedmont. The outset of 1848 saw Austria and Piedmont as firm allies. King Charles Albert of Piedmont was no more a friend of liberalism than Metternich, and he, as well as the entire Piedmontese officer corps, had been brought up to regard Austria as the fount of legitimate authority. The only consideration that might lead the king to cast aside these legitimist scruples was the thought that, were either Lombardy or central Italy to throw off Austrian dominance, they might easily enter into Piedmont's own sphere of influence. In March 1848, Milan rose up and, after five days of fighting, drove out the Austrian garrisons under Marshal Radetsky. This had given Charles Albert a chance: if he supported the revolution, he might add Lombardy to his Piedmontese territory.

Yet the king hesitated: his distrust of the leaders of the Milan revolt, men whom he regarded as dangerous liberals, struggled in the balance against his desire for glory and for the aggrandizement of his realm. The notion of aiding a popular insurrection was repugnant to him; he even tried to convince England that he was really thinking of marching to Milan only to suppress the republicans and to "restore order."[4] He delayed his attack until his ministers forced the provisional government of Milan to swallow annexation to Piedmont as the price for military support. When he finally crossed with his army into Lombardy, he failed to pursue Marshal Radetsky's retreating forces, allowing the enemy to regroup in the fortresses at the mouth of the Brenner Pass. After months of wasted opportunities and ineffectual campaigning, he was finally defeated at Custoza and forced to fall back to Milan. Although he promised to defend the gallant city with his life, he soon sued for peace, and then, amidst the general contempt of the Milanese, whose hard-won liberty he had done nothing to protect, retired shamefacedly back to Turin.

The defeat at Custoza was a serious blow to Piedmont's prestige and a check on its hopes of emerging as the dominant power in a new Italian order. In the spring of 1849 the Piedmontese tried again, sending their army once more into the Lombard plain. Here they met with an even more serious defeat at Novara. With this, Charles Albert chose to abdicate in favor of his son.

The new king, Victor Emmanuel, belonged to a different generation. Although hardly a liberal, he was less haunted by the fear, typical of those brought up during the first years of the Restoration, that any compromise with liberal ideas would sound the death knell of legitimate monarchy. Withstanding Austrian pressure, he therefore refused to abrogate the constitution that his father had reluctantly granted in 1848—the Albertine Statute. Thus, in 1849 Piedmont remained the sole constitutional regime in Italy.

This made Piedmont the natural focus of nationalist hopes of Italians everywhere, especially as, by now, Pius IX's rejection of reform had shown that the project of an Italian league under papal leadership, which had so inflamed public opinion in early 1848, was now a dead letter. Victor Emmanuel was flattered to find himself at the center of patriotic attentions. For all his faults, he wished to be a popular king. He also saw himself as a soldier; he often said that he was more comfortable in a military bivouac than at court. Thus, the thought of a new war with Austria, one in which he not only would enlarge his kingdom and redeem the humiliations suffered by his father but also might reveal himself as a national hero and liberator began to grow in his mind.

The Piedmontese king's ambitions coincided with those of one of the ablest politicians and astutest diplomats in nineteenth-century Europe. During the 1850s, Count Camillo di Cavour emerged as Piedmont's leading statesman and architect of its domestic and foreign policy. Cavour was a reformer, and under his administration Piedmont began to enjoy a new measure of stability and prosperity. Cavour was no democrat, however, and if, with his guidance, Piedmont moved away from its traditional policy of friendship with Austria toward an alliance with France and England, it was not because he objected to absolutism in principle. Cavour was rather an opportunist who perceived that the political order imposed by the 1815 Treaty of Vienna could not remain intact much longer, and who foresaw that, if Piedmont played its diplomatic cards with enough skill, it might become the major beneficiary of a changing political climate.

Standing between Cavour and the fulfillment of his ambitions were three men. The first two were Giuseppe Mazzini and the emperor Napoleon III of France. The project of a united Italy under Piedmontese rule had enjoyed considerable support among Italian liberals and patriots. As it became clear, however, that King Charles Albert had no intention of uniting Italy but desired simply to enlarge the borders of his own kingdom, this support had evaporated. Cavour realized that if Piedmont wished to gain advantage from the changing climate, it would have to put itself forward as the champion of Italian unity. Doing so, however, meant siding with the revolution. This, in turn, must bring him into conflict with Mazzini.

Mazzini's moral authority within the revolutionary movement stood in the way of Cavour's plan to seize the leadership of that movement for Piedmont. Although widely regarded as a republican conspirator and international terrorist, within the democratic party Mazzini was, in fact, a moderate. He had long broken with the *carbonaro* tradition; he had denounced political assassinations; he had even repeatedly proclaimed his willingness to support a monarchy in Italy, provided that it was a constitutional monarchy that agreed to fight for national unity. The Piedmontese police, who had been opening Mazzini's letters for decades, knew all this, and Cavour doubtless knew it as well. Nevertheless, he continued to harass Mazzini publicly, denouncing him as a communist, an enemy of religion, a terrorist and incendiary. He falsified incriminating evidence and sequestered Mazzini's newspapers.[5]

Assuming the leadership of the struggle for Italian unity was a dangerous business, and Cavour realized that, sooner or later, his policy was bound to provoke an open breach with Austria. The army of Piedmont was not strong enough to take on the Austrian army on its own. This meant that Piedmont needed an ally. Logically, this ally could only be France. Cavour's ambitions thus required the consent of Napoleon III.

The need to bring both the Italian democrats and France into his projects required a certain degree of duplicity. Courting moderate liberal opinion, Cavour spoke of Mazzini as an enemy of the state who, if he were ever captured on Piedmontese territory, faced certain execution. Yet in June 1856, when the Piedmontese police discovered that Mazzini had slipped back into his native Genoa, they not only failed to apprehend him but actually tried to sound him out over a scheme to set off an insurrection in the duchy of Modena.[6]

The whole policy came close to blowing up in Cavour's face. By no means did all of the revolutionary party support Mazzini in his renunciation of political assassination as a revolutionary weapon. The radical Felice Orsini had been in close contact with Mazzini in London since at least 1853, and in 1854 had been part of a dinner party whose guests included Garibaldi, Mazzini, the Hungarian patriot Lajos Kossuth, and the American consul in London.[7] The translation of his memoirs, which recounted his revolutionary activities and, above all, his escape from the impregnable Austrian fortress at Modena, had given him a celebrity in England rivaling that of Mazzini himself.[8] Yet along with dash, charm, courage, and resourcefulness, Orsini suffered from the vanity and jealousy common among nineteenth-century revolutionaries; his memoirs are filled with bitter attacks on his co-conspirator and fellow exile Mazzini.[9] Aware of this rivalry, and thinking, perhaps, that a line to the terrorists might prove useful, Cavour had been in secret contact with Orsini since 1853.

Cavour could not have been privy to all of Orsini's schemes: on January 14, 1858, three bombs were hurled at Napoleon and the empress Eugénie, who were driving in their carriage to the opera in Paris. Their horses fell dead; around them lay 156 wounded, of whom 8 later died; yet the imperial couple stepped from the carnage miraculously unhurt. On hearing the news of this terrorist outrage, Cavour was heard to exclaim, "If only this is not the work of Italians." His worst suspicions were soon confirmed: The attack had been planned and executed by Orsini and his associates.[10]

Although Napoleon never guessed that Cavour had actually been subsidizing Orsini from his secret service funds, he suspected enough. Enraged, he demanded that Cavour expel the democrats from Piedmont and silence their press. The situation was saved by a spirited letter from Victor Emmanuel: were I, the king told the emperor, "to use violence in my own kingdom . . . I should lose all my influence, and [the emperor] all the sympathies of a generous and noble nation."[11] Surprisingly, not only did the emperor relent, but the incident seems as well to have helped precipitate his decision to accept a Piedmontese alliance against Austria.

The reasons for Napoleon III's change of heart have always been a matter of historical debate. A veteran of sects and plots himself, the emperor may have been impressed by the tenacity and recklessness of the republican opposition. This may have convinced him that Cavour's policy of orchestrating the energies of the radicals to his own ends was wiser and more profitable than pure repression. In any event, in July of the same year, traveling incognito and with a false passport, Cavour slipped into France. At Plombières he met the emperor, and during a carriage ride through the woods, the two leaders worked out the details of a new Franco-Piedmontese entente and laid out plans for a joint war against Austria.

There was a risk attached to a French alliance. Were Piedmont's victory over Austria to be achieved by French arms, France might claim a voice in Italian affairs as large as Austria's had been. An Italy dominated by Austria would then be succeeded by one dominated by France, an eventuality that neither Cavour nor the democrats relished. To lessen this risk, and to solidify Piedmontese leadership over the revolution, Cavour turned to the third figure: in 1856 Garibaldi returned from exile and met Cavour.

Like Mazzini, Garibaldi was a genuine democrat, and one, moreover, with several death sentences hanging over his head. He had been sentenced to "an ignominious death" by Piedmont for his participation with Mazzini in a revolutionary plot in Genoa in the early 1830s.[12] For this he had received a pardon in 1848. He was still wanted, however, by Austria and the Papal States for his defense of the Roman Republic in 1849.

Yet the defense of Rome against the combined armies of France, Naples, and Austria had made Garibaldi a popular hero. Cavour foresaw that if he could induce Garibaldi to endorse Piedmontese policy openly, liberal opinion throughout Italy would surely follow. In 1848, when first returning from exile with his companions from South America, Garibaldi had offered his sword to Charles Albert. That time it had been refused. In 1856, returning now from a second exile, Garibaldi met with a different reception. Cavour arranged a meeting with Victor Emmanuel. Despite inevitable differences in their political perspectives, the two men seem to have taken to each other.

Cavour needed tangible proof of Garibaldi's support, and so in the summer of 1857, Garibaldi agreed to become vice president of the National Society. Originally founded by Daniel Manin and Giorgio Pallavicino, the National Society had been intended as a link between moderate liberals and the members of Mazzini's more revolutionary "Party of Action." By the mid-1850s, however, it was falling under Cavour's influence. Pallavicino had enlisted the support of the Sicilian Giuseppe La Farina, who, fleeing from Bourbon repression, had emigrated to France, where he made contact with Mazzini. By 1854, La Farina had broken with Mazzini and fallen under the influence of Cavour. Taking advantage of La Farina's prestige as a revolutionary leader and his network of contacts within the revolutionary party, Cavour let La Farina remodel the National Society into an instrument of Piedmontese power.[13]

Mazzini was under no illusions. By making Garibaldi vice president of the National Society, Cavour had outmaneuverd him and he knew it. Garibaldi, he complained, had ingenuously allowed himself to become Cavour's tool. "Garibaldi is good," he wrote; "he loves his country and hates the Austrians; but Garibaldi is *weak*. Therefore changeable. I believe he has been really ensnared by the Piedmontese Ministry."[14]

Yet Garibaldi had his own reasons for siding with Cavour and Victor Emmanuel against Mazzini at this juncture. Garibaldi had seen in 1849 that the mass of the Italian people, though sympathetic or even enthusiastic toward the nationalist cause, had neither arms nor military experience. He was disillusioned with the plots and scheduled insurrections of the secret societies. Asking the people, as he perceived Mazzini to be doing, to rise up and attack large and well-equipped Austrian or Bourbon regiments was to send them needlessly to the slaughter. Italian liberty, he believed, needed to be won with Italian bayonets, and the only state that might provide him with these bayonets was Piedmont. He thus accepted the necessity of involving the Piedmontese army in the struggle, and was willing, at least for the time being, to leave political matters in the hands of Cavour.

In purely military matters, Garibaldi's judgment was superior to that of Mazzini. In 1857 Mazzini had tried to interest Garibaldi in a new venture. The Neapolitan revolutionary Carlo Pisacane was planning to land a small expeditionary force on the Calabrian coast. The party would first attack the Bourbon prison fortress on the island of Santo Stefano, there to liberate the political prisoners held in chains, and then incite a peasant uprising on the mainland. Garibaldi wanted no part of it. He told his friend Jessie White Marino that he had no wish to send men to their death just "to make the *canaille* laugh."[15]

Pisacane's subsequent adventure justified all of Garibaldi's foreboddings. Like Orsini, Pisacane was hungry for public attention, even if it led to his own martyrdom. It was "deeds," he had written, not "doctrines" that "manifested the life of a nation."[16] He set off toward the end of June 1857, though not before handing over his "Testament" to Jessie White Marino, a document that, as one biographer admits, is nothing more than a long suicide note.[17] He condemned his critics, those who sleep comfortably in their beds and judge the deeds of others; they have always called the men whose ideas are ahead of their times "mad imbeciles." Doubtless these same critics would label him a "mad, ambitious, and turbulent spirit," and if he failed, they would write of the many imperfections and shortcomings of his plans. Yet, recommending himself to the good wishes of all his friends and true patriots, he proclaimed his readiness to join the "noble ranks of martyrs." In his final words, Pisacane offered himself as a holocaust to the revolution. "If I die," he wrote, "Italy can be proud that she still produces sons ready to immolate themselves for her benefit. . . . I unite under my banner all the affection and all the hopes of the Italian revolution. . . . [F]ighting by my side will be all the sorrows and all sufferings of Italy."[18] With that he sailed.

When the political prisoners at Santo Stefano refused to be liberated by Pisacane and his crew, the group proceeded to a second prison colony on the island of Ponza. Here, in addition to the dozen political prisoners, they released about two hundred common criminals. The party then landed at Sapri and marched into the hills of Basilicata. Here they met with disaster. Their sudden arrival alarmed the peasantry, who had no idea what the unexpected appearance of this party of armed men could mean. Incited by the local clergy, who thought them a party of Freemasons, peasants from Padula and Sanza attacked the plotters. Pisacane and most of his followers were killed. Rosolino Pilo, in charge of a second ship, was lucky to escape with his life.

Garibaldi was set on more effective means of achieving the revolution. In 1858 he and Cavour came to an agreement: Garibaldi was to recruit a small force—the Cacciatori delle Alpi—using volunteers from Austrian Lombardy, from Venetia, from the Papal States and duchies. In the event of a war, the presence of a patriotic force of Italian volunteers fighting alongside the regular Piedmontese army would lend the struggle a national character; this would make it harder for the French to refuse to recognize Italy's aspirations at the negotiating table. All the better if this patriotic force were to be led by the great democratic leader himself, especially if it were to capture the public imagination by some romantic feat on the battlefield.

In April 1859, Austria foolishly let itself be provoked into invading Piedmont, precipitating a new war. Garibaldi and his Cacciatori fought in the Alps. Their operations were all that Cavour could have wished for; outmaneuvering far larger forces, the Cacciatori achieved brilliant victories in Varese and Como. These were propaganda victories as well: three thousand young volunteers, with old muskets and no cannon, had defeated large Austrian regiments, excellently armed and fully equipped with artillery.[19]

In military terms, the operations had little influence on the outcome of the conflict. The 1859 war was decided by two battles on the Lombard plain—at Magenta and Solferino. These were regular army battles, and the second was a scene of carnage providing a foretaste of those of the American Civil War. Although the Austrians were defeated, the armies of the French and Piedmontese were scarcely less mauled. Shortly afterward, the emperors of France and Austria met at Villafranca and there arranged the terms for peace.

By the Treaty of Villafranca, Austria ceded Lombardy to Piedmont while still retaining Venetia. The rest of Italy was to remain as it had been before the war. Yet this latter provision was to prove unenforceable. At the beginning of the 1859 war, Tuscany, the Romagna, and the duchies of central Italy had all expelled their rulers. In the summer of 1859, the populations in these areas showed that, regardless of what the Treaty of Villafranca might stipulate, they had no desire to have them back again. Since no one—neither the French nor the Austrians nor the pope—was in any condition to impose them upon an unwilling populace, moderate governments, friendly to Piedmont, were allowed to remain in power, waiting for Cavour and Napoleon III to work out a new bargain that would allow these regions to be annexed by Piedmont.

If the 1859 war enhanced the prestige of Piedmont, it also whetted Cavour's appetite. In August of that year he was heard to exclaim, "I shall take Naples in hand."[20] The successful conclusion to the Austrian war put the South at the top of the democrats' agenda as well. The idea that the national revolution might commence in Sicily and work its way up the peninsula had first emerged in the late 1830s, when the cholera riots had shown the island's potential for popular violence. From his conspiratorial base in Malta, Niccola Fabrizi had long been a proponent of a Sicilian strategy. Mazzini had become interested, though he was worried that popular violence in Sicily was more likely to be expended in the cause of Sicilian independence than for Italian unity. Returning to Italy in 1854, Garibaldi stopped to visit Mazzini in London, and Mazzini took the opportunity to press on him the idea of leading an invasion of Sicily. Garibaldi replied that he would "gladly" do so, but only if it were to coincide with a major rebellion on the part of the Sicilians themselves.

By the end of 1859, Garibaldi too had acquired something. Cavour may have regarded the successes of Garibaldi's Cacciatori delle Alpi as merely reestablishing Piedmontese prestige among Italian liberals, but Garibaldi's dream was to lead the Italian nation-at-arms. To the handful of red-shirted followers who had accompanied him from his South American exile, Garibaldi could now add his Cacciatori. It was the nucleus of an effective revolutionary force. Mazzini thus took Garibaldi at his word. He put his considerable powers of persuasion and his skill at knitting together insurrectionary plots to work, aiming at stirring up a rebellion in Sicily that would be impressive enough to induce Garibaldi to lead his revolutionary force to its aid.

## Conspiracy in Sicily after 1849

Meanwhile in Sicily, revolution had become a suicidal prospect. In January 1850, Palermo saw an abortive uprising, an uprising that might be considered the final act of the 1848 revolution. Its organizers were *squadra* leaders and officials of the last Sicilian government who had sworn never to accept the reimposition of rule from Naples, and who had participated in the last-ditch attempt to defend their independence in September 1849.

The uprising was intended to be a repeat of the uprising of January 12, 1848. The plotters created four committees, one for each of the city's four quarters. They contacted radical leaders in the surrounding countryside who were to recruit new *squadre* and lead them into the city. They called for the rebel forces to converge at the Fieravecchia, which was to serve once more as the heart of the rebellion.

The conspirators were thorough; even the British consul, William Goodwin, seems to have been in on the scheme.[21] At the appointed hour, 7:00 P.M. on Sunday, January 27, the armed bands appeared at various points in the city and found well-armed contingents of government troops awaiting them. The Neapolitan government had learned from its past errors; no longer would it keep the army confined to barracks to await developments and orders from Naples. The government was determined now to act quickly and aggressively, nipping any insurrectionary attempt in the bud before it could gain momentum or win popular support.

The insurgents were surprised when the government troops opened fire on them without warning. Some of the bands returned the fire; a band led by Nicolò Garzilli, one of the original plotters, even managed to fight its way to the Fieravecchia. Most of the plotters threw down their arms, however, and fled into the alleyways, where their escape was facilitated by the gathering dusk.

Many of the leaders escaped this way; but six, including Garzilli, were captured and marched off to the Castellammare. There, at dawn on the following morning, Filangieri held a council of war; he ordered that the six be punished in an exemplary manner. They were brought from their cells and given a summary trial in which their council was allowed time neither to prepare a defense nor to make objections. They were then all condemned to death by firing squad. The sentence was to be carried out that very evening in the Fieravecchia itself.

The severity of the reaction caught the city by surprise. Bourbon justice had frequently been cruel and arbitrary, but it had rarely been swift. Usually political prisoners, even those accused of insurrection, had been dumped in one of the island's innumerable prisons, often without ever being formally charged. Conditions in these prisons could be dreadful, but there was always hope that with the intervention of powerful friends, or simply with the passage of time, the government would decide on an act of clemency. The prospect of immediate public execution meant that the rules had unexpectedly been changed.

Such a prospect seemed to traumatize the city, especially as the execution was to take place publicly. As soon as the sentence was announced, shops, cafés, and taverns hurriedly closed their shutters. The streets were deserted. It was said that as the barefooted prisoners were marched the short distance from the Castellammare to the Fieravecchia, women fainted or grew delirious behind barred windows. In the following weeks a number of other individuals connected with the attempt were arrested, and nine more men were eventually executed.[22]

One of the leaders who escaped was the young Baron Francesco Bentivegna from Corleone. Bentivegna had organized a *squadra* in 1848 and had led it into the capital on the heels of Turi Miceli and his Monrealesi. He was appointed major in the Sicilian militia, and became, successively, military commander and deputy for Corleone.[23]

Although there was now a reward on his head, Bentivegna was more determined than ever to free Sicily from its Neapolitan oppressors. He saw that the chances for an exclusively urban uprising were now slight. He fell back into the area surrounding his native Corleone; here he was protected both by his family and friends, and by the unbroken network of secret committees. He sent "emissaries" to Monreale, Belmonte, Parco, Piana dei Greci, Misilmeri, Bagheria, Carini—"all those towns," Filangieri reported to Naples, "which form a circle around Palermo where there lurks a class of persons always ready for insurrection and disposed to swoop down upon and sack this city."[24] By 1853, Bentivegna had recruited a new *squadra* of about fifty men whom he hoped to lead in a new attack on the capital. In early February he assembled his recruits in a barn near Santa Maria di Gesù. Here he sketched out his program: "Brothers!" he began. "The revolution is raging in Italy; the Imperials [Austrians] have been expelled from Milan; Hungary has risen up in arms at the generous cry of Kossuth; a powerful flame burns through all of Europe."[25]

This was pure fantasy. If Bentivegna credited his own words, it was only because, in an access of passion, his will to believe had overcome his sense of reality. Nonetheless, his speech electrified the assembly of *villici*—agricultural workers and cowherds, who knew nothing of such things. They believed Bentivegna when he went on to tell them that they were to descend into Palermo and, armed with little more than scythes and daggers, overpower a company of soldiers and seize the artillery in front of the Palazzo Reale. The men opened the cask of wine they had brought and, toasting their leader, gave their word that they would be ready at the appointed hour.

Unfortunately there was a spy in their midst, and Bentivegna's plans were soon known to the police, who took energetic measures. Political prisoners were transferred from the Palermo prison to the fortress at Messina or taken to the island prison of Santo Stefano. There was a wave of new arrests, including a number of monks and friars. Realizing that he had been betrayed, Bentivegna returned to Palermo, where he too was soon arrested. As he had only preached insurrection, Bentivegna was charged with "illicit association" and "plotting against the security of the state," for which he received a sentence of five years' imprisonment.

He was released in August 1856. Though required to report regularly to the police, he soon slipped their surveillance. By now he was in touch with Salvatore Cappello, an elderly conspirator, originally from Messina, who had organized a "Secret Revolutionary Committee" in Palermo in 1855. This was the major channel of communication between the conspirators in Palermo and Mazzini, Crispi, and Pilo, who were now together in London.[26] Soon Cappello, Bentivegna, and the other conspirators were ready to try a new adventure.

On November 22, 1856, Bentivegna led a *squadra* into Mezzoiuso, a town in the interior of Palermo province. Here they opened the municipal prison and disarmed the local guards, none of whom seem to have resisted. The band then set off in the direction of Villafrate, stopping a mail coach on the way, seizing the horses, and disarming the guards. They arrived in Villafrate the following morning. Under an improvised *tricolore*, Bentivegna addressed the local populace. He promised that English ships were sailing to the revolution's assistance—another triumph of his will to believe.

While this was happening, one of Bentivegna's fellow conspirators, Luigi

La Porta, staged uprisings in nearby Ventimiglia and Ciminna. The two leaders met to confer in Ciminna. As yet the revolution had spread through only the smaller towns of the interior of the province. The next step would be to try to raise some of the larger towns—Lercara, Prizzi, Corleone, and Marineo. They sent off emissaries in these directions, and the enlarged *squadra* began to march toward Corleone on the evening of November 24.

All these actions made sense, however, only if there was an insurrection in Palermo. And indeed, Bentivegna had marched on Mezzoiuso believing that his actions had been timed to coincide with an insurrection in the capital organized by the Secret Revolutionary Committee there. In fact, it is certain that the secret committee in Palermo was indeed preparing some sort of insurrection, and that Bentivegna had been assigned the task of raising the interior in support of the revolution in the capital. Nonetheless, on the evening of the twenty-fourth, Bentivegna was informed that the committee had decided to postpone the insurrection due to take place in Palermo. He had thus set off the revolt prematurely.[27]

With this news, Bentivegna realized that he was, to say the least, in a precarious position. He had a *squadra* of about two hundred men, plus arms and money. By 1848 standards this was a sizable force; yet unless a major insurrection intervened to pin down the huge garrison in the capital, it did not stand a chance. As soon as he discovered that the capital had not arisen, Bentivegna hurried back in the direction of Mezzoiuso. From the surrounding heights he espied a large contingent of Bourbon troops heading for the town. Bentivegna now realized that he had failed. He had genuinely believed that English warships were sailing to the aid of Sicily, that Palermo would rise up, and that the insurrection would be supplied with the 1,200 rifles, 42,000 cartridges, and four pieces of artillery promised by expatriate committees in France and England.[28] When he discovered that these were nothing but illusions, he dissolved his *squadra* and tried to make his way alone back to his family in Corleone.

His march, however, had set off tremors throughout the entire province. On learning of Bentivegna's activities, the Secret Revolutionary Committee had hurriedly sent out emissaries to other towns. One of the emissaries was waylaid by brigands, who killed him and stole his horses. Another reached as far as Cefalù, where local revolutionaries opened the prisons and released prisoners jailed there. From here, new emissaries were sent to provoke an uprising in Termini Imeresi. Armed bands and revolutionary committees began springing up around Monreale as well.

For two days, rumors of revolution spread through the countryside like wildfire. Yet with the news that a large body of troops was arriving in Mezzoiuso, and that Bentivegna had dissolved his own *squadra* and fled, the revolution collapsed as rapidly as it had begun. The would-be revolutionaries panicked. Some took the time to bury their arms and ammunition in a safe hiding place, but most seem merely to have abandoned them as they vaulted over stone walls and scrambled through gardens and orange groves. Most of those in the Monreale area escaped in this manner. Their fellow revolutionaries in Cefalù were not so lucky. The brief insurrection there was cut short by the arrival of a government troopship. The rebels tried to escape into the hills, but many were captured. Bentivegna, by now too tired and disillusioned to hide any longer, was captured as well. He and one of the leaders from Cefalù were tried for participating in an armed insurrection and convicted. The following year they were both executed by firing squad.

## Maniscalco

It should have been apparent to everyone that, on their own, the conspirators stood little chance against the regular Bourbon troops. Yet there were some less apparent lessons to be drawn from the conspirators' failures as well.

Arriving in Sicily in September 1848, Filangieri discovered a handful of loyal Bourbon officials remaining in Messina, and from these he began to create his new administration. Chief among them were the *intendente* of Messina, Giovanni Cassisi, and the young captain of the Royal Gendarmes, Salvatore Maniscalco. Appointed civil commissioner for Sicily, Cassisi revealed himself as the leading proponent of heavy-handed and repressive policies. He soon returned to Naples, where he became Filangieri's chief critic in the state bureaucracy. Maniscalco, by contrast, remained in Sicily to become the new chief of police, a position he held uninterruptedly from his appointment in November 1848 until the Bourbon surrender to Garibaldi.

Maniscalco proved himself an excellent civil servant. Hardworking, taciturn, spartan in his personal habits and dress, he threw himself into the work of creating a new police force with zeal and punctilious attention to detail. Though serving in Messina, he came from a Palermitan family and had a good grasp of Palermitan society. Filangieri gave him a free hand, and, especially after Filangieri himself had been recalled to Naples, Maniscalco emerged as the nodal point of all Bourbon operations in Sicily and virtual dictator of the island.

Maniscalco is an interesting figure who has not lacked his defenders among historians.[29] Though unswervingly loyal to the crown, he exemplified the reformist outlook of the Bourbon civil service. He was closely associated with the administrative reforms and new initiatives which benefited Sicily during the 1850s. Yet it was hardly without significance that the impetus for these reforms should now be emanating from the police. Maniscalco's conception of reform was authoritarian: power was to be concentrated exclusively in the hands of officials of unquestionable integrity, like himself. Ordinary Sicilians were to kept at a distance. Only in this way could power be protected from their corrupting influences. This, he argued, was what Sicilians really wanted anyway. "The people of Sicily," he claimed, "really want nothing more than public security, minimal taxation, religious festivals, and a cheap life."[30]

Like many Neapolitan administrators, Maniscalco held the Sicilian aristocracy in contempt. Although he was in no position to show open hostility toward Sicilian nobles, some of whom had connections to the court of Ferdinand II, he worked quietly to void traditional aristocratic institutions of any real content. These were the institutions that had served as the basis on which the nobility had tried to assert Sicilian autonomy in 1812, 1820, and 1848. Pushing the aristocracy into a marginal or merely ceremonial position meant that they could no longer play their traditional role as buffer or intermediary between the state and Sicily.

It was during Maniscalco's tenure in office that Sicilian society began to reshape, or perhaps distort, itself in response to police pressure. Ruling Sicily directly from police headquarters in Palermo was a formidable undertaking. There was little in the way of population records: there were no detailed census reports; tax records and land transactions, courtroom proceedings, sentences, and prison records were all registered unsystematically. There were neither indexes nor catalogues. What records there were, moreover, had largely been burned in 1820 and 1848. The police lacked concrete information. Proper names were seldom used among the Sicilian lower classes; individuals were usually called by their nicknames (*ingiurie*). Scientific methods of identification, such as photographs, anatomical measurements, and fingerprints, all lay in the future, and it was difficult for the Neapolitans to know who was who in Sicily. In such a situation, police control over the population inevitably came to rest on an extensive network of spies and informers.

Maniscalco was remembered in Sicily as the official who extended and perfected this network. Already before 1848, the police informer (*delatore*), had become a typical, and much-hated, figure in Sicilian society. Under Maniscalco there was not a community in Sicily, large or small, that lacked an informer who reported to him directly. He cast his nets as widely as he could: priests, concierges, tavern keepers, and coach drivers were all brought in. In the eighteenth century, in an effort to stop the spread of dangerous ideas among the lower classes, the clergy had ordered servants to stop up the keyholes in drawing rooms and boudoirs.[31] Maniscalco reversed this directive. Servants were now expected to report on their masters.

Much of the cooperation, however, was halfhearted. Maniscalco knew ahead of time that Bentivegna was preparing an insurrection in 1853; this much he had learned through reading the letters that political prisoners tried to smuggle out of jail. He was also able to plant a spy in Bentivegna's following, who, by transcribing Bentivegna's words at Santa Maria di Gesù, performed an unintentional service for future historians as well. Yet, as long as he remained in the countryside, protected by family, friends, and fellow conspirators, the police were unable to capture Bentivegna himself.

The police also knew about the Secret Revolutionary Committee in Palermo; they knew that it was planning a new adventure in 1856. Yet they were not able to prevent Bentivegna from contacting it or keep him under surveillance. Bentivegna returned to Corleone, traveling to Misilmeri and to the coastal towns around Cefalù, everywhere recruiting followers and organizing conspiracies. The police were apprised of his every movement; yet they could never quite lay their hands on him. Spies who had turned informer out of fear or self-interest rather than out of loyalty to the regime more than once seem to have given Bentivegna and his fellow conspirators a day or two's head start before reporting their presence to the police.[32]

Sicilians in government employment were also expected to inform on their fellow citizens. Sicilian officials pardoned in extremis for their part in the 1849 defense of Palermo may have preserved their lives in exchange for a promise to collaborate with the restored regime; this may explain why the police had so much advance notice of the January 1850 uprising. Yet Sicilians who had to save their jobs or their lives in this manner could prove reluctant collaborators, passing on at least as much information to the conspirators as they did to their superiors. Maniscalco relied heavily on the telegraph as a means of receiving information and issuing orders promptly. Yet telegraph operators and mail couriers might remain true to the revolution, using the government's own telegraph lines to send encrypted messages to conspirators in other cities. In this way the Secret Revolutionary Committee in Palermo kept in touch not only with London and Turin but also with their fellow conspirators in Catania, Messina, and Trapani.

Ironically, the police provided the revolutionaries with the means to pursue their ends. According to Raffaele de Cesare, Naples might well have lost Sicily sooner had not Maniscalco and his spies kept up their constant vigilance.[33] Yet the network proved a double-edged weapon. In principle, the hounds should be distinct from the hares; yet in Sicily the two species overlapped. Sicilians who might have condemned Bentivegna as a "mad, ambitious, and turbulent spirit," as Carlo Pisacane put it, still would not have betrayed him if they thought that their own friends or family might be involved in his plot.

On the occasion of Bentivegna's second attempt, Filangieri could marvel that revolutionary conspiracies "are the hundred-headed Hydra; the more they are decapitated, the more they are born anew."[34] Yet revolution had come to Sicily through official channels. The Carboneria was brought to Sicily by the Neapolitan army, who had learned of it through contact with the French army. Even in the provincial towns, there were by now few leading families that did not have at least one branch with Masonic, or even sectarian, connections. These families had official connections as well. Thus, the forces committed to repression and to the maintenance of the established order and the forces committed to the revolution coexisted in the same families. Inevitably this made repression an unpredictable affair; repression unfolded within a delicate balance in which personal ambitions and family loyalties counted at least as much as the call of duty. Inevitably Maniscalco's network of spies and informers functioned as a permeable membrane open to both sides. Designed to keep the police informed about the population, the network of spies also kept the population informed about the police. Maniscalco was reputed to be the man who knew "everything"; yet somehow the revolutionaries seemed to know everything and more. Inevitably the revolution was transmuted by this dependence.

It was a transmutation, however, that was not readily apparent. Before 1848, the Bourbon government had tolerated a certain amount of open dissent, especially among the upper classes. By late 1847, barons, university professors, underworld bosses, and even the Sicilian Jesuits were openly manifesting their desire to be free of Naples. The repressive atmosphere of the 1850s made such open manifestations of revolutionary and anti-Neapolitan sentiments impossible. As power became more and more concentrated in Maniscalco's hands, and as the political importance of Sicily's traditional ruling classes declined, revolutionary leadership passed to the sectarians themselves.

Curiously, Maniscalco failed to see this. He continued to assume that revolutionary leadership could arise only from the upper classes. The Franco-Piedmontese war did excite the upper classes in Palermo. A public subscription in favor of Piedmont was launched, and there were rumors that a group of nobles planned to offer their congratulations to the French consul. The prospect of Italian unity was guardedly discussed in clubs and noble salons, and the younger nobility talked of revolution and even of forming new *squadre*. A leading center of liberal discussion in 1847 had been the Casino Geraci, an aristocratic club. Although the Casino Geraci was situated virtually next door to the main police station at Piazza Bologni, the police never dared interfere with its proceedings. By the late 1850s, however, the deference had disappeared. Shortly after news of the Franco-Piedmontese victory at Solferino arrived in Palermo, the club's members ordered a celebration, placing torches at the door of the club-house. The gesture so enraged Maniscalco that he descended from his office at police headquarters and tore down the lights himself.[35]

Such upper-class activities may have represented disloyalty, even sedition, but they hardly constituted a revolutionary threat. Nevertheless, during the summer of 1859, Maniscalco had fifteen young Palermitan nobles and patricians flung into prison. But he was looking out for revolution from the wrong quarter. Maniscalco believed that by effacing every trace of dissent from Sicilian society and marginalizing Sicily's native ruling class, he had "decapitated" the revolution. With each successive "decapitation," however, leadership moved farther down the social scale.

### The April 4 Uprising

Like Bentivegna, the young Giuseppe Campo and his two brothers had fought in the September 1849 defense of Palermo. In January 1850, Giuseppe was part of the group led by Nicolò Garzilli that had fought its way into the Fieravecchia. Unlike Garzilli, however, he was lucky enough to escape, running straight past the Bourbon troops and out the Porta di Termini, where he hid in the house of relatives.[36]

Campo spent most of the 1850s managing his family's property in Bagheria. In 1856 he acted as the intermediary between Bentivegna and the Secret Revolutionary Committee in Palermo. The police never learned of this connection, however, and therefore Campo remained undisturbed. In late 1858 he returned to Palermo and made contact with the Secret Revolutionary Committee, which at this time was composed of Salvatore Cappello, the five de Benedetto brothers, their cousin Onofrio di Benedetto, and the young baron Casimiro Pisani. The following year, prodded by Mazzini and Crispi, the committee decided on a new insurrection.

The Campo family had property and relatives both in the Bagheria-

Villabate region and the region around Misilmeri, and the de Benedetto family had property in nearby Ciaculli. Accordingly this was chosen as the starting point. The committee entrusted Campo with a large sum of money donated by Baron Pisani (who excused himself from any further part in the uprising), with which he was supposed to recruit *squadre*. The insurrection was scheduled to take place on the October 9, 1859.

Militarily, Campo's insurrection was a farce. He had given the committee's funds to various overseers (*castaldi*) in the Bagheria-Villabate area, telling them to hire *squadristi* among the agricultural laborers. The overseers had done as they were instructed, and by October 7, a number of *squadre* had duly been formed. Yet no order of march or battle plan had been prepared. On the evening of the ninth, what was supposed to be a march on Palermo unfolded as a series of uncoordinated local demonstrations. *Squadre* emerged from the coastal villages waving *tricolori* and firing their muskets into the air. Campo led an attack on a guards' barracks in Villabate; there was a similar attack in Ciaculli. These two attacks, in which no one was injured, were the only real incidents that took place.

The Bourbon authorities, however, mistook these uncoordinated demonstrations for a general uprising, and in a moment of panic seem to have dispatched the whole garrison of twenty thousand to the Villabate-Bagheria area. Naturally, this only increased the confusion, as the troops had no idea whom they were looking for. The *squadristi* hid in the gardens whenever the troops approached, and there were no exchanges of fire. Once in Villabate, the troops maltreated the populace, beating up the men and raping some of the women. Other than that, all they could do was to rip down the *tricolori*, which were springing up everywhere.

Campo hid out for two days before returning home dressed as a priest. His family had dug out a cellar under the kitchen table; here he hid for a month, fed by the maid, as his family had all been arrested. He finally escaped on a ship to Genoa.

Campo had naturally planned his revolt to coincide with an uprising in Palermo. Once again, however, the capital had failed to ignite. By now, the failure to produce a Palermo uprising was becoming an embarrassment to the Secret Revolutionary Committee, under pressure from both Mazzini and Garibaldi. In August 1859, wearing false spectacles and carrying an Argentinian passport in the name of "Manuel Pareda," Francesco Crispi had returned to Sicily to solicit a revolt.[37] He also brought instructions for the fabrication of "Orsini bombs." For their part, the conspirators were soliciting Garibaldi through Niccola Fabrizi in Malta. In September, Garibaldi replied that he would "come with pleasure, with joy." Yet he also repeated his conditions. "If you can do it with any chance of success, then rise." Garibaldi wrote diplomatically and encouragingly, yet he was nonetheless determined to avoid the possibility that his expedition might end in a disaster like that of Pisacane.[38]

Even Cavour got into the act. In February 1860 he sent Enrico Benza to Palermo. Benza was an intimate of Victor Emmanuel; he met with the upper classes in Palermo, assuring them that a successful insurrection would enjoy the support of Piedmont. He also provided funds for arms, some of which, through Baron Pisani, were passed along to the Secret Revolutionary Committee.[39] With money, arms, and promises of military assistance, all seemed in readiness for a new revolt. The only element missing now was an individual reckless enough to set this revolt in motion.

G. M. Trevelyan identifies Francesco Riso as "plumber Riso," but this is surely going too far. From the accounts of Giovanni Paolucci and Marietta Campo, it is clear that Riso was the son of a prosperous contractor in Palermo. The difference is important: the Riso family had workmen in their employ; they owned carts and rented magazines and storage depots in the center of the old city. These provided Francesco Riso with the means to smuggle arms and munitions from the countryside into the city, and to store them undetected. Still, it is significant that the man who undertook to produce the event that not just Palermo but, by now, London, Turin, Genoa, and, no doubt, Naples were expecting came from a comparatively humble social background. In a report of March 8, 1860, the lieutenant governor, Paolo Rufo, prince of Castelcicala, wrote to Naples that "even the city plebs [in Palermo] have become familiar with ideas such as *nonintervention, popular sovereignty, universal suffrage*, and similar such extravagances."[40]

The houses of the Riso and Campo families, both of whom were involved in the insurrection, were near the Convent of Gancia, whose bells, on January 12, 1848, had answered the tocsin from the Convent of Sant' Ursula sounded by La Masa. The cloister enclosed a disused garden surrounded by vaults. In these Riso began to stockpile arms and ammunition, as well as trumpets. The activities passed largely unnoticed by the friars themselves, who, believing that Riso was merely storing building supplies, had let him have the keys to the front entrance and the vaults. The munitions were largely those commissioned by the Secret Revolutionary Committee and made in the Colli district to the north of the city. Along with the deposit in the Convent of Gancia, there were smaller deposits in the Piazza Magione and in the street on which the mint was located.

The decision to commence an uprising in April was probably taken at the beginning of 1860. The aristocracy was informed of it by Ottavio Lanza di Trabia, a priest and son of the prince of Trabia, who, along with a certain Baron Riso (not Baron Pietro Riso, who was captain of the Sicilian National Guard in 1848–49), channeled Piedmontese and Palermitan contributions to the Secret Committee.[41] The exact date was yet to be fixed, for the committee in Palermo was awaiting the arrival of Rosolino Pilo, whom Mazzini had sent to lead the insurrection. Francesco Riso, frightened lest his stock of guns be discovered by the police, pressed for immediate action. The final decision seems to have been taken at a meeting at the end of March. It was prompted by a letter from Mazzini urging: "Wait? For what? Do you really think that Napoleon or Cavour is coming to set you free? Dare and you will be followed. But dare in the name of National Unity; it is the condition sine qua non. Garibaldi is bound to come to your help."[42]

As in 1850, the plan was to form three bands, each taking its arms from one of the three deposits, and then assembling at the Gancia convent. From there the combined parties would march to the Fieravecchia, which was once again chosen as the center of the uprising. At the Fieravecchia the rebel formation would then be joined by *squadre* from Carini, Piana, Misilmeri, Bagheria, Villabate, the Colli, and one from the immediate garden suburbs, all entering from the Porta di Termini.

By now the whole city was expecting a revolt: the banks had been emptied as people cashed in their savings, and food stores had been bought out as residents stocked up on supplies. On the night of April 3, three bands of seventeen, fifty-two, and thirteen men assembled in their hiding places. The police had been informed as well, and during the night, they surrounded the Gancia. The police knew that insurgents were assembling at other points as well, though they did not know exactly where. They sent out large patrols of soldiers to prevent these groups from uniting. Informed of police maneuvers, and realizing that he was surrounded, Riso decided to attack anyway, hoping that at least a heroic gesture would serve as the signal for the rest of the city to rise up in revolt.

At five in the morning of April 4, he marched his little troop into the dark street. They were soon stopped by a police patrol. When, to his challenge, the police replied, "Viva il re!" Riso shouted, "Viva l'Italia e Vittorio Emanuele!" and opened fire. The four or five policemen fled, but the sound of the shots quickly brought reinforcements. Riso and his band ran back into the convent. Riso ordered someone to ring the tocsin while he climbed the bell tower and there planted the *tricolore*, firing shots into the air.

By now the second *squadra* from Piazza Magione had left their hiding

*The capture of Francesco Riso, April 4, 1860.*

place. Almost immediately they encountered a large contingent of police and soldiers. A ferocious fight ensued and the *squadra* was forced to retreat. The third and smallest of the *squadre*, seeing that their way to the Fieravecchia was barred by a large concentration of troops in the Piazza Marina, did not even attempt an assault.

The *squadre* had hoped to clear the way with the Orsini bombs and small cannons; but the bombs were almost entirely defective and refused to go off, and in the confused melee the cannon was never fired.

By dawn it was all over; the police and soldiers were searching the convent for members of Riso's party, most of whom had been killed or wounded. Palermo woke up on the morning of the fourth to see the few surviving prisoners being marched through the popular quarters to the music of a military band. Maniscalco fired off a jubilant message to Naples: "I've seized the revolution by its hairs."[43]

To prevent the rural *squadre* from entering the city, the authorities ordered the city gates to be closed and guarded by cavalry patrols. Yet these *squadre* fared far better than Riso's three bands. They were far more numerous—there were three hundred men from Carini alone—and they were able to ambush cavalry patrols and then melt into the countryside. Although the authorities soon added two additional battalions of cavalry (roughly 2,400 men, if we calculate 1,000 men per battalion), they were still hard-pressed by a largely invisible enemy.

Defeated in the city, the revolution had better success in the hill towns. Misilmeri and Villabate immediately declared for the revolution. On the evening of April 3, *squadre* from Misilmeri and Villabate made ready to depart for Palermo. These, with other *squadre*, assembled at the pass of Gibilrossa, overlooking Palermo at the foot of Mount Grifone. Here they bade good-bye to their families and received a blessing from the local clergy. Their leader, Domenico Corteggiani, carried a *tricolore*, and as the *squadristi* filed past him in review, each took up an edge and kissed it. With additional *squadre* coming in, the number of Misilmeri insurgents reached about two hundred.[44]

The Albanian-speaking communities around Piana and Montelepre joined the uprising as well. Traditionally the Albanians had held themselves aloof from conspiracies and revolutionary politics; in 1860, however, they joined with a will. They had been forbidden to celebrate Mass according to the Greek rite by the Bull of Gregory XIV, *Etsi pastoralis*. Issued in 1843, the Papal Bull had not been enforced until the 1850s at the orders of the Neapolitan government. Not only were the Albanian *squadristi* to prove themselves brave and determined fighters, but also the acquisition of the Piana region provided the revolutionaries with links to the south and the west, making Piana the meeting point between the Conca d'Oro towns and the interior.[45]

Provisional governments were declared in both Piana and Corleone, which sent their *squadre* to join the insurgents at Misilmeri. Here, on the eleventh, there was an attempt to create a unified revolutionary command under La Porta. Yet even these larger *squadre* could not hold their gains against concentrations of Bourbon troops. By nightfall on the eleventh two battalions of royal troops had arrived and Misilmeri had been retaken.

On the fifteenth, the government sent out a column of three thousand men against Piana, where around seven hundred insurgents were concentrated. These rebels escaped to Partinico, where, uniting with other *squadre*, they continued on to Montelepre. Here they debated whether to retire to Monte San Giuliano (modern-day Erice) or proceed to Carini, still flying the *tricolore*. Hoping that they were now strong enough to risk a pitched battle, they agreed to march to Carini.

Over a week's resistance in the countryside had given new heart to the Palermitans, who staged a public demonstration in solidarity with the revolution. Yet Maniscalco speedily shocked the city back into submission by publicly executing the thirteen surviving prisoners from Riso's uprising (including Riso's father, who had taken no part). When they reached Carini, the combined *squadre* learned that Palermo was quiet and that the government had offered amnesties to all those willing to lay down their arms. At this news, most of the *squadre* went home, leaving a nucleus of about five hundred to face an attack of three battalions on the eighteenth. After a fierce fight the *squadristi* were dislodged, and the town of Carini was sacked by government troops.

The countryside was still far from quiet. *Squadre* continued to skirmish, and local revolutionary committees continued to crop up, hoisting the *tricolore* over municipal buildings to proclaim their solidarity with the revolution. The leaders of the *squadre* were also still at large, as were most of their followers. Yet with the defeat at Carini, the revolt had been effectively contained. The *squadre* were powerless against flying columns of two to three thousand soldiers. These had been successful against the uprisings that occurred in Trapani province as well as in Messina and Catania. So long as the government had the means to deploy effectively the 25,000 troops they maintained in Sicily, the revolution had little chance of success.

After Carini, the bulk of the Albanian *squadristi* under their leader Pietro Piediscalzi, along with remnants from other *squadre* who had fought two days before, retired to bivouac around Piana. Morale was low. The Bourbon commandant in the area, Chinicci, refrained from attack, calculating that in a few days' time, taking advantage of the proffered amnesty, most of the rebels would disperse of their own accord. Many undoubtedly would have, had not Rosolino Pilo arrived to save the revolution from sputtering out entirely.

Pilo had been sent to lead the revolution. He had left Genoa on March 25, and after being nearly lost at sea during a storm, had landed in Messina on April 10. He arrived in the company of Giovanni Corrao. Corrao came from a merchant navy family in Palermo; in 1849 he had fled Sicily for Malta, where he eventually met Pilo. Together with Corrao, Pilo made his way from Messina to the Conca d'Oro, encouraging revolutionary committees and reorganizing *squadre* on the way. On the twentieth of April, the pair reached Piana.

Pilo's presence had a galvanizing effect on the dispirited rebels. He was Sicily's leading revolutionary, a close associate of Mazzini, and a representative of the Sicilian aristocracy. He provided a rallying point around which the *squadre* could regroup. Soon there was a new rebel base camp between Piano and Monreale.

More than his presence, however, it was the news that Pilo brought that lifted the morale of the revolution. Garibaldi, he declared, would soon be in Sicily. This was what the revolutionaries had been waiting to hear. The news traveled rapidly to Palermo, where it gave renewed heart to the political prisoners languishing in the Vicaria prison. They posted lookouts at the windows on the prison's upper stories, hoping to catch sight of the smoke of battle in the surrounding hills. In the town itself, the revolutionary presses sprang back into action, instilling new hopes and inciting the citizens to fresh actions. By the beginning of May, the lieutenant governor reported that the news had "spread to the remotest villages of the island." Word spread in official circles as well; but here it provoked fear and consternation. Naples sent out its fleet to patrol the waters around Sicily, and the lieutenant governor issued proclamations declaring that the noted *fillibustiere* (pirate) Garibaldi would soon be captured and shot.[46]

Pilo's announcement was, to say the least, premature. On April 20, Garibaldi's departure still lay over two weeks in the future.

### Garibaldi and the Thousand

Shortly after April 4, Niccola Fabrizi telegraphed Crispi from Malta with the news of Riso's rebellion. Rejoicing that Palermo had risen at last, Crispi set to work feverishly, organizing ships and supplies, and contacting volunteers for the expedition that Garibaldi was to lead. On the twelfth, Garibaldi met in Turin with his lieutenants Giacomo Medici and Nino Bixio, who urged the Sicilian project upon him. Garibaldi provisionally agreed and the next day set off for Genoa, where he installed himself at the Villa Spinola three miles outside of town. Here he awaited the arrival of volunteers, especially from the Cacciatori whom he had led several months before.

Garibaldi also awaited news of events in Sicily. On April 27, he received a new telegram from Fabrizi: "Complete failure in the provinces and in the city of Palermo. Many refugees received by English ships that have come to Malta."[47] This was too discouraging. The next morning he called Crispi, Bixio, and La Masa into his chambers and regretfully told them that it would be "folly" to proceed.

Garibaldi's decision to call off the expedition was greeted with rage and confusion. Bixio and La Masa declared that they were willing to go ahead without him; other volunteers began to pack their bags to leave. The situation was saved by Crispi, who well understood that, whatever the situation in Sicily might be, it would be true "folly" to embark on an expedition without Garibaldi. Crispi appreciated Garibaldi's state of mind. He was haunted by the specter of the disaster that had overtaken Pisacane; he had reluctantly called off the expedition at the last minute only because he felt that he had no right to squander the lives of his volunteers on a hopeless enterprise. Yet he still wished to proceed. Advising the volunteers to put off any decisions until "new facts" could be ascertained, Crispi telegraphed coded messages to conspirators throughout the island. On the twenty-ninth, armed with more optimistic assessments, he and Bixio asked to meet with Garibaldi the following morning.

Whatever Crispi's "new facts" may have been, they instantly had the desired effect. Garibaldi read through Crispi's dispatches, then, rising from his chair, announced, "We'll go."[48] Shortly before midnight on May 5, Garibaldi and his volunteers began boarding two steamers "borrowed" for the occasion.

Garibaldi's first plan had been to make a wide circle around the Bourbon cruisers and land somewhere on the south coast of Sicily. At the last moment he seems to have changed his mind and decided to make a dash straight to Marsala. It was a stroke of fortune that he did; not only had two Neapolitan warships just left Marsala to patrol the south coast, but also the Marsala garrison had been withdrawn two days before to reinforce Palermo. When Garibaldi's two ships arrived at Marsala, the harbor was occupied only by local fishing boats and some English merchant ships. Outside the harbor were anchored the HMS *Argus* and HMS *Intrepid*, recently arrived to protect British residents in Marsala. On the morning of Garibaldi's arrival, some of the officers had gone ashore to view "Mr. Woodhouse's wine establishment," and some were still in town, peacefully eating ices in a café. Theirs was the only military presence in the town when Garibaldi and his thousand volunteers arrived on the eleventh of May.[49]

To replace the Marsala garrison, the Neapolitan authorities had dispatched three battalions plus artillery and cavalry under the seventy-year-old General Francesco Landi. Landi had proceeded slowly, believing that the "moral effect" of the mere sight of three thousand regular troops marching in formation would be enough to frighten away any lingering Sicilian *squadre*. By the time of Garibaldi's landing in Marsala, these troops had barely reached Alcamo, midway between Palermo and Marsala. When Landi learned of Garibaldi's landing, he advanced to the little town of Calatafimi. Here he remained, uncertain of what to do next. Meanwhile, at Garibaldi's camp, the first Sicilian *squadre* were arriving to offer their services. When Landi discovered that Garibaldi was in front of him and that *squadre* had torn down the telegraph lines and broken the semaphores that connected him with his headquarters in Palermo, he nervously elected to remain in the town with two battalions, sending the third out to reconnoiter.

Garibaldi and his volunteers had marched to the hill town of Salemi. Here he learned of the presence of three thousand Neapolitan troops in

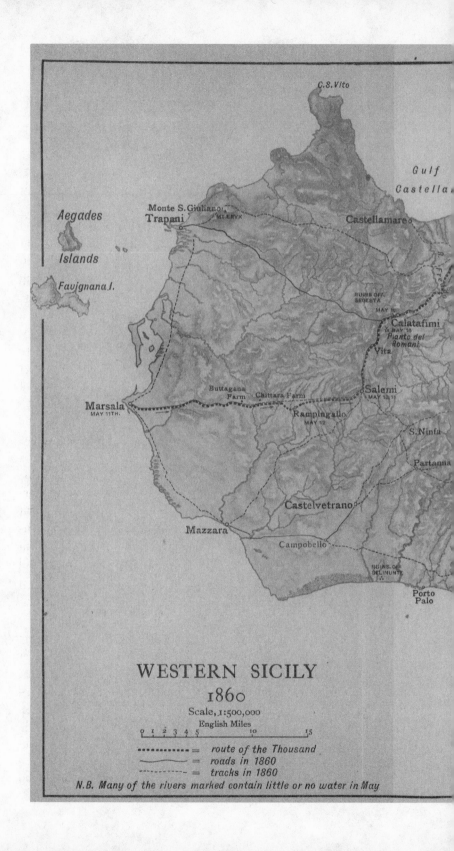

C.S.Vito

Gulf
Castella.

Aegades

Islands

Favignana I.

Monte S.Giuliano
Trapani        MT.ERYX

Castellamare

RUINS OF
SEGESTA
X MAY 16

Calatafimi
X MAY 15
Pianto del
Romani
Vita

Buttagana
Farm     Chittara Farm

Salemi
MAY 10,11

Marsala
MAY 11TH.

Rampingallo
MAY 12

S.Ninfa

Partanna

Castelvetrano

Mazzara

Campobello

RUINS OF
SELINUNTE

Porto
Palo

WESTERN SICILY
1860
Scale, 1:500,000
English Miles

0 1 2 3 4 5        10        15

········· = route of the Thousand
————— = roads in 1860
- - - - - = tracks in 1860
N.B. Many of the rivers marked contain little or no water in May

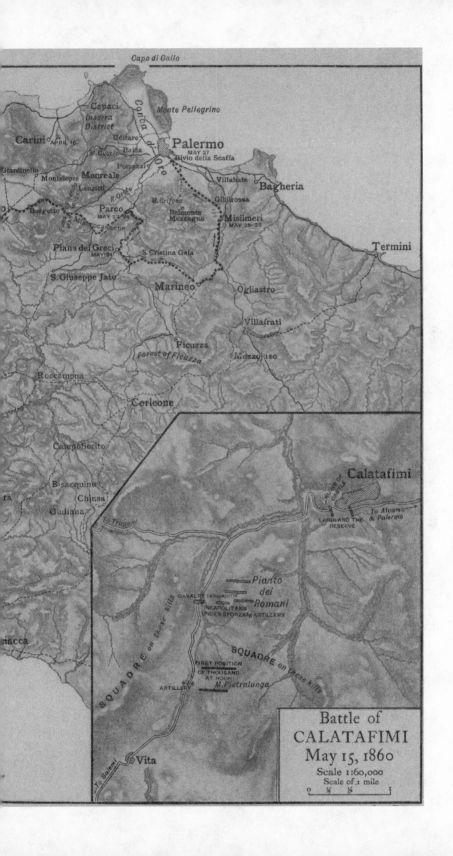

Capo di Gallo

Monte Pellegrino

Capaci
Insera
District

Carini
APRIL 16.
Uditare
Baida
M.Cuccio
Palermo
MAY 27
Bivio della Scaffa

Giardinello
Montelepre
Monreale
Lenzitti
Porrazzi
Villabate
Bagheria

Borgetto
Parco
MAY 23-24
M.Grifone
Gibilrossa
Belmonte
Mezzagno
Misilmeri
MAY 25-28

Piana dei Greci
MAY 24
S. Cristina Gela
Termini

S. Giuseppe Jato
Marineo
Ogliastro

Villafrati

Ficuzza
Forest of Ficuzza
Mezzojuso

Roccamena

Corleone

Campofioritos

Bisacquino
Chiusa

Giuliana

To Trapani
RUINS OF CASTILE
Calatafimi
To Alcamo
& Palermo
LAND AND THE
RESERVE

Pianto
dei
Romani
CAVALRY MONUMENT
NEAPOLITANS
UNDER SFORZA
ARTILLERY

SQUADRE on these hills

SQUADRE on these hills
FIRST POSITION
OF THOUSAND
AT NOON
M.Pietralunga
ARTILLERY

To Salemi
Vita

Battle of
CALATAFIMI
May 15, 1860

Scale 1:60,000
Scale of 1 mile
0    ¼    ½    1

Calatafimi. Garibaldi assumed that the Neapolitans would attack his position at once. When it became evident that Landi intended to do nothing more than sit on his position, Garibaldi decided that he would launch an attack instead. On the morning of May 15, he led his Thousand down from Salemi to the little village of Vita on the road to Calatafimi. Here they temporarily halted, and as the day was already sweltering, Garibaldi's volunteers took the opportunity of stuffing their pockets with oranges and lemons. After a short rest, they resumed their march along the Calatafimi road. As they reached the watershed, Garibaldi turned off the road and, leaving his few pieces of artillery behind, began to ascend the Pietralunga, a hill situated just to the north of the road.

From its summit, Garibaldi scanned the northern horizon with his binoculars. He made out a party of Neapolitan troops. They, in fact, were the Eighth Cacciatori, one of the best regiments in the Neapolitan army, who at this moment happened to be at the top of the Pianto dei Romani, a high hill directly opposite Garibaldi's position.

Seeing the Garibaldini on the hill opposite him, the Neapolitan commander, Major Sforza, sounded the advance. He had no order to attack, and at this point intended only to explore Garibaldi's position. Descending from the Pianto dei Romani, crossing the narrow valley, and starting their ascent toward their enemy's position, however, Sforza and his officers soon began to catch a clear sight of the volunteers. The Neapolitans had feared that Garibaldi was leading a detachment of regular Piedmontese army troops; what they now beheld, however, seemed mere rabble. Other than a line of green-coated Genoese carabinieri, there were no regular soldiers among them. Most of the volunteers wore their civilian clothes; some were even in their top hats. They took the red shirts worn by others to be the red uniforms worn by prisoners confined in the prison hulks. Concluding that these irregulars constituted an enemy no more formidable than the Sicilian *squadre*, Sforza and his soldiers took heart and began to charge up the Pietralunga.

At first the Garibaldini maintained their position without firing. Only the Genoese riflemen advanced in skirmishing order, firing at the advancing Neapolitans. Suddenly, however, without any order having been given, the leading companies of the Thousand leaped to their feet and charged down upon the Neapolitans. Faced with this unexpected behavior, the Neapolitans wavered, then turned and fled to the lower slopes of the Pianto dei Romani as the Garibaldini sped across the valley in hot pursuit.

At the outset of the battle, the Garibaldini enjoyed a slight superiority in numbers, for fighting alongside the Thousand were around two hundred Sicilian irregulars, the *squadra* of Baron Sant'Anna from Alcamo. Yet this advantage was quickly reversed, for, from Calatafimi, Landi dispatched one of his two remaining battalions. Thus, for the remainder of the afternoon, the thousand-plus Garibaldini were pitted against two thousand Neapolitan soldiers. The Neapolitans had other advantages as well. They were able to fall back onto an eminently defensible position and shoot down upon Garibaldi's volunteers as they charged from below. Above all, they were better armed. Of the Thousand, only the Genoese Carabinieri possessed modern rifles; the rest had to make do with antiquated smooth-bore muskets with fixed sights.

The slopes of the Pianto dei Romani were covered with rough terraces, which provided the Garibaldini with much-needed cover. Still, to win, the Garibaldini needed to advance up the slope, and this meant exposing themselves, leaving the cover of the lower terraces and running or slithering through the parched grass to the terrace above. They were desperately short of ammunition as well; yet this did not matter much, as Garibaldi had already decided that if the heights of the Pianto dei Romani were to be taken at all, they would be taken at bayonet point.

The Neapolitans hung on stubbornly; yet they could scarcely credit what they were beholding. For ten years the "moral effect" of the sight of regular soldiers had usually been enough to cow a frightened populace into submission. Sicilian *squadre* had rarely held their positions under fire, much less dared to charge straight into Neapolitan fire with fixed bayonets. Yet this was precisely what the Garibaldini were now doing. Garibaldi's venture in Sicily stood little chance of success. The numbers against him were simply too great. Yet Garibaldi must have realized that were his ill-armed and comically clad volunteers to put two of the best regiments in the Neapolitan army to flight on the Pianto dei Romani, the odds might begin to change in his favor. And there was always the hope that, faced with such unexpected tactics, the Neapolitan general staff, never noted for its energy, might panic and be provoked into the mistakes that would give Garibaldi the opportunities he needed.

After two hours of unremitting torture, Garibaldi found himself under the cover of the last terrace. With him was a party of about three hundred, including Bixio, the Hungarian Stefano Türr, the remnants of his staff, the surviving Genoese, and a group of students from Pavia. They were now so close to the summit that they could make out the commands of the Neapolitan officers as they ordered their men to aim lower. Garibaldi remained here for a quarter of an hour, catching his breath and waiting for stragglers. When Bixio had suggested a retreat earlier that afternoon, Garibaldi had replied, "Here we make Italy or die." In context it was no more than a simple statement of fact; had Garibaldi and his followers fallen into the hands of General Landi, they would have been shot. Cavour would have done nothing to save them from their fate.

Above, some of the Neapolitan troops, short of ammunition, began picking up stones and hurling them down onto the terrace below. Garibaldi happened to be leaning forward, bent toward the ground, when one of the stones struck him in the back. He straightened up and ex-claimed, "Come on. They're throwing stones. Their ammunition is spent." Unsheathing his sword, he dashed up the last hill, his men follow-ing as closely as they could. Many of his volunteers and a few of the Sicil-ian *Squadristi* fell wounded, for the Neapolitans were not out of ammuni-tion after all. Yet Garibaldi's charge had overrun the last Neapolitan defense. More of the volunteers followed the first party into the breach, at-tacking the Neapolitan positions with bayonet and sword. The Neapoli-tans "fought like lions," as Garibaldi later generously wrote; but their posi-tion had fallen. After a furious combat, the Neapolitans came streaming down the other side of the Pianto dei Romani toward Calatafimi.[50]

If Calatafimi was a stunning military victory, its moral effects were every bit as devastating as Garibaldi could have wished. Major Sforza accused General Landi of betrayal; there were wild stories that he had secretly been bribed by Garibaldi. The old general was thoroughly confused: he wired Palermo asking for help; he announced that his troops had "killed the great captain of the Italians"; he panicked. He was growing increas-ingly alarmed at reports that new *squadre* were forming around him. They had destroyed the telegraph lines and his military semaphores; now they were waylaying his couriers. The first to read the report announcing Garibaldi's death was, in fact, Garibaldi himself. Landi's forces still greatly outnumbered those of Garibaldi; at the very least, he could have held his position and blocked Garibaldi's further advance. Instead, he ordered his troops to abandon Calatafimi.[51]

The Neapolitan troops had fought bravely, but with defeat, demoraliza-tion set in. Some of the noncommissioned officers deserted. The gigantic Neapolitan sergeant who had charged the Garibaldini from the Pianto dei Romani, killing Garibaldi's flag bearer and wounding his son Menotti be-fore carrying off the banner in triumph, was soon fighting on the side of the Garibaldini. Yet the majority of the Neapolitan troops were now more intent on wreaking vengeance on the Sicilians than on joining them under Garibaldi's banner. On May 16, Landi's troops entered Alcamo; from here they set off for Partinico. At the little village of Massa-Quarnero they began killing the population in reprisal for their defeat. By the time they reached Partinico, they found the alarmed population awaiting them in arms. The townspeople attacked the retreating columns, and a massacre followed in which neither the Neapolitans nor the Partinicesi asked or gave quarter. When the Thousand passed through the town a few days later, they were appalled at the sight of the gutted and burnt houses and the mutilated corpses lying in the streets.[52] Repulsed from Partinico, Landi's troops took the mountain road to Montelepre. Here they were attacked by local *squadre* who took much of their baggage.

With the sight of Landi's defeated troops straggling back into the capital on May 17, demoralization and panic began to grip the Neapolitan authorities. The aged and incompetent lieutenant governor had been replaced by the even more aged General Ferdinando Lanza, who was said to have been empowered to offer the Sicilian aristocracy the 1812 constitution once again. Certainly he offered a peace on the basis of the conditions that Ferdinand II had offered in February 1849.[53] But such issues were by now out of date; even if the Sicilian nobility had been disposed to accept these concessions, the situation was out of their control. On the fifteenth, Maniscalco wrote a despairing message directly to the king:

> Public spirit in Palermo is worsening, the revolutionary faction, becoming all-powerful, threatens to massacre all those devoted to the cause of legitimate monarchy; all are filled with terror; functionaries are deserting their posts; the call of duty is no longer heeded; society is falling apart; all are fleeing on packet ships fearing a general massacre in the case of a conflict.[54]

By May 1860 the reports from the Bourbon governor Castelcicala, Maniscalco, and General Lanza were all converging on one point: Palermo was preparing to rise again. This time the uprising would not be another quixotic venture. It would be a full-scale revolt like that of January 1848. What is more, when Palermo arose, the *squadre* from the countryside would once more fall upon the city. Garibaldi had sent off La Masa and Crispi to raise new volunteer bands in communes throughout the western part of the island. He wrote Pilo, announcing that they would soon be meeting. Yet even without these initiatives, the *squadre* were increasing every day. From the top of the Castellammare and the Palazzo Reale, Neapolitan officials could see the bonfires lit each night at Gibilrossa on the road to Misilmeri.

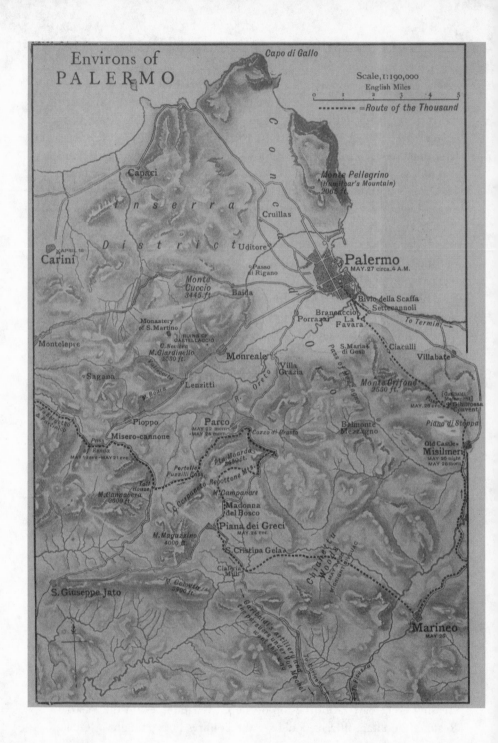

Environs of
**PALERMO**

*Capo di Gallo*

Scale, 1:190,000
English Miles
0   1   2   3   4   5

------- = *Route of the Thousand*

*C
o
n
c
a
d*

Capaci

*Monte Pellegrino*
*(Humilcar's Mountain)*
*2065 ft.*

*I n s e r r a*

Cruillas

*D i s t r i c t*

× APRIL 18

**Carini**

Uditore

Passo
di Rigano

**Palermo**
MAY 27 circa.4 A.M.

*Monte
Cuccio
3445 ft.*

Baida

Bivio della Scaffa
Settecannoli

Monastery
of S.Martino

Brancaccio
Porrazzi      La
Favara

To Termini

RUINS OF
CASTELLACCIO

C.Neviera

*M.Giardinello*
*2550 ft.*

Montelepre

Monreale

S.Maria
di Gesù

Ciaculli

Villa
Grazia

Villabate

*Sagana*

*M.Boira*

Lenzitti

R. Oreto

*Monte Grifone*
*2550 ft.*

[Garibaldi
Monument]
F.Ghirlrossa
Convent

Pioppo

Parco
MAY 22 morn.
MAY 24 morn.

Cozzo di Crasto

Belmonte
Mezzagno

Piano di Stoppa

Misero-cannone

Pass
of Renda
MAY 19 eve–MAY 21 eve

Portella
Puzzilli Pass

Pta.Moarda
2650 ft.

Old Castle
**Misilmeri**
MAY 26 night
MAY 26 morn.

Toll
House

C.Carbonello Repottone M.ta

*M.Cannonera*
*3000 ft.*

M.Campanare

Madonna
del Bosco

**Piana dei Greci**
MAY 26 eve.

*M.Magazzino*
*4000 ft.*

S. Cristina Gela

*Chiarella
woods*

Ciaforia
Mill

*M.Calvelta*
*2500 ft.*

**S. Giuseppe Jato**

Garibaldis Artillery
went across under Von Mechel
pursues

To Bolognl

R. Eleuterio

**Marineo**
MAY 26

From Calatafimi, Garibaldi marched to Alcamo. As he rode into town, people fell to their knees before him. Then, from Alcamo, the Thousand climbed to Renda, a high, narrow, and barren plateau at the edge of the Conca d'Oro.

From Palermo, the Conca d'Oro fans out to the south like a roughly shaped scallop shell. Its interior, a jumble of hills, valleys and steep ravines, is dotted with villages and towns knitted together by a network of roads, mule tracks, and footpaths. It is a landscape well adapted to the hit-and-run tactics of guerrilla warfare, and to the blood feuding to which the villagers had long been partial. On its outer edge, however, the Conca d'Oro rises precipitously in a ring of mountains whose passes lead to the high plains of the Sicilian interior. It was over these outer ridges that Garibaldi and the Thousand plodded for the next week, often with large detachments of Neapolitan troops close at their heels.

From the outset Garibaldi's intent had been to attack Palermo. He first thought of attacking Monreale, at the center of the Conca d'Oro, and then falling on Palermo by way of the Monreale road. He sent a message to Pilo to take his *squadre* and occupy the heights above Monreale at the Monastery of San Martino, hoping draw off part of the Monreale garrison.

The plan proved impracticable: the Monreale garrison stood at three thousand, and there were another two thousand troops in the area. To make matters worse, a further three thousand troops had been sent from Palermo under the command of a Swiss officer, Colonel Luka Von Mechel. Von Mechel had been sent to reinforce Monreale; finding Garibaldi's forces in an extended line in front of him, however, he sent only one battalion ahead toward Monreale. He dispatched the bulk of his forces against Pilo's *squadre*. The first battalion encountered Garibaldi's vanguard as it descended toward Monreale and, in a short encounter, managed to push it back up toward the ridges. His second two battalions, pushing toward San Martino, fell upon Pilo's *squadre* before they were ready for battle. Pilo was killed in the attack, shot dead as he sat on a rock, pen in hand, writing Garibaldi for help.

With Von Mechel now in command of Pilo's position overlooking Monreale, Garibaldi's own position on the ridges was threatened. Ordering Sant'Anna to cover his movements by lighting campfires on the ridges above Monreale, Garibaldi swung around to the road connecting Palermo to Piana and Corleone and marched to Parco, where he formed a new camp. The march was an extremely difficult one, and Garibaldi's followers, who had spent the last three days camping and marching on the exposed peaks and plateaus under an incessant rain, were by now exhausted; but the maneuver gave Garibaldi two days' respite, which he used to fortify his position at Parco.

Soon his position there became untenable as well. Discovering that Garibaldi had escaped from the heights above Monreale toward Parco, Von Mechel set off in pursuit. He was joined by the Monreale garrison plus another two thousand troops dispatched from Palermo. Apprised of his enemies' movements, and fearing entrapment in a pincers movement, Garibaldi retreated toward Piana.

Garibaldi was now practically in flight, and had the eight thousand troops of Von Mechel immediately set off after the Thousand on the road to Piana, it might well have spelled the end for Garibaldi. Fortunately for him, such were not the methods of the Neapolitan military establishment. They had developed a garrison mentality, and as soon as they learned that Garibaldi and his volunteers were withdrawing over the mountainous rim and into the wild and inhospitable plains of the Sicilian interior, where few of them had ever been, they went home. They were undoubtedly a bit afraid as well: it was said that Garibaldi took no prisoners; that he shot every soldier, police spy, and Neapolitan official who fell into his clutches. In any case, Neapolitan authorities were obsessed with concentrating as many of their troops as possible for the defense of the capital, even if this meant leaving the interior unguarded. Thus, the two battalions sent out from Palermo simply returned there, while the Monreale garrison returned to its post as well.

This left Von Mechel and his two battalions. The Swiss officer paused to re-form the troops under his command, increasing their strength with detachments from the Palermo garrison. In the end, his forces numbered something over three thousand men. They were handpicked men. These delays, however, had cost Von Mechel a day, and a day was all that Garibaldi needed.

As soon as he reached Piana, Garibaldi called a council of war. He observed that by now the cannons and carriages the Thousand had brought with them were an impediment which limited their mobility by constraining the volunteers to stick to the high roads. Garibaldi had arrived in Piana along the road from Palermo to Corleone. The road led through the upland valley in which Piana lay before winding southward toward Corleone over the next set of peaks. Yet Garibaldi had learned that before the road started its ascent, there was a spur track leading eastward to the little town of Santa Cristina Gela. That evening, Garibaldi sent his artillery ahead down the Corleone road, accompanied by several Sicilian *squadre* and by his injured. He followed with the main body of the Thousand shortly behind. By the time they passed the Santa Cristina Gela road, night had fallen. Garibaldi continued on the Corleone road to the foot of the mountains, then wheeled off sharply to his left. Under the cover of the hills and the darkness, they rejoined the track to Santa Cristina.

From Santa Cristina the Thousand continued due east, making their way by footpaths to the town of Marineo. From here there was a good road leading straight to Misilmeri. Garibaldi sent a courier ahead telling La Masa to meet him with his *squadre* at Gibilrossa the following morning and gave his men a much-needed rest. Later that afternoon, however, he thought better of it, and, rousing his men, set them marching again. Garibaldi and his footsore volunteers reached Misilmeri before midnight on May 25.

Several hours before, Von Mechel had arrived in Piana. He was told that Garibaldi had left by the Corleone road twenty-four hours earlier; indeed, the tracks of the artillery were still clearly visible. Von Mechel scented blood; Garibaldi seemed clearly to be fleeing into the interior, and it would be only a matter of time before he could corner him and finish him off. Von Mechel paused just long enough to send a triumphant telegram to Palermo, and then marched off to the south. He continued on for several days. Outside Corleone he was bombarded by Garibaldi's five cannons, and this made him even more convinced that he was closing in for the kill. He was fifteen miles from the south coast of Sicily when a messenger reached him with the news that Garibaldi was in Palermo.

On the twenty-sixth, Garibaldi finally gave his men a much-deserved day of rest while he considered the problem of how to enter Palermo. He was encamped on the plain below Gibilrossa. Ferdinand Eber, a Hungarian by birth but now the *Times* correspondent in Sicily, arrived from Palermo. From Eber, Garibaldi learned that the majority of the Neapolitan troops were concentrated to the north and the west of the city walls. The southeastern approaches were guarded only by a small detachment, and if Garibaldi could descend into the valleys of the Conca d'Oro without detection, there was a good chance that he could enter the city by Porta Termini or Porta Sant'Antonino. Garibaldi also discovered that there was a precipitous footpath leading from the pass at Gibilrossa to the village of Ciaculli. Using this, Garibaldi and his volunteers would be able to avoid the public roads from Misilmeri and Bagheria.

Eber was not even the first visitor to Garibaldi's camp that day. Three English naval officers who happened to be driving along the coast road near Villabate were challenged by an advance party and then invited to the camp. They readily accepted, and soon found themselves sharing wild strawberries with Garibaldi. They told Eber that they were struck by the informality of the camp and the youth of both the volunteers and the *picciotti* (Sicilian volunteers). The place had the appearance more of a Gypsy encampment than a military base. The volunteers lounged on blankets, eating a stew made from the carcass of a calf and a mountain of onions with hunks of bread, washing it down with draughts of Marsala. Eber arrived later that afternoon, accompanied by two officers of the United States warship *Iroquois*. He had learned where the camp was located, but was worried about going alone. The Americans were happy enough to accompany him; it sounded like an adventure and they were hoping to get a chance to meet the famous Garibaldi. One of the two officers gave Garibaldi a revolver which he carried into Palermo the next day.

Garibaldi had sent La Masa out to raise *squadre* in the countryside, and La Masa had performed his task well. Marching with the Thousand—now reduced to about seven hundred—were over three thousand Sicilian *picciotti*. Garibaldi had put Giovanni Corrao in charge of Pilo's remaining forces, for Corrao had revealed himself as an able organizer and guerrilla fighter. He was ordered to bring his men down through the northern suburbs and be ready to attack at the Porta Macqueda on the north.

After the Battle of Calatafimi, peasants came forward to give the Garibaldini information, helping them elude Von Mechel at both Renda and Parco. The network of Bourbon spies had collapsed; yet, so isolated had the Bourbon high command become, so accustomed to relying on spies and informers as their sole source of information about Sicily, that they had little inkling that their network had abandoned them to their fate. By the twenty-sixth, all of Palermo knew of Garibaldi's presence at Gibilrossa—everyone except Lanza and Maniscalco. Even though the merest Palermo street urchin by now knew better, they continued to believe that Garibaldi was in flight somewhere south of Corleone with Von Mechel in hot pursuit.

## The Battle for Palermo

Garibaldi and his forces began their climb into the pass of Gibilrossa shortly after nightfall on May 26. From here they followed the path of a riverbed as it descended sharply to Ciaculli. After this, the party split up into columns (which continually lost one another as they stumbled through the dark citrus groves) and made their way to the next rendezvous

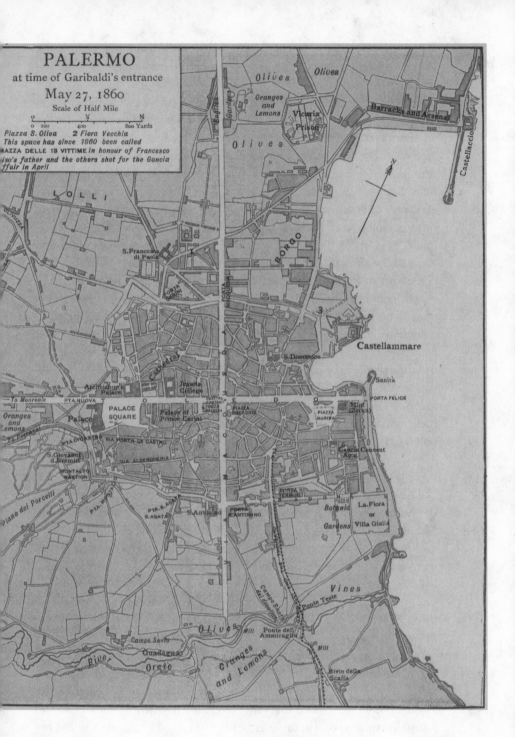

at the crossing of the Oreto River. At the twelfth-century bridge, the Ponte dell'Ammiraglio, they met their first detachments of Bourbon troops.

Garibaldi had placed some of the Sicilian *squadre* in the vanguard, and these, in their excitement, now began to yell and fire their muskets into the air. Forewarned, the Neapolitans were prepared for the assault. When they made out the approaching Garibaldini in the moonlight, they opened fire. The leader of the vanguard, the Hungarian Louis Türkory, threw himself flat on the ground with about fifty of his men. The Sicilians, however, ran for cover in the surrounding vineyards. Seeing a dangerous hole opening up between the vanguard and the rest of his forces, Garibaldi galloped straight for the bridge with the two companies of volunteers and some of the *picciotti*. The Neapolitans broke off the engagement and scattered back to Palermo. The element of surprise had now been lost, however, leaving the Garibaldini with no option but to dash for the Porta Termini, about a mile away, before the Neapolitans could organize a defense.

Unlike the northern and western sides of Palermo, the southern side presented the attackers not with walls and bastions, but rather with a row of houses built up against the old walls. In front of this row ran a wide street (the present-day via Lincoln) leading to the seafront and to Palermo's public gardens (the Villa Giulia, where, in November 1847, the public performance of Donezetti's *Gemma di Vergy* had been held). The only access was by the Porta Sant'Antonino, at the southern end of via Macqueda, or, farther east, by the Porta Termini, which led to the Fieravecchia. It was toward this latter gate that Garibaldi was now running.

The gate at Porta Termini had long since disappeared, but in its place the Neapolitans had constructed a high barricade. There were only a few Neapolitan troops guarding this barricade, but perched on top, they were well positioned to direct an enfilading fire at Garibaldi's followers, who ran up to try to dismantle it. Not only that, but to approach the barricade one had first to cross the wide street fronting the row of houses, thereby exposing oneself to cross-fire from cannons placed in front of the church at Porta Sant'Antonino and from the blasts of the Neapolitan warships in Palermo harbor.

Many of the *picciotti* had needed to be coaxed or driven out of their hiding places where they had fled after the first encounter with Bourbon troops at the Ponte dell'Ammiraglio. Faced now with the barricade at Porta Termini and, more than anything else, terrified by the din of the Neapolitan war cannons, these same *picciotti* balked a second time and refused to cross the road. The situation was critical; several of the advance party had already been wounded, and the leader of the vanguard, the brave Hungarian Türkory, lay dead at the foot of the barricade. Fortunately it was still dark, and, despite the superiority of their weapons, the Neapolitans were notoriously bad shots. The fusillades from Porta Sant'Antonino and the cannonades from the port were noisy but had little effect. As Eber wrote in his dispatch to the *Times*, "I never saw so little damage done by so much shooting."[55]

Finally Bixio, ignoring a musket ball that had lodged in his chest, with the remaining volunteers managed to throw down the barricade, allowing Garibaldi to charge through and into the city astride his great horse. Outside, Eber and some of the other volunteers took it upon themselves to escort the still petrified *picciotti* in twos and threes across the road and through the breach. Finally, one of the youngest of the volunteers, the seventeen-year-old Francesco Carbone from Genoa, planting a chair in the middle of the road and, hoisting a *tricolore* above it, sat down and calmly crossed his legs, letting the bullets and cannonballs whiz harmlessly by. Convinced at last that it was possible to survive the crossing with their skin intact (or perhaps too ashamed to hold back any further), the bulk of the *squadre* began to rush across, entering the city and joining Garibaldi and Bixio in the Fieravecchia.

It was about four in the morning, but the scene at the Fieravecchia was pandemonium. Palermo had been awaiting Garibaldi, and when it heard the sounds of the predawn battle, people knew that it could only be he. Some stood still with tears streaming from their eyes, others fell to their knees, but the majority could not contain their joy. They danced, whistled, clapped, and shouted. The crowd grew as more and more people rushed into the still darkened piazza and surged forward to kiss their deliverer's hand. Garibaldi stood awhile, impassively bearing this acclamation, then he walked over and hugged Bixio, who had toppled the barricade and who, having ripped the musket ball from his chest with his own hands, was now nearly fainting from exhaustion and loss of blood.[56]

From the Fieravecchia, Garibaldi sent his volunteers and the leaders of the *squadre* to rouse the town. At first there was no response. The citizens remembered the outcome of the uprising less than two months earlier; they remembered the execution of the thirteen victims a week afterward, and probably also remembered the executions at the Fieravecchia ten years before. The reception at the Fieravecchia had been misleading; as the volunteers ran through the town, they found the streets silent and empty and the shutters barred. Yet as more peasant *squadre* poured in through Porta Termini, firing their muskets into the air, shouting and waving *tricolori*,

Palermo began to take heart. Emboldened, the brave, or merely the incorrigibly curious, ventured from their houses, running after the volunteers and the *picciotti*, and, in the excitement, receiving confused and exaggerated accounts of what was happening. Excited citizens burst into the churches and convents, banging the bells with stones or bits of pipe, anything they could find (the Bourbon police had thought to remove the clappers from all the city's bells, thinking that, in this way, the tocsin could not be rung). Then the shuttered windows burst open. Mattresses and old furniture rained down upon the streets below. Palermo was about to erect its barricades.

Barricades had probably been on Garibaldi's mind from the start. He knew that even with the help of the Sicilian *squadre*, his thousand volunteers could not survive for long in the open against 25,000 Bourbon soldiers. Once he was inside the city, behind barricades, with the city's population solidly behind him, his chances would be much improved.

*Barricades in Palermo. Courtesy Pitre Museum, Palermo.*

Trevelyan describes Palermo on the morning of the twenty-seventh as the "devil's kitchen," as "its 160,000 inhabitants and 4,000 friendly invaders clashed and roared and shrieked and banged."[57] Into this throbbing sea of exulting humanity the Bourbon warships and the artillery in front of the Palazzo Reale now began to direct a murderous and indiscriminate fire.

The Neapolitan troops had no intention of storming the barricades. As General Lanza had calmly and frankly told the British admiral Sir Rodney Mundy at a meeting two days before, if the rebels did succeed in barricading themselves in the heart of the city, the Neapolitans would respond by reducing the city to rubble with their artillery and warship cannons. It was during this meeting that Maniscalco asked the British consul William Goodwin if he did not concur that a population that rose up against constituted authority ought to be annihilated. Goodwin voiced the sentiments of the British, and doubtless most of the other foreign residents in the city; he replied that "when a people were tyrannized over they had an inherent right to take up arms, and to fight against their oppressors."[58]

The damage resulting from the bombardments was frightful. Worse were the depredations of the soldiers, who, instead of venturing into the center of the city, had burned and sacked the houses in the Albergheria quarter adjacent to the Palazzo Reale as well as the houses in the western suburbs. Families died trapped in the collapsing rubble or were choked to death by smoke and charred into unidentifiable blackened masses.[59] Typically, these atrocities were committed for their "moral effect"; they served no military purpose.

Garibaldi soon seized both police headquarters at Piazza Bologni and the municipal building near Quattro Cantoni; these were both tucked away in the center of the city, where the Neapolitan artillery could only lob their shells blindly. Still, shells kept raining down, though none hit Garibaldi, who in any event seemed to take no notice of them. Soon the superstitious came to reason that he had the magical power to ward off bullets and artillery shells. The timorous crouched as close to him as they could get when they heard the whistling of falling missiles. His power, they decided, came from the strange whip that he had carried from South America and always wore looped to his belt.[60]

Like General Landi, who, after Calatafimi, had retreated to Palermo instead of blocking the further advance of Garibaldi and the Thousand, General Lanza now thought of reinforcing the Palazzo Reale rather than of dislodging Garibaldi from the town. He ordered the troops guarding the large port to the north of the city to join him, marching around to the

*Bourbon warships shell the Albergheria district of Palermo, May 1860.*

western gate. By this maneuver he deprived himself of communication with the sea. The order was doubly unfortunate, for, as the troops were leaving the northern suburbs, they were fallen upon by Giovanni Corrao leading Pilo's *squadre*. Corrao secured the northern suburbs as well as the northern gate, Porta Macqueda. The rebels held most of the town plus the major north-south axis. By now there were eighteen thousand Bourbon soldiers crammed into the area around the Palazzo Reale and the western suburbs.

Despite these successes, the situation seemed, at very best, a stalemate. The troops around the Palazzo Reale were too numerous and too well armed to attack. Worse, Garibaldi was running short of ammunition. Curiously, however, it was General Lanza who decided that his position was untenable. He had cut himself off from the port to the north of the city. He could no longer communicate by semaphore with the ships in Palermo harbor, as the rebels had blocked the view by hanging a gigantic curtain across Porta Felice, the city gate facing the harbor. Two hundred of his soldiers had been killed in the fighting; around him were eight hundred or so wounded. Belatedly he decided to launch a frontal attack against the barricades.

On the third day, May 29, Garibaldi's followers managed to gain the cathedral. From here they were able to move one stage farther west and take the archbishop's palace as well. The south side of the archbishop's palace looked onto the piazza in front of the Palazzo Reale. Thus, by the morning of the twenty-ninth, though Garibaldi's forces were hardly in a position to attack Lanza's headquarters, at least they had it in their rifle sights.

It was this threat that rallied the Neapolitans. They brought in reinforcements from Porta Nuova, the western gate. Soon their counterattack had driven the Garibaldini out of the archbishop's palace and out of the cathedral as well. The situation was once again critical, for the momentum of the Neapolitans' attack was threatening to carry them eastward, toward the rebel enclaves in the heart of the city. Learning of this, Garibaldi gathered about fifty Sicilian *squadristi* and led his own counterattack. At first the Neapolitans stood their ground, but Garibaldi ordered the bugler to sound a charge and drove the Neapolitans back to the cathedral.

The result of this battle in the northwest corner of the city was that, having lost what they had taken that morning, the rebels were now back to where they had started from. Lanza, however, seemed to draw a different lesson. He was running low on food, munitions, and medicines. The relative failure of his one attempt to storm the rebel positions convinced him that no fresh attempts could be undertaken. He had already approached the British; now he asked whether he and Garibaldi might make use of the *HMS Hannibal* for a conference. When he received a favorable reply, he sent a message to Garibaldi proposing a meeting and offering a cease-fire effective at the stroke of noon on the thirtieth.

*Garibaldini posed by a fallen Bourbon soldier, 1860, in a retouched photograph.*

For Garibaldi, who expected nothing better than an even more determined assault on his positions from the Neapolitans the following day, the offer of a cease-fire was a last minute reprieve. The offer was even more miraculous than Garibaldi realized, for shortly before he had dispatched the message, General Lanza had learned that Von Mechel was returning from his wild goose chase and was near the Ponte dell'Ammiraglio.

Unaware that the rebels now held the city, Von Mechel set up camp outside the Porta Termini. On the thirtieth, he marched his men into the Fieravecchia, where he was stopped by some of the volunteers who tried to explain that they now held the city and that the Bourbon commander in chief had declared a cease-fire. Von Mechel found the very idea preposterous; he opened fire on the rebels and was about to march forward toward the center of town when he was stopped once again, this time by a certain Lieutenant Wilmot, one of the English officers sent to arrange the meeting between Garibaldi and Lanza. Ignoring the shooting, Wilmot strode indignantly up to Von Mechel pointing to the hands of his watch. Von Mechel, he expostulated, was in violation of the truce. This was an affront to the British Admiralty. Wilmot's frantic remonstrations only seemed to deepen Von Mechel's perplexity. Fortunately, two Neapolitan officers now arrived; they blandly informed Wilmot that it was all a mistake, and then told the "Bavarians" (Von Mechel's divisions) that everything that the Sicilians and the British lieutenant had claimed was the truth. Von Mechel was at last convinced.

The rebels took advantage of the day's truce to reinforce their barricades. General Lanza drew up plans for an attack the next day, but at the last moment decided to extend the truce for another three days. He dispatched some of his generals to consult with the king in Naples. Subduing Palermo was still possible, he believed, but only at a high cost in blood. The English, American, French, and Piedmontese consuls were openly sympathetic toward the rebels. The Austrians had turned their back on their old allies. It is likely that neither the king nor General Lanza had any desire to shoulder the moral and political opprobrium they would undoubtedly incur if they were to resume the shelling of the old city. The truces were a tacit admission of defeat. On June 6, Naples capitulated, and on the following day began to evacuate its forces. Although Garibaldi still had months of fighting ahead of him, it is June 6 that marks the end of Bourbon rule in Sicily.

# 4

## 1866: The *Sette Mezzo* Uprising and the Week's Republic in Palermo

Despite Palermo's rejoicing over the defeat of the Bourbons, nothing had yet been settled. The political future of Sicily still hung in the balance and would remain so throughout the long summer of 1860.

The situation had been ambiguous from the start. On the day after landing in Marsala, Garibaldi began his march into the interior. On May 13 he halted at the hill town of Salemi; here, "upon the invitation of the noble citizens and upon the deliberations of the free communes of the island," he proclaimed himself dictator in "the name of Victor Emmanuel, king of Italy." It was a bold gesture, but it was also a confusing one; no such person as "Victor Emmanuel, king of Italy," existed. There did exist, of course, a King Victor Emmanuel, but he was only king of Piedmont. If it was this Victor Emmanuel that the proclamation was referring to, why had the king lacked the courtesy to inform the chancelleries of Europe that Piedmont was invading the Kingdom of the Two Sicilies?[1]

Providing Piedmont with the pretext for a territorial grab was the last thing on Garibaldi's mind when he set sail for Sicily. His goal was nothing less than a unified Italian state with its capital at Rome. By September 1860, Garibaldi and his volunteers had arrived in Naples. Here they were joined by Mazzini. The two men immediately began to talk of an imminent invasion of the Papal States. This was something that Cavour wished to avoid at all costs. Cavour was worried about a possible French, or even Austrian, reaction. Napoleon III was already sufficiently irked at Turin's annexation of Tuscany, the Romagna, and the central Italian duchies earlier that year. An attack on the papal territories—territories that France was supposedly protecting—might well provoke him into a military intervention, placing all of Piedmont's new acquisitions at risk.

Privately, Cavour was also worried that the democrats were growing too powerful. Were he to conquer Rome, Garibaldi would doubtless keep his promise and offer the crown of a united Italy to Victor Emmanuel. Yet accepting the crown from the hands of the revolution would be tantamount to a public humiliation for the king. If, however, the opposite were to happen and the Bourbons pushed Garibaldi back into the sea, the prospects were even more unpalatable. By launching the invasion in the name of "Italy and Victor Emmanuel," Garibaldi had dragged Piedmont into the struggle. If the Bourbons drove Garibaldi back into the sea, they would throw all of Cavour's own ambitions in with him.

Garibaldi's victories meant, as the Tuscan, Count Bettino Ricasoli, observed to Cavour, that the revolution was now making all the running. If Piedmontese hegemony was to be preserved, Cavour needed to assert his authority over the revolutionaries.

## Crispi

One of Garibaldi's first acts on becoming dictator in Sicily was to appoint Francesco Crispi his secretary of state for the interior, making him effectively the prime minister of Sicily. It was a role that Crispi had been grooming himself for since 1849.

Crispi was forty-one when he set sail with Garibaldi for Sicily. A thin, excitable man, he had put aside the stiff collar and frock coat of a jurist for the revolutionary expedition, wearing instead a simple black blouse secured at the waist with a wide belt. He also brought his wife along, the only woman among the Thousand; if we are to believe Giovanni Paolucci, he brought her along to wash his shirt.[2] He rarely carried a musket. This was not owing to cowardice, as his later detractors ungenerously charged, for Crispi was often in the thick of the action. He had brought from Genoa a portable writing desk, and while the others were busy fighting, he would sit with the writing desk on his knees, busily drafting orders and proclamations.[3]

We find him in this posture on the May 23, 1860, on the high, windy, rainy saddle of Renda, atop Monreale. He was pausing here to write a long letter of instructions to the newly appointed governor of the Palermo district, making sure to include with it a copy of the new laws for municipal governors as well as instructions on taxes and on the militia. Well able to imitate the imperious tones of high officialdom, Crispi added, "The dictator wishes that, as the country gradually emerges from the struggle against the Bourbons, it will be found to be in good order and free."[4] Brave words from a "prime minister" whose leader was, at that moment, running from Von Mechel's Bavarian battalions.

Yet the letter itself is also emblematic. Crispi's intent was to proceed as La Masa had done in 1848, associating the revolution with the ruling classes, inviting the leading notables to participate in the revolutionary government. In 1860, however, this was not so easy. In 1848 the ruling classes in Palermo still retained their hold over power. After 1849, however, Salvatore Maniscalco as chief of police had dismantled their power in Sicily and forced the revolution underground. Ruling-class participation in the 1860 struggle had been fitful: individuals had rallied to the revolution, but the upper classes as a whole had remained aloof.

Nor was there a younger generation ready to step in, for repression and the revolution had taken a dreadful toll. It had claimed the lives of the two natural leaders of the revolution, Francesco Bentivegna and Rosolino Pilo. It had also claimed the life of Pietro Piediscalzi, the brave leader of the Albanians, as it had claimed the lives of other *squadra* leaders. And it had claimed the lives of two of the de Benedetto brothers, who had died in each other's arms defending the cathedral on the last day of the battle for Palermo.

The revolution had, of course, thrown up some leaders of its own. Luigi La Porta had survived prison and participation in the Bentivegna uprising to become the acknowledged leader of the revolution in the Misilmeri area. He was to serve in the revolutionary government in 1860 and, later, had a distinguished career in the Italian parliament. Abele Damiani had organized the uprising in Marsala, though he fled to Malta when a flying column of Bourbon soldiers arrived to suppress the revolt. He returned shortly after Garibaldi's landing, however, in time to be one of the first to

charge through the Porta di Termini beside Nino Bixio. He was also destined to become one of Sicily's leading parliamentary deputies in the 1870s
and 1880s.

Yet men like La Porta and Damiani were too young, too inexperienced,
and too few in number to serve immediately as the basis of a new political
ruling class. Worse, they were all provincials; there was not a Palermitan
among them.

This is the final irony of Crispi's May 23 letter, for the man to whom
Crispi addressed it, the newly appointed governor of the Palermo district,
Paolo Migliore, was a nonentity. He had played a minor role in the 1848
revolt in Palermo. As revolutionary governor for the district of Palermo he
was destined to leave no trace. Crispi was hard-pressed to find enough
governors to go around.

The 1848 revolution had convinced Crispi that effective government
required a strong executive; yet he brought with him copies of the laws
passed by the Sicilian parliament in 1848–49, and continued to hold the
amended 1812 Sicilian constitution, with its guarantees of freedom of
the press and trial by jury, in high esteem. His ambition was to draw up a
new set of fundamental laws for Sicily, combining what was best in the
Bourbon and Piedmontese administrations with the 1812 Sicilian constitution. Crispi left for Sicily in 1860 with sheafs of proclamations under
his arm.

Once in office, he immediately set to work. Yet almost equally immediately, his plans were stymied. On June 7, Giuseppe La Farina arrived in
Palermo. He had been sent by Cavour to stir up trouble.

Cavour sent him in an unofficial capacity; he was there to build up the
National Society in Palermo, making it a party favorable to annexation by
Piedmont. For this he was provided with money enough to launch his own
newspaper and, perhaps, told to whisper in the ears of Sicilian notables
promises of honors and positions that might fall to those who endorsed the
right course of action. Whatever his exact instructions, his presence soon
poisoned the political atmosphere in Palermo, a fact from which he
seemed to derive considerable personal satisfaction. His letters back to
Cavour are filled with sarcastic references to the revolutionary government, described as "a chronicle of follies."[5] So divisive was La Farina's
presence in Palermo that Garibaldi was soon forced to intervene and take
the unusual step of expelling him from the island.

Yet La Farina was also astute; he had immediately perceived the weakness in the revolutionaries' position and had set about exploiting it. Inspired perhaps by Plutarch's account of Quintus Fabius Maximus,

Garibaldi had declared himself dictator.[6] His dictatorship, however, was intended as a military expedient, lasting only as long as the campaign lasted. Once the emergency was over, Garibaldi desired nothing better than to return to his island retreat of Caprera, for he had little liking for politicians and politics.

Although the idea of a dictatorship was Garibaldi's, it had been Crispi who had orchestrated "the invitation of the noble citizens" of Salemi, and Crispi who had drafted the proclamation of May 13 "in the name of Victor Emmanuel." But what did being dictator "in the name of Victor Emmanuel" mean? La Farina pointed out that if it meant that Garibaldi was commander of the expedition and military governor of the island only for the duration of the campaign, then it did not follow that Garibaldi's prime minister had any right to reform legal codes or make important appointments. These were all prerogatives of Victor Emmanuel and his duly appointed ministers.

The legal systems of Sicily and Piedmont had many differences. Educated Sicilians understood this, and though they knew that some sort of union with Piedmont was in the cards, they assumed that they would be allowed to keep much of Sicily's traditional customs, laws, and administrative structures, at least for a time. Leading Sicilian liberals such as Michele Amari and the marquis of Torrearsa favored convoking a constitutive assembly that would meet to iron such problems out. Even Cavour at first assumed that some sort of constituent assembly of Sicilian notables would need to be held to ratify Sicily's annexation and to work out a way to merge the two different systems.

Again it was La Farina who perceived the political dangers of such a delay. A constituent assembly would be an alternative center of power, a center that, while not hostile to Turin, would not be subservient to it either. Palermo might well turn to the friends of Garibaldi and Crispi for leadership. As soon as Cavour saw this possibility, his attitude hardened. There would be no discussions, no constituent assembly, as these would only further Crispi's projects. Sicilians, he proclaimed, had a duty to accept Piedmontese sovereignty as a condition of national unity.[7]

By the end of August, the constitution of Piedmont, the 1848 Albertine Statute, had been promulgated in Sicily. According to the first article of the statement prefacing the decree of promulgation, the extraordinary powers of the dictator existed only to consolidate the victory and end the revolution. The dictator lacked the power to modify or alter "the fundamental law of the Italian Monarchy"—the Albertine Statute—as this was the law that "informs the entire order of the new laws, their authority, and their jurisdictions, both those that are already in place as well as those that need to be enacted."[8] The revolutionary government was declared to be only administrative. Crispi's ambitions to create a new constitutional synthesis were definitively overthrown.

In October 1860, in a hastily organized plebiscite, Sicily voted overwhelmingly to become part of the kingdom of Piedmont. In Cavour's original design, the voters were to be asked whether or not they accepted annexation into Piedmont. Crispi fought a rear-guard action and succeeded in having the wording changed. The voters were asked instead whether they accepted the unity of Italy under the House of Savoy. This at least preserved Sicily's dignity: Piedmont was only the *primes inter pares* among the regions under the crown of Savoy, and Sicily was not required to acknowledge that it was subject to the government in Turin. It was merely a formal victory, however, one that Cavour could easily concede, and it is perhaps indicative of the legalistic cast of Crispi's mind that he set so much store by it.

### Aspromonte, the Murder of Corrao, and the Flight of Badia

The revolutionaries around Crispi in the summer of 1860 were no longer a band of brothers. Many were returned exiles. During the last-ditch defense of Palermo in 1849, Crispi and La Farina had been comrades in arms; in 1860, however, they were bitter personal enemies. This helps explain the sense of acrimony in the summer of 1860. The struggles of the revolutionary government were often those of disgruntled men who had passed their years in exile nursing their grievances in obscurity. Yet the acrimony was also a reflection of a political vacuum.

The nobles, professionals, and landowners who made up Sicily's ruling class were spread like a single drop of oil over an ocean of humanity, an ocean that remained largely unfathomed and uncharted.[9] Sicily's struggle for independence had initiated with the ruling classes; yet already in 1820 and 1837 the rest of the population had made it clear that it was not going to be denied its rights. In 1848 alliances had been forged between the revolutionary leadership and men of the lower classes, alliances that permitted the revolution to drive the Neapolitan army out of Sicily and helped keep the island from the brink of chaos in the months that followed. Little was known, however, about the hopes and wishes of such men. They revered Garibaldi, but would not take it kindly if the Piedmontese tried to brush aside the obscure men who had made the revolution.

In April 1862, Garibaldi returned to Turin to address the new Italian parliament over the treatment of his Red Shirts and to denounce the government for its refusal to consider his proposal to form a volunteer army to liberate Rome and Venice—a proposal that was anathema to the king and the general staff. Wearing his own red shirt and his gray poncho, Garibaldi began his speech sonorously; the text had probably been prepared for him by the opposition leader, Urbano Ratazzi. Yet his eyesight was weakening, and even with his spectacles and a huge magnifying glass, it became difficult for him to make out his own notes. Finally, unable to contain himself, Garibaldi threw away his papers and launched into a passionate and almost incoherent denunciation of Cavour.[10]

In June, Garibaldi returned to Sicily. After a rapturous welcome in Palermo, he set off to tour his old battlefields, retracing his steps to Marsala. Believing him a living saint, the country people grew delirious in his presence. Everywhere he went he was accompanied by brass bands, cheering children, weeping women, and men struggling forward to kiss his hand (a gesture of obeisance that he had declared abolished two years earlier). In Marsala Cathedral the congregation began to chant his slogan "Roma o morte" (Rome or death) before the altar. Soon volunteers were flocking to him, and convinced by Mazzini's Party of Action that all Sicily was ready to rise at his call, he let himself be persuaded to lead a new attempt to liberate Rome.

By August, Garibaldi had entered Catania at the head of an army of three thousand volunteers. The government made no attempt to interfere, and indeed, it is likely that Garibaldi had received covert encouragement from both Victor Emmanuel and Prime Minister Ratazzi, who hoped that Garibaldi could be persuaded to use his volunteers against the Austrians in the Balkans. But when Garibaldi crossed the Strait of Messina and demonstrated that he was fully in earnest about leading his volunteers to Rome, the Turin government grew alarmed, especially when the French made it clear that it was up to Piedmont to stop Garibaldi or bear the consequences.

Garibaldi's first reaction on learning that several Piedmontese army battalions had been sent after him was to assume that it was all a sham, that the army would only pretend to chase him, but that it would finally let him escape and continue his march northward. This was a costly error. On August 28, Garibaldi and his volunteers drew up in a defensive position in the mountainous Aspromonte region in the toe of Italy, bottled up by the Piedmontese troops of Colonel Pallavicini. Garibaldi might easily have defended his position; in his April address to parliament, however,

*Garibaldi at Caprera, recovering from his wounds at Aspromonte. Courtesy Museo del Risorgimento, Rome.*

he had denounced the government for provoking a "fratricidal war" in the South, and now he did not wish to be the one to fire the first shot.

He stepped forward shouting "Don't shoot!" sending messengers to his son Menotti and Giovanni Corrao on the wings. He told the bugler to blow the "cease-fire." Suddenly he was seen to clutch his hat to his thigh and fall to the ground. He had received two wounds, a musket ball in his thigh and another under the bone of his left foot.[11]

Giovanni Corrao, in charge of the expedition's left wing, was one of the 1860 *squadra* leaders who had shown military talent. He had received a commission in the Piedmontese army, where he was quickly promoted to the rank of colonel. When Garibaldi's call came, however, he resigned his commission and returned to Palermo to recruit volunteers. The "Corrao Brigade" included the elite among its volunteers; it contained the three remaining De Benedetto brothers, the duke of Cesarò (who had led a *squadra* in Agrigento province in 1860), the prince of Niscemi, the marquis Maurigi, and Enrico Cairoli. These prominent young men were all members of Mazzini's Party of Action. Raffaele de Benedetto was so enraged at the wounding of Garibaldi at Aspromonte that he broke his sword rather than surrender it to a Piedmontese officer.[12]

For their participation in the expedition, Corrao and the other members of his brigade were arrested and sent to a military prison at La Spezia on the Tuscan coast. They were pardoned several months later, returning to Sicily to be welcomed as heroes. They were lucky; certain of their followers had been summarily executed.

After returning from prison, many of those who had marched with the Corrao Brigade forswore further revolutionary adventurers. The duke of Cesarò, the marquis Maurigi, and Enrico Cairoli were all later elected to parliament. Their decision was supported by the Crispian and Mazzinian press in Sicily as well, which argued that revolutionary adventures had now become a threat to the unity of the new state. Corrao, however, persisted. He was the son of a merchant sailor who had grown up in the Borgo, the port outside the old city's northern gate, and his sympathies and political opinions were closer to those of most of the revolutionaries and ex-*squadristi* than to those of his upper-class followers.

Returning to Palermo in late 1862, Corrao was accepted as unofficial leader of the revolutionary party. As second in command, first to Pilo and later to Garibaldi, Corrao could lay claim to a revolutionary descent pure enough to satisfy any of the Mazzinians. This allowed him to serve as the bridge between those who, whether out of unitarian idealism or because they saw no practical alternative, had accepted Piedmontese annexation, and the revolutionaries and ex-*squadristi* who had not. Still, the situation was becoming increasingly unstable. Corrao was rumored by the police to be in contact with *tristi* and ex-*squadristi*. By early 1863 he was living in semi-clandestinity, having narrowly escaped arrest. On the second of August, he was ambushed while returning in his carriage to Palermo and murdered. The circumstances of his death have always remained a mystery.[13]

Without Corrao's unifying presence, the solidarity of the Palermo democrats disintegrated. Leadership of the revolutionary wing passed to Corrao's own lieutenant, Giuseppe Badia. Badia was a popular figure who had fought in the 1848 and 1860 revolutions; he had taken part in the Aspromonte expedition and was also the leading figure in Palermo's Workingmen's Society (Società Operaio). Yet Badia could claim no direct link to Garibaldi.

Nor was Badia an intellectual or a member of Mazzini's Party of Action. Leadership of this group passed to Mazzini's chief disciple in Palermo, Francesco Perroni Paladini. Soon the Palermo Mazzinians began to suspect that Badia and his associates were cooking up schemes for a new insurrection. What was much worse, the aim of this insurrection was not the liberation of Rome but the independence of Sicily. In January 1865, Perroni Paladini delivered a speech in which he denounced the "reptiles who spread their *word* without daring to lift their heads." The "word" in question was Sicilian separatism; and by accusing Badia's group of harboring separatist intentions, Perroni Paladini was pronouncing anathema against them.

The following day, Perroni Paladini organized a public meeting at Palermo University in support of the government. Before the conference could get under way, however, it was broken up by a group of hecklers. Scuffles broke out, and the National Guard had to be called in. The friends of Perroni Paladini identified the thugs as Badia's followers from the Workingmen's Society. They issued a complaint, and soon Badia was wanted by the police on the serious charge of conspiring to change the government by force. Badia and his followers were pressed into hiding.

If Badia was not plotting an insurrection before January 1865, he certainly was plotting one afterwards. He spent the next six months in Palermo and the surrounding countryside. A reserved police memorandum speaks of Badia inciting his friends "to maintain their promise to assemble men and to ready the necessary supplies and munitions to start the revolution."[14] He issued a fiery proclamation from his hiding place. The plan was for an insurrection led by the *squadre* from the countryside and some of the men from his Workingmen's Society in the center of Palermo. There were rumors that the date of the insurrection was set for the summer of 1865.

With whom did Badia meet during the first six months of 1865? If we knew the answer to this we would probably know more about the uprising that took place the following year. In fact, using the police files, we can make some educated guesses. To understand these, however, we must look at what was happening in Palermo province from April 1860 onward.

## The Squadre

Around Palermo there was, as Rosario Romeo puts it, an "extensive underclass of men ready to rob and murder, hiding behind political motives."[15] In April 1860, liberal committees had augmented their *squadre* by opening the jails and offering liberty to any who would participate in the struggle against the common enemy. Local committees were sometimes happy simply to see these men leave. The town of Carini had already contributed one *squadra* in early April. When the town committee received a summons from Rosolino Pilo to assemble a new *squadra* to reinforce his position at the Monastery of San Martino delle Scale, the committee simply released the inmates from the town prison and from those of the surrounding towns, offering them a salary of six *tarí* a day. They later defended their action, saying it was best to send these men to fight in order to "leave the rest of the citizens in peace."[16]

It was not always easy to separate the revolutionaries from the *tristi*. The leader of the Revolutionary Committee for Ciminna was Luigi La Porta, who, in mid-April, was elected leader of the provisional government in Palermo province. Ciminna also contributed a second *squadra*, led by another young revolutionary named Santo Meli. At the beginning of May, this *squadra* fell on the town of Baucina, near Corleone. One observer reports:

> [The *squadra*] consisted of a bunch of montagnards with neither discipline nor morale that was apt to dissolve or reunite itself every time news of a new opportunity presented itself or a rumor spread that they had been betrayed. The town [Baucina] was in a state of perfect anarchy; no one was to be seen: all the doors were shut; the mob had joined the *squadra* and had assaulted the town hall, burning all the documents that they found there; the rest of the *squadra* roamed the town with nei-

ther order nor subordination, making a tremendous commotion. The *caposquadra*, who was called Santo Meli, attacked the Castellaccio [the town citadel] near to the Ficuzza and, entering it, arrested the jailkeeper and his two guards. He had these unfortunates brought into the town square and ordered them shot. But the confusion of people milling about was so great that they were only wounded while instead a number of bystanders were killed when the firing squad opened fire.[17]

Still, Meli answered La Masa's summons and presented himself at Gibilrossa on the nineteenth of May, expecting to lead his *squadra* into Palermo. The leaders of the Thousand took an extremely severe view of revolutionary freebooting; it was said that Garibaldi would order looters shot "without even taking the cigar out of his mouth." Meli was arrested and placed in custody. Shortly before the march on Palermo, he escaped. He returned the following month, calmly riding up to General Türr's headquarters at Villafrati, near Misilmeri, with six of his companions. Türr was lying ill in bed, conversing with Alexandre Dumas père, when Meli rode under his window. He was arrested, and Türr decided to court-martial him on the spot.

Surprisingly, Meli defended himself very ably. He had proudly flown the *tricolore* since the fifth of April, he said, remaining in the field when other *squadre* had disbanded and fled. He had extorted nothing, merely requisitioned arms, money, and supplies. He had murdered only spies, informers, and reactionaries, burned only the houses of noted Bourbon sympathizers. What is more, he had been in constant contact with the Revolutionary Committee in Palermo, which had approved all he had done. When the court-martial asked Meli to substantiate this last claim, he pulled out a sheaf of documents released by the revolutionary committees of various towns attesting to his good conduct and patriotism, and to the fact that he had indeed been acting under their authorization.

The court-martial judges were taken aback by these proofs that Meli had been operating hand in glove with the revolutionary committees. Their chagrin was increased when they discovered that the witnesses they found to testify to Meli's misdeeds had all developed cases of amnesia. No one could remember having seen or heard anything against him. Türr was forced to defer Meli's case for further investigation.[18]

Meanwhile, in the countryside, Aspromonte was a watershed in more than one sense. When Corrao and his followers returned to Sicily after their brief imprisonment, they discovered that the western part of the island was occupied by the Ninth division of the Piedmontese army. The government had used Aspromonte as an excuse to declare an emergency and dispatch the troops. They were to remain there for the next fifteen years. The pretext was that the army had been sent to round up draft dodgers, for Piedmont's law requiring military service had been extended to Sicily. The minster of the interior, Ubaldino Peruzzi, justified the inclusion of Sicily, arguing that the increase in draft dodging there had rendered the presence of the army necessary. He added, almost as an afterthought, that the army would be useful because the two extremist parties, the *rossi* and the *neri*, were encouraging Sicilians to avoid military service.[19]

The campaign soon provoked a storm of protest.[20] General Giuseppe Govone, chosen to command the troops in Sicily, was later charged with illegalities and brutality.[21] The charges were probably untrue, at least as far as Govone himself was concerned, for he was a scrupulous officer. He had served in the Naples region from mid-May 1861 to the end of September 1862; he then passed several months in Palermo before returning home around Christmas. In the spring of 1863, with the new emergency legislation in place, he returned once more to Sicily with a larger contingent of troops.

The government regarded the Govone expedition as an unmitigated success. His troops had flushed out an impressive number of draft dodgers. While they were at it, they managed to capture a large number of outlaws and common criminals. Some 1,300 *malfattori* were captured, he reported, "among whom were many having 5 to 10 homicides on their conscience, one who had 30, and one who even had 37!" Govone also captured sixty members of a band that was terrorizing Castellammare.[22] Best of all, there had been no riots, no pitched battles or shoot-outs, and almost no injuries—or so he claimed.

Govone wished to limit the use of violence as far as possible, preferring to awe the population into submission by a massive show of force. His usual method was to round up all able-bodied men and demand that they produce either evidence of service or an exemption. The result was that prospective draftees melted into the hills, leaving their lands untended. Where the young men had disappeared, Govone sent out patrols to comb the countryside and set up watches outside their homes. He sealed off the entire mountainous peninsula of Capo San Vito, near Castellammare, and patiently searched every square yard of it—a notable achievement in military logistics.

In a letter to Peruzzi on June 10, 1863, he described his *retata* (dragnet) in Misilmeri, "one of the worst towns in the district." The troops around Misilmeri had been repeatedly foiled in their attempts to catch draft dodgers. Govone sent in a spy to see if they were still in their homes. They were, and with the permission of the prefect, he sent in three battalions together with ten *carabinieri* sergeants to surround and seal off the town. The troops then searched a total of 1,150 houses, one by one. They came up with about 200 young men. Govone summoned the municipal council for information concerning these men:

> But the Council did not wish to give any information and tried to stall. It was then necessary to call the notaries and other officials; but they did not wish to help us any more than the Council did. We then had the priests summoned with their parish registers. We took the young men in front of the Council and asked them to state their names. . . . Then they passed in front of the notaries and officials who had to tell us their names. We cross-checked it all against the parish registers. Yet even this way we failed to achieve much of anything. The Council, the notaries, and officials remained mute; the registers were in total disorder. We had to release almost everyone on account of the impossibility of proving anything, or on account of documents that they produced. I saw that many of the documents were false, and therefore we refused to accept them. The result of this desperate work was the arrest of two or three draft dodgers and six or seven suspects, a result which, Your Excellency sees, is pretty meager.

At this point, Govone left the town, putting everything in the hands of a major with the orders to search the houses of the well-to-do every day, and to patrol the countryside continually, arresting any young men they found. The army and police were later accused of beating up prisoners and raping their wives. After two or three weeks of constant harassment, resistance began to cave in, and the draft dodgers started to present themselves.[23]

Govone was convinced that the presence of the army was justified and, indeed, was having a salutary effect. The true source of unrest, he wrote, was the rapaciousness and unscrupulousness of the newer, non-noble landowners—the *signorotti*, as he called them. They had risen through violence and murder. They had corrupted judges, bought witnesses, and suborned officials. They held the population in submission. It was their abuses that were driving the poor and powerless to commit what he called "social *vendette*."

This, of course, was the argument that Neapolitan reformers had been using from the late 1770s to the time of Maniscalco. There was certainly a great deal of truth in it. Yet Govone went on to conclude that by striking at

these culprits directly, without worrying about legal formalities, disregard-
ing the corrupt magistrates, officials, and political bosses who protected
them, the army was earning the gratitude of ordinary Sicilians.[24] That was
a different matter.

In 1812 the Sicilian nobility had been careful to include trial by jury
among the civil rights they wrote into their new constitution. These rights
were strengthened when the constitution was recast in 1849 and confirmed by Crispi in 1860. This, and the fact that Sicily had risen up in
three bloody and costly rebellions, ought to have been enough to convince
anyone that the Sicilians were not, in fact, grateful to see these rights tram-
pled upon by a military commander, however well intentioned. Govone's
campaign undoubtedly earned him the gratitude of a few Sicilians; yet it
earned him the enmity of a great many more.

Three years later the town of Misilmeri rose up, killing twenty-seven
police officers and *carabinieri*—virtually every public security official in the
town. In 1868, fifty-six individuals were tried in Palermo for participating
in the massacre. The state represented the riots as *fatti criminosi*, criminal
acts. The attorney for the defense replied that the majority of the rioters
were the poor, the illiterate, and the disenfranchised, whose only means of
expressing their political convictions was to take to the streets. Much to
the outrage and scandal of the government, the Palermo jury agreed with
the defense. Of the fifty-six men accused, only nineteen were found guilty
of crimes of violence; twenty were freed on the grounds that their participation was merely an *attentato politico*, or political action, while seventeen
were fully acquitted.[25]

## The Nicolosi Family of Lercara Friddi and Don Peppino il Lombardo

Govone's diagnosis may often have been exact. The *signorotti* who urged
their followers to sack public buildings and gut the palazzi of pro-Bourbon
families were rarely acting from purely disinterested motives. Yet it was a
diagnosis that failed to perceive the effects of his own presence. He was
candid enough to admit that his campaign was widely unpopular. What is
more, it was uniting political troublemakers against the government.
These were troublemakers, moreover, who had considerable practical experience in conspiracies and in organized violence. By 1865, they were
conspiring once again.

One of the largest of the Sicilian *squadre* taking part in the liberation of
Palermo were the 412 *picciotti* from Lercara Friddi, a town deep in the in-

terior of Palermo province. So large was the Lercara contingent that La Masa offered their leader, the priest Agostino Rotolo, a place in the vanguard. Rotolo good-naturedly refused the offer, stating that his age, corpulence, and total unfamiliarity with firearms disqualified him from such an honor.[26]

In the town of Lercara itself, the local Revolutionary Committee was dominated by the Nicolosi family. Before 1860 the family had been noted for their pro-Bourbon sympathies, and, during the 1848 revolution, a mob had gutted the family's palazzo. The father, Nicolò, served the Bourbons as magistrate and *sottointendente* of Cefalù. He was part of Maniscalco's network of local confidants, and had, in fact, led the party that arrested Francesco Bentivegna. Nicolò died shortly before the 1860 revolt, however, just in time for his sons to switch sides.

Since the 1840s, the Nicolosi family had been struggling against their rivals, the Sartorio family, who, as the richest and most powerful family in the town, monopolized many of the offices and government sinecures. It may have been the prospect of outflanking their rivals that drove the young Nicolosi brothers into the arms of the revolution. The leader of the Revolutionary Committee in Lercara was the eldest of the Nicolosi sons, Giovanni, later mayor of the town. He was assisted by his brother Francesco, who also became mayor of Lercara, *consigliere provinciale*, and parliamentary candidate, and by the third brother, Luigi, who was the town treasurer throughout the 1860s and 1870s. The fourth brother, Vincenzo, was the administrator of the large Nicolosi estate, including sulfur mines, as well as the administrator of the vast estates of the Prince of Palagonia. Their cousin, Calcedonio, was an important investigating magistrate in Palermo.[27]

Giovanni and Francesco took charge of raising the money to form the *squadra* to march to Palermo in 1860. Before leaving, however, they organized their own revolution back home. The revolution was aimed less at the symbols of Bourbon power than at the Sartorio family, who had personified these symbols for the previous two decades. Their properties were devastated, and they were deprived of their offices and honors. Only then did the Nicolosi brothers dispatch Father Rotolo to lead the *squadra* to Palermo. The brothers remained behind, Giovanni becoming the captain of the National Guard and Francesco becoming acting mayor.[28] A police report from the beginning of 1861 describes this coup:

Emboldened like a band of crime-hardened running dogs, [the Nicolosi brothers] have managed to grab for themselves, and for their cronies, all the administrative jobs in the town. Last January, Don Francesco Nicolosi and his armed following terrified the voters into electing him town councilor. To keep Lercara in tumult, he and his friends told the taxpayers not to pay the government anything. He has prohibited the civic council to meet. . . . Decent citizens refuse to take part in the National Guard so long as Giovanni Nicolosi remains its captain, and [his brother-in-law] Don Antonino Orlando (so honored by the Bourbons for his services in 1848) remains its inspector.[29]

The police report is clearly partisan—which does not make it untrue. True or not, the Nicolosi family remained within the conspiratorial network of the revolutionary groups long after 1860. This solidarity gave them the political protection of other revolutionary groups plus that of some politicians and magistrates.

In 1865, several months before the date set for the outbreak of Badia's rebellion, we also find the Nicolosi brothers trying to enlist the services of the brigand Angelo Pugliese. Pugliese was born in 1832 in Lungro, a small Calabrian town near Cosenza.[30] His parents were shepherds. Accused in the early 1850s of writing *lettere di scrocco* (extortion letters), he fled his hometown and joined the brigand band of the Bellucci brothers. Soon he was captured, and in 1856 he was condemned to the prison colony on the island of Santo Stefano—the same prison, in fact, that Carlo Pisacane and Rosolino Pilo were planning to assault the following year.

Here the Bourbon government had placed both brigands and political prisoners; thus Pugliese found himself in the company of leading Neapolitan liberal intellectuals, men such as Silvio Spaventa, Luigi Settembrini, and Gennarino Placa. Placa, in particular, discovering in Pugliese "a mind not entirely vulgar, a heart not entirely corrupt" (as Pugliese later wrote), undertook his instruction.

Pugliese was transferred to the arsenal in Palermo, and from there he escaped in December 1861. Arriving at Uditore in the northern suburbs of Palermo, he assumed the identity of Giuseppe del Santo, a Garibaldino from Bergamo.[31] He worked here for a year as an elementary school teacher. Here he was befriended by Antonino Giammona, leader of one of the 1860 *squadre* and future *capo* of the Uditore mafia, and the councilor Giuseppe Palazzolo, later to become a member of the Republican Insurrectionary Committee of September 1866.[32]

On the recommendation of Palazzolo, Pugliese/del Santo found his next job as an overseer in the region of Alia in the interior of Palermo province. He worked on the lands of the Matteo Guccione, Matteo's son Benedetto, and his son-in-law Santi Lo Cicero. The Guccione–Lo Cicero families formed an extensive network of *gabelloti* (tenants) and professionals. By the early 1860s they had emerged as one of the richest and most powerful groups in the province.[33] They controlled thousands of hectares in west-central Sicily as well as monopolizing the municipal offices in the town of Alia. This combination was useful in another of their activities—horse and cattle theft.[34]

In nineteenth-century Sicily, livestock theft was an organized crime, a sort of preindustrial version of a hot car ring.[35] By the 1830s, the cattle theft industry had become organized at the interprovincial level.[36] The "industry" employed a network of accomplices that extended from the western part of Palermo province, through Caltanissetta province, and into Agrigento province. This was also the sulfur mining area. It was a zone that, by the 1870s, had become a virtual "brigand corridor" across western Sicily. One center of operations was Lercara Friddi. Thieves here ran a profitable business stealing horses and mules and reselling them to mining companies. In the 1860s, the stolen livestock ring around Lercara was led by Giuseppe Anzalone and Antonino Petta, two young men from landowning families; the Anzalone family owned an important mine as

*Nineteenth-century brigands counting their loot.*

well.[37] Their association worked in collaboration with the Guccione–Lo Cicero families in Alia.

Pugliese remained with the Guccione–Lo Cicero families throughout the summer of 1863. He was certainly involved in cattle theft, for, when Petta was arrested toward the end of 1863, Pugliese was chosen as the band's new leader.[38]

Pugliese inherited a band made up largely of fugitives and *campieri* (estate guards). He enlarged it, bringing in, among others, a police official from Alia.[39] He reorganized it as well, providing arms and extending its range of operations. His literacy and his cultured and gentlemanly bearing were valuable assets, for they allowed his band to dispense with the mediation of local notables in the disposal of stolen goods. Pugliese was able to build his own personal network of friends and contacts which ran from Palermo to the south coast, and westward to the town of Partinico. This made the Pugliese band more autonomous, less dependent on the protection of large landowners, and therefore less amenable to their control—a fact that the Guccione–Lo Cicero clan seems to have noted with alarm.

Pugliese later called his band a *masnada*—a literary term for armed brigands. It was divided between the fugitives, draft dodgers, and ex-*campieri* who made up the main body of active and permanent members, and their *fiancheggiatori* ("flankers," i.e., accomplices). Among these last were landowners who offered the band hospitality and protection in exchange for being left alone. Also included, however, were landowners previously involved in the stolen livestock ring, and, in all likelihood, in kidnapping and extortion as well.

Except for the original Guccione–Lo Cicero component, the band came mainly from the town of Mezzoiuso. Its nucleus were the ex-*campieri* of Giuseppe Valenza and the D'Angelo brothers, rich landowners and violent "men of honor" from Prizzi, who knew Pugliese through their mutual participation in the stolen livestock ring of Anzalone and Petta.[40]

In January 1865, Valenza and the D'Angelo brothers led the Pugliese band in an assault on the house of the Alessi family in San Giovanni Cammarata. About thirty men, including a local priest, took part. The Alessi family had recently given their property in *gabella* (short-term rental contract) to the Guccione family. The Prizzi landowners had wanted the *gabella* for themselves. The band sacked the house, while Valenza and the D'Angelo brothers tortured the elderly Alessi brothers. The assault yielded the band a rich haul, which was divided between Pugliese and D'Angelo.[41]

Just before Easter 1865, the Pugliese band was invited to a party at Gerbina, the so-called "giardino Nicolosi," complete with prostitutes.

Their host was a *campiere* named Antonino Miceli. Pugliese later wrote in his deposition that he reprimanded Miceli over this, telling him that he had no business wasting his time and his goods over "quella canaglia" (that riffraff). He might, Pugliese warned him, even end up in prison. Miceli reassured Pugliese. Signore Giovanni Nicolosi, he said, "had told them [the *campieri*] to go to the ex-*feudi* [estates] Santo Luca e Riena and get bread, wine, and barley every time the lads [*picciotti*] showed up in Gerbina."[42]

Why was the Nicolosi family offering hospitality to Pugliese and his brigands? It has been suggested that, as land and mine owners and as political bosses of Lercara, the Nicolosi wanted to form some sort of criminal partnership with Pugliese. This would be logical; Lercara was the center of livestock theft, and the Nicolosi were the bosses of Lercara. Yet there are two considerations against it. First, there is no indication in the police reports and the actual trial documents that the Nicolosi family were directly involved in this sort of crime. Second, it is notable that, after accepting the hospitality of the Nicolosi family, Pugliese seems to have abandoned his career as a brigand and cattle thief.

There is another, more intriguing possibility: Giovanni Nicolosi may have seen Pugliese as the potential leader of a *squadra* he was recruiting. It was a *squadra* that was to be used in a new uprising scheduled to take place that summer. Giovanni Nicolosi had in fact already recruited a *squadra* for the Aspromonte expedition in 1862. Padre Rotolo had even resigned from the municipal government to lead it. The family pulled out in time, however, and when the expedition ended in debacle, Giovanni managed to make peace with the government, making a show of severing his revolutionary links. The break may have been less than complete, however, for the Nicolosi were rumored to be still in contact with republicans and ex-*squadristi*. There was even a rumor that they had accepted money or arms from the Bourbon committees. Pugliese confirmed this interpretation himself when he commented in his deposition that he had received an invitation to march on Palermo in the spring of 1865, but, though tempted by the prospect of loot, he claimed that he had no desire to take part in an operation led by "*neri* and reactionaries."[43]

The date, of course, coincides with that of the revolution which Badia and his friends were plotting. The information about the Nicolosi and Pugliese helps answer the question of whom Badia was conspiring with in the early summer of 1865. It is probable that the Nicolosi had been one of the families asked to participate in Badia's insurrection, and that they planned to send a *squadra* led by Pugliese. The conspiratorial network thus included not only Badia's Workingmen's Societies, but also revolutionary republican groups, some of them from as far away as Lercara Friddi.

All this planning came to naught, however. On July 21, 1865, Badia's second in command, Carlo Trasselli, invited Badia to a secret meeting at the house of Gaetano Amoroso on the outskirts of Palermo. When Badia arrived, he found the police waiting for him.

## New Conspiracies

Pugliese referred to the "*neri* and reactionaries" as supporters of the insurrection. The Sartorio family suggested that the Nicolosi brothers were in contact with reactionaries. Perroni Paladini's group accused Badia of forging links with clericals, reactionaries, and Bourbons. These accusations are less bizarre than they might seem. The bond between Mazzini and the revolution in Sicily had never been very deep: the goal of Mazzini's Party of Action was a popular revolution that would unify Italy; the goal of the revolutionaries in Sicily was to throw the Neapolitans off of their island. If expelling the Bourbons required the help of Piedmont, then the revolutionaries had to obtain that help. If the price for this help was union under the House of Savoy, then this was the price that the revolution had to pay. Two years later, however, many concluded that the price had been too high.

The break with the Mazzinians allowed other conflicts to surface as well. Unlike the majority of Sicilians, the Mazzinians supported the draft. There were those who agreed with Nino Bixio that since the North had sent its sons to liberate Sicily, Sicily had a debt to the nation to send its sons to free Rome and Venice. Although the followers of Crispi and the Party of Action in Palermo supported the draft, the rural population opposed it totally—their opinion being expressed in the Sicilian proverb "better a pig than a soldier."

Another problem was that of the monasteries and the religious estates. Anticlericalism had never been part of Sicily's revolutionary tradition. The Sicilian clergy had supported the revolution. In 1848 this support was nearly universal. Even in 1860, only the higher clergy, whose appointments had been carefully scrutinized by both the Vatican and the Neapolitan government, remained loyal to Naples; the lower clergy and monks rallied to the cause of Sicilian independence.[44]

There was, by contrast, a strong streak of anticlericalism on the Continent; the followers of Garibaldi would never forget the defense of the Roman Republic in 1849. One of the last proposals presented before Crispi's revolutionary government in 1860 was that of expropriating the monastic estates. The new government accepted this idea and, in 1865, decided to break up the estates and sell them at auction. The Mazzinians were enthusiastic, especially over the closure of the monastic schools, which they regarded as sources of monkish influence. So delighted were they at this blow to clerical dominance over the masses that, replying to those who argued that the expropriated lands should be given away to the poor rather than sold at auction, the pro-Crispian journal *Il Percursore* argued that the "moral effect" of this blow to the roots of reaction outweighed such "materialist" considerations.[45]

This again was not the opinion of the majority of Sicilians, who remained attached to their church. The monasteries and convents of Palermo were a source of employment and of charity to the poor. According to Giacomo Pagano, "The 19 nunneries in Palermo spent 327,000 lire per annum to keep alive 919 families."[46] The idea that these convents were to be expropriated and no form of compensation would be offered to the monks and nuns, the employees, or the poor who depended on their charity infuriated the Palermo populace.

Much of the rumor and speculation over the background to 1866 revolved around the possible connection between Badia and the 1848 *squadra* leader from Monreale, Turi Miceli. Honored by the Sicilian government in 1848–49, Miceli had accompanied Baron Riso to Bagheria to meet with the Neapolitan general Filangieri to negotiate the peaceful surrender of the capital. The restored Bourbon government rewarded Miceli, nominating him chief government tax collector in Lercara Friddi. His duties in Lercara must have put him into contact with the Nicolosi family, though we have no information about this. His part in the surrender of Palermo and his nomination as a Bourbon official may have earned him the opprobrium of the radicals, for there is no record of his participating either in the conspiracies or in the 1860 revolt.[47]

Miceli, however, enjoyed important connections. Although his job was in Lercara, he seems to have spent most of the 1850s in his native Monreale. He had lands and family here, and apparently became an important local notable, perhaps even, as Paolo Alatri suggests, the local mafia boss. He was well connected, with friends from the 1848–49 revolutionary government as well as contacts among Neapolitan officials. Thus it is not surprising that, after 1860, the Bourbon court in exile in Rome tried to get in touch with him.

The exiled government had created a secret insurrectionary committee in Malta whose purpose was to feed money and arms into Sicily. The head of the Bourbon committee in Rome, the same Pietro Calà Ulloa who had reported on the secret societies in the 1830s, was also in contact with Maniscalco, now living in exile in Marseilles.[48] Maniscalco knew Miceli. He had been in close contact with Nicolò Nicolosi until 1860, and even though the sons had abandoned the Bourbon party on the death of their father, were an appropriate opportunity to arise, Maniscalco would have had no difficulty in passing them a private message. The principal Bourbon agent in the Palermo region was the lawyer Gioacchino Grasso, who was Turi Miceli's cousin. It seems probable that it was Grasso who offered Bourbon arms and money to Miceli, Badia, and other revolutionary leaders.[49]

It is impossible to believe that either Badia or Miceli ever desired a Bourbon restoration. What is more, it is highly unlikely that either Ulloa or Maniscalco ever thought that they did. It is more likely that the Bourbon court in exile noted that these men were stirring up trouble and decided to take the opportunity to give them a little help.

Another of Miceli's contacts was the head of the Bourbon insurrectionary committee in Monreale itself. This was Padre Placido Spadaro, who was, curiously enough, also the chief confidant of the Palermo chief of police, Felice Pinna. Pinna seems to have known of his friend's Bourbon connections; if he was unconcerned about them, it was because he did not take the Bourbon threat very seriously. Pinna was much more interested in capturing Badia and his associates. He probably reasoned that, if they wanted to stir up trouble, the Bourbons would try to channel arms and money to the revolutionaries. If this were true, the best way of capturing the revolutionaries would be to shadow their Bourbon benefactors. Thus Padre Spadaro might show him how to get his hands on Badia.

It is also possible that Pinna tried to get some information from Miceli himself. Miceli was arrested about the same time as Badia, yet he was not charged with anything and was soon released. It seems that the police simply pulled him in for a chat about his circle of friends, and before releasing him, they may have had extracted some sort of promise to keep them informed.[50]

If we have little documentary evidence about the network of conspiracies preceding the 1866 uprising, or about the counterintelligence measures that the police used against them, it is not because this documentation never existed. It is rather because Pinna personally destroyed all the confidential reports in his keeping shortly after the uprising—a fact that is in itself suggestive, to say the least. The only contacts that we can actually demonstrate are those between Padre Spadaro and Pinna, for though the documents themselves are missing, many are still catalogued in the police registers as reports on private conversations between the two men.[51]

The arrest of Badia had decapitated the revolutionary party and forestalled any insurrection planned for 1865. Revolutionary leadership passed from Badia to another of his lieutenants, Lorenzo Minecci. By now, however, the revolutionaries had become shadowy figures, men we know only from police lists. Francisco Brancato comments of Badia's committee that they "were all obscure men, some of them on the run from the law."[52] By the late 1870s, however, as we shall see, some of these obscure men had achieved a considerable notoriety for themselves as leaders of the mafia.

It is perhaps significant that Pinna's Bourbon connections contributed nothing to Badia's arrest. The Bourbon conspirators may well have preferred him on the loose, making trouble for the Piedmontese, rather than in their custody. Badia was trapped by one of Garibaldi's original Red Shirts, Giacomo Medici, serving as military commandant for Palermo province. It was Medici who persuaded two wavering revolutionaries, Enrico Albanese and Carlo Trasselli, to join the government side and turn Badia over to the authorities.

With Badia taken care of, Medici now turned his attention to Angelo Pugliese. But Pugliese was already gone. There had been a series of murders within the band, and Pugliese had disappeared about a month before Badia was captured.[53] Medici wanted to know where Pugliese had gone, and to find out, he began to put pressure on the Nicolosi brothers.

In fact, Pugliese had gone all the way to Sousse in Tunisia, where he set himself up as a grain merchant under the name of Gabriele Micato. Once again he passed himself off as a persecuted revolutionary. He claimed to have taken part in Agesilao Milano's attempt to assassinate Ferdinand II in 1856. He also claimed to have been part of Carlo Pisacane's expedition the following year. This, at least, was a half-truth, for, had Pisacane landed at Santo Stefano as originally planned, he might have freed Pugliese. From Sousse he sent letters to the administrators of the larger estates in Agrigento province, who had evidently been his associates in his cattle rustling days, as well as to his Masonic colleagues.

Giacomo Medici had fought by Garibaldi's side in the South American pampas. Here he must have learned something of the combination of politics, brigandage, cattle rustling, and struggles between landowning families typical of that region. He now offered the Nicolosi an ultimatum: either cooperate with the government or suffer the consequences. The brothers decided to cooperate. They first turned over the members of the band from Lercara; next they revealed Pugliese's hiding place in Sousse. Most of the gang members from Mezzouiso and Prizzi were captured, though the Guccione–Lo Cicero nucleus escaped. Some of them emigrated to America; others, together with some returned emigrants, remained to become the nuclei of the bands that operated in western Sicily in the late 1860s and 1870s. Medici showed his gratitude by recommending the Nicolosi brothers for gold medals and official citations.

## The 1866 Uprising in Palermo

The arrest of Badia and Pugliese did nothing to calm the province. On the contrary, during 1865, public security in Palermo province was deteriorating rapidly. By the summer of 1866, wrote an English resident in Palermo:

> The power of the local administration to protect life and property in the province of Palermo, at least beyond the walls and immediate suburbs, seemed almost entirely to have ceased; and this powerlessness was most notable within ten or twelve miles from the city. Gang-robberies in houses and on the highways, murder of police officers and other official, *sequestrations* . . . , attacks upon the mails and other public conveyances . . . were a daily occurrence.[54]

He added that even the road to Monreale had become unsafe, and that travelers were forced to organize themselves in armed convoys. A significant observation this: the Monreale road was one of the routes by which *squadre* had entered the city in 1820 and 1848. The fact that this road had become insecure was an ominous sign for the capital. In fact, it was on the night of Saturday, September 15, 1866, that *squadre* entered the city, arriving by the Porta Nuova, the Monreale gate.

Like that of 1848, the revolt of 1866 was announced in advance. Handbills mysteriously appeared on September 8. On September 12 the head of the National Guard, General Gabriel Camozzi, warned the prefect, Carlo Torelli, and the chief of police, Felice Pinna. They were totally incredulous. Still rumors of an impending uprising were rife. Already in the summer of 1865 there had been panic buying as Palermo housewives tried to lay in a stock of bread and macaroni.[55] The same thing began to happen in September 1866: "A friend of ours," wrote the English resident in Palermo, "about a week before the disaster, was consulted by a family as to what had been told them by a countryman who supplied them with garden-stuff. 'Now ladies,' he had said, 'lay in your supplies for a week at least, for they are going to have four days of republic, and then Francesco [Francesco II of Naples] will be back.' "[56]

Pinna was specifically informed that *squadre* were assembling in Monreale. An officer of the *carabinieri* was, in fact, murdered in Monreale several days before the uprising. Yet either Pinna was misled by Padre Spadaro or, as some of the witnesses darkly hinted, the formation of *squadre* in Monreale was part of a carefully orchestrated police provocation that misfired.[57] Whatever the case, Pinna, dismissed these and the warnings of General Camozzi as "rubbish" (*balle*), and refused to take any action.[58]

According to the statements later made by members of the Monreale municipal council, by the summer of 1866 the town had been in the hands of the "Mafia" for months. During the night of September 15, a red banner bearing the word "Repubblica" was unfurled over the Chiesa delle Croci. Men began to don the red berets or red scarves that identified them as partisans, members of the Monreale *squadra*. Soon a band of thirty or more had assembled and started clamoring to be on their way, down the hill to the capital. Their progress was, at first, very slow. They paraded through the town, stopping to acknowledge the cheers of their wives and children. After this, the procession slowly wound its way through the hamlets on the Monreale road, picking up recruits as it went along.

The atmosphere was more that of a *festa* than a military operation. The marchers stopped at the innumerable taverns and drink shops along the way; many became too drunk to continue. As the remainder neared the city gate, they began to fire their muskets in the air. By now they numbered several hundred. The guards at the Porta Nuova, terrorized by the approach of an armed throng whose arrival had long been predicted, fled without resistance. Thus, when the marchers entered Palermo shortly before dawn on the sixteenth, they were unopposed.[59]

The city was expecting them. Although one witness mentions forty men who had entered the city earlier and remained hidden in houses,[60] it was the arrival of a drunken and rowdy band of Monrealesi that seems to have provided the spark that touched off the rebellion. Some sort of plot certainly existed; for soon after the Monrealesi had entered from the west, they were joined by Palermitan *squadre* arriving from the Carini gate in the Borgo district near the Convent of San Francesco di Paolo. With these additions, the number of *squadristi* was about four hundred. At the news of the arrival of the Monrealesi, the various workingmen's associations brought out their arms as well. They were joined by the *bassa gente*, or lower classes, who now swarmed into the street. According to the English resident: "The bands as they entered carried red flags, some of which bore *Viva la Repubblica*, and some in addition, it is said, a figure of Santa Rosalia, the local *diva* of Palermo. Some of the men wore red scarves and red night-caps, and they scatted copies of a proclamation on red paper, containing vague and bombastical denunciations of the monarchy."[61] The red flags, red bonnets, and red sashes were all recognizable republican symbols. So too, of course, were the "bombastical denunciations" written on red paper. These, it turned out, were the work of a certain Francesco Bonafede.[62]

Bonafede was a genuine republican conspirator. His first arrest dated from 1847, when he was accused of conspiring against the Bourbon gov-ernment of Naples. The 1848–49 uprising in Sicily turned him into a fer-vent follower of Mazzini. In 1856 he took a leading part in the abortive Bentivegna uprising. With its failure, Bonafede went into hiding. The po-lice responded by putting his entire family in prison, and this forced Bonafede to give himself up. He was sentenced to be executed, though his sentence was later commuted to eighteen years in irons in the prison colony on the island of Favignana. Following the landing of Garibaldi in 1860, he was set free; yet he was too reduced by his ordeal to take an active part in the 1860 uprising.[63]

Bonafede's role in the 1866 rebellion resembles that of Francesco Bag-nasco, the *carbonaro* plotter who had taken it upon himself to announce the date of the 1848 revolution in the name of the "Directive Committee." Al-though the 1848 "Directive Committee" was a fiction, it turned out to be a highly efficacious one. In 1866, however, this ruse did not work quite so well. Although it did help the revolt get under way, no one stepped for-ward to take the lead afterwards. In reality, there was no one left who could credibly have stepped forward. There was no La Masa or Pilo in 1866.

Nor was there anyone to play the role of Ruggiero Settimo or the mar-quis of Spedalotto. The Palermo aristocracy expressed its opposition to Piedmont's treatment of their island by forming a Sicilian "autonomist" party, which had won a landslide victory in the 1865 parliamentary elec-tions. Although there were rumors of contacts between Badia and leading Palermo nobles, it is unlikely that these nobles gave the revolt any real support. When they were called to testify before the 1867 inquiry into the causes of the uprising, they used the opportunity to condemn government policy in no uncertain terms; yet they had no sympathy for the republican revolutionaries and their red-capped and red-scarfed followers.[64]

This left only Bonafede himself. By 1866, the irascible Bonafede had quarreled and fallen out with nearly everyone in Palermo's conspiratorial world. Nevertheless, he certainly aspired to leadership of the revolution. On the third day of the uprising, after the insurgents had taken and sacked the Palermo *municipio*, Bonafede moved in, ensconcing himself in the main office. From here he issued orders in the name of the revolution and declared Palermo a republic. It was a quixotic form of leadership, however, for he had no following, and his pronouncements were ignored even by his fellow revolutionaries.[65]

In fact, the 1866 uprising had no leader. According to the English resident, the rebels were "the ordinary *bassa gente* of the city" together with a mixture of those "of better appearance."[66] Other accounts are more specific. In a letter to his brothers written from Palermo during the uprising, the baron Michele Pasciuta, from Ribera in Agrigento province, mentioned seeing "coachmen, builders, butchers, tailors, and municipal employees" running through the streets with rifles in their hands.[67] Giovanni Raffaele presented a similar list, adding to it porters, carters, and other trades working in the open markets.[68]

With no leader, the revolution had neither a goal nor a strategy. The English resident also commented that in the uprising were all those who thought that "Revolution [was] a lark that every good fellow was bound to take part in." There is probably a certain truth in this. Rebellion generated its own momentum. As soon as the common people convinced themselves that a rebellion was indeed taking place, they joined in with a will, using their experience of past revolutions. They set up barricades, for barricades were the symbol of Palermo in revolt. Yet having set the barricades up, they failed to man them or even post sentries. Sightseers wandered through them freely. They risked being hit by a stray bullet, "but [were] otherwise exposed to neither harm nor insult."[69]

An obscure priest from Monreale, who happened to be questioned by the parliamentary committee, summed this all up the situation. The insurrection, he said, had been a popular one; he then went on to explain that the uprising had been caused by the conviction that there was a revolution, and there ought to be a revolution.[70]

The revolution thus spread because there was nothing to stop it. The *squadristi* from the countryside and the republicans from Palermo's workingmen's clubs probably numbered no more than a thousand. Yet witnesses put the number of rioters at between fifteen and twenty thousand.[71] For the first two days these rebels were almost unopposed. The government forces remained besieged inside their strongholds, leaving the insurgents free to do as they wished. They wandered about the city looking for government offices. Whenever they found one, they sacked it and burned all its records.[72] They attacked police stations and even the fire station. They sacked the military hospital and marched the 130 cadets from the Istituto Militare Garibaldi to the Convent of the Santo Spirito as prisoners. They later took the *municipio* next door and destroyed all the documents they could find. This was the high-water mark of the revolutionary tide.

The rebels failed, however, to mount an attack on the Palazzo Reale, the office of the prefect and the nerve center of the government. They neglected even to destroy the government telegraph office.

The mob materialized so quickly that, in the first two days, the mayor, the young Marchese di Rudinì, found himself trapped in the *municipio*. He remained besieged until the prefect, Carlo Torelli, arrived from the Palazzo Reale with half a company of soldiers. The city was in a panic, so Rudinì and Torelli decided to make a tour of the city with their small band of troops to inject courage into the population and rally the National Guard. They succeeded in their first objective; along the via Toledo they were greeted with Italian flags and applause. They failed in their second; the National Guard preferred to remain closed in their homes.

There were four convents in the center of old Palermo, the Madonna degli Stigmati, San Vito, San Giuliano, and Santo Spirito. These, according to the English resident, "formed a sort of rebel Quadrilateral."[73] When the little party of Rudinì and Torelli approached the Convent of the Stigmati, it came under rebel fire. The top floor of the nunnery was crowned with a projecting latticed balcony to protect the modesty of the nuns. It was tailor-made for snipers. Their fire proved too much for the young soldiers; they fell back, and Rudinì and Torelli were forced to follow, making their retreat to the Palazzo Reale.

The sally of Rudinì and Torelli was one of the few acts of courage on the government side. Certainly they had been brave, yet Rudinì was forced to pay a high price for his opposition to the mob. On Monday afternoon, the mob gutted the Rudinì palazzo, located next to the *municipio*. The marquis's pregnant wife was forced to escape from a first-floor window. The English resident reported that the rioters sacked the palazzo because Rudinì had shown so much energy in prosecuting smugglers and petty criminals. Francesco Brancato gives a different, and probably more accurate, interpretation. The traditional role of the mayor of Palermo during a popular uprising, he notes, was to show solidarity with the populace and try to shield them from reprisals. Spedalotto had been a hero to the people of Palermo; Rudinì, by contrast, had opened fire on his own citizens. Even though Rudinì went on to become one of Sicily's most illustrious statesmen, the people of Palermo never forgave him for this insult.[74]

Although the intentions of the vast majority of the crowd were peaceful, Badia's followers were out to settle old scores. Perroni Paladini was one of them. Just three days after Badia's arrest, Perroni Paladini had been stabbed in the streets of Palermo. About forty days before the outbreak of the revolution itself, during a meeting of Badia's followers, called by Lorenzo Minecci, in a house on the outskirts of Palermo to prepare for the forthcoming uprising, the republicans also discussed a proposal to assassinate Perroni Paladini. During the September uprising, his house was gutted by the mob. Perroni Paladini was comparatively lucky. It was Badia's second in command, Carlo Trasselli, who had led his friend into a police trap in the early summer of 1865. Trasselli had been rewarded with a commission in the National Guard. He had little time to enjoy it. During the 1866 uprising, Trasselli was picked up by the *squadra* of Vincenzo Grimaldi and murdered.[75]

The rebel *squadre* were encamped around the Convent of San Francesco di Paolo, outside the old city walls in the northwest corner of the town. The encampment soon took on the aspect of a popular fair. Here the rebels remained, undisturbed. On Wednesday, September 19, about one thousand government troops landed and tried to force their way into the rebel enclave. Army howitzers shelled the area for about a half an hour. Then the government forces began their advance.

With the rebels under fire for the first time since the uprising had commenced, Turi Miceli reappeared and took command. We do not know when Miceli arrived in Palermo. Although members of his family may have been part of the Monreale *squadra*, Miceli himself was not among them. Still less do we know the reason why Miceli decided to join a revolt that had no attainable political goal. We do know, however, that when the old *squadra* leader arrived, he galvanized the rebellion. He regrouped the rebels and led them in a counterattack. The soldiers were completely taken by surprise, and soon were in full retreat. They fell back toward the port, near the prison, with the rebels in hot pursuit. At this point Miceli decided to assault the prison itself.[76]

Built in the 1830s and 1840s, Palermo's Ucciardone was a model prison, constructed according to the latest Benthamite criteria.[77] The prison block was surrounded by a high wall, mounted with bastions and parapets. It was located near government barracks. It was eminently defensible. That was lucky for the government, for it contained 2,500 inmates who would not have hesitated to fall on the city, just as the freed prisoners had fallen on the city in the 1848 uprising.

One of the inmates was Giuseppe Badia, and it is possible that Miceli

*An ex-voto from 1866 depicting a fight between the inmates and guards in Palermo's Ucciardone prison. Courtesy Pitre Museum, Palermo.*

considered him the *capo* of the rebellion. Miceli, however, was almost immediately mown down by automatic rifle fire from gun emplacements on the walls. His legs were smashed. His companions picked him up and carried him to the prison hospital located outside the prison compound, and therefore in rebel hands.

Vincenzo Mortillaro, the marquis of Villarena, was also in the hospital. He had been there since May, when he had been arrested by the magistrate Calcedonio Nicolosi, who accused him of being the leader of the Bourbon party in Palermo. Mortillaro later wrote that Miceli was a man of "great heart and tenacious resolve, whose mere appearance, musket at his shoulder, was enough to spread panic in town and country." Miceli, the marquis reports, "was carried into the hospital, and I saw him there, in the midst of unspeakable torments, surrounded by his desperate comrades, give up the ghost, without, even once uttering a cry of pain."[78] With the death of Miceli, the *squadre* ceased their attack. Effectively, this marked the end of the uprising.

The murder of Trasselli and the knifing of Perroni Paladini were a settling of accounts within the revolutionary party. For the majority of insurgents, their participation in the riot had a different meaning: they were angry with the government and sought to punish a state that was guilty in their eyes of both injustices and neglect. An urban riot was the common people's means of shaming the government and heaping public humiliation upon it.[79]

Pro-government writers of course interpreted the crowd's participation in a different light. They claimed that, for the mob, the revolution was no more than an excuse to rob and kill.[80] Yet this claim is contradicted by virtually all sources. The only private houses to be attacked were those of Rudinì and Perroni Paladini. Even the sackings, wrote the French consul, were limited to "très peu de chose."[81]

Appropriately, it was left to the French consul in Palermo to observe that the populace seemed to be acting in accordance with their own perceived revolutionary traditions. The crowd, he noted, had destroyed documents and government property. Beyond this, destruction had been minimal. None of the prisoners taken by the insurgents had been mistreated; the lives and property of foreigners in Palermo had been respected. He went on to comment that "this conduct is certainly not that of brigands but of true revolutionaries [*véritables révolutionaires*] whose very excesses arise from an idea and a political goal."[82] One wonders whether he remembered these generous words five years later, when it was Paris's turn to arise.

The analogy between their uprising and the Paris Commune of 1871 was something that Palermitans themselves noted. Writing in the late 1870s, Palermo's new chief of police was scandalized to discover that "The deplorable events of 1866 are for the masses here a comforting historical memory, which, with blustering rodomontade about the people's initiative, serves as a source of pride, almost as if that sorrowful event stood as a precursor for the Commune of Paris."[83]

It required a chain of improbable coincidences and unlikely alliances to permit a leaderless gang of Monrealesi to seize control of Palermo for a week, especially as the chief of police knew everything already. Yet improbable coincidences and unlikely alliances could result from years of conspiracy and police counterintelligence. Today, events such as Pisacane's expedition to Saprì or Bentivegna's uprising have a fustian quality about them that renders them almost comic. Yet the heroism was in earnest, and the outcomes were often tragic enough. Pisacane and Bentivegna were revolutionary saints, fallen martyrs in the pantheon of heroes, stretching out their hands to those who remained behind, beseeching them to carry on the struggle. This was the revolution as it saw itself and as it was seen by those in Palermo who tried to behave like "véritables révolutionaires" rather than common brigands. This was the tradition into which the mafia was now about to slip.

# 5

## Cosche and Mafiusi

The first official reference to the "so-called *Maffia* or delinquent association" appeared in a report of April 1865. We saw that its author, Count Gualterio, had then been puzzled by the new and mysterious term. Two years later, in May 1867, a parliamentary commission was convened to inquire into the causes of the 1866 uprising. By now, the novelty had vanished; everybody had heard of the mafia—though not everybody agreed what it was. Nevertheless, witness after witness, northerners and Sicilians alike, testified that 1866 was a mafia uprising.

The inquiry's star witness was the former mayor, now prefect of Palermo, the marquis di Rudinì. Rudinì started by fielding questions about public administration of Palermo; then he launched into what the inquiry had been waiting to hear—his thoughts on public security. Crime in the Palermo region, he began simply, was stronger than the law and stronger than the government. In order for the citizens of Palermo to live and work in safety they needed to ensure their own protection. This is why they turned to the mafia, and this, he said, is why "the *Mafia* is powerful, perhaps more powerful than is believed."[1]

Rudinì was under no illusions. The protection that the mafia was selling was largely a protection from itself. Such "protection" might seem hardly more than a polite term for extortion. Yet Rudinì understood that it was more complicated than that: "In order to defend one's life and property in the countryside it is necessary to seek out the patronage of criminals, and—he added significantly—to associate with them in a certain way."[2] It was not, in other words, simply a matter of paying the mafia to leave you alone; sometimes it was more a matter of playing ball with them, doing things their way, protecting the mafia in exchange for their protecting you. In this way one might pass from an innocent victim of mafia extortion to what Angelo Pugliese had called a *fiancheggiatore* or what the police called a *manutengolo* of the mafia.

Rudinì was both troubled and impressed by the strength of the ties of solidarity and mutual interest that bound the mafia to their victims/friends. These were the same ties of *omertà* that Pietro Calà Ulloa had described in the case of the "sects" or "brotherhoods" he wrote about in the 1830s. The mafia, said Rudinì, was a network of semiautonomous local groups, each under the direction of one or more *capi*, who kept in contact with the *capi* of neighboring groups. There was nothing, he continued, to stop the police from arresting these *capi*; their identities were all locally well known. It was impossible, however, to obtain any evidence against them.[3] This was confirmed by police official after police official. Whatever the crime may have been, and however certain the official may have been that a particular mafioso was behind it, the only witnesses that could be produced were those who provided the mafioso with alibis or testified to his good character.

But what had crime and extortion rings to do with a political uprising such as the one Palermo had just experienced? Later on, Sicilians who testified before the 1875 government inquiry into criminal violence or who wrote during the Notarbartolo scandal in the 1890s and early 1900s would develop the claim that the mafia had arisen out of Sicilian patriotism and hatred of Bourbon oppression. The mafiosi were nothing more than the *picciotti* who rallied to the revolution in 1848 and 1860. This claim was always an ingenuous alibi, for Sicilians knew that things had not gone precisely in this manner. The mafia reflected patterns of crime that had existed in Sicily long before the struggle against Naples had begun. Still, the claim had a certain plausibility, for an association between the revolution and the mafia really did exist.

It existed in the first place at the level of names, dates, and places. Turi Miceli was by all accounts the boss of Monreale from 1848 to his death in 1866. He was the center of politics, revolution, and extortion there. Miceli would no doubt have contested the inclusion of the term "extortion" here, arguing that all he did was to assist his friends and foster the interests of the community. Yet however civic-minded Miceli's activities may have been, they were still activities that made him rich and powerful. They also made him the center of a network of political friends and allies. This gave him a position that he could bequeath to his heirs, for we find members of Turi Miceli's family mentioned in police reports related to the mafia up until the murder of his son Francesco in 1892.

Turi Miceli is simply the most illustrious example of a general connection between revolution, politics, and the mafia throughout Palermo province and into the neighboring provinces as well. Towns such as Monreale and Misilmeri that had strong revolutionary traditions before 1860 become mafia strongholds afterward. Many of the leading mafiosi in the 1870s could boast of participation in the *squadre* in 1860 and, in some cases, as far back as 1848.

Even the role of Palermo's central prison remained unchanged. Some of the first *carbonaro* conspiracies had taken shape there. We saw that during the disturbances of September 1847, Rosolino Pilo heard that the prison bosses had issued the order that "he who dared commit thefts during the supreme days that were probably to follow was a traitor to the Fatherland."[4] During the 1867 inquiry, Rudinì told his colleagues that the "Vicaria," as the Palermo prison was called, was "a sort of government. From there is issued dispositions, orders, . . . etc.."[5] Palermo's central prison remains the nerve center of the Sicilian mafia to the present day.

All these particular connections between revolution and mafia are symptoms of a more general link. Revolution, we saw, was a *carrière ouverte aux talents*; it provided a short cut. The risks were very high, but then so were the potential rewards. The same is true of politics and crime; they were *carrières ouvertes aux talents*. Although politics and organized crime are different sorts of activities, the talents they require are broadly similar. Sneak thieves, pickpockets, and thugs need courage, physical agility, and brute strength. A successful mafia boss or politician, by contrast, needed social skills; he needed to be a good organizer and good at dealing with people.

What brought the mafia and the politicians together was the fact that they were all in the business of controlling people.

The same might be said of Sicily's revolutionaries. They were very good at organizing conspiracies and at jockeying for position with rival secret societies; yet their record as practical revolutionaries was, to be honest, spotty. They were much better in the backroom plotting than under fire on the battlefield. This again brought them closer to the politicians. Thus, as different as revolution, politics, and crime may have been in theory, in Sicily the three seemed to mesh together quite nicely. The existence of a considerable continuity between revolutionaries, *squadristi*, mafiosi, and politicians indicates that, in one form or another, all these men were in politics from the start.

Saying that revolution, politics, and crime are all *carrières ouvertes aux talents* implies that, for an individual, any might serve as a vehicle for social mobility. It is not surprising then that many of the generation that began to come into power in Sicily in the late 1870s, the "homines novi," as they liked to call themselves, started their careers in the struggle against Naples. This is true equally for those who became successful politicians and those who "made their bones" in the mafia. In either case, a good war record seemed a prerequisite for a successful career.

It is just as well that it was, moreover; someone had to take over. Twelve years of ferocious repression under Maniscalco had marginalized Sicily's traditional ruling class. The disaster of the 1862 Aspromonte expedition and the repression under General Govone which followed hard on its heels had split the revolutionary party into two warring halves—a pro–Italian unity group and a pro–Sicilian autonomy group. It was this second group that was responsible for the 1866 uprising. We saw that it consisted of obscure individuals, many of whom were on the run from renewed police repression. Obscure as they may have been, however, by now many of them possessed considerable practical revolutionary experience. This group may well have included men who had been recruited by Pilo and his associates in 1847, or men who, a month later, swore in front of the Duomo of Palermo to help maintain order in the coming uprising. It may have included others who had listened to Bentivegna's exalted fantasies in 1853, or had followed his lead in the abortive uprising of 1856. It certainly included men who had been part of *squadre* in 1860 or of Badia's revolutionary network in 1865.

It is easy to dismiss the 1866 uprising as a farce, but this misses the point. What is remarkable is that it happened at all. When the fathers and the grandfathers of the 1866 rebels had fallen upon Neapolitan soldiers in

1820 and 1848, they had hacked them to death and stripped them of all their belongings. The 1866 rebels, by contrast, were *véritables révolutionaires*: they wore red caps and scarves; they had leaders and plans; they erected barricades; they refrained from bloodshed and looting. They were even, under the leadership of Turi Miceli, capable of charging straight at a Piedmontese regiment and setting it to flight. And they did it all themselves. They did it this way because there was no one left to lead them—no Giuseppe La Masa, Rosolino Pilo or Francesco Crispi, no old-fashioned baron or revolutionary intellectual or "emissary" from the continent. They had to use their own revolutionary know-how; they had to organize themselves. And this is what made the mafia different from other criminal underworlds.

Palermo was not the only nineteenth-century city with a criminal underworld. Naples had its camorra; New York had Tammany and the Tweed Ring. Criminals underworlds were more the rule than the exception in this period. Yet in Naples and New York a sense of hierarchy and social order always prevailed. Politicians were one class of gentlemen; crooks were no gentlemen at all. Politicians were involved in white-collar crimes like graft, bribery, market fixing, and payoffs; criminals were involved in low-rent crimes like prostitution, extortion, illegal gambling, and various forms and violence and theft. The two classes needed each other; they traded favors and protected each other. But the social barrier remained intact. Politicians and crooks did not mix socially.

In Sicily, by contrast, the barrier was beginning to crumble. Twelve years of persecution under Maniscalco had weakened Sicily's traditional ruling class; a bout of further repression under the Piedmontese from 1862 to 1876 made it difficult for a new, predominantly middle-class, revolutionary leadership to establish itself as a legitimate ruling group. All these factors—the weakness of the traditional ruling class, the inability of the new middle class to establish its legitimacy, and the practical experience of the lower classes and the underworld—allowed the mafia to emerge. When it did so, moreover, it emerged not as a more powerful lower-class underworld; it emerged rather as a semiautonomous form of political control alternative to the legitimate control of the new Italian state. This is what frightened Rudinì, General Medici, and some of the more perspicacious of the witnesses in 1867. They had caught glimpse into Sicily's political future, and they did not like what they saw.

The extension of mafia power was a gradual process. We shall see in the final chapter that even by 1900 at the highest level of Sicily's ruling group, that of the parliamentary deputies, there were many who appeared blissfully unaware that the process was taking place at all. In retrospect, this seems amazing, for the evidence was all there.

Up to now we have concentrated on politics and revolution, treating crime as a side issue. It is now time to reverse these priorities. For the rest of this book we will focus as directly on the mafia as our sources allow. We can begin by looking at the word itself.

## Etymology and Legends

Where did *mafia* come from, and what did it mean?

The term first appears as slang; it referred to something that was "flashy" or "eye-catching." According to the playwright Gaspare Mosca, *mafia* or *mafiusu* could be applied to things such as bright, shiny plaits, a well-tied necktie, or even a substantial potbelly.[6] The great Sicilian ethnologist Giuseppe Pitrè first heard the term in the 1860s in the Borgo suburb of Palermo. He remembered hearing peddlers hawking their wares as "real *mafia* stuff." Although he glosses the term as "bello, grazioso," it is clear that there is more to it than this, for he continues, noting that "a girl who is not only pretty, but strikes the observer as being self-consciously so, one who bears herself well, . . . who has a certain I don't know what that makes her better or superior, has the quality of *mafia*. She is *mafiusa* or *mafiusedda*."[7]

The masculine, *mafiusu*, has even more of this "I don't know what" quality. Young *mafiusi* were not only flashy; they were also menacing. Later in the century, the Sicilian policeman and criminologist Antonio Cutrera would write that the *mafiusu* "wears a brightly colored shirt, keeps his hat at a rakish angle, has his well-pomaded hair combed so that a curl falls on his forehead; his mustache is well trimmed. When he walks he swings his hips, and with his cigar in his mouth and his walking stick in hand, he keeps his long knife well hidden . . . from the police."[8]

This is a description that might equally fit the *guapo* on the streets of Naples. A Palermitan *mafiusu* was someone who knew how to *nacari*—another characteristic Sicilian term meaning to swagger insolently or menacingly. A *mafiusu* was a young "man of honor," a man who, as Sicilians put it, won't put up with a fly on his nose.

Despite his air of menace, however, all authors agree that the *mafiusu* was not a criminal or mere *triste*. Nor was he a gangster, for the associations to which he belonged were never simply criminal conspiracies. Typically he was young, and was someone who demanded that everyone he met show him and his associates proper "respect." He was also someone whose behavior was likely to lead him into trouble—into fights or those bouts of wanton destructiveness undertaken for what Sicilians call "u currivu."[9] When this happened, both Pitrè and Cutrera observed, the young *mafiusu* might land in prison, and it was there that he could meet real members of the criminal milieu and initiate his career in the underworld.[10]

*Mafiusi* had their good side as well. They could be gallant and generous; they were loyal to their friends. A connection between mafia and chivalry was repeatedly drawn: a judge, Giuseppi de Menza, described the young *mafiusi* in the 1870s as "the *enfants terribles* of the criminal world ... [T]hey represent, one might even dare to say, the chivalresque side of crime."[11]

Concerning the origin of the mafia, opinions differed. It was claimed that the mafia had its origins in the Middle Ages, if not remote antiquity. This was the opinion of the American gangster Joe Bonanno, for example, who wrote that the mafia (which he calls "the Tradition") began as a sect of noble avengers sworn to protect Sicily's common people against the abuses of foreign dominators.[12]

According to a well-known story, the mafia was born in the outbreak of the Sicilian Vespers in 1282. Like the police of Maniscalco, the Angevin troops who occupied thirteenth-century Sicily were concerned over the possibility of a popular insurrection. On the morning of the uprising, they posted guards at all the city gates with instructions to search the carts and baskets of the peasants coming into the market for concealed weapons. It seems that one Angevin soldier took his duties too seriously. Not only did he search the basket of a buxom young Sicilian *viddana* (wench), but he thrust his hand inside her blouse as well. This was more than her young husband was prepared to take. He withdrew his concealed sword and, thrusting it into the belly of the hapless soldier, shouted the words "Maledizione Ai Francesi Italia Anela!" (Maledictions to the French; Italy is yearning). This call was taken up as the battle cry for the entire uprising; soon its initial letters—M/A/F/I/A—were to be seen scribbled on walls throughout the city. In this way the term *mafia* ever after stood for Sicily's determination to rid itself of foreign oppression.[13] (According to another version, the first three letters of MAFIA stood for "Morte alla Francia"— Death to France.)

It is hard to imagine how anyone can believe such nonsense. Leave aside the unlikeliness of illiterate *popolani* of 1282 Palermo chalking up graffiti on the city walls like modern-day student revolutionaries. Leave aside the total improbability of the incident itself: Would a medieval Sicilian husband enraged by a sexual assault on his wife be likely to shout out a slogan for Italian unity? Consider only the question of language. The phrase is in modern Italian; yet in 1282 modern Italian did not yet exist. It did exist, of course, in the 1870s, at a time, that is, when both the story and the political sentiments would have been much more appropriate. The same might be said of another contemporary explanation—though one that is no longer current today. According to this, *mafia* actually stands for "Mazzini Autorizza Furti Incendi Abigiati" (Mazzini authorizes thefts, arson, cattle rustling; or, instead of *abigiati, avvelenamenti*—poisoning).

Apocryphal legends are nonetheless significant. They associate the mafia with Sicily's tradition of rebellion and resistance to foreign dominance—a tradition that, according to Sicilians, dates from 1282. In another story, the mafia is derived from the semi-legendary sect of noble avengers—the Beati Paoli.[14] Although this is merely another legend, it is interesting that it is a legend that centers on the church of San Francesco di Paolo in the old Borgo. The church was the focus of the 1866 rebellion and would later have important ties to the mafia as well.

The mafia did owe something, of course, to the Carboneria. Again, it is interesting that this obsession with medieval pedigrees is something that the mafia shares with (or even borrows from) the Carboneria.[15] Thus it is not surprising that, after 1860, we find dozens of Masonic clubs in Sicily called "The Vespers" or "The Sons of the Vespers."

Even if the story of the medieval origin of the mafia was a legend, most Sicilians took it for granted that the word itself was as old as the Sicilian character. After all, the word evoked a particular combination of stylishness, chivalry, and truculence that was perceived to be uniquely Sicilian. Yet, Sicilian sensibilities notwithstanding, not even this seems to be true.

The widespread belief that the word derives from Arabic rests on nothing more than the fact that words beginning with ma— seem to resemble Arabic participles, and the notion that the Arab occupation of Sicily in the early Middle Ages made Sicilians culturally and genetically different from other Italians. The Sicilian linguist Giuseppe L. Messina has pointed out, however, that this argument does not stand up to philological analysis.[16] Unlike Spanish, the Sicilian language has few words deriving from Arabic.[17] Moreover, Sicilian dialect has been a literary language since the eleven hundreds; its earliest vocabularies date from the sixteenth century. Despite this long history, no Sicilian dictionary contains the term *mafia* before 1876.[18] When it first came into common use in the late 1860s, authors could not at first decide whether to spell the term *mafia* or *maffia*, with two *f*'s. None of this supports the argument for the term's antiquity. If the term had really been in the Sicilian vocabulary since the early Middle Ages, it is surprising that neither the poets nor the lexicographers make any reference to it, especially as the term supposedly sums up the Sicilian character.

Pitrè's observation that the term first appears around Palermo's port district is pertinent, for it indicates that the word might have entered Palermo by sea. During the 1860s and early 1870s, use of the term was restricted to Palermo and the Conca d'Oro. From here it spread inland, aided by itinerant puppeteers who enlivened their performances by making their characters speak in the tough-guy *mafiusu* slang of the capital.[19] The term was also spread by police officials, who were instructed by the Ministry of the Interior to compile lists of all "mafiosi" (the Italianization of the Sicilian *mafiusi*) in their jurisdictions, and by journalists whose misinformed articles in the northern press filtered back to Sicily and were credited in those parts that were unfamiliar with the Palermitan term. It is thus possible, as Vincenzo Mortillaro and the first commentators originally asserted, that *mafia* derives from Tuscan or even Piedmontese dialect.[20]

Whatever its origin, it was the 1866 uprising and the 1867 inquiry that focused wider attention on the mafia. A link was made between the *mafiusi* of 1866 and the *squadre* of 1860 and 1848. Vincenzo Maggiorani, for example, reported that he had been told that the *squadre* who had descended on the city in 1866 were the same as those who had arrived in 1860 and, in many instances, even in 1848.[21] Once the mafia became associated with the *squadre*, the association could be extended back to the 1860 and 1848 uprisings as well. All rebellions in Palermo—including especially the Vespers uprisings of 1282—became mafia uprisings.

Taken in this sense, "mafia" turned into a political symbol. It stood for the Sicilian people, oppressed, disenfranchised, and despised under the Bourbon yoke, yet never wavering in their determination to regain their liberties at whatever cost. Although in Palermitan slang the word *mafiusu* still summoned up an image of a flashy young tough, with his well-oiled hair and hidden knife, the rhetorical *mafiusi*, the freedom fighters of 1848 and 1860, became the Palermitan counterpart of the sansculottes and communards of revolutionary Paris. The *mafiusi* were the Sicilian nation-in-arms.

One version of the "nation-in-arms" theme was illustrated by duke di Cesarò, elected as deputy from Aragona in Agrigento province. When he was asked by the 1876 parliamentary inquiry to explain the origin of the mafia, he expressed little doubt that

> in Sicily every class was united in the common struggle [against Naples]; and indeed it is the proud boast of the Sicilian aristocracy that

they have always been united with the people. . . . Look at Sicilian history: you will find that the barons assumed the leadership of every revolutionary movement, and that the people refused to swear fealty to anyone except their barons. When we wanted to make a revolution, it was natural that we weren't going to be too fussy about examining all the scrapes that those we were recruiting had gotten themselves into. . . . This for me, gentlemen, is the origin of the mafia.[22]

Although this may have been what the barons wanted to believe, the claim that the common people of Sicily "swore fealty" to their barons, letting them lead the struggle against Naples, is debatable to say the least. Still it is significant that di Cesarò can equate the mafia with the common people struggling for liberty under the leadership of these barons. Here the theme of the alliance between the influential and the dangerous classes becomes transformed into an image of national unity.

In this image it is really immaterial who assumes the role of the influential classes. The mafia can "swear fealty" to their barons or to any other revolutionary claimant. Describing the 1860 uprising from the perspective of Alcamo, Giuseppe Fazio writes that the members of the Sant'Anna *squadre* were all mafiosi. He cautions the reader, however, not to be scandalized by this assertion. The reader should not confuse the true mafioso with the negative stereotype appearing in the northern Italian press.

> The mafia had its origin, I believe, as a form of Freemasonry or of Carboneria. [Its members] hated all despotic governments, all the instruments of such governments, and all their laws, even those that were good. This was the state of things. Thus the mafia ought to be looked at as an excess of profound hatred toward the Bourbons, enlarged and sustained by the pride and punctiliousness of the Sicilian character.[23]

Significantly, Fazio's description was written in 1901, when, as we shall see, Sicilians were concerned with upholding their political traditions against northern charges that Sicilian politics was incurably corrupt and mafia-ridden. Fazio was probably aware that calling the *picciotti* of Sant'Anna "mafiosi" was anachronistic; the word would not have been used in Alcamo in 1860. His insistence on using it anyway probably had more to do with his desire to defend the honor and good name of Sicily than with faulty memory.

In describing the mafia as originally a *carbonaro* sect, Fazio was referring specifically to the *carbonari* in Palermo's central prison. There were, we saw, reports of sects being organized by political prisoners in the jails of Naples and Palermo from the Napoleonic era.[24]

During this period, prisons were simply places of confinement, fortresses in which inmates of all categories were promiscuously locked up together. These prisons were run by the inmates themselves, who maintained order and organized the provision of food and clothing. Shortly after his incarceration, an inmate in the old Vicaria in Palermo would be asked to contribute money for "the lamp." The request referred to the lamp that hung in front of a painting of the Madonna in the entrance hall of the prison for which the prisoners provided the oil. In reality, of course, the prisoner was being taxed; prisoners had to pay a tribute to the prison bosses. These bosses not only constituted the prison government but controlled the market for goods inside the prison as well. If a prisoner lacked either food or bedding, these, as well as other luxuries to mitigate the rigors of incarceration, could be bought from the bosses.

Traditionally, the head of the "Mala," or underworld, in either Naples or Palermo was the head of this prison government. He was a man treated with the greatest respect and consideration by prisoners and police alike; indeed, the police seem not to have interfered with his activities either inside or outside the prison.[25]

It was into this world that Sicilian political prisoners were thrown in the first decades of the nineteenth century. Those from the upper classes seem to have been treated with deference and respect by the prison bosses. It is not surprising that, as liberals and patriots suffering for their belief in liberty, equality, and brotherhood, some attempted to redeem their fellow inmates, either by teaching them to read and write (as in the case of Angelo Pugliese) or by proselytizing for the revolutionary sects.

Rosolino Pilo's story that, on the eve of the abortive revolution in of September 1847, the prison underworld sent out messages can be matched by similar stories from other sources. These stories form part of the popular legends of both the mafia and the revolution, stories that, though impossible to prove or disprove, color Sicilians' own conception of the mafia.

The most notable of the stories of solidarity between the underworld and the revolution comes from a dialect play written in 1862 and presented in Palermo the following year. In this play a young lawyer, thrown into prison for conspiratorial activities on the eve of the April 4 uprising, is befriended by two young *picciotti da sgarro* (what today might be called gangland "soldiers"). After various adventures, including their betrayal by the villain of the piece, and after lively discussions on the subjects of religion, the underworld, patriotic love for Sicily and Palermo, and hatred of

*Poster advertising* I Mafiusi de la Vicaria. *Courtesy Pitre Museum, Palermo.*

tyrants, injustice, and *sbirri*, the young lawyer is finally revealed as Francesco Crispi. In the final act, the gangland soldiers are represented as reformed, patriotic citizens, happy in the bosom of their families.

The original title of the play was to be *I Camorristi di la Vicaria*, using the Neapolitan term *camorrista* ("gangster," "racketeer," from *camorra*, "racket"). In the summer of 1862, however, the playwright Gaspare Mosca witnessed an altercation between two young Palermo toughs; one grabbed the other shouting, "E tu vulissi fari u mafiusu cu mia" (So you want to play the mafioso/wise guy with me). It occurred to him that it was inappropriate to use the Neapolitan term *camorristi* in a play dramatizing how Sicilian criminals earn their redemption by fighting in the struggle for independence against Naples. Mosca had the genial idea of changing the title to *I Mafiusi di la Vicaria*. It was just the touch the play needed, for it enjoyed an enormous success: it was revived repeatedly in Sicily itself, was brought to Sicilian audiences in America, and was adapted for puppet theater so that even shepherds in remote mountain villages might learn how hardened members of the Palermitan underworld had redeemed themselves and joined the patriotic struggle.[26]

## The Mafia in Official Sources

Nineteenth-century sources associated *mafiusi* with two sorts of Sicilians. There were the *squadristi* of 1848, 1860, and 1866. And there were the laborers, employees, small landowners, and tenants involved in the agrarian economy in the Conca d'Oro, especially in the citrus groves. These were hardly distinct groups, for in times of peace, *squadristi* worked the land. Still, the contrasting definitions are interesting both for what they include and for what they exclude.

If we compare the occupations of men who participated in the *squadre* with those of the men listed as "second-category" mafiosi by the police in the 1870s, we find a predominance of occupations that might be translated as "overseer," "custodian," "watchman," or "guard." Included are *campieri* (estate guards), *soprastanti* (overseers), *castaldi* (caretakers), and local police guards. To these can be added itinerant categories such as coachmen and carters, as well as various merchants, shopkeepers, and artisans from the towns and men listed as "small proprietors."[27]

Included here are employees and a fair cross-section of the suburban middle and lower-middle classes; excluded are the sharecropping peasants, agricultural laborers, and the poor generally. Neither revolution nor organized crime was associated with the very poor or the marginal classes; both arose rather from groups well integrated into their local societies, those whose jobs connected them with landowning families and with municipal factions. Within this larger grouping, however, it is also notable that both *squadristi* and *mafiusi* represent a relatively unskilled though mobile subgroup—estate guards rather than specialized gardeners, coachmen and carters rather than coach builders and carpenters.

The differences are as interesting as the similarities. Crime and brigandage were *carrières ouvertes aux talents*; Angelo Pugliese was proof of this. Among the lists of mafiosi there are a number of men listed as "deserters" or "draft dodgers," as well as those listed merely as "propertyless." The peasants and rural proletariat had, of course, participated in the rebellions, and the police documents make frequent reference to the "mass" of lesser mafiosi. Thus a certain Salvatore Alfonso, a smallholder from the small town of Castronovo, is listed not just as a second-category mafioso but as "a *capomafioso* of the most dangerous sort owing to the ascendancy that he exercises over mafiosi of the lower sphere."[28] These "mafiosi of the lower sphere," however, usually remain an anonymous mass of unnamed hooligans and troublemakers, whose low social positions did not permit them to become members of the various clubs, Masonic conspiracies, and religious confraternities that articulated the networks of local power. They were the sort of men who, especially before 1866, were referred to simply as *tristi*.

Noticeable too is the comparative absence of the professions in the lists of mafiosi. The *squadre*, of course, had included the educated sons of local landowners, usually in positions of leadership. Where educated men do appear in the lists of mafiosi, they always appear as "mafiosi of the first category." The only exception in the 1870 lists is a certain Gioacchino Prinzivalle from Scillato, a veterinarian turned cattle rustler and sometime kidnapper. A veterinarian was an educated professional, yet cattle rustling smacked of manual labor; so, despite his status as an "intellectual," the police relegated Prinzivalle to the second category.[29]

Insofar as professionals or members of the upper classes are listed at all, they are most likely to be listed under either the heading of "republicans" or that of *manutengoli*. Thus in Bivona in 1871, the police report mentions the "republican element . . . led by unscrupulous men who are under suspicion by the police." These "are followed by deluded young men and by students, but the above-mentioned men [the leading republicans] are more interested in having contacts with suspected criminals and evildoers capable of every sort of crime."[30]

The term *manutengolo* ("protector" or "accomplice") specified landowners and officials who protected brigands and criminals, using them as enforcers in their private feuds, perhaps even sharing in their criminal gains. The police wrote of Giuseppe Boscarini Prato, for example, a landowner and leader of the opposition in Valguanera in 1894:

> He shares the defect of the great majority of landowners of the Island, that is, he does nothing to help the authorities purge the countryside of evildoers. It is known, for example, that the fugitive Michele Bruno spent a great deal of time on the premises of the ex-*feudo* Conazzo, his property. Another fugitive, Antonio Muratore, haunted this same ex-*feudo* for a long time. Whenever the baron was questioned about the above-mentioned fugitives, he always responded that he knew nothing about them. By means of this sort of *omertà* he has gained a great ascendancy over the *contadini* and the *mafiosi*.[31]

The term *manutengolo* was applied to the Nicolosi, Guccione, and Lo Cicero families, men whom Angelo Pugliese identified as being his band's "flankers." In fact, the police list as the absolute *capo* of the mafia in the Termini Imeresi region the leading protector and *manutengolo*, the ex-mayor of the town of Caccamo and its contemporary deputy, Giuseppe Torina.

The police reports also give us an insight into the networks that supported both the revolution and the mafia. Much of the violence issued from rivalries between landowning families.[32] The heads of such families were also the leaders of local factions, and municipal politics was tormented by their property disputes and personal rivalries. One 1875 witness observed that "Partinico had become a den of thugs," writing, "There isn't a week that passes without one or the other [party] shedding tears over the murder of one its members."[33]

The provincial deputy Enrico Albanese described Partinico's problems in more detail to the 1875 parliamentary commission investigating criminal violence in Sicily. "If you look closely at the little towns in Sicily," he began, "you'll find there a medieval struggle in the true sense of the word—an eye for an eye, a tooth for a tooth, each family at war with all the others."[34] He went on to describe how behind the town's political divisions were a set of blood feuds within the local ruling élites.[35] When the deputy from Corleone, Paolo Paternostro, interrupted him here to ask why the lower classes felt themselves involved in such feuds, Albanese replied:

> The little people are divided as well. You might say that, in general, the little people are more in favor of the Scalia party than that of Cannizzo, because the Scalia family gives a lot of work to people. But they're divided into parties anyway, for what happens everywhere else also happens here: whoever works for such and such a person has his own group of friends, and these friends have their own friends, and so on.[36]

It was this sense of "and so on" that helped spread party conflicts in Sicily beyond the bounds of the ruling classes.

Nevertheless, the mafia was more than just the outgrowth of local ruling-class feuds. Smuggling in the Conca d'Oro, for example, had existed as an independent activity for centuries. In 1864 Baron Turrisi-Colonna described the smugglers and traffickers operating there as united in a "sect."

> [It is] a sect that finds new affiliates every day among the brightest of the youngsters from the rural classes, from the custodians of the field, from the *agro palermitano* [the city's agricultural hinterland], and from the vast numbers of smugglers. It is a sect that gives and receives protection from anyone who is obliged to live in the countryside, from tenants to stock herders, that gives protection and receives assistance from certain men, that lives by trafficking and petty commerce. The sect has no fear of the public forces, for it believes that it can always sidetrack their investigations. It little fears judicial persecution, flattering itself that proofs will never emerge owing to the pressure that it can put upon witnesses.[37]

He finished this description with the comment that the "sect" was presently "looking toward another revolution, because those of 1848 and 1860 earned it two *General Amnesties* for first offenders and for common crimes."[38] A prophetic comment in 1864.

When Turrisi-Colonna returned to testify in the 1867 parliamentary inquiry, he confirmed his earlier observations, though by now he naturally called this sect the "mafia."[39] Giovanni Maurigi, one of Palermo's leading judges, testified that there was a "Mafia" in every one of the towns around the capital, usually formed around a nucleus of two or three men and their following. Taken together, he thought, there were probably four or five thousand mafiosi in the Palermo region. They were involved in robberies and with the taking of the *componendum*. Traditionally, the police had come to arrangement with the mafia: so long as they remained well behaved, the police did not interfere with their rackets. This tradition, he finished by observing, had continued into the 1860s.[40]

### Protection Rackets

Maurigi's reference to the *componendum* is significant. Although Turrisi-Colonna described the mafia as living "by trafficking and petty commerce," it is clear that their range of activities was wider than this. Strictly speaking, a *componendum* was an illicit demand for money. It was a legal term used to cover a wide set of practices that we might call kickbacks, bribes, or protection money. Nevertheless, although bribery and extortion were crimes, the *componendum* resembled practices that, in their more licit forms, were deeply ingrained in the traditional Sicilian economy.

The landed aristocracy, living in Palermo or the other coastal cities, rented their estates on three- or five-year leases, payable in advance, to *gabellotti*. Although the term *gabellotto* is usually translated as "tenant farmer," the term *gabella* actually means "tax" or "toll." In this sense a *gabella* was a franchise, and the *gabellotto* who bought the franchise was a tax farmer who had bought the right to tax the peasants.

This, in fact, was how many Sicilian *gabellotti* behaved: rather than investing in or even managing their lands, they simply squeezed the peasantry for as much as they could. This was a scheme replicated at every level of the hierarchy: the overseers (*soprastanti*) and guards (*campieri*) whom the *gabelloto* hired were paid little or no wages; they received instead a living on the estate where they worked. The larger *soprastanti*, for example, might be provided a house or rooms in the estate buildings (*masserie*), a vegetable garden, a share of the wine, olive oil, and fruit produced on the estate, cheeses and wool from the shepherds, as well as a horse or a mule. Significantly, much of this was directly provided by the peasants whom these overseers and guards had been hired to supervise. Beyond this, the *soprastanti* and the *campieri* had a right to a scoop of grain from the threshing of each peasant. This was called their *pizzu*, or "beakful"; taking the cut was called "wetting the beak."[41]

As a way of organizing agricultural production, the system was hopelessly inefficient. Yet it cost nothing to run. The landowner did not need to make investments. There were few employees or laborers to pay. It was less of an economic system in itself than a form of political dominance founded on a division between a minority who held power, and who therefore exercised the right to impose taxes or the *pizzu*, and a majority of peasants who had to suffer these tributes.

The police used a variation on this same system. Local policemen were municipal not state employees, and were apt to be ill paid or often not paid at all. Instead, they worked for tips. In practice, this meant that a local police force was a company of guards, sometimes mounted, sometimes on foot, organized, commanded, and paid for by local landowners and merchants. So long as such police units could be kept under control, the system worked tolerably well. Yet repeated complaints about abuses indicate that, through most of the nineteenth century, the system did not work well.

Local ruling classes often split into Bourbon and anti-Bourbon factions, and, either during revolts or in the bouts of repression that followed, the faction in power would not hesitate to use the police to despoil their local enemies.

The high-crime area in western Sicily followed the coastal strip from Termini Imeresi in the north to Marsala in the west. It also followed the roads into the interior: the road from Monreale through Corleone to the south coast over which Garibaldi had dispatched his cannons; the road from Termini Imeresi through Caccamo and on to Caltanissetta; the road from Partinico to Alcamo. These arteries linking the interior to the coast were every bit as essential to the livelihoods of smugglers, livestock thieves, and brigands as they were to the landowners and merchants. On these desolate stretches of highway it was often difficult to differentiate local guards, who might appear and demand payments from travelers passing through their territories, from the highwaymen themselves. Nor would travelers who had suffered thefts think very highly of the local guard who arrived at their doorstep to inform them that their property "might" be found in return for a payment of about 50 percent of its value.

These were customs that made it easier for organized crime to impose the *pizzu* and to disguise their rackets as licit forms of tribute. The Neapolitan term for underworld or racket is *camorra*; the term probably derives from *capo e morra*, or those who ran the game of *mora*. Anyone who wished to operate a gambling den was required to pay a percentage of his takings to the underworld; he needed, in the parlance of the American mafia, to give the bosses their "end." The terminology was the same: the underworld needed to "wet their beaks," and their "end" was called, in Sicily, and often in Naples and America as well, the *pizzu*.

The underworld imposed its protection on innumerable activities:

coachmen had to pay a *pizzu* for the fares they took; tavernkeepers, stall-holders, and artisans had to pay protection money for the right to practice their trades. The underworld controlled the market in casual labor as well; a job was considered a "favor," and anyone seeking a job as a laborer or attendant needed to ensure the benevolence of the underworld bosses who "protected" the activity.

Protection was, of course, a two-way street: anyone who paid his *pizzu* to the "organization" might consider that, having paid his taxes, he was entitled to enjoy the benefits of protection. In 1874 the Palermo prosecutor's office discovered an association called the Mugnai della Posa, which we might roughly translate as the "dues-paying millers."[42] According to the prosecutor Carlo Morena, in order to prevent price wars and competitive undercutting, the young millers in the Conca d'Oro and the Orto Botanico suburb of Palermo had been organized into a sort of guild in which all members agreed to charge their customers the same amount. Although contrary to Italian commercial law, this was simply a price-fixing ring organized by the millers themselves. Yet, as a price-fixing ring, the association needed some way of enforcing its fixed prices and excluding outsiders. It was this necessity that turned the Mugnai della Posa into a protection racket.

The word *posa* referred to the dues that all members paid; on each cartload of grain brought to the mill, the miller paid a certain percentage to the association. Like the sharecropping peasants, the millers paid their *pizzu*, though in their case they received a tangible benefit in exchange. In the 1870s the millers' associations had expanded to include the carters as well. The principle remained the same: the carters paid their *posa* on each cartload of grain or flour that they carried to or from the mills. The two occupational groups supported each other: the millers refused to accept grain from carters who were not a part of the association; the carters were guaranteed that, if they paid their dues, they could practice their trade.

One suspects that these practices were the accepted norm and that there were innumerable associations like the Mugnai della Posa in the Palermo area. Most of them, of course, did not attract the attentions of the police by murdering those who refused to join. In the case of the Posa, however, a certain miller named Angelo Celona was told by the head of the association, Morello, that if he refused to join the society and abide by its rules, he would be shot. Celona refused, and for this he was killed by Morello and a party of carters.[43] It was the murder rather than the price fixing that brought the "dues-paying millers" to the attention of the ministers of the interior and of justice.

The mafia's protection rackets were similar to, and indeed an extension of, those of the underworld's bosses who ran Palermo's prison or of the *gabellotti* who managed Sicilian agriculture. This explains why so many mafiosi are described as "guards" or "caretakers." They were, in reality, mafia "partners" who "protected" an estate or sector of commerce for the mafia family, possibly receiving some sort of direct payment from the landowner as well as imposing a *pizzu* on everyone whose employment they "protected." What the police viewed as extortion was, from the mafia's perspective, almost a natural right that accrued to anyone who organized control. It followed (as we shall see in more detail later) that mafia violence usually arose from a struggle for control. Once the mafia had established a "protectorate" over a certain territory or activity, violence usually declined.

## I Casi di Malaspina

The situation in the orange groves around Palermo was complex. Here mafia control meant control over both the work force and the land itself, that is, not only over the comparatively defenseless agricultural workers but over the orange grove owners as well. These were men of substance, better able to defend themselves against the underworld's demands for tribute. Yet these were also men who might well find uses for the underworld's ability to control the economy. Once again, protection was a two-way street, and even for property owners there might be advantages in co-operating with the mafia. In the countryside around Palermo, Dr. Gaspare Galati wrote in 1875,

> the *mafiosi* impose themselves on property owners as custodians or caretakers. In this capacity they steal, engage in rackets on the products of the land, on the sale of these products, on those who buy them, on, in fact, everything. Beyond this they squeeze the purses of their bosses with threatening letters [*lettere di scrocco*] or, to keep them from performing an unwelcome surveillance, prevent them from even visiting their own lands. . . .
>
> What is more, landowners placed in the painful position of losing the profits of ownership, and maybe even their lives, are not even permitted to free themselves from these dilemmas by renting or selling their lands. The organization is involved in this field as well. It would never permit an outsider to come up with a reasonable offer, either for rental

or for purchase. Bidders stay away; even if they don't already know it, they're warned that he who refuses to obey will be eliminated. Meanwhile, working through its clients, the society comes and makes a miserable offer for the rental or purchase, and the poor owner, afraid of losing everything, has to bow to circumstances . . . Thus it is that almost all the citrus groves around Palermo have been either bought or rented by powerful *mafiosi* at miserably low prices.[44]

This description is part of an account of Galati's own struggle against "the mafia in the Palermo countryside" which he sent the 1875 parliamentary commission. Galati is one of the few who did try to stand up against the mafia.

Galati lived in Malaspina in the suburbs north of the Porta Macqueda. Originally Malaspina had been part of an area of parkland in which the Palermitan aristocracy had build their suburban villas in the late seventeenth and eighteenth centuries. In the early nineteenth century, however, parkland was replaced by citrus groves, whose profits and productivity increased until the land rents in areas such as Malaspina and Uditore became among the highest in Europe. Relations between citrus-growing families were often violent, as were the relations between the growers and the workers. It was the murder rate in this area that prompted Leopoldo Franchetti to remark in 1876 that here "the odor of orange and lemon blossoms was tainted with that of cadavers."[45]

Galati was the administrator of the *fondo* Riella, one of the richest properties in the area. The legal owners were the two Riella sisters, the younger of whom was Galati's wife. He had become the administrator following the death of his brother-in-law, a man whom Galati described as "by nature indescribably weak and pusillanimous." When this brother-in-law had received an anonymous threatening letter, he had shut himself in his house in terror, dying shortly afterward of heart failure.

On taking over as administrator, Galati discovered that the actual manager of the lands was the caretaker, Benedetto Carollo. Carollo was a *mafiusu*, who, following the "usual racket of the mafia" ("consueta camorra della mafia in generale"), creamed off 25 percent of the receipts from fruit sales for himself. Carollo practiced another racket as well: shortly before picking, he arranged to have half of the harvest stolen. He later sold the stolen fruit privately.

Seeing that the profits were being eaten by the mafia, Galati decided to sell the property. Carollo, however, objected, and frightened away prospective buyers. He was working, according to Galati, on behalf of the

Uditore mafia, who wished to force him to sell the property to them for a derisory sum. Galati then tried to sack Carollo, but he refused to go, claiming that Galati had no right to fire him. The job, he said, had been his *pane* (bread) for ten years. Carollo invited two friends to stay with him on the property; together, the three men hung around Galati's property, trying to intimidate him.

Undeterred, Galati hired a new caretaker. Shortly afterwards, the new caretaker was murdered, ambushed by assailants hiding behind the wall of the neighboring property.

Galati turned to the police for help. They were sympathetic and assured him that they would take immediate steps to protect him. With this promise, Galati hired another caretaker, named Cusumano. This provoked a new threatening letter: Benedetto Carollo, it said, was a "man of honor"; Galati had no right to dismiss him and hire a "rotten snitch" (*infame spia*) in his place. Galati was told to chase Cusumano off the property.

Galati believed that he had material evidence linking this letter to Carollo. He returned to the police, who, renewing their assurances, promised to arrest Carollo. Instead, they again did nothing, and Galati soon received a new letter saying that if he ever again "mounted the steps" of the police station, he would be "killed without mercy." Eight days later; as Galati informed the parliamentary committee, "on Sunday, January 24 [1875], as Cusumano was driving in a cart, unarmed, proceeding toward my house at Malaspina, he was shot three times in the back at close range. The ambush occurred in the middle of an inhabited street at one o'clock in the afternoon immediately outside the Porta Macqueda." No one, of course, "saw" anything.

The wounded caretaker was taken to the hospital, where his wounds were diagnosed as not fatal. When he learned that he would probably survive, he decided not to risk cooperating with the police and refused to identify his attackers. After three more days, however, infection set in. Believing his end to be at hand, Cusumano summoned the police and dictated a statement identifying his attackers as Benedetto Carollo and two of his friends.

The police needed Cusumano to survive and testify in court. The hospital was unsafe, so Galati had him removed from the hospital and placed in a rented room. There, as he wrote, "with my own hands and my own money, I pulled him back from the mouth of the tomb." This prompted a particularly violent response from the anonymous letter writer. He sentenced Galati and his entire family to be stabbed to death: if they left their home, they would be murdered on the open streets; if they tried to barricade themselves in their house, the assassins would break down the barricade and finish them off in their own sitting room.

According to the police, everything depended on the testimony of Cusumano. If he accused Carollo and his friends in open court, the local mafia would be dealt a stunning blow. Cusumano, however, had other ideas. As soon as he was well enough to walk, he slipped out of the room where Galati had hidden him and went to Uditore to parley with the families of the men whom he had identified. They soon arrived at an understanding, which Cusumano and his new friends sealed with a banquet. The next day Cusumano visited the police and withdrew his statement. For Galati there seemed no further alternative. On May 6, "without even taking leave of our dearest friends," Galati and his family abandoned Palermo and set sail for Naples.

Galati claimed to be able to unveil the secrets of the Uditore mafia which was persecuting him. This mafia, he said, hid behind the mask of a lay religious confraternity organized by a Franciscan friar named Padre Rosario. Padre Rosario had taken part in the 1848 uprising, and was afterward imprisoned by the Neapolitans as a "raving demagogue." He seems to have retained his radical political sympathies after 1860, for Galati describes him as organizing a *squadra* from the members of his confraternity and using his church as the general headquarters for the 1866 uprising in the Uditore area.

During this uprising there was a skirmish between Padre Rosario's *squadra* and government troops. Several government soldiers were captured and, bound together, paraded from Malaspina to Uditore, where they were held in Padre Rosario's church. Leading these prisoners was none other than Benedetto Carollo.

The information that Carollo was among the many ex-*squadristi* in Padre Rosario's confraternity is interesting; yet this has no direct relevance to Galati's case. In fact, there is nothing in Galati's memorial to the 1875 commission to link him personally with Padre Rosario, who had no interest in acquiring Galati's lands either for himself or for his confraternity. Curiously enough, all of Galati's information about Padre Rosario's confraternity came from Padre Rosario himself. Before composing his memorial, Galati, who had never met Padre Rosario, wrote him a letter asking about the membership and past history of his confraternity. The friar ingenuously responded with a long letter describing his confraternity, its members, and its past history. He seems to have been totally unaware of the use to which Galati intended to put this information. Nevertheless, it was on the basis of Padre Rosario's information rather than Galati's that, three years later, the police were finally able to proceed against some of the members of the Uditore mafia.[46]

It is not at this point clear why Galati chose to tell the commission so much about Padre Rosario, for it emerged that it was not Padre Rosario who was responsible for Galati's troubles but rather the two lay leaders. The first of these was the confraternity's president, Antonino Giammona. Galati has little to say about Giammona; he was apparently well-off, for Galati describes him as a boorish, semiliterate peasant and leaves it at that. We shall see later that, in reality, Antonino Giammona was far more than this.

The other lay leader of the confraternity was Francesco Paolo Sardofontana, described as the protector and leading *manutengolo* of the Uditore mafia. Galati was more forthcoming about him:

> By nature a squanderer, little remains of his paternal and maternal inheritance beyond a bit of agricultural land around Uditore, and even that is mortgaged to the tune of over 45,000 lire at 7 and 8 percent interest. Beyond this, he has a number of unsecured debts. And so seeing himself well and truly ruined, standing on the brink of a precipice, he threw himself body and soul into the association as one of its protectors.

He was a man, Galati wrote, struggling to maintain his large family. He was "inept," though finally perhaps "more lazy than inept," a wastrel, in fact, who "will never succeed in making his way in life." This may seem a bizarre tone to use in describing a leading protector of the mafia. It also seems surprising that Galati knew so much about Sardofontana's financial problems. Yet both the avuncular tone and the detailed knowledge are explained by the fact that Galati was Sardofontana's brother-in-law. Sardofontana was the half-brother of Galati's wife, Marianina Riella.

Galati did not inform the commission about this connection; nor did he tell them that the wall from behind which the shots were fired that killed his first caretaker was the wall that separated the *fondo* Riella from that "bit of agricultural land around Uditore" still owned by Sardofontana.

This and other information can be gathered from a letter appended to Galati's memorial, sent from police headquarters in Palermo. The police wrote that they were responding to a request from the commission to "supply information concerning Dr. Galati and his motives for leaving this city." Considering the accusations that Galati had leveled against the police, it is hard to believe that this was all the commission wanted to know. Although the letter specifically states that Galati was "of good character," it is evident that the police were writing to discredit his version of events. They supplied the information about property disputes within the Riella-Sardofontana families that Galati had preferred to leave out. The police also wrote that the threatening letters had not been written by Carollo at all but by Giammona. What is more, although the first letter was addressed to Galati, all subsequent letters were addressed to the legal owner of the property, Galati's wife.

The mafia, wrote the police, wished to force Galati's wife to "rent the rich and fertile *fondo* Riella either to Giammona or to someone else in his criminal organization at a miserable price, and so started to terrorize her with threatening letters." Galati knew where these letters were coming from; he choose to fire Carollo as a message that he was not going to let his wife give in. After he did this, the mafia passed from threats to direct action, eventually forcing Galati and his family to flee Sicily.

Galati must not have wished to see his connections with Sardofontana revealed; thus he deflected suspicion onto Benedetto Carollo and Padre Rosario rather than toward Giammona and Sardofontana. For their part, the police failed to bring up the murder of the first caretaker and the attempted murder of the second. These were, of course, incidents that cast their own activities in an unfavorable light and led Galati to suspect them of complicity with the Uditore mafia. It was later demonstrated that Galati was correct in identifying Carollo as the assailant in the second shooting. What the police information does manage to reveal, however, is that Galati was not merely the victim of mafia persecution, but that his dispute with Giammona and Sardofontana was part of a family feud.

It was a family feud with local repercussions. The police wrote that Francesco Paolo Sardofontana was the only offspring of his mother's second marriage. Shortly before dying, his mother had cut him out of her will. The police made clear that local opinion was divided into two parties over this. Some considered it a mother's "just scorn at seeing her son intimate with the mafia of Passo di Rigano and Uditore headed by Antonino Giammona."

We have already encountered Giammona as the man who befriended Angelo Pugliese in 1862 and introduced him to the Guccione family in Alia. Giammona was also a "patriot"; he had fought in the 1848 revolt and had led a *squadra* in 1860.[47] He was appointed captain in the Sicilian National Guard after 1860, but, though his followers had formed a rebel *squadra* in 1866, Giammona does not seem to have supported the uprising. After the rebellion, Giammona in fact received a government encomium for the part his National Guard unit played in restoring order. We shall see in the next chapter that it was not uncommon for mafia bosses to have friends in government and in the police department; this probably explains why, despite their promises to Galati, the Palermo police failed to arrest either Carollo, Giammona, or Sardofontana.

By the 1870s, Giammona was the most important mafia boss in the Malaspina and Uditore areas.[48] He did not lack for influential friends and supporters. During the 1875 hearings, the lawyer Francesco Gestivo explained how Giammona had had the courage to form a "league" of property owners against the cheap thugs (*scroccatori*) who were infesting the zone. So successful had Giammona's league been that it had provoked the jealousy of other property owners, who now insinuated that Giammona was a mafioso.[49]

One imagines that it was the men in Giammona's "league" of property owners and the members of Padre Rosario's confraternity who formed the other party mentioned in the police letter—the party that sympathized with Sardofontana. This party believed that Galati had exercised an undue influence over his dying mother-in-law. The mother's will disinheriting the Sardofontana family and leaving everything to Galati's wife had been altered, they claimed, "at the suggestion of Dr. Galati," who had only recently become intimate with the family.

## The Sangiorgi Report

Galati's description of the mafia of Malaspina and Uditore was confirmed, both in its general outline and in many of its particulars, by trials, police reports, and inquiries from the mid-1870s onward. Although the mafia evolved in the course of the century, its aims and methods of operation always remained the same.

At the end of the century, between 1898 and 1900, a new chief of police in Palermo, Armando Sangiorgi, wrote a series of reports to the minister of the interior in Rome. According to Sangiorgi, the mafia imposed on the property owners, "caretakers, guards, [and] workers, rents as well as the sale price for citrus fruits and all other products of the land."[50]

Sangiorgi gave a much more extended picture than Galati. In Palermo and the Conca d'Oro, dialect terms such as *cosca* and *nassa* were, by 1890, in use to designate a mafia group as a specific criminal association. Both words had the sense of "gang." *Cosca*, deriving from the Latin term *costula*, "rib," meant a tight bundle or bunch, as with an artichoke, whose leaves were said to form a *cosca*. Already by the 1870s this idea had been extended to a tightly bound bunch of criminals as well.[51] Sangiorgi's reports are the first attempt to map the over-all structure of the mafia *cosche* in the Conca d'Oro.

Sangiorgi represented the *cosche* as, in principle, organized territorially—one *cosca* for every village, suburb, or quarter of the city. This territorial organization was always in a state of flux, however: stronger *cosche* might control more than one territory, or a single territory might be divided into more than one *cosca*.

Within each territory, affiliates of a particular *cosca* would frequently belong to some association—a political club, friendly society, or religious confraternity. In other cases the mafia was grouped around taverns. The *capo* of a particular *cosca* would not necessarily be the president of the mafia association, though he was usually an officer. In any case, his status as a *capomafia* was generally known to everyone locally—to members and nonmembers of the association alike.

As in the case of Padre Rosario's confraternity in Uditore, these clubs were genuine associations, not criminal gangs or even simple mafia front organizations. In both Bagheria and Villabate, the local mafia was also connected to a political party which was represented in, and actually won, municipal elections.[52]

There was thus a continual ambiguity between the *cosca* as a specifically criminal association and the mafia as a larger association. This was an ambiguity that constantly annoyed the police, who, on occasion, would round up all the members of an association connected to a mafia *cosca*. Yet it was apparent that only a proportion of the membership was materially involved in the crimes perpetrated by the particular *cosca*.

Ideally, the criminal nucleus of any *cosca* was a group of brothers, and it is in fact noticeable how many such groups appear in the Sangiorgi report.[53] Yet only in a minority of cases were the criminal members of a *cosca* limited to men from a single family; it was more usual to find men from several families involved. Generally, a *cosca* was composed of a leading family, which provided the *capo* and some of his immediate lieutenants. This family was usually flanked, however, by at least one other family, which provided the *sottocapo* (second in command). Beyond this, the *cosca* might include other men, affiliated as individuals, usually as friends of the *capo* or of a *sottocapo*. As Sangiorgi described them, *cosche* seemed to number between five and ten men, though some may have been larger.

This division between *cosca* members and members of the larger association connected to it left a somewhat ambivalent space between a minority who managed the *cosca*'s criminal activities and the majority who belonged to the mafia association without taking part in its crimes. In this space were younger men who might help in the *cosca*'s protection rackets and turf wars without being fully accepted, as it were, as part of the family. In the American mafia, the status of these men as "soldiers," and "connected guys," eventually became clear and regularized. To judge from the Sangiorgi report, however, their position in nineteenth-century Sicily was still not formalized. There are often references to the *cagnoli* (dogs) and *cagnolazzi* (puppies); the terms seem to mean "associates"—perhaps in the sense of faithful followers. Salvo Lupo interprets the distinction between *cagnoli* and *cagnolazzi* as between "made guys" who had a right to a certain percentage of the *cosca*'s takings and "connected guys," the American mafia term for aspiring members. This distinction is possible, though it is not directly supported by any documented source.[54]

From the Sangiorgi report (as well as from a comparison with the American mafia), it seems that the non-family members of the *cosca* were divided between old friends and trusted associates of the *capo*, and younger men who wished to run their own protection rackets or commit their own crimes in the *cosca*'s territory and who were willing to cooperate with the *cosca*, acknowledge the supremacy of its *capo*, and split their take with him.

A *cosca* might engage in a variety of activities; still, its raison d'être was always protection. Ideally, the *capo* would place a member of his immediate family—a son, a nephew, or son-in-law—as the mafia "partner" on each of the estates that the *cosca* controlled. These "protectorates" were the chief source of a *cosca*'s earnings.

The most obvious example was livestock theft. As we have already seen, much cattle and horse theft was organized in the interior of the province, around towns such as Lercara and Prizzi. The stolen animals would be moved singly or in small groups from property to property until they were either sold or, in the case of the cattle, butchered in clandestine slaughterhouses for sale in the city. This form of livestock theft depended on the consent and cooperation of many individuals; not least it required the consent of the *cosche* that protected the various properties through which the animals passed. Typically, the mafia protectors would expect some present or cut, most of which would be passed along to the *capo*.

Sangiorgi tried to assign a *cosca* membership to all those involved in this theft; yet this may have been an overrationalization. The organizers of livestock-stealing rings usually considered themselves independent entrepreneurs. They had cordial and mutually profitable relations with the *cosche* with which they habitually worked; yet in the event of a feud between rival *cosche*, they would usually try to remain neutral.

From a *capomafia*'s point of view, livestock theft might appear as simply another form of economic activity in which he might "wet his beak." Sangiorgi indicated the *fondo Gentile* (Gentile estate), in Mezzomonreale—between Monreale and the Porta Nuova of Palermo—as one of the centers that received stolen animals. He also indicated Villabate as an area that controlled the clandestine slaughter of animals. Unlike the thieves themselves, the mafia protectors of the *fondo* Gentile seem to have been *cosca* members; in particular, they were related to the Villabate *cosca*. Nevertheless, they had a fair amount of autonomy. Depending on circumstances, the thieves might approach the *capo* for permission to pasture animals on lands he protected, or they might ask the mafia partner himself, who would make his own arrangements, either going into partnership with the thieves or simply demanding a *pizzu* for his acquiescence and hospitality. In any case, the partner understood that he was earning money for the *cosca*, not simply for himself.

In representing the *cosche* as organized territorially, Sangiorgi was following local convention. This is a scheme that makes the spread of the mafia easy to visualize. The scheme was a convenience, especially to the police, used to thinking in terms of precincts, districts, and tidy administrative boundaries. Nevertheless, the scheme is something of a misrepresentation. The structure of the mafia might be better described not as a jigsaw puzzle of tiny *cosca* states but as a network of personal relationships. This network was formed from the friendships and understandings between bosses (*capi* and *sottocapi*) and between these bosses and their more important associates and "clients" (we shall look more closely at this relation in the next chapter). Although it is harder to visualize the mafia in this way, thinking of it as a network of personal contacts helps explain how the *cosche* actually operated.

One difficulty with the territorial scheme of the mafia is that it is based on demographic units: each community has its own *cosca*. Thus, Sangiorgi duly provided a list of the *capi*, *sottocapi*, and members of the mafia of Malaspina, Uditore, and Passo di Rigano (to name the three towns mentioned by Galati) as well as six others in this particular area.[55] Yet it is clear from this and other reports that the center of a *cosca*'s principal interests—and rivalries—was not its community but the estates over which each *cosca* strove to impose a protectorate.

The confines of these estates did not even remotely correspond to the territorial boundaries of the communities. A *cosca*'s power was measured in the size and number of properties it controlled, and it did not matter if these properties were not contiguous, or even if they were scattered throughout various parts of the Conca d'Oro. It followed that there were no natural boundaries that separated the territory of one *cosca* from that of another. Demography was at best a weak indicator: an estate that drew the bulk of its work force from Malaspina might be expected to have a protector from the Malaspina *cosca*, while those whose workers came from Uditore might be protected by the Uditore *cosca*. Yet even by Galati's time the two communities had begun to overlap, and estates in the northern suburbs might, conveniently, find workers in any of a number of nearby communities.

This does not mean, of course, that a *cosca* did not fiercely defend its territory; it merely means that the territories that a *cosca* did defend were those it controlled (wherever they might lie) rather than those that happened to be located in the communities in which the *capi* or *sottocapi* lived. Furthermore, the most important factor determining the shape of a *cosca's* power was usually the kinship network of the *capi* and *sottocapi*. By the 1890s, Sicilians were spreading out, and families whose kinship network a hundred years before might have been limited to the territory of a single village, now had cousins, nephews, and in-laws in the city, in towns and villages throughout the province, and even in far-off America. Sicilians who, to judge from Sangiorgi's territorial representation, should have been members of their local *cosche* frequently turn out to have been allied to rival *cosche*. One frequently discovers that these "traitors" were cousins or nephews of the leading families of rival *cosche*.

The ambivalence of a *cosca* as, on the one hand, a territorial unit and, on the other, a "clan" or "family" whose younger generation was constantly seeking new properties to protect and new activities to control helps explain the mafia wars that broke out in the Conca d'Oro. Much of Sangiorgi's report is devoted to elucidating the war that took place between the Siino and the Giammona clans in the 1890s.

According to Sangiorgi, until 1894 the *caposupremo* of the Palermo mafia (or at least of the northern suburbs) was the fifty-year-old Francesco Siino, *capo* of the Malaspina *cosca*. Allied with him was the Uditore *cosca*, whose *capo* was Francesco's elder brother Alfonso, and whose *sottocapo*, Filippo Siino, was both nephew and son-in-law to Francesco.[56] The Siino clan had other allies and branches of the family that extended its power throughout the Conca d'Oro and even into continental Italy.

The power of the Siino clan was contested, however, by younger families. First, it was challenged by the Colli mafia, whose *capo*, Giuseppe Biondi, wanted to eliminate the Siino protectorate over the ex-*feudo* of the Bracco-Amari family, located in the Colli area. They were rivals for the ex-

*feudo* Politi in nearby Pallavicino as well, whose protector, Rosario Gentile, was first affiliated with the Siino clan but later changed sides. These younger *capi* tended to be allied with the Giammona family. The *sottocapo* in Colli, Gaetano Cina, was, in fact, one of Antonino Giammona's sons-in-law.[57] Antonino's son Giuseppe Giammona was the *capo* of the Passo di Rigano *cosca*. His *sottocapo*, Salvatore Bonura, was the head of another mafia family with ambitions to take over the Siino protectorates.

By the 1890s, the role of Antonino Giammona was that of patriarch and elder statesmen. Sangiorgi referred to him as "the directive intellect" behind the mafia, for which "he sets the course, thanks to his long experience as an old ex-con, giving instructions on how to commit crimes and create defensive positions, especially by alibis."[58] He played no part in the war against the Siino clan. It was rather Giammona's allies, Bonura, Biondi, and Cina, leaders of the younger *mafiusi*, bent on taking over all of the Siino territories, who initiated hostilities. They started by robbing and vandalizing properties under the protection of the Uditore *cosca*. According to Sangiorgi:

> Among the canons of the mafia there is one regarding the respect for the territorial jurisdictions of other [*cosche*]. The infraction of this canon constitutes a personal insult. Hence the encroachments of the Giammona group were perceived by the Siino family as an atrocious personal insult. . . . [The Giammona group] was trying to shame the Siino family toward whom they felt personal hatred out of jealousy in regard to Gaetano Cinori, son-in-law of the old Giammona [i.e., Antonino], and also on account of an old blood feud and for conflicts of interest.[59]

This reference is not entirely clear. In a later report, however, Sangiorgi wrote that from 1892 to 1895, the Giammona clan had committed a series of murders of *mafiusi* who had insulted them by violating their territories. This may explain the reference to the "old blood feud" and "conflicts of interest."[60]

By the beginning of 1897, according to Sangiorgi, "the economic resources [of the Siino clan] had begun to run dry. Not even the various expedients proposed by this or that *capo* managed to restore their earnings."[61] This reference to "various expedients" is again, at this stage, obscure; we discover its probable meaning in a later report. Just as in the 1960s, when the Palermo mafia realized that contraband cigarette smuggling rings could be transformed into a drug smuggling network, so in the 1890s the Siino family found that the extensive network of personal contacts involved in livestock theft proved useful in establishing a counterfeiting ring.[62]

At the center of this ring was the Falde *cosca*, whose *capo*, Giuseppe Gandolfo, was closely allied with Francesco Siino.[63] In December 1896, however, the Falde *cosca*'s counterfeiting workshop was raided by the *carabinieri* of Resuttana Colli. There followed a series of arrests in the Conca d'Oro, in Lercara Friddi (which, as the center of the livestock theft ring in the interior, was drawn into the counterfeiting operations as well), and from as far away as Venice.[64]

The breakup of the counterfeiting ring resulted in a chain of killings. Francesco Siino may have suspected that the Giammona clan had tipped off the police. This was a natural enough suspicion, though it was probably untrue. Antonino Giammona's contacts with the livestock theft rings of the interior can be traced as far back as 1862; Siino had based his counterfeiting operations on a network that remained closely tied to Antonino Giammona. Siino may have particularly suspected that the tip-off came from the Villabate *cosca*, another group of associates that retained its links with Giammona. In any case, in January 1897, Francesco Siino called a mafia assembly. "All right," he is reported to have told the members, "since no one any longer respects me as they should, let every group fend for itself."[65] This was taken as both a renunciation of his position as *caposupremo* and a declaration of open war against the Giammona clan.

Up to now, neither Antonino Giammona nor even his son Giuseppe seems to have intervened in the feud that had been initiated and carried out through their allies and subordinates. In 1897, however, there were four mafia murders in the Palermo area (popularly called "the case of the four disappearing bodies") in which the victims were collectively murdered and (in three cases) dumped in a well, where they were not found for several months.

A *cosca* war typically unfolded as a series of ambushes. Single *mafiusi* were virtually always gunned down by three or four of their rivals, armed with shotguns and lying in wait for their intended victim. These killings might take place in broad daylight, for no one would "see" anything. The reason why *cosca* killings were sometimes public was that a vendetta itself was public. A *cosca* wanted to kill publicly because it needed to "sign" its deeds, to let its rivals know that a vendetta had been enacted and by whom.

The public nature of a vendetta encouraged an element of ritual to enter into mafia violence. The mutilation of a victim's face was a *sfregio*, a deadly insult and an act of gratuitous aggression. Yet a *sfregio* was equally a sign, a public announcement, that the aggressor considered his victim as being without honor.

This announcement could take other forms. Concealment or elimination of the victim's corpse meant that the victim's family could not honor it with a religious burial. This was a terrible insult, and one of the reasons why "the case of the four disappearing bodies" aroused so much interest in Palermo was the public sympathy for the families who were unable to bury their sons. The offense was so tremendous that the father of one of the victims threatened to go to Rome and see the minister over it.[66]

In at least the first three cases of the disappearing bodies, when the victims were shot repeatedly by a large group of assailants and their bodies dumped in a well, the insult was fully intentional. By denying their victims honorable treatment, the mafia was announcing that, now that the war was over, transgressors were no longer considered members of feuding *cosche* but simply scum that needed to be eliminated without mercy. The added insult, in other words, was intended to show that the murders were not vendetta killings but an official execution.

The victims were all minor *cosca* members accused of betrayal or of encroaching on the territories of neighboring *cosche*. What was remarkable about these murders was not the identity of the victims but the fact that they did not receive their punishment at the hands of the *capi* or the *cosche* they had offended; instead, according to Sangiorgi, they were executed by order of a commission of *capimafia*, assembled to put an end to the spiral of violence and feuding, which by now was reaching dangerous proportions. The executions were carefully planned: on Sunday evening, October 4, 1897, while the *capimafia* who had formed the commission were publicly attending a banquet in one tavern, three of the victims, believing that they too had been invited to a banquet, were driven to various locations in Palermo. They left their carriages and walked with their escorts into a tavern filled with a large number of men. As soon as they entered, the doors were closed behind them; the victims were surrounded by their escorts and the men inside the tavern and shot. Their murders had a collective, public, almost ritualistic character: every man present fired his bullet into the body.[67]

The murders were a signal that the commission of *capimafia* was out to enforce peace between the warring *cosche*. They also signaled that the Giammona family, which had assembled the commission of *capimafia*, was now reasserting its place as the leading mafia family in the northern and northwestern districts of Palermo and the Conca d'Oro. If Sangiorgi gives no information about whether the new peace had been brokered by Antonino and Giuseppe Giammona or whether they helped arrange the four murders, it may have been because his sources of information were closer to the Siino family.

In any case, the peace came too late to save the Siinos. The mafia commission ordered the two families to make peace. In October 1897, shortly after the first attempt on Francesco's Siino's life, the leading Siino and Giammona family members arrived with their bodyguards at the old 1866 rebel headquarters, the church of San Francesco di Paolo in the Borgo. Here both Antonino Giammona and Francesco Siino solemnly swore to end their feud. The ceremony did little to reassure Siino; he declared that he wanted to move to Livorno, and advised his nephew and son-in-law Filippo to do the same. Filippo, however, refused to abandon Palermo and leave the Siino family interests undefended. His house in Malaspina was too exposed, however, so he moved with his cousins Giuseppe and Michele into the city, to a house in the Borgo, where he remained, surrounded by bodyguards.

He was now being hunted by the Bonura family and by the *cosca* from Colli. They tried to persuade Francesco's *sottocapo* in the Malaspina *cosca*, Giuseppe Lombardo, to murder him. Lombardo preferred to remain loyal to his old friends, and seems to have refused. In the end, the murder was planned and executed by Giuseppe Biondi of the Colli *cosca*. Throughout 1897, his followers had been systematically murdering the Siino guardians on neighboring estates. At twilight on June 8, 1898, as he was getting ready to mount his carriage and ride to Porta Macqueda, Filippo Siino was ambushed and killed by four shotgun blasts fired at close range. His carriage driver was severely wounded.[68]

Francesco was inconsolable. He had delayed his departure, and now the murder of Filippo marked the irrevocable defeat of himself and his family. "We counted ourselves and we have counted the others," he declared. "We're 170, including the *cagnolazzi*; they're 500. They've got more money than we do, and they've got influence that we don't have. We've got to make peace."[69]

Leopoldo Franchetti later wrote that the mafia wars in Palermo in the 1890s resembled the Squarcialupo rebellion in the 1500s. Anyone who knows the story of the Palermo baronage, especially in the sixteenth century, will recognize that, in its economic motivations and methods, and perhaps most in its human drama, this is indeed the truth. This may be the reality behind the references to the mafia as a form of feudalism or a form of chivalry. Those who maintain that the mafia was an aspect of Sicilian feudalism have this point in their favor.

We might end with a footnote. Much work certainly might be done on the relation between the *squadre* in 1848 and 1860 and the growth of the mafia from 1866, for there are likely to be documents still untouched in local archives. Yet such information will always be hard to interpret, and its survival is such a matter of chance that it seems unlikely that any statistical conclusions can ever be drawn. We will probably never be able to definitively answer the questions, "How many *squadristi* became mafiosi?" or "How many mafiosi had revolutionary backgrounds?" Witnesses in the 1867 inquiry did not go into the matter very deeply; they took the link between the rioters in 1866 and the *squadristi* in 1860 and 1848 as a matter of common knowledge and left it at that. In the case of the Monrealesi, and doubtless others as well, there can be little doubt that a link existed. By 1866, the dangerous classes had begun to operate on their own.

# 6

## Violent Brotherhoods:
## The Mafia from 1866
## to the Stoppaglieri

After 1860 it would take more than the simple promulgation of the Albertine Statute to force Sicily into the Piedmontese mold. Even in the most favorable of circumstances, Sicily's assimilation into the Piedmontese state could only prove a long and awkward business.

Circumstances, too, were anything but favorable. Political necessities had forced Cavour into a preemptive strike, a miniature coup d'état which negated the Sicilian revolution's grasp for power. It was a maneuver that forestalled his enemies, but one that would also render Sicily all but ungovernable for the next fifteen years.

The victory of Cavour and La Farina changed nothing; the problem facing the Piedmontese in December 1860 was the same as the one that had confronted Crispi six months before: What was the new state to rest upon? Where were the intermediaries? What was to function as, in the words of

a later political generation, the transmission belt, bringing orders and reforms from above to the masses waiting below?

On December 14, Cavour wrote to Victor Emmanuel: "Our aim is
clear; it is not susceptible to discussion. It is to impose unity upon the
weakest and most corrupt part of Italy. About the means there is not much
to discuss either; we will use moral force and, if that is not enough, physical force."[1] In context, Cavour was intending simply to express his determination to take the situation in hand, whatever the cost. Seen from the
vantage of hindsight, however, it seems a dismal prospect: lacking cadres,
lacking friends, lacking even trustworthy sources of basic information, the
government would quickly be forced to fulfill its mandate through "physical force" alone.

## Sicily under the Right

The English resident in Palermo observed in 1866 that the Bourbons
had coped with crime either "by exceptional laws, or by systematic compacts with the criminal population."[2] Cavour never contemplated continuing in such a fashion. Northern liberals agreed with the Neapolitan historian Pietro Colletta that "the vicious circle of crimes, savage punishments,
amnesties, and worse crimes"[3] was the result of state mismanagement. The
first governments of the unified Italian state were dominated by the party
of Cavour and his successors—the Historic Right. This was the party that
first sought to impose order on Sicily. How well did they succeed?

For Turin in 1860, Sicily was politically uncharted territory. In that year
Cavour sent his friend and confidant Diomede Pantaleone on a mission,
first to the continental South, and then to Sicily. Pantaleone was to make
contact with members of Cavour's National Society, asking them their
opinions about the political climate on the island and, in particular, the
electoral prospects of the National Society. Cavour died in 1861, before
Pantaleone had finished, and Pantaleone addressed his final report to
Cavour's successor, Bettino Ricasoli.

Pantaleone was diplomatic; the tone of his letter is subdued and re-
strained, yet it is also frank. Those with whom he talked in Palermo felt
uncomfortable about Cavour's policy of purging the followers of Garibaldi
and Crispi. Despite the government's victory in the plebiscite of 1860,
they knew that Sicily's attachment to the House of Savoy was anything but
deeply rooted. Whatever their demerits, Garibaldi and Crispi were firm

unitarians who had agreed to accept Piedmont's Victor Emmanuel as their constitutional sovereign. Besides, who was the government going to replace them with? Garibaldi was popular, and the most youthful and energetic elements of Sicilian society were following his lead. Sicilians were not nearly so enthusiastic about Cavour's National Society, nor could it be said that all of its Sicilian members had a past that would bear much scrutiny. "Tied to this party," wrote Pantaleone, "though certainly without the knowledge or consent of its leaders as to any organization of a politically sectarian character, are crooks, thugs, and cutthroats, who often, with great scandal and damage to the Government, are seen appointed even to government office on account of the protection that a sect can always offer to its adepts."[4]

Pantaleone is almost certainly alluding to La Farina, who, in his eagerness to counteract the influence of Mazzini's Party of Action, had made it clear that members of the National Society would get preferential treatment when the time came to hand out government jobs. As we saw, according to the duke di Cesarò, when the barons wanted to form a *squadra* in 1848 or 1860, they were not inclined to be "too fussy about examining all the scrapes that those [they] were recruiting had gotten themselves into." Evidently La Farina used the same no-questions-asked principles to build up the National Society.

The results could be seen in the police force. The area most affected seems to have been the Colli district in the northern suburbs of Palermo. Here public security had been in the hands of the sons, grandsons, brothers, and nephews of Salvatore Licata. Not only did the Licata family organize thefts in the Colli, but also they sent *lettere di scrocco* to the richer families in the area and vandalized the villas of those who refused to pay up.[5]

Like Antonino Giammona, Salvatore Licata had led a *squadra* in 1860, a fact that surely accounts for his appointment as head of the district police in Colli after 1860. The district included Uditore and Malaspina, whose *cosche* were already in the 1870s emerging as the dominant forces in the Palermo underworld. We are told nothing about the relations between the Giammona and the Licata families; but it is impossible to imagine them as other than cordial and mutually profitable. This may help explain why neither the police delegate nor the district prosecutor in Malaspina could help Dr. Gaspare Galati in his struggle against the Uditore mafia. It may also help explain why neither the prefect nor the state prosecutor nor the chief of police in Palermo was ever informed about what was happening in the Colli district. Licata and his family had a network of friends, and Giammona was a captain in the National Guard, patron of a large religious confraternity, and head of a local landowners' association. He had been decorated by the government for his services in 1866. Although local officials were aware of the situation, they thought twice before denouncing such well-connected and influential men.

As a result, nothing was known or even suspected at the top. When Giacomo Pagano, who had inherited some lands around Malaspina, went to police headquarters in 1875 to complain about the thefts of fruit that he suffered at the hands of the Licata family in league with his caretakers, the chief of police, Pietro Biundì, refused to believe him. He denied that the thefts could have been the work of the Licata family and told Pagano, most unhelpfully, that it was a matter for the local police in Colli to deal with.

Obviously dissatisfied with such a reply, Pagano demanded to see the prefect, Count Rasponi. Rasponi commiserated with Pagano, but said there was nothing he could do. He lacked information about the suburbs of Palermo, and in any case, he did not have the manpower to investigate the complaints. Commenting on this matter before the 1875 parliamentary investigative committee, Pagano remarked that it seemed strange that he, as a private citizen, should have been so much better informed about organized crime than the prefect, who, all his reports and police confidants notwithstanding, lacked any clear picture of what was going on.[6]

Nor was this criminal infiltration limited to the police. Di Cesarò testified before the 1875 hearings how, in the early 1870s, "one of the most esteemed citizens of Sicily," and, *caso raro*, "someone blindly devoted to the government," Francesco Vassallo Paleologo, had visited Rasponi's predecessor as prefect, Giacomo Medici, to inform him confidentially of "certain matters that were going on in Piana dei Colli." At the end of the week, when he returned to his suburban villa, he was visited by a *contadino* who warned him that he should keep clear of the area for a while as it had become known that he had denounced "some influential people" to Medici. Surprised, Paleologo asked the man what he had heard, and the *contadino* repeated all the details of the conversation that he had had with Medici.[7] Like the sectarians in the 1850s, the underworld had tapped into the state's own network of confidential information, and were usually one step ahead of the state. If Paleologo wished to see his properties protected, he would be well advised to come to terms with the men who were really in charge.

Most of this infiltration had taken place without the knowledge or desire of senior Sicilian police officials—but not all of it. We have seen that the Bourbons maintained control not only through "exceptional laws," but also through "systematic compacts with the criminal population." During the 1875 inquiry, one of the judges from Palermo testified that the police had "fallen into the error of thinking . . . that they could control one half of the mafia by having the other half under their control and at their disposition."[8] This was confirmed by the jurist and senator Andrea Guarneri, who testified that the government had tried to base the lower ranks of the police force on the mafia. This, he continued, "was a serious mistake," for "the government counted upon those elements to keep police officials informed, paying them—in a moral sense as well—in favors—making them rural guards, giving them arms permits, the sorts of little favors that police officials can do."[9]

Tacit forms of cooperation between the authorities and the *malavita*, or criminal underworld, had existed for centuries. In the 1850s, however, in the hands of Salvatore Maniscalco as chief of police, they blossomed into a close and effective working relation. Maniscalco could use his network of informers, confidants, and friends as an instrument of pressure. If an important crime occurred—a vendetta killing, a major livestock theft, the kidnapping of a son or the dishonoring of a daughter—and the perpetrators were thought to be protected by local and family solidarity, Maniscalco would set this instrument in motion, arresting the family, friends, and protectors of the suspects and detaining them until they either gave the suspect up or, alternatively, came to a settlement with the injured party. These settlements were informal, extralegal agreements; they were intended less as a means of punishment than as a means of avoiding protracted blood feuds that would disrupt public security and prove costly to both parties.

It was a technique of pressure and informal arbitration that extended to crime as well. Since a *cosca* was likely to regard the encroachment of another *cosca* as "a deadly insult," such encroachments were a major cause of *malavita* wars. Maniscalco realized this, and understood that one way of preventing such wars was to treat established underworld bosses with "respect," helping them to keep the younger *cagnoli* and *cagnolazzi* in order.

During the 1867 inquiry, the newly appointed chief of police in Palermo, Giuseppe Albanese, went out of his way to praise Maniscalco for the way in which he had "involved the *capi* of the Mafia in the maintenance of security."[10] It does not seem far-fetched to infer from this that Albanese had already decided to imitate Maniscalco's tactics himself. Yet Maniscalco had been backed by an absolutist government; he could arrest anyone he liked for as long as he liked, and could see to it that his actions would never be made public knowledge. After 1860, however, such methods were no longer possible.

In 1857, Maniscalco had been knifed as he was entering Palermo Cathedral for Sunday Mass. His would-be assassin, never apprehended, was an underworld figure working with the sectarians.[11] Albanese, who probably never imagined that his emulation of Maniscalco would lead this far, was similarly wounded in 1869. In this case, however, the assailant was immediately apprehended. He was revealed to be "one of the most dangerous mafiosi, knife wielders, and men of violence" in Palermo. When asked to state his motives, he explained that Albanese had been putting pressure on him to work for the police. When he refused, Albanese had threatened him with *domicilio coatto*, a form of internal exile available to the police under emergency conditions. The man had influential connections who intervened for him, but Albanese still remained firm: "either the police or *domicilio coatto*." Unable to contain himself, he attacked Albanese in the street (and received a sentence of twenty years' hard labor as a consequence).

This information was revealed during an 1875 parliamentary debate on public security in Sicily by Diego Tajani, state prosecutor in Palermo during the early 1870s.[12] Tajani declared that in 1870 he had found evidence that police officials in Palermo, Monreale, and Misilmeri were involved in thefts and extortion. He had discovered that some of these officers were either confidants of Albanese or involved in his contacts with the underworld. He had received a letter from the two young sons of a property owner in Monreale who were in hiding from a murder warrant that had been issued against them, though they had assured the police in Monreale that they would appear for their trial. In their letter to Tajani, the two boys claimed that the real murderers were police officials. They asked for safe conduct in order to present their evidence to Tajani himself.

Tajani decided to grant their request. Several days later, he learned that they had both been murdered. He discovered evidence which led him to suspect that the order to murder the two boys had come from the Palermo police. With this he decided on the unusual step of making out a warrant for the arrest of Albanese himself.[13] The government intervened in time, and the matter was hushed up before a scandal could break out, though Albanese was forced to resign, his career ruined.[14]

## The Fall of the Right

The government's inability to take control in Sicily, its inability to obtain information or even know who were its friends and who were not, lay behind the "deep and prolonged misunderstanding between the Country and Authority" Count Gualterio complained of in his 1865 report. The report was written in the spring, while Giuseppe Badia was still hiding out in the countryside. Thinking perhaps of the political unrest stirred up by the revolutionaries, as well as the robberies and kidnappings of Angelo Pugliese and his band, Gualterio noted that various political factions had all been involved in recent crimes. He continued that, on his return to Sicily, Giovanni Corrao had sought out the mafia, and, once he was assured of its support, the revolutionaries and the mafia had passed over to the Bourbon party. The alliance with the mafia and the Bourbons was maintained after Corrao's death by Badia. Seeing these links develop, Gualterio wrote, the followers of Crispi and Mazzini, as well the editors of the pro-Crispi *Il Percursore*, grew alarmed—so alarmed that they had ceased to oppose the government and had now become firm supporters of the moderates in Turin.[15]

By 1865 the state was virtually besieged: the army could not guarantee public security; "gang robberies in houses and on the highways, murder of police officers and other officials, *sequestrations* . . . , attacks upon the mails and other public conveyances, had," as the English resident noted, "become a daily occurrence."[16] Public confidence in the authorities had plummeted. The government, as Gualterio continued in his report,

> has found itself without the due moral authority to request the support of the numerous class of influential and authoritative citizens, . . . and, therefore, during the recent outbreak of crime and unrest (which has many links with the various parties) has found itself unable to reassure the populace concerning the efficacy of its acts and bring to an end the unfortunate results that this outbreak of crime has produced.

It was this isolation that was leading to the "deep and prolonged misunderstanding between the Country and Authority" which "contributed to make it possible that the so-called Maffia, or dishonest association, was able to grow in audacity." Two years later, in a report to the prefect, a police deputy from the interior put matters much more succinctly. "Let us be frank," he wrote. "Authority and the Government have very few friends here."[17]

We can see the truth of this most easily in the interior. The band of Angelo Pugliese was the nucleus from which new brigand bands, active in the late 1860s and early 1870s, formed. By 1875 the network of complicity, already existing under Pugliese, had hardened into a veritable brigand corridor extending from the hinterland beyond Termini Imeresi and Cefalù all the way to the south coast around Sciacca.[18]

Here the police and army could make little headway, for local landowners refused their cooperation. Certain of these landowners, such as the Guccione family, acted from self-interest and for criminal gain. This could not be said of all, or even most, of the landowners, however. Most landowners simply paid protection money to the bands. Why were they so reluctant to help the police free them from the brigands? What did they gain from acquiescing to extortion? When the question was debated in 1875, the deputy from Aragona in Agrigento province, the duke di Cesarò, gave a very simple explanation: "In the eyes of the ignorant local populace, a government that receives taxes without guaranteeing lives or property plays the part of . . . the bands! Bands that receive taxes and guarantee public security play the role of legitimate government!" The parliamentary record notes that this speech was received with cries of *"Bravissimo!! Bravo!* on the left—noises on the right."[19]

The idea that landowners in the interior cooperated with brigands because they trusted them more than the police and preferred dealing with them was, of course, totally unacceptable to the government. Yet even the police had to admit that it was sometimes true. In the 1890s, Antonio Cutrera was sent as police delegate to Cammarata. His mission was to capture one of the last remaining brigand leaders, Francesco Paolo Varsalona. He approached the mayor, who turned out to be surprisingly unenthusiastic over the prospect of Varsalona's capture. When asked about it, records Cutrera, the mayor replied:

> "They say that Varsalona is a great evil, but it doesn't seem that way to me. Instead, I find it all quite logical; while the state is incapable of defending our persons, thanks to a contribution that doesn't cost our communal budget a thing, Varsalona guarantees us our lives and our possessions. Besides, what harm does he do? He doesn't kidnap anybody; he doesn't"—at least according to the mayor—"kill anybody. He just lives and lets live."[20]

Di Cesarò and the mayor of Cammarata were not, of course, defending brigandage per se. They were rather arguing that, scandalous and amoral as it may have seemed, many Sicilians *trusted* local brigands far more than they did the police.[21]

The situation was, if anything, worse in the Palermo region. Partinico was emblematic. In 1868 the prefect, Giacomo Medici, wrote to the min-

"... What harm does he do? He doesn't kidnap anybody; he doesn't—at least according to the mayor—kill anybody. He just lives and lets live." Posed portrait of Francesco Paolo Varsalona after his capture. Archivio Lo Presti.

ister of justice complaining about the behavior of the local prosecutor, Cuneo.[22] The Palermo police chief, Giuseppe Albanese, had ordered the mounted guards of Partinico to arrest a certain Vito Celeste, charged with the attempted murder of the public security agent of Salemi. Celeste, however, was a *squadra* leader from 1866, a party boss in Partinico, and a close friend of prosecutor, Cuneo, who simply countermanded Albanese, ordering that the mounted guards be jailed instead.

According to an accompanying letter from Albanese,[23] the mounted guards had been sent in to clear out the brigands who had been infesting the Partinico area. Some of these brigands were Cuneo's cousins, and it was to protect his friends and family that Cuneo had ordered the arrest of the guards, seven of whom were currently languishing in Partinico's jail. According to Medici and Albanese, Cuneo had ordered their arrests on the basis of totally fabricated charges, using depositions of false witnesses who turned out also to be cousins of Cuneo and Celeste.

Medici and Albanese had ample grounds for demanding the removal of Cuneo. Partinico had lapsed into a state of lawlessness: municipal administration was corrupt and ineffectual (Albanese characterizes the town clerk as "indescribably venal"); there were gang shoot-outs in broad daylight; local factional leaders hired assassins to eliminate their rivals; and the former mayor was a fugitive from justice.[24] Yet the only local help forthcoming issued from groups with precedents and motives as unappetizing as those of the brigands the state wished to prosecute.

Sometimes the state simply tried to push past these obstacles. The report includes a letter from the army commander in the Partinico area, under whose direct orders the mounted guards were almost certainly operating. The commander confirms Medici's version; he goes on to confirm as well, however, that the stories about the "excessive zeal" of the mounted guards and their "none too regular treatment of their prisoners" were all too true, adding only the pharisaical justification, "Should not the rigors of the law be attenuated in respect to the end achieved."[25]

How could the state clean up this mess without local support? Medici had little choice. In 1869, repeating his pessimistic assessment of the public security situation, he requested even more stringent police powers to enable him to circumvent the local magistrates and politicians who were hampering his efforts.[26] Between 1870 and 1875, in fact, pressed continually by Medici and Albanese, the government conceded to the police in Sicily ever more ample powers of search, seizure, and arrest without judicial warrant.

In 1874, under pressure from its own officials in Sicily, the government of Marco Minghetti proposed once again to strengthen emergency legislation in Sicily. The government's proposals were debated before the Chamber of Deputies in the late spring of 1875. Prior to this debate, the government seems to have leaked some of the prefectural reports on Sicily, calculating, perhaps, that the dire conditions revealed in these reports would convince waverers that urgent measures had to be taken. The maneuver, backfired, however: instead of rallying support to the government, it united southern, and particularly Sicilian, deputies, deeply offended at the arrogant language with which certain northern officials had described Sicilian society.

These officials, probably never imagining that their words would be rendered public, made no effort to disguise their true feelings. For example, in response to the question of what was the cause of the mafia, the prefect from Caltanissetta, Guido Fortuzzi, had cited the "pervertimento morale" of the Sicilian population, "for whom the ideas of justice, honesty, and honor are dead letters, and who, in consequence, are rapacious, bloodthirsty, and superstitious."[27] This was plainly insulting. Luigi La Porta stood up in the chamber to rebut the insinuations: "Sicily, o signori, is not offended. Its honor stands well above the words of one such as Signor Fortuzzi." At this point Saverio Friscia from Sciacca cut him short. He jumped to his feet and shouted, "The *civiltà* of Sicily lies in its glorious deeds!"[28]

"Glorious deeds" was a clear reference to Sicily's tradition of insurrection. In a debate on the deteriorating conditions of public security in Sicily, this was more than most northern deputies were prepared to take. Yet Friscia was an anarchist— the only anarchist ever to sit in the Italian parliament. He was convinced that it was Sicily's destiny to regenerate Italy, and perhaps the rest of the world as well, by violent revolution—just as it had in the time of the Vespers.

During his speech, La Porta listed some of the excesses committed by the police in Sicily. He included the story that, before the 1866 uprising, the police in Misilmeri had raped the wives of prisoners before their husbands' eyes. This was a charge that had already been brought up in the 1867 inquiry, where the witness who recounted it was none other than Giovanni Nicolosi, testifying as mayor of Lercara Friddi.[29]

La Porta's reference to the story in the 1875 debate, as well as Friscia's evocation of Sicily's insurrectionary tradition, were emblematic. By now the opposition was no longer divided between autonomists, ex-Garibaldini, Mazzinian unitarians, and revolutionaries; its members were speaking as Sicilians in the name of an aggrieved Sicilian nation. The opposition had at last found its voice. During the debate, not only did virtually the entire Sicilian contingent in parliament (the silence of marchese di Rudinì was the notable exception) rise to condemn the activities of the police in Sicily, but the followers of Crispi took pains to declare as well their solidarity with revolutionaries, brigands, and mafiosi—all victims of governmental oppression.

## The Stoppaglieri of Monreale

Martial law was a failure. The presence of troops on the island meant that the state would be able to suppress any attempted insurrection, but as 1866 had shown, it could not prevent attempts from taking place. In towns such as Partinico, where factional rivalries ended in public shoot-outs, mounted guards might restore order; but they were not enough to resolve the original disputes or even ensure that the gunmen would not be back on the streets the minute they rode out of town. Guards might sometimes chase down brigand bands; but they could not prevent a brigand corridor from developing. Martial law kept chaos at bay, but this was not control. Control meant inducing Sicilians to accept the government as the legitimate authority and to settle their disputes through legitimate means. This Sicilians were reluctant to do, often trusting brigands and criminals more than the authorities.

What could the state do about this? If it did nothing, the mafiosi who collected their pizzu and the bands who, as di Cesarò put it in his speech before the parliamentary committee "receive taxes and guarantee public security," would continue to "play the role of legitimate government." If it tried to restore legality, however, it would be accused of "excessive zeal" and a "none too regular treatment of . . . prisoners."

What the state really needed was information. The prefects needed to know who was on their side and who were their enemies, even when these latter were decorated with medals, even when they were part of the police force. If the state did not know this, its claim to represent legitimate authority was largely theoretical. The mafia held all the advantages: the mafiosi may not have had legitimate authority, but they knew what was going on. The state must have realized this. This is why, it is likely that well before Gualterio's 1865 report, the Palermo police had begun to cultivate underworld contacts. There were difficulties in this policy, however. How could the state be sure that the mafia could be trusted? The state authorities did not really know who they were dealing with. Nor did they even seem to care.

Studying the mafia in either the Sicilian or the national archives in Rome, one finds it striking that the Ministry of the Interior and the Ministry of Justice were interested in crimes only when they had a political connection. Prefects and police chiefs regarded nonpolitical crimes as the responsibility of the local police. Their job was rather to report on republicans and Bourbons supposedly plotting the overthrow of the new Italian state. Had the state cultivated the mafia to learn about Sicily, it might have learned more. Instead, the state authorities cultivated the mafia as a stalking horse to lead them into the Bourbon and republican camps.

As in 1848, the 1866 rebels appointed a "provisional committee" to act as the revolutionary government. The leader of this committee, the elderly prince of Linguaglossa, was largely a figurehead. The true leader was neither Francesco Bonafede nor Badia's second in command, Lorenzo Minecci (though both were on the committee), but Linguaglossa's secretary, Domenico Corteggiani.

Corteggiani was the revolutionary leader from Misilmeri who, on the night of April 3, 1860, had stood at the pass at Gibilrossa holding a *tricolore* while two hundred *squadristi* from Misilmeri and Villabate filed past him, each taking the corner of the flag and kissing it.[30] Corteggiani was a friend of the de Benedetto brothers, and a member of the Revolutionary Committee in Palermo since 1859. He had been chosen by the committee to lead a combined *squadra* from Misilmeri and Villabate into Palermo in support of Francesco Riso's uprising. Several months earlier he had been selected for the same role in the uprising of Giuseppe Campo. In both cases, Corteggiani had been wise enough to turn back before it was too late.[31]

Corteggiani and his brothers were important landowners in the Misilmeri area. Domenico was also a pharmacist. This was a piece of information that made a nineteenth-century police official prick up his ears; weapons and munitions were still made by hand, and a pharmacist possessed a license that entitled him to purchase the ingredients for gunpowder. Just as today a chemist with shady connections is automatically suspected of refining drugs, so a nineteenth-century pharmacist with radical opinions was automatically under suspicion as a cartridge and bomb maker. The Revolutionary Committee had contacts with ironmongers who cast cannons and muskets and pharmacists who clandestinely manufactured powder for them. This was still true in 1866, for, according to the police, the Misilmeri *squadra* in the 1866 uprising were supplied with munitions manufactured by the Corteggiani brothers on the Calamisi estate.[32]

Another member of the Revolutionary Committee in 1866 was Rosario Miceli from Monreale, who may have been Turi Miceli's nephew. Rosario Miceli was also a *squadra* leader in both 1848 and 1860. Sometime in the early 1860s, angry at his failure to obtain a state pension, Rosario Miceli went over to Giuseppe Badia's group.[33] He led a *squadra* in 1866, and was possibly one of the leaders of the original group of thirty or so Monrealesi who set off for Palermo on the night of September 15, 1866.

Most of the members of the 1866 committee—Bonafede, Minecci, Corteggiani, Rosario Miceli, Father Spadaro, and others—were jailed for their parts in the uprising.[34] They found themselves in prison alongside Badia and the others arrested with him in 1865, as well as republicans—such as the Buscemi brothers and Salvatore di Paolo—who had harangued the crowds or led the *squadre* during the uprising, or those who were later reported to have been part of the original revolutionary plot.[35]

Most of these revolutionaries were released around 1869. Yet their political history kept them under police surveillance. This fact has proved to be an advantage for us. The police reports on these marked men allow us to enter the shadowy world where the revolution, the police, and the mafia met.

Soon after his release in 1869, Badia and his associates paid a visit to Medici to tell him they were renouncing all further political activity. Medici took their declarations with a large grain of salt—rightly so, for soon he discovered that, inspired by schemes of Mazzini's followers in the Romagna for a "universal republic," Lorenzo Minecci and the two Buscemi brothers were drafting a constitution for such a republic in Sicily.[36]

Corteggiani and Bonafede were Mazzinians of long standing. They were in at least indirect contact with their master, and played a part in his final attempt to provoke an uprising in Sicily in 1870.[37] Corteggiani and his brothers had a house in Palermo near the Porta Macqueda. Here, in August 1870, following a tip-off, army engineers excavated under the floor and found a workshop and a number of men making cartridges. Bonafede, the Buscemi brothers, and the Amoroso brothers were involved in this cartridge-making scheme as well. In his report Medici described them all as followers of Badia, though he did not cite any evidence directly linking Badia with this conspiracy.[38]

Medici did not reveal the name of the informer who tipped off the police about Corteggiani's munitions workshop. We might suspect, however, that this informer was a certain Salvatore Marino from Monreale, for we know that it was Marino who told the police the details of Mazzini's plot for an insurrection.

Marino constitutes another link in the bizarre network of clerico-republican-mafioso spies which had so completely misled Chief of Police Felice Pinna about the imminent rebellion in 1866. If this network had indeed come into existence as a way of using the mafia as informers and agents provocateurs, it would explain Marino's presence in the group of plotters around Corteggiani and Bonafede. It was Tajani who, in his 1875 speech, identified Marino as the "mole" who had informed the police about Mazzini's plot in 1870. He described him as one of the "false republicans" the Palermo police had planted in the republican camp. He also mentioned that Marino had led the gang that had earlier broken into Palermo's municipal pawnshop, making off with a large haul in cash and pawned goods, though he did not say if the proceeds from the robbery were supposed to fund the impending uprising.[39]

In 1874 there was a new wave of arrests, as Medici discovered the existence of a socialist, or, as it was called at the time, "internationalist," circle in Palermo. The first to be arrested was Badia. His arrest was soon followed by those of Corteggiani, Minecci, and a Palermo student named Giuseppe Ingeneros. Also arrested was Pasquale Quattrocchi, a pharmacist from Termini Imeresi described in an 1871 police report as a "mafioso of the 1st category."[40] Shortly afterward, Bonafede and Gabriele Amoroso were arrested too.

Although Marino had been in close contact with many of those arrested, and although followers of Badia were said to have recruited adherents in Monreale, by now Marino seems to have ended his services as "false republican" and police informer and been allowed to return to Monreale, where he played an important role in the mafia.[41] In or shortly before 1875, the Monreale police arraigned him as the murderer of a certain Giovanni Piazza. The parliamentary deputy for Monreale, Michelangelo Caminnecci, promised to intervene for him, though for some reason he was unable to prevent the murder case from being scheduled for trial—a failure for which Marino never forgave him.[42] Marino still had friends at the Palermo Tribunal Court, however, and he managed to have the prosecution's documents against him stolen and destroyed. These friends also supplied him with a false passport. With this he fled to New Orleans, where he joined the community of emigrant Monrealesi living there.[43]

So far our research has brought to light a group of revolutionary plotters and one police spy. We have no reason—as yet—to label any of them, with the exception of Marino, "mafiosi." Since Salvatore Marino provides a connecting thread that will lead us into the Monreale mafia, it is worth recapitulating what we have learned about him so far.

First, he was involved in revolutionary politics and had a number of republican and socialist friends. Second, after 1870 he became an important mafioso in Monreale. Third, by 1875 he had been indicted for murder. Fourth, he must have had important connections, because he arranged to have the evidence against him destroyed and obtained a false passport which he used to emigrate to New Orleans. Fifth, he was described by Tajani as a police spy. We do not know whether or not he maintained his connections with the police after he returned to Monreale. Maybe not: Albanese was interested in him only insofar as he provided information about republicans and socialists. By tipping off the police about Mazzini's projected insurrection, he might have blown his cover, rendering himself of no further use to the police. Yet even if the police had no more use for Marino, Marino might have had a use for them.

Finally, as we shall see, Marino died in New Orleans, though not before claiming that he was the *capo* of an organization numbering some 45,000 men.

In 1878 Marino was joined in New Orleans by another Monrealese in trouble with the law, Rosario La Mantia. According to La Mantia's subsequent statement, he knew no one in New Orleans when he landed there. Nevertheless, he soon managed to find a job working in the store of a certain "Francesco Alessi." His employer later confided to him that this name was an alias, and that in reality he was Salvatore Marino. It was La Mantia to whom Marino bragged of heading an organization numbering 45,000 men.

During the summer of 1878, Marino caught yellow fever. In September his condition deteriorated, and he began to fear that he would not survive the illness. He called La Mantia to his bedside and gave him a packet of secret papers. He asked La Mantia to burn these in front of him. La Mantia, however, surreptitiously switched the papers with a pile of unimportant bills, burning those instead. Evidently the ruse worked, for when Marino died on September 29, La Mantia was able to depart with the papers.

According to La Mantia, when he left New Orleans he had intended to go to Marseilles. When he docked in Le Havre, however, he suddenly decided to go to Barcelona instead. From here he traveled to Zaragoza, where he contacted the Italian consul and showed him the documents in his possession. Eventually La Mantia was taken to Rome, where he made a statement describing his contact with Marino.

The police were principally interested in two letters among the papers that La Mantia was carrying. The first letter had not been written by Marino, nor was it even addressed to him. It was signed "Pippino," and was written by Giuseppe Maraviglia.[44] This was a letter to Salvatore Matranga, another Monrealese in New Orleans.[45] The second letter was to Marino and was signed "Totó," which is short for Salvatore. The police thought that this might be either Salvatore Amoroso or Salvatore di Paolo. Eventually, with the help of calligraphic experts, they decided the writing belonged to Salvatore di Paolo's.

All four Monrealesi—Marino, Matranga, Maraviglia, and di Paolo—were described by the state prosecutor in Palermo as *tristissimi* and as "members of the association of the Stoppaglieri."[46] What was this "association"? We shall return to Marino, Rosario La Mantia, and the two letters presently; for now we must stop and try to answer this latter question.

The prosecutor who wrote these words was Carlo Morena, state attorney in Palermo between 1875 and 1878; previously he had served in Messina. During these three years much of the prefect Antonio Malsuardi's time was taken up with his campaign against brigands in the interior. This meant that the campaigns against the mafia associations were largely left in the hands of Morena. It is from Morena's letters, compiled from reports of other state prosecutors and investigating magistrates, that we can form a picture of the Stoppaglieri.[47]

The Monreale police had been hearing rumors about the Stoppaglieri since 1874, though it was not until the 1876 murder of Simone Cavallaro, a police officer and member of a rival group, that they began their investigations in earnest. Malsuardi had been hearing stories too, and had encountered similar associations in the towns of the interior. On January 30, 1877, he wrote Morena a letter informing him about the associations he had discovered in the brigand towns south of Cefalù and Termini Imeresi. These reminded him of the Stoppaglieri of Monreale and the Oblonica of Sciacca, about which he had been gathering information for two years.

Although there were certain differences between them, Malsuardi discovered that these organizations all had a similar structure. What is more, despite their differences, they employed identical passwords and recognition devices. Malsuardi thought he had discovered the center of diffusion in the mountain town of Castelbuono, and added that in particular the members of the Castelbuono association swore to help the brigands and all those in hiding from the law, and to assist in enacting vengeance against anyone found helping the police. In fact, the Castelbuono association had already issued two death warrants, one for a mounted policeman and another for a municipal guard in Castelbuono. Fortunately, neither sentence had yet been carried out.

Malsuardi regarded the associations as politically subversive; the members were sworn "to rise up in arms against the government if ever an occasion should present itself."[48] That revolution remained one of the goals of these associations was confirmed by a report that Morena sent to the minister of justice later that year in which he listed the most important cases being investigated by the prosecutor's office in Sicily. These included associations or gangs (we cannot always tell which) among whose crimes was that of "rebellion": a group of twenty-five from Syracuse province, fourteen from Trapani province, and five from Caltanissetta province. Later in the year, he found sixteen more rebels in Caltanissetta.

In March 1877, Morena replied to Malsuardi's letter.[49] After giving the matter a great deal of study, he now attempted to reconstruct the history of these associations from their origins at the beginning of the 1870s onward. The Stoppaglieri, he confirmed, was indeed one of a number of similar associations. These included the Fratuzzi of Bagheria, the mafia of the Fontana Nuova quarter of Misilmeri (which seems also to have been called either the Fratellanza or the Fratuzzi), the Oblonica in Sciacca and Caltabellota, as well as a number of others.

As they all seemed to have identical statutes and initiation rites, Malsuardi had assumed that all these associations were branches of a single organization. It was not that simple, Morena told him. Referring probably to the Carboneria, Morena argued that similar revolutionary and/or criminal brotherhoods had existed throughout Sicily since the 1830s and 1840s.[50] In fact, certain of the passwords and rituals associated with these associations derived from the *carbonaro* oaths current in that period. Salvatore Maniscalco, he wrote, had known of their existence, and had been content to use "some of these criminal congregations to exterminate others." Normally these associations only fought one another, and thus were not a real revolutionary threat. Morena added:

On only one occasion do the associations in question show an ability for common action and for a common interest. This is whenever they join to launch a local war against the police and the *Evil Government*. This is what happened during the days in September 1866; the associations formed themselves into as many *squadre*. After this, however, after they were expelled from this city, they took up their ancient rivalries where they had left off and resumed their bloody wars. This is what happened in Bagheria and other towns.[51]

Although Morena does not specify this, either these associations or their direct antecedents had supplied *squadre* in 1848 and 1860 as well. What he is describing, of course, are the offspring of the revolutionary sects that had developed out of the Carboneria before 1848 and that afterward continued to exist as secret societies with a predominantly lower-middle-class and working-class membership.

Morena went on to tell Malsuardi what he had found out about the Stoppaglieri of Monreale, which he described as the "young mafia of Monreale." In fact, most of the associations described by Morena could be similarly characterized as "young mafias." All were founded around 1870; all used similar passwords and recognition devices; all were committed to the ideal of the "universal republic." This was the ideal that, as we saw, in late 1869 or early 1870 had been borrowed from Mazzinian groups in the Romagna and adopted by Badia's followers in Palermo. Thus the Stoppaglieri and similar associations were not only "young mafia" associations but also examples of the new generation of revolutionary sects that had begun to spread into the interior of Sicily after 1870.

There were, nonetheless, a number of peculiarities about the Stoppaglieri of Monreale. First, Morena explained that the association had been founded in order to exterminate the older mafia association in Monreale, the Giardinieri. Second, unlike other mafia associations, the Stoppaglieri had been founded by the police, specifically by the police delegate in Monreale.[52] These two peculiarities were connected.

The Stoppaglieri of Monreale had indeed been founded in 1871 by the police delegate, Paolo Palmieri, together with his brother, who is not named in the reports. Its first president was a friend of Palmieri's named Giovanni Minesala,[53] who was succeeded by Saverio Spinato. We should bear in mind the date. In 1871, Albanese was still chief of police in Palermo, and though the conflict with Tajani still lay two years in the future, relations between the Palermo police and the office of the state prosecutor in Palermo had already begun to deteriorate. Thus, though Morena refrains from saying so explicitly, he leaves the clear impression that he believed the Palermo police to have been deeply compromised in the Stoppaglieri and frightened that their involvement was about to be revealed by the state prosecutor's office.

Evidently the problem remained unresolved, for Morena went on to complain that the Palermo police were still refusing to help the prosecutor's office in arresting members of the Stoppaglieri. For his part, the new chief of police in Palermo wrote to complain to Malsuardi that the state prosecutor in Monreale had refused to act against an individual identified as the leading mafioso there, Pietro di Liberto. Morena countered that there was no evidence against di Liberto. He added that the previous Monreale police chief had had nothing against him and that the last prefect under the right, Luigi Gerra, had said that about di Liberto there existed two contrasting currents of opinion.

It thus appears that there was not one but two mafia associations in Monreale, one of which had connections with the police. Even this is an oversimplification: it turns out that both had connections with the police. According to Tajani, in 1875 six of the major public security officials in Monreale were noted mafiosi. These included the commander of the rural guards, the commander of the suburban guards, and four captains of the National Guard. Although Tajani did not specify whether these men were Stoppaglieri or Giardinieri, it is noteworthy that several of the Giardinieri were later described as "captains" in the National Guard.[54] Both the Giardinieri and the Stoppaglieri were thus connected with the Palermo police; their connections, however, arose in different periods.

The old mafia of Monreale, the Giardinieri, was the mafia of the *squadre* in 1866, the mafia of Turi and Rosario Miceli. Presumably the red-capped and red-scarfed Monrealesi who had marched to Palermo in 1866 were Giardinieri. Presumably this was an association with roots in 1848 and probably 1860 as well. That would explain why so many of the Giardinieri were also captains in the Sicilian National Guard, for the National Guard became a sort of veterans' association for ex-*squadristi*.

The Stoppaglieri, by contrast, was a new mafia, founded in 1871 by the police delegate of Monreale, Paolo Palmieri. Although Tajani was not aware of the Stoppaglieri when he spoke in 1875, presumably the mafia of Monreale with which Albanese had formed links was the Stoppaglieri. Even if the connection between Albanese and the Stoppaglieri cannot be proved, a connection between Albanese and Palmieri demonstrably existed. What, one wonders, did Chief of Police Albanese think of the fact that his subordinate was organizing a mafia in Monreale? Could Albanese have decided that the only way to get a reliable mafia in Monreale was to found one himself?

Connecting Albanese with the Stoppaglieri helps explain the rest of the evidence. The first piece concerns Palmieri and Albanese.

Already in 1865 Palmieri was the focal point of Police Chief Pinna's intelligence system in Monreale. Owing to the disappearance of the files, we are unable to specify what his exact role was; nevertheless, among the documents that the acting police chief, Biundì, described as missing in October 1866 was "a closed package upon whose cover was written: 'documents sent by the Delegation of Public Security of Morreale [*sic*], official-in-charge, Palmieri Paolo.' "[55] Since Pinna was interested almost exclusively in republicans, we can assume that the missing documents contained Palmieri's reports on republican activity in Monreale assembled by his mafia contacts.

That Palmieri had mafia contacts during the 1860s can probably also be inferred from a letter to Pinna's successor, Albanese, in January 1867. The letter was from the chief of police in Naples, and concerns a police attempt to use agents provocateurs to implicate the anarchist deputy, Friscia, in a republican plot. Involved were Nicasio Palmieri (or Palmeri) and Lauro Arbitale, both identified as "republican agents." Palmieri's son had in fact taken part and been wounded in the assault on Palermo in September 1866. Nothing came of the plot, and there would be no reason to suspect either Palmieri or Arbitale of being mafiosi, had not the prefect of Naples telegraphed Medici informing him that "Palmieri is with the *maffia* and Abitale is its treasurer."[56] If the Nicasio Palmieri working as a police spy in 1867 was the brother of Paolo, then he would be the brother that Antonio Cutrera identified as the co-founder of the Stoppaglieri.

In any case, Paolo Palmieri was considered to have invaluable contacts with both the revolutionary party and the underworld, and this explains not only why he emerged unscathed from Pinna's fall but also why he hung on to his office for three years after Albanese's own disgrace. During this period there was no lack of complaints: in May 1871, Medici was notified that Palmieri had revived the Bourbon practice of arresting the families of fugitives, a practice that was now illegal.[57] The complaints had been forwarded to the Palermo prefect by the minister of justice, a fact that, incidentally, helps confirm that the state prosecutor's office in Palermo had its own sources of confidential information—sources that were independent from, indeed decidedly hostile to, the Palermo police.

Particularly hated was the extensive use of agents provocateurs against suspected republicans, as this was a policy that led the police into alliance with, and into granting immunities to, the underworld. In 1870, before arriving in Sicily, Tajani had read a newspaper article describing how the uncovering of a vast republican conspiracy in Palermo had been due to the vigilance of Albanese. When he arrived in Palermo, he discovered that this conspiracy had been invented by police agents.[58] Using the network of informers who had attached themselves to the office of the Palermo prosecutor, Tajani soon uncovered other abuses which formed the basis of the accusations he leveled against Albanese several months later.

All this brings us back to Salvatore Marino, who, we should remember, was both a Stoppagliere and a police spy. It seems likely that if Albanese considered the Stoppaglieri a revolutionary sect under his control, he would have used it to force the hand of Mazzinians and internationalists. The fact that the Stoppaglieri were also killing off the Giardinieri might not have been entirely displeasing to him, for the Palermo police had something of a grudge against the Giardinieri for leading them down the garden path in 1866. If this hypothesis is true, it is testimony to how little the Palermo police had learned in the meantime. The Monreale mafia was about to take them for another ride.

In 1876 the Stoppaglieri ambushed and murdered Simone Cavallaro, a leader of the Giardinieri. The only description of this murder comes from Cutrera, and is infuriatingly obscure. While passing through Monreale one night, Cavallaro's eighty-year-old father was supposedly ambushed and taken to the house of a certain "P.D.," there to take the oath of the Stoppaglieri, "who, tired of the Italian government, wanted to make a republic."[59] The father argued that it was too late to take the oath, but promised to meet his assailants the following evening at the house of the "Grand Master." Instead, the old man went to the house of his son Simone, who sent his father to the town of San Giuseppe Jato. In the middle of the night three days later, Simone Cavallaro was shot. Although he refused to name his assailants, shortly before he died he stated that they were all Stoppaglieri.[60]

We know that Cavallaro had been one of the *squadra* leaders in 1866, and that afterwards he found a position in the Monreale police force, where he became a close friend of the captain of the mounted guards.[61] After 1874 he also became one of the first internationalists in Monreale.[62] He was thus an important local figure, and it was his murder and his denunciation of the Stoppaglieri that led the prosecutor in Monreale to open an investigation into the association.

Again we should pay attention to the date. By 1876, Palmieri, Albanese, and the government itself had all fallen, and there was a new state prosecutor in Monreale, one who was liable to regard the murder of an important Giardiniere in a different light. The prosecutor soon discovered that Palmieri's successor in Monreale, Nigri, had been submitting reports about the Stoppaglieri since 1874. Having learned from his own investigations that the association had existed since 1871, he wrote to the chief of police in Palermo, asking if there were also reports from the period between 1871 and 1874. The chief of police proved unhelpful; he denied that any such reports existed, and refused to help the Monreale prosecutor any further.[63] If the prosecutor found this attitude surprising, it was because he was still unaware how compromised the police were.

Another important murder was that of the leader of the Giardinieri, Salvatore Caputo. According to Cutrera's account, in 1874 Caputo had been told by the police delegate in Monreale that he would be put under police sanctions unless he brought in Salvatore Marino. Caputo turned to Marino's father. As both the father and the son were Stoppaglieri, Marino's father put the matter before an assembly of the association. The assembly refused the request and declared Caputo to be an *infame* (traitor), ordering his death. As a result, Caputo was killed in a Stoppaglieri ambush.[64]

Again, Cutrera's version is maddeningly obscure; as it stands, it makes little sense. If Caputo was the leader of the Stoppaglieri's rivals, the Giardinieri, why should the police have asked him to bring in Salvatore Marino? Why, if one of the principal functions of the Stoppaglieri was to protect its members from the police, would Salvatore Marino's father have put Caputo's proposal before the assembled Stoppaglieri at all?

The story becomes clearer when we learn that the police official who approached Caputo was the same Nigri who succeeded Palmieri in 1874. It was Nigri who, soon after his arrival in Monreale, first began to file reports about the Stoppaglieri. If Nigri suspected that Albanese and Palmieri had been using Marino and the Stoppaglieri to attack the old mafia in Monreale, then it would have been logical for him to approach this old mafia for information about these connections. Besides, Salvatore Caputo was no common criminal; in addition to being the head of the Giardinieri, he was a captain in the National Guard. He was also a large landowner and influential local man with many friends, especially in the Monreale police force.

Nigri had evidently collected enough evidence to have Salvatore Marino arraigned on a murder charge. At first Marino was confident that, with the promised help of his parliamentary deputy, he could beat the charge. Later, after it had become evident that his friends were either powerless or afraid to move, Marino discovered that he still had a friend who could help him remove the documents from the court records and get him a false passport. That friend may have been Salvatore di Paolo, the "Totò" of the 1878 letter to Marino. Di Paolo had been an 1860 *squadrista* who remained in the revolutionary party, and who eventually took part in the 1866 uprising, serving on the insurrectionary committee. When he was released from prison in 1869, he returned to his native Monreale, where it is likely that he was also among those who first helped organize the Stoppaglieri.[65] Before 1866, however, di Paolo had been concierge at the Supreme Court of Justice in Palermo. Di Paolo may still have had the connections that Marino needed.

It is notable that the war that the Stoppaglieri waged against the Giardinieri seems equally to have been a war against the old Monreale police. The first victim of the Stoppaglieri was a policeman, Giuseppe Lipari, murdered in April 1873. His murder was followed the year after by that of a vice brigadeer in the state police force. Simone Cavallaro was a police officer as well. Shortly before his murder, the Stoppaglieri had killed Stefano di Mitri, a rich property owner, another ex-captain of the Sicilian National Guard and another member of the old mafia.[66] One cannot help suspecting that these former captains of the Sicilian National Guard whom the Stoppaglieri were systematically liquidating were the *squadre* leaders of 1866.

If this reconstruction is correct, the Stoppaglieri were not simply an example of the new breed of republican brotherhoods that began to spread in 1870; this was also an association that enjoyed the patronage of the police delegate in Monreale, who, working in close collaboration with the Palermo police chief, wished to use it to destroy the old Monreale mafia, the Giardinieri, whose connections with both the revolutionaries and the Bourbons in the 1860s as well as with Albanese's predecessor, Felice Pinna, had allowed it to grow powerful and autonomous. Against this reconstruction, however, there is Giuseppe Guido Loschiavo's statement that the first president of the Stoppaglieri was none other than Rosario Miceli.[67] Loschiavo was a Sicilian judge writing in the 1930s. By then both the name Miceli and the Stoppaglieri had become legendary in Monreale. Although we shall see that someone named Miceli may well have been a leader of the Stoppaglieri, none of the contemporary sources associates either Turi or Rosario Miceli with the Stoppaglieri. It seems possible that, by the 1930s, Monrealese memory found it more appropriate to commemorate Rosario Miceli as the president of the Stoppaglieri rather than of the defeated Giardinieri.

There is one final problem. The records of the 1878 Stoppaglieri trial in Palermo are very incomplete; we seem to possess only the parts pertaining to the murder of Salvatore Caputo in 1876. Yet in these sections there is hardly any mention of the Stoppaglieri at all.[68]

There is an explanation for this. Since the late 1860s, Italy had passed a number of statutes designed to make membership in an association with a criminal scope a crime in itself. These were statutes specifically drawn up for use against organized crime and brigandage in southern Italy and Sicily. Yet, as Morena's predecessor had already argued in 1873, these statutes were ineffective.[69]

In 1877, Morena exchanged letters with the minister of justice. They both came to the same conclusion. It was not enough to say that an association such as the Stoppaglieri had a criminal scope; the state had to prove this by demonstrating, for example, that it was the Stoppaglieri who had murdered Cavallaro and Caputo. If the state made arrests without such proofs, either it would be denied indictments or the defendants would be acquitted by the jury. The minister of justice was particularly annoyed by the large and well-publicized show trials in which thirty, forty, or even one hundred defendants, all charged with belonging to an association with a criminal scope, had all been set free.[70] It was pure frustration, Morena agreed:

> It's always the same story! As long as it's only a case of whispering into the ear of the Delegate names and facts (sometimes implausible and contradictory), you're sure to find a thousand individuals who lay claim to the Medal of Good Citizenship. As soon as you want these names and facts repeated in a clear voice and placed on a regular deposition, which, apart from a vendetta, might cause a regular trial to take place, with witnesses and cross-examination by the defendants' attorneys, then it's a different matter. Then it's the Delegate who's made some *mistake*. . . . Nothing, nothing can be gotten out of them. Those thousand have become zero. In the end all that remains is a wearisome contrast: the moral conviction in the mind of the Judge that the crime exists, and the material lack of any proof of it presented before the court.[71]

In these circumstances, Morena thought it wiser simply to ignore the Stoppaglieri as a criminal association and try to convict its members for specific murders. This approach was not much better, however. The Caputo family no doubt would have been glad to see all the Stoppaglieri hanged, but they were not going to admit to things in court that might lead the police to investigate their own activities. Consequently, the Caputo family and their followers invented a story about a mysterious stranger seen hanging about Monreale on the morning of Salvatore Caputo's murder. The stranger, they said, was wearing a black cloak and a large straw hat, so they could not see his face. Still, they were all sure that he was the murderer. The police dutifully made inquiries, and of course found nothing.

The trial documents are nevertheless very revealing. Typically, both the police reports, which form the basis for Cutrera's description, and Morena's letters concentrate exclusively on the political aspects of the crimes of the Stoppaglieri. They express no interest in either group as an extorsion ring. The trial documents, by contrast, place the groups in their larger social context. We can see from them that most of the Stoppaglieri were in fact employed in tending or guarding the citrus groves around Monreale. Alongside the political feuds described by Morena and Cutrera, we discover a turf war such as the one between the Giammona and Siino clans. We also discover that, there were heads of large landowning families in Monreale who, like Francesco Paolo Sardofontana in Uditore, were willing to support these associations, hiring their members as part of their schemes to enlarge their holdings.

Several years after the trial, the real circumstances behind the murder of Salvatore Caputo were revealed. The instigator of the murder was identified as Teresa Miceli, the sister of a patron of the Stoppaglieri, Davide Miceli.

Davide Miceli had been murdered by the Caputo family in early 1874. His sister Teresa offered a prize of 750 lire to whichever of her family's employees would murder the head of the clan, Salvatore Caputo. Caputo was, in fact, murdered in a Stoppaglieri ambush later in the same year. Soon after Caputo's murder, the murderer himself was accidentally killed when he was struck by a falling roof tile. On his body was found the 750 lire Teresa Miceli had paid him. The victim's family offered to give the money back to her, but Teresa Miceli proclaimed publicly that they could keep it with her blessings.[72] This was taken as a public acknowledgment of responsibility. The revenge of the Stoppaglieri and the Miceli family forced the entire Caputo clan to flee from Monreale to Bagheria.

We possess little information about Davide Miceli. We know that, like Salvatore Caputo, he was a well-off landowner. He was also one of the patrons of the Stoppaglieri association. Miceli is not an uncommon name in this area, so we do not know if Davide Miceli was related to Turi and Rosario Miceli. In fact, we cannot even demonstrate that Turi and Rosario Miceli were related, though one supposes that they were. We do know, however, that the family of Turi Miceli remained important in Monreale, for in 1892 Turi's son Francesco Miceli was murdered in a mafia ambush.

The prosecutor in Monreale also discovered that branches of the Stoppaglieri were being founded in the towns around Monreale, as well as in Borghetto, Marineo, and Misilmeri, and that the association was founding branches in the Palermo region as well. This final piece of information takes us back to the two letters that Rosario La Mantia took from Salvatore Marino in 1878, which told about the Stoppaglieri's relations with other societies.

To begin with, La Mantia's own account of how he got the letters raises more questions than it answers. Monreale is not that big a town, and it is not conceivable that La Mantia would not have known who Salvatore Marino was, especially as they were both Stoppaglieri. La Mantia's story that he just happened to turn up in New Orleans, where he just happened to get work with Salvatore Marino and just happened to end up with his two letters, is not in the least credible. We can safely assume that no one— neither the police nor the various ministries and magistrates involved— ever believed it.

Salvo Lupo assumes that La Mantia was a police spy. He points out that, though under police restrictions and surveillance, La Mantia had no trouble obtaining a regular passport.[73] Furthermore, after his interrogation, the police let La Mantia disappear. He was not present as a witness in either of the trials of the men accused on the basis of his evidence, a fact that was exploited to good effect by the defense attorneys.[74] We might add that when La Mantia was interrogated, no one questioned him about his implausible cover story. Nor was the matter ever raised in correspondence between the state attorney in Palermo and the ministers of justice and interior concerning La Mantia.

But who were these state officials? The state prosecutor in Palermo was, of course, Carlo Morena. His superior, the minister of justice, was none other than his predecessor in Palermo, Diego Tajani. After the Albanese scandal, Tajani had left the state prosecutor's office and was elected to parliament in 1874. His speech during the debate on public security in 1875 caused a sensation, and in 1876 the young Tajani suddenly found himself minister of justice. Morena and Tajani thus knew exactly who Marino and the Stoppaglieri were. The minister of the interior was Giovanni Nicotera. An old Neapolitan sectarian, companion of Crispi, and one of the few survivors of Pisacane's ill-fated expedition in 1857, Nicotera would certainly have been told about the relation between the Stoppaglieri and the Palermo police. If all three refrained from making reference to either, it was probably because they also knew that relations between the police and the state prosecutor in Palermo, already strained during the 1860s, had broken down completely as a result of Tajani's attempt to arrest Albanese. It was important to reestablish good relations between the police and the prosecutor's office in Palermo, and they would not have wished to reopen old wounds. One can imagine that the three officials must have conferred privately; for official purposes, however, these cases were closed.[75]

What about La Mantia? Normally, we are never permitted to catch a glimpse of police informers at work: the police might write that they obtained their information from a "friend" or through "confidential channels"; yet they were careful to avoid mentioning these confidential sources by name. Had La Mantia really been a spy, the police would have allowed him to fade back into anonymity. Instead, La Mantia's sudden appearance at the Italian consulate in Zaragoza seems to have taken everyone by surprise. Morena even wired the Italian consulate in New Orleans to check on La Mantia's story.[76] Yet why had La Mantia gone to New Orleans in the first place? Who sent him? Did whoever sent him also know that La Mantia had left New Orleans with Marino's letters? Finally, why did La Mantia decide en route not to go to Marseilles, as originally planned, but to go to Barcelona instead? Could his change of plans have had anything to do with the fact, reported to the prosecutor's office in Palermo, that in December 1878 two other men from Monreale, Salvatore Di Paolo and Giuseppe Maraviglia, had traveled to Marseilles looking for him?[77]

Maraviglia and Di Paolo were, of course, the two Stoppaglieri who had written the letters that La Mantia was carrying. A reluctance to meet Maraviglia and di Paolo with their letters in his possession may help explain the sudden change in La Mantia's travel arrangements.

Unfortunately, the two letters are missing from the dossier, and we are forced to reconstruct their contents from the statement La Mantia made in Rome. We know that they concerned the assassinations of the Buscemi brothers and others as well as the recent arrest of the Amoroso brothers. In both letters Marino is referred to as the "president" of the association.[78] They also speak of a struggle in Monreale, presumably the war between the Stoppaglieri and the Giardinieri. Evidently the bloody chain of killings in Monreale was causing concern in the Palermo underworld, for, according to Maraviglia's letter, "the uncle of Marino" had come to Monreale to mediate between the warring groups. La Mantia's interrogators asked about this: Who was Marino's uncle? It turned out to be the son of Antonino Giammona, Giuseppe Giammona. La Mantia explained that Giuseppe Giammona was not Marino's real uncle, but was only called such owing to the special affection he had for Marino. Giammona had visited Monreale to make peace between what he called "the party of the *cagnolazzi*" and what he called "the contrary party."[79]

Maraviglia's letter mentioned a number of other "friends" as well. La Mantia also explained this reference. The term, he said, was being used ironically; Maraviglia's letter listed the men who had been murdered on Marino's orders. These killings had taken place not in Monreale, however, but mostly in the Orto Botanico district, immediately outside the city walls near the old Porta Montalto. The murders listed in Maraviglia's letter were the casualties in a new mafia war between the Amoroso and the Badalamenti clans.

According to Raffaele De Cesare, almost all those that the Revolutionary Committee chose to lead the *squadre* on the morning of Francesco Riso's revolt were, like Domenico Corteggiani and the de Benedetto brothers, "persons above any suspicion." Not all the *squadra* leaders enlisted by the Revolutionary Committee enjoyed such good reputations. De Cesare mentions a certain Lupo and a certain Badalamenti. Better known under the nickname of "u' zu [Uncle] Piddu Rantieri," Badalamenti was a goatherd working on the de Benedetto estates. The brothers had recruited him into their revolutionary conspiracies, and Badalamenti had led a *squadra* in 1860.[80] De Cesare calls him

> a goatherd of extraordinary courage, a ruffian and a mafioso upon whom the police had recently inflicted a ferocious penalty: they had suspended him head downward and applied I do not know how many lashes to the soles of his feet, so that the feet themselves had grown strangely swollen while the soles had become covered with calluses. They were trying to extract from him a confession for I do not know what sort of nonpolitical crime. But "u' zu Piddu" took it all, responding without emotion "I don't know nothin." [Nun sacciu niente].[81]

By 1870, "u' zu Piddu" had become *capo* of the Orto Botanico mafia. Starting in 1873, however, his *cosca* was challenged by a younger group with connections to the Stoppaglieri of Monreale. This was the mafia of the six Amoroso brothers.

During the 1860s, the Amoroso family was closely linked to Giuseppe Badia. Badia, in fact, was arrested in the house of Salvatore Amoroso. Salvatore himself had no part in the trap, however, for during this period he was also hiding from an arrest warrant. He was captured shortly thereafter, and, like Badia, was in prison during the 1866 uprising. His family's connection with the revolutionary party remained solid. When Lorenzo Minecci and his followers met to discuss the assassination of Francesco Perroni Paladini, they met in the house of Salvatore Amoroso. During the revolt, the insurrectionary committee met in this house as well.[82] Later, Gaetano Amoroso was party to Domenico Corteggiani's bomb-making project, and, as we saw, was arrested along with Francesco Bonafede for his membership in Badia's "internationalist" circle. The Amorosos were also friends of the Buscemi brothers, whom we saw drafting a constitution for a universal republic in 1869, and whose subsequent murder in the Stoppaglieri wars was alluded to, but not explained, in Giuseppe Maraviglia's letter to the leader of the New Orleans Stoppaglieri, Salvatore Matranga.[83]

Cutrera identifies the Amoroso brothers in the 1870s as the leaders of the Palermo branch of the Stoppaglieri. This is not impossible. The Amoroso brothers were closely linked to Badia and his circle, from which the idea of an association devoted to the "universal republic" first spread. They were particularly linked with Salvatore di Paolo. According to La Mantia, after Marino himself, the leaders of the Stoppaglieri were di Paolo and Michele Amoroso.[84] La Mantia in fact believed that the "Totó" of the letter to Marino was Salvatore Amoroso, not di Paolo. The Amoroso brothers were also connected with Giuseppe Maraviglia, and both di Paolo and Maraviglia were later charged and convicted of material involvement in the nine homicides that the Amoroso clan committed in their feud with "u' zu Piddu" Badalamenti.[85]

The war between the Amoroso and Badalamenti clans was a turf war similar to the war between the Siino and the Giammona clans described in the Sangiorgi report.[86] As always, the issue was protection: the Amorosos played the role of the "young mafia" challenging an older *cosca* by encroaching on its territories. The Amoroso-Badalamenti war started in 1873 with the wounding of Gregorio Fanara, the guardian of the Turrisi-Colonna land for the Badalamenti-Cerrito *cosca*. His assailants were Salvatore Amoroso and Salvatore di Paolo.[87]

Antonino Giammona was not directly involved in the attempt of the new mafia of the Stoppaglieri association to seize control of the Monreale region and the suburbs around the Porta Montalto. We can probably take the decoration that Giammona received for helping keep the peace during the 1866 uprising as evidence that the Giammona family was no longer actively supporting the revolutionary party by this date. Hence, although the Monreale prosecutor described the Stoppaglieri as expanding, forming branches in the Uditore and the Colli regions,[88] it is unlikely that either Antonino or his son Giuseppe was ever a member. Despite this, the Giammona family did not seem to view the rise of this "young mafia" in Monreale and Palermo as a challenge to their own authority. Indeed, the Stoppaglieri of Monreale as well as the Amoroso brothers continued to respect the Giammona family and accept them as mediators.

## The "Brotherhoods"

Morena was understandably surprised by what he was uncovering. Like Maniscalco, officials of the new Italian state conceived of political threats as coming from disaffected segments of the ruling class. In the 1860s and

1870s, this meant Bourbonists and clericals on the right, or Mazzinians and internationalists on the left. The Bourbons and leaders of the Italian state that followed were, of course, well aware of the lower classes' capacity for destructiveness. Yet, as traumatic as these frenzies could be, they were not seen as revolutionary threats, for a rabble of leaderless plebs had nothing to put in the place of constituted order. After the lootings and burnings, after the tax registers had been destroyed and the prisons opened, after the mob had marched through the streets with the head of some poor unfortunate on a pikestaff, they would simply disperse and go home. Without leaders from the ruling classes, there was nothing else they could do. It was only when disaffected segments of the ruling class entered into an alliance with the unruly plebs that not just a political threat but a true revolutionary threat came into being.

The idea that, without proper leaders, the lower classes of Palermo were incapable of staging an uprising ought to have died in 1866. But it did not. After 1866 the state continued to look in the same directions. By now, however, officials were beginning to ask another question: Which side was the mafia on? It was clear that the mafia was historically connected to the revolution; this did not mean, however, that it was obliged to remain politically linked to any revolutionary group. A particular *cosca*'s set of alliances was determined by its struggle to extend its protection as widely as possible. So long as the state ignored this aspect of the mafia's activity, only wanting to know whether it was on the side of the *neri* or the *rossi*, it could make little sense of the mafia.

Morena had discovered that the Stoppaglieri belonged to a revolutionary sect whose links to the Carboneria he took great care to elucidate. But he also discovered that making revolution was not the Stoppaglieri's real goal. Instead, the association was trying to establish control over Monreale by physically eliminating its rivals, the Giardinieri. From this we might conclude that, from 1866 on, mafia *cosche* treated revolutionary associations as front organizations. They were nothing more than convenient ways of organizing control. Certainly there is a good deal of truth in this conclusion. But was it all really that simple? Could mafia and revolution be so easily separated?

In their letters, neither di Paolo nor Maraviglia ever used the name "Stoppaglieri," much less "mafia." The latter term, in the sense of criminal underworld, was coined by journalists and police officials; it was never part of the vocabulary of the Sicilian underworld itself. Members of that underworld might use terms such as *mafia, mafiusu,* or *mafiusedda* as slang in a manner described by Pitrè; but there was never a sense that "mafia" denoted an association, or even a social class, to which they belonged. The underworld had its own terminology. We saw that Giuseppe Giammona called the Stoppaglieri "the party of the *cagnolazzi*." The term "Stoppaglieri," by contrast, was not so much slang as a nickname that was applied to the association in Monreale, and which, on occasion, its members came to accept. "Stoppaglieri" suggested either something like "fast-talkers" or (as Loschiavo proposed) "those who keep their mouths stopped up."[89] Cutrera adds that the Giardinieri also had a nickname— "Scurmi fitusi," or "Rotten Mackerels." Probably it was not a nickname that the Giardinieri were very happy about.

In any case, the name Stoppaglieri eventually stuck. As we saw, the letter from Maraviglia was addressed to Salvatore Matranga. The Matranga clan was the leading family in the New Orleans underworld, and were possibly behind the assassination of the New Orleans chief of police in 1890, a crime that they tried to pin on their adversaries, the Provenzanos. It was a murder that provoked the slaughter of thirteen Sicilians in Parish Prison in New Oreleans a few months later. In defending themselves, the Provenzanos accused the Matrangas of being the leaders of the "Stoppagliere Society."[90] The letter from Maraviglia to Matranga indicates that this was indeed the case.

Nevertheless, the members of the associations described by Morena never called one another *cagnolazzi* or Stoppaglieri; the most common term they used was *compare*, or "fellow godfather," denoting an important relationship between Sicilian men. The associations themselves were usually referred to as the "society of the *compari*" or else as the "Fratellanza" or "Fratuzzi"—the Brotherhood. The idea of brotherhood had its roots in the revolution and could never be reduced to a code word synonymous with criminality. It was a powerful idea that the mafia could neither monopolize nor control. The fact that no Sicilian joined an organization called "La Mafia" but joined instead organizations called "La Fratellanza," organizations that, even when there was a mafia *cosca* at their heart, required their members to call one another *compare* or *fratello*, showed that the ideals of the revolution were far from dead.

In 1859 the Bourbon police discovered a new conspiracy in Agrigento province. Its nature was alarming: instead of the usual group of student firebrands and sons of landowners with time on their hands, its members were peasants and sulfur miners. They met in taverns and spoke of how the entire island was again ready to rise and "set up a Government of equality, which is their way of saying robbing the property of others, taking the possessions of the well-off, who, they say, ought all to be put to death, removing all distinctions of class, and dividing among themselves, brothers in equality, the booty."[91] The police estimated the membership of the sect to be about four hundred.[92]

During the 1870s, Agrigento province became a hotbed of sectarian activities; "universal republican" societies were founded in Sciacca, Caltabellota, and the surrounding towns. These societies soon spread among the sulfur miners of Favara, where, as elsewhere in Sicily, a democratization of the republican ideology led to violence. In principle, the sects existed to fight tyranny; in reality, their attempts to extend their control led them to quarrels and bloody *vendette* among themselves.

By 1880 the "universal republic" sect was spreading among the republican brotherhoods in Favara; the largest of these was called the Fratellanza or the Mano Fraterna (the "Brotherhood" or the "Brotherly Hand"). In 1885, in the first of a series of trials, 168 of the Fratellanza's members were tried in Agrigento under the charge of belonging to a group "associated for a criminal purpose and with the sole scope of evil-doing"—a strengthening of the conspiracy statute that had been expressly formulated to meet their case the year before by Palermo's Court of Appeals. Of the 168 men accused of being members of a criminal association, 30 were also charged with the more serious matter of being involved in the ten murders laid to the credit of the Fratellanza.[93]

Like the Stoppaglieri, the Fratellanza was a mutual aid society whose members contributed a small monthly dues. Although the bulk of the membership was composed of sulfur miners and peasants, the society included shopkeepers and a schoolteacher. Its leader was a priest, Don Angelo Lo Coco, who first made his reputation as a rabble-rousing politician in near-by Canicattì, from where he had later been forced to flee when he was accused of commissioning a murder.[94] Since we know that Canicattì was one of the first towns in Agrigento province where the doctrine of the universal republic spread, we might guess that it was Don Angelo who that had brought the doctrine to Favara.[95]

Don Angelo is described as "intelligent and learned, acquainted with Latin and Greek." He seems to have been an engaging figure, "tall, complex, uninhibited, and sympathetic. When he arose to speak in his own defense, he tried, with sonorous voice and dramatic gesture, to demonstrate that he was the victim of a political intrigue."[96]

The real leader of the Fratellanza of Favara was not Don Angelo Lo Coco, however, but a landowner named Calogero Sanfilippo Rinelli. A born revolutionary, Rinelli spent much of the 1870s and 1880s either in prison or in exile on the smaller islands, where he was beaten and tortured, losing most of his teeth.[97] Yet, as Francesco de Luca remarks, he always came back, "more vigorous and audacious than before."[98]

The ultimate goal of the Fratellanza may have been the universal republic; yet the means by which it pursued this end included intimidation and, in all likelihood, extortion. The series of killings with which the Fratellanza was involved seems to have stemmed from its attempt to organize and control Favara's sulfur miners in the face of competition with two rival republican brotherhoods. A failure to understand its origins results in a failure to understand its crimes. Repugnant as the violence was, it had little to do with robbery, vandalism, or bestiality; it was rather a chain of killings and injuries connected with a turf war between rival sects.

After the murder of a member of his Fratellanza, Rinelli is described as summoning his followers and asking them to remove the "shame." He ordered them to murder a member of the offending sect and return with his right ear, cut off as a "sign." Rinelli, of course, did not need an ear to be sure that his followers had killed their victim; news of the killing would have spread instantly through the town. What he was really demanding was that his henchmen symbolically mutilate their victim's corpse. The mutilation was a *sfregio*, an insulting act of gratuitous aggression. It was this murder of a member of Rinelli's group, followed by the murder and mutilation of a member of one of the rival groups, that set off a war in Favara which ended only when all three leaders of the republican brotherhoods in Favara met to establish a truce and, under the leadership of Rinelli, unite their forces against the police.[99]

Whatever his political convictions, Rinelli's methods of recruiting were those of gangsters. According to one witness, Rinelli simply asked individuals if they had enemies, and if so, would they like to join a secret society that would protect them. Anyone who refused to join would be threatened until he gave in.

In 1880, Vittorio Urbani, a railway worker, was approached by Giovanni Fanara, one of his work mates, and invited to attend "a meeting in a secret place." When Urbani, together with a stonemason, arrived at the spot, they found Fanara and three unknown men. Fanara led the new recruits to an abandoned lime kiln and there invited them to join a republican brotherhood. Urbani later claimed that he tried to refuse, but, seeing that he was outnumbered, finally agreed to undergo the initiation ceremony. The police discovered a description of the initiation ceremony in the house of Rinelli:

> The oath was sworn in the presence of three members, one of whom having bound the finger [of the candidate] with a thread, pricked it,

and sprinkled a few drops of blood upon a sacred image [a picture of the Virgin]. This was then burned and the ashes thrown into the wind. The thread denoted the indissoluble bond that united each member to the others; the ashes signified that, just as it was impossible to give back the paper its original form, so was it impossible for a member to leave the society or to fail in the performance of his contracted obligations.[100]

The candidate held the image of the Virgin in his hand as it burned. When it was entirely consumed, he blew the ashes away and pronounced the Fratellanza oath: "I swear on my honor to be faithful to the Fratellanza, just as the Fratellanza is faithful to me. And just as this Saint and these few drops of blood burn, so will I pour out all my blood for the Fratellanza. And just as these ashes cannot return to their original state and this blood to its original state, so I may never leave the Fratellanza."[101]

Not only was this oath and initiation ceremony similar to those of other republican brotherhoods formed in this period, but also they are similar to mafia initiation rituals performed today.[102] The ritual is virtually identical, for example, to the one in which Joe Bonanno initiated Joseph Valachi into the Cosa Nostra in New York in 1930, and the one in which Jimmy Frattiano was made a member of Joe Dagna's "family" in Los Angeles. Even the term *compare* is retained, though in a garbled form. Joe Bonanno stood as Valachi's "gombah"; he thought the word was Yiddish.[103]

We saw in Chapter 2 that, in 1819, *carbonaro* initiates swore "to respect the rules of the Carboneria, to help one another in case of need, and all this under pain of being cut into pieces and incinerated in a furnace." This was an oath that probably went back originally to the *carbonari* of Naples under Napoleonic rule, and the practice of the Favara brothers of calling one another *buoni compari* and the universal republic "the republic of *buona gente*" seems to refer to the French sectarian practice of using the term *bons cousins*.

The relation between the Favara Brotherhood and the Carboneria can also been seen in the oath of the "Pugnallatori," a term that is itself derived from the first secret societies formed by Filippo Buonarroti in northern Italy in the 1820s. The Pugnallatori was a sect formed by Giambattista Falcone before he followed Carlo Pisacane on his fatal expedition to Saprì in 1857. Although Falcone was not among the lucky few who lived to tell the tale, a copy of the statutes of his sect has survived. Members of the Pugnallatori were required to recite to one another the following catechism:

The head?
Of the Tyrant!

What do you hold higher?
Equality, Fraternity, Patriotism!

What do you hold more sacred?
Liberty or Death!

What is your Law?
God's Ten Commandments!

Quote them to me.
Death to all Tyrants, to their Followers, and to their Henchmen![104]

This catechism also functioned as a recognition device. The Fratellanza had a similar catechism ending with the question, "What is your goal?" and the response, "The Universal Republic, Brotherhood, War against Kings!"[105]

Morena described the passwords and initiation ceremonies of these associations as old Carboneria formulas, transmitted either in the Palermo prison or through a puppet theater. He specifically mentioned the puppet-theatre version of novel by Dumas *père* about the famous Sicilian brigand Pasquale Bruno. The Monreale prosecutor had also heard a long description of the Stoppaglieri initiation from Salvatore d'Amico, who befriended the Caputo family when they fled to Bagheria.[106] Nevertheless, the best description of these rites emerged in the trial of one of the Fratellanza of Favara.[107]

The Fratellanza shared its set of passwords with the Stoppaglieri and the other contemporary sects. At first sight these passwords seem absurd. When a member wanted to signal that he was a member of the sect, he put his right hand to his chin and said, "It hurts!" His companion might naturally respond, "What hurts?" and he would reply, "U sagghiuni" or "U scagliuni," that is, the canine tooth. Morena noted this reference to a painful canine tooth and added that this had for many years been part of Sicilian criminal slang.[108]

It is hard to see how this password might actually have worked in practice. Fortunately, in his description Cutrera supplies a somewhat longer exchange:

"Oh, how my canine tooth hurts."

"Is it a long time that your canine tooth has been hurting?"

"Since the Feast of the Annunciation."

"Who was there?"

"Tom, Dick, and Harry who received me like a brother [*fratuzzu*]."[109]

The reference to the Annunciation is to the time when all members were symbolically "made" and received as a *fratuzzu* into the association. What about the reference to the *sagghiuni* or canine tooth? This may refer to the fact that sectarians or *cosca* members were known as *cagnoli* or *cagnolazzi*—dogs. It is noticeable that included in Cutrera's and Loschiavo's lists of mafia groups are the Scagliuni of Enna.

Contemporaries could make little sense of these rituals. The political notions of the sulfur miners did not, the police reported, go beyond a desire for "looting and vandalism" and an understanding that "political tumults" could provide them with the "means to satisfy their dark and brutal desires."[110] For followers of Cesare Lombroso's fashionable school of scientific criminology, it was axiomatic that the violent criminal was a neurophysiological degenerate. How else, asks Tommaso Colacino rhetorically, can we explain why members of the Fratellanza skinned the body of a *maresciallo* of the carabinieri, roasted it over charcoal, and ate it seasoned with vinegar. The violence of the Fratellanza was an expression of "the beast" that always lies "in a latent state" in the heart of man.[111]

Yet if this was all there was to it, why did the Fratellanza trick out their "bestiality" with oaths and passwords? Why had the Fratellanza adopted a statute, a tight organizational structure, and an elaborate set of rituals?

In support of his argument that the Fratellanza represented bestiality, Colacino quotes the toast that, according to him, new members of the Fratellanza were offered at the banquet following the initiation ritual. "Sweet is wine, but sweeter by far is the blood of men," citing it as example of vestigial cannibalism. This toast may well have existed, but not with this significance.

Giuseppe Lestingi gives the same words, but in the context of another story.[112] A member of the Fratellanza, Rosario Alaimo Martello, found himself accused by his fellow "brothers" of betrayal. A criminal under special police surveillance, he was specifically accused of informing the police about thefts committed by the Fratellanza in exchange for a greater measure of personal liberty. When the brothers learned of this betrayal, they declared Alaimo Martello an *infame* who deserved to die. As a brother of the sect, however, Alaimo had the right to a hearing. He pleaded for his life, denying that he had ever intended to betray the brotherhood. His brothers decided to put his loyalty to the test. Alaimo had to persuade his nephew to become a brother in the Fratellanza, offering to stand as his sponsor himself.

Alaimo succeeded in convincing his nephew, and a date for his initiation was set. The nephew agreed to meet his uncle at a certain house at sunset on the appointed day. As soon as he arrived, Alaimo took him into a house and led him into a darkened room. The moment the young man entered, he was set upon by assailants who threw a cord around his neck and strangled him. They placed his corpse in a sack and gave it to his uncle, who threw it away amidst the ruins of a deserted castle. Later, fearing that the body might yet be discovered, Alaimo returned to the ruin, doused the sack containing his nephew's remains with gasoline, and reduced them to ashes.

The theme of an execution disguised as an initiation ceremony is a cliché in stories about the mafia. It is used to good effect, for example, in the film *Goodfellows*. Each of the first three victims in the "case of the four disappearing bodies" discussed in Chapter 5 entered his appointed tavern believing that they were about to be treated to a banquet. Very plausibly, they also entered believing that they were about to be initiated into their *cosche*.[113]

Usually, of course, the victim is executed on account of a *sgarro*, a deviation from the code. In this case, however, it was not the victim who had committed the *sgarro*. The narrator, in fact, insists not simply on the nephew's innocence but on his complete extraneousness to the Fratellanza and all its misdeeds. This makes little sense. Like Cutrera's accounts of the murders of Simone Cavallaro and Salvatore Caputo or Galati's account of the murder of his first caretaker, Lestingi's account of the murder of Alaimo's nephew seems to have omitted some essential details.

In this particular case, Lestingi wishes to argue that the Fratellanza was a large organization that did evil deeds just for the sake of doing evil. Thus it ordered a ritualistic killing in which the victim was totally innocent and totally extraneous to the organization. The only motive was to put Alaimo's loyalty to the test by requiring him to lead his own unsuspecting nephew to his execution. It is certainly possible to believe that the Fratellanza was testing Alaimo's loyalty by forcing him to lure his nephew into the false initiation. It is hard, however, not to imagine that the Fratellanza had a more concrete motive for wishing to see the nephew dead.

Certainly, the story is gruesome. Yet is it an example of "bestiality"? Terms such as "brutal," "savage," and "bestial" seem to indicate acts of sub-human, uncontrolled, irrational violence, supposedly typical of cannibals and other primitives. Yet not only does such a description seem unfair to cannibals, but also it seems entirely to miss the point of the example itself. This was not a spontaneous act of blind violence; it was an execution.

The difference between an execution and an act of spontaneous violence is that an execution is constrained to follow a set of procedures. Alaimo de-manded, and evidently received, some sort of trial. A judicial execution is also a public act, and one usually surrounded by a number of rituals. It is difficult for a mafia execution to be public in the same way. Yet there is still a need to distinguish an execution from a murder in a *cosca* war, for the two types of killings have very different connotations. It is in this context that the theme of the execution disguised as an initiation finds its meaning. The initiation ceremony (in which the candidate is to swear to "pour out all my blood for the Fratellanza") provides a setting that is formal, even solemn enough for an execution. What is more, the candidate/victim ar-rives at the ceremony of his own free will and with the intention of sub-mitting to the will of the Fratellanza.

There remains only the problem of choosing the executioner. For the murder to be an act of collective justice, the relation between the execu-tioner and the victim must remain impersonal. The executioner should not know, much less have a grudge against, the victim. In the case of Sicilian mafia executions, the executioner was traditionally chosen by chance, through a round of *tocco*, a Sicilian drinking game. The players were usu-ally younger members or aspirant members of the *cosca*, and it was the cus-tom of the *cagnolazzo* selected by this method to signify his willingness to undertake the task by proposing a final toast: "Sweet is wine, but sweeter by far is the blood of men."

It appears that, showing far more political autonomy than contemporaries credited them with, the common people of Sicily were remodelling the Carboneria into a new sect. They even made their own distinct contribu-tion to these traditions. According the Fratellanza statute, when a brother was sent to another town, he was to present himself to the local *capo* and answer a number of questions. To the question, "Where were you made?" he was to respond with the name of town in which he was initiated. To the question, "Who was there?" he responded, "Bona gente," good people. In response to the question, "What day was it?" he was to respond, "The twenty-fifth of March." This was the date of the Feast of the Annunciation. The image burned in the initiation ceremony was in fact that of Santa Maria Annunziata. Francesco de Luca captures the significance of this very well:

> To rid themselves of all their curses, [the Fratellanza] formed themselves into a brotherhood with the Universal Republic as its object, whose advent they flattered themselves that they might hasten by *commencing* on the day when the good news was announced to all mankind—on the day of the *annunciation* of Mary, when She was told that She was to be the mother of the redeemer. Thus, during their *initiation* they like to asperse the image of *Maria Annunziata* with their blood. In this way they became indissolubly bound through a genuine primitive religious ceremony. Offenses done to any member are reputed to be offenses against the entire society, which united and compact against the minority which upholds the so-called order and justice, avenges its wrongs and comes to the aid of the *Sons of the Family*.[114]

# 7

## Mafia and Politics:
### The *Caso* Notarbartolo

The mafia offered concrete advantages. Those who cooperated with it and paid, their *pizzu* were protected and permitted to carry on with their work. There were also definite liabilities for those who refused to co-operate; they were bullied and harassed and sometimes even murdered. In this way, associations such as the Posa in the Conca d'Oro, the Stoppaglieri in Monreale, and the Fratellanza in Favara exercised control over much of the western Sicilian economy. Yet this alone could never have been enough; the mafia could never have dominated these millers, carters, laborers, and miners had Sicily's own ruling class seriously opposed it. Why in the forty years after unity, did Sicily's ruling class fail to make any real attempt to do so?

During the 1880s and 1890s, the deputies from western Sicily were divided into two parties: the followers of Crispi and the followers of Rudinì. Crispi represented the men of 1860 and the deputies who had spoken out in 1875; Rudinì stood for the political legacy of Cavour and for monarchy and stability. By now, however, the political divisions of 1860, though not forgotten, were muted; deputies from both parties knelt at the shrine of Mazzini, Garibaldi, and the "effulgent generation of heroes" who had made Italian unification a reality.[1]

However it may have appeared in Italian constitutional theory, Sicily was still a political hierarchy. In the minds of the Sicilian ruling class, this meant that those who held power had a duty to act in a spirit of paternalistic liberality, dispensing patronage and benefits to those below. Elected officials from any party were regarded as the particular advocates of those who had elected them. A good advocate busied himself finding jobs for his constituents, writing recommendations, dealing with the bureaucracy, and guiding the documents that requested pensions, permissions, licenses, loans, and so on to a favorable outcome. None of these obligations required officeholders to look into the details of the lives of their clients. Indeed, any such scrutinization would have been regarded as a hostile act. Sicilian political life was based on the fiction that the officeholder acted out of disinterested benevolence and that the client always deserved whatever favor he was petitioning for—a fiction that few believed completely but that all sides found convenient to maintain.

According to the Neapolitan deputy Rocco de Zerbi, the southern elite lived their lives like "oysters": their lives had "nothing in common with that of the rock to which they were attached," for the population in whose midst they lived "had other habits, other beliefs, other tastes, other inflections in their voices: they don't know us and we don't know them."[2] Marcella Marmo and Olimpia Casarino, who cite de Zerbi, take him to task, pointing out that the deputies from the coastal cities of the old Neapolitan kingdom had plenty of contacts with the urban plebs, and de Zerbi, a conservative deputy later involved in a banking scandal, surely knew this. Yet this is perhaps to misunderstand the point. Southern political notables indeed had plenty of opportunities for contact with the lower classes, for these classes continually bombarded them with petitions for jobs and favors. But this did not mean that the élites really knew what the people in the streets were doing.

In the early 1880s a Neapolitan docker named Pasquale Cafiero was fired from his job when the police found out that he belonged to a socialist cell. Cafiero petitioned Saverio Friscia, the anarchist deputy from Sciacca, who wrote a recommendation from Palermo. But Cafiero did not neglect to petition his local deputy too, and, his conservative and monarchist convictions notwithstanding, Rocco de Zerbi did not hesitate to add his recommendation to that of Friscia. Their combined weight proved sufficient, and Cafiero got his job back.[3]

Sicily's élites thus knew very little about the lives of the sorts of people whom the mafia organized. This lack of knowledge, plus their disinclination to delve too deeply into the activities of their constituents, helps explain why Sicilian deputies remained unconcerned about the mafia until it was too late. Like the ministers of justice and the interior, they conceived of threats as coming from the political cabals around them. For Sicily's political leadership in the first decades after unity, the mafia stood beyond their political horizon.

Part of the explanation for this lies in the limitation of the franchise. For the first two decades of unity, the franchise in national elections excluded the sectors of the population that the mafia controlled.[4] Throughout these decades, Sicilian politics was dominated by the nobility, who, though they represented only 1.6 percent of the eligible voters, made up 22.9 percent of those elected to office.[5] Nevertheless, a political threat did exist. Even under the old electoral law, the franchise had tended to grow. In 1861 there were 1,050 voters in Palermo; in 1880, two years before a new electoral law was passed, there were 9,280. How so many new voters got onto the electoral rolls is somewhat of a mystery. Conservatives were later to claim that the rolls had been consistently inflated by corrupt local machines that extended the vote to their clients whether or not they met the legal requirements. In any case, there is no mystery about where the new votes were coming from; they came from the suburbs.[6] However they obtained their votes, Sicilian politics was moving in this direction. The new voters were connected to the fastest-growing sectors of the Sicilian economy: the coastal plains.[7] These were also the most mafia-dominated zones of the entire province. Although unrecognized at the time, the mafia was already making inroads.

The franchise was enlarged in 1888, during Crispi's first government,[8] and the new electoral rolls were ready in time for the 1892 elections. By now, 30 percent of the adult male population was eligible to vote.[9] This only extended the vote further in the direction of the mafia. The electorate continued to grow most rapidly in the mafia-dominated regions of Palermo, Trapani, and Agrigento provinces.

With the new electoral laws in place, and with the assistance of a police force friendly to the government, the 1892 elections were a resounding success for the Crispian bloc. By now, however, the mafia's influence in the elections was too plain to be doubted. Curiously, this did not seem to trouble the majority of the deputies: to them, the mafia simply seemed a feature of a particular landscape that they, as deputies, had been elected to represent. They accepted the mafia's support, accepting thereby a duty to look after its interests without indiscreetly inquiring what these interests actually were.

As the party that had stood up to the government and trounced it in the 1874 elections, the Crispian bloc had made itself the natural majority party of Sicily, especially in the west. As a result, the mafia-dominated areas of western Sicily were politically dominated by Crispian deputies.

It was a good fit. The mafia and the Crispians shared a revolutionary past and a common political culture. They also shared an inclination toward Freemasonry; while mafia *cosche* were running protection rackets from local Masonic lodges, Crispian deputies, such as Camillo Finocchiaro-Aprile, the father of Andrea (see Chapter 1), were becoming the Grand Masters of Italian Freemasonry.[10] These, however, are analogies, not material connections. From the perspective of the Crispian deputies, the mafia was simply part of their political clientele. The mafiosi could be very helpful; their associations organized political rallies and sponsored patriotic celebrations; mafia-elected mayors acted as political agents, getting out the vote, placing the municipal parties at the candidates' disposal, and juggling electoral lists in their favor. The Crispian deputies continued to see themselves as the political patrons of these mafia-dominated municipalities and so failed to see how dependent upon them they were growing.

From the perspective of Rudinì and the conservatives, this alliance between the Crispian deputies and their clientele, whether dominated by the mafia or not, presented a bleak prospect. With the tendency for Sicilian electoral rolls to swell ever larger, there seemed little hope for the conservatives of increasing their vote. They needed a break: a public security crisis grave enough to declare a new emergency situation in Sicily or a political-mafia scandal clamorous enough to provoke general indignation. Although Rudinì could not have foreseen this, the conservatives were about to get both.

### The Sicilian *Fasci*

Between 1888 and 1892, along with republican and radical factions, the newly formed Socialist Party in Sicily began to organize groups called the "Fasci dei Lavoratori." The model was Emilia-Romagna.[11] The first *fasci* formed in Palermo and Catania closely resembled the earlier mutual assistance societies. Yet there were also differences: the brotherhoods founded in the 1870s and 1880s were autonomous. Even the Stoppaglieri was unable to extend its control much beyond the Monreale area. The *fasci*, by contrast, were organized by trade; each category was represented in a Camera di Lavoro, modeled on the French Bourse du Travail, which served as a labor exchange for all the members. This meant that the *fasci* were closer to trade unions, in which each member of a local also belonged to a larger organization.

By early 1893, the movement had spread into the interior, gaining new adherents among the sharecroppers and agrarian laborers too poor and socially marginal to be brothers in associations such as the Stoppaglieri. In the late Spring of 1893, the leader of the *fascio* at Corleone, Bernardino Verro, led the sharecroppers and laborers in a strike, demanding reform of the contracts between sharecroppers and landowners (the *patti*) as well as reforms and guarantees for the agrarian laborers. Taking place immediately before the harvest, the strike caught the landowners and *gabellotti* at their most vulnerable moment. Faced with the prospect of losing their entire harvest, they capitulated, accepting all the strikers' demands.

The successful strike brought the pent-up resentments of the poor boiling to the surface. The number of interior *fasci* increased dramatically. There were outbreaks of violence as peasants struck or attempted to occupy fields which they claimed had been illegally enclosed. The strikes and agitations of 1893 exacerbated municipal rivalries; there were riots in which, once again, town halls were sacked and tax registries burned.[12] The movement spread to the sulfur miners as well, as the spring of 1893 revived old memories of the spring of 1848.

In May 1893, the Sicilian Socialist Party held its first congress in Sicily. Later that same year it sent the leader of the Palermo *fascio*, Rosario Gabriele Bosco, to the second national conference of the Italian Socialist Party in Reggio Emilia. All eyes were on events in Sicily, and Bosco was asked to open the conference. He gave a stirring description of events on the island, finishing off with a grandiose flourish. "It will be a struggle," he proclaimed from the podium, "a tragic struggle, a hecatomb: but if Sicily falls, it will fall wrapped in a red flag!"[13]

The *fasci* crisi brought Francesco Crispi back to power. By now an old man of nearly seventy years, approaching the end of his political career, he had first served as prime minister from August 1887 to January 1991. During his first government, Crispi had busied himself with foreign policy, strengthening Italy's ties to Austria and Bismarckian Germany. He pressed through rearmament and tariff measures designed to make Italy militarily autonomous and economically autarchic. It was a policy that soured Italo-

French relations, setting off a trade war. In December 1890, Crispi's government was weakened when the leader of the northern left, Antonio Giolitti, resigned as minister of the treasury. Shortly thereafter, Crispi alienated the right by accusing it of having followed a policy of "servility to the foreigner." Enraged, the right proposed a vote of confidence. Opposed by the right and abandoned by the northern left, Crispi was defeated. His militaristic dreams rebuffed, he stalked out of parliament muttering, "Tiny! Tiny men!" to deliver his resignation to the king.[14]

Crispi was a formidable constitutionalist, with a vision of his country as a land of free people, living in self-governing communities, under the protection of a strong and unified state. It was a vision that he derived, in part, from Republican Rome, and, in even greater part, from his study of the independent Italian communes of the Middle Ages. It was a vision, however, that looked back to an older Italy, an agrarian Italy of small towns and cities, an Italy that had existed in the 1840ss, and that still existed in many parts of the South. Yet with the first factories appearing in the North, and with improved roads, railways, and steamships laying the foundations for economic integration, it was a vision increasingly out of date. By the time Crispi was allowed to put it into practice, much of his political philosophy was already obsolete.

By now, however, his monarchism and protectionism, his truculence toward France, and his colonialist adventurism had earned him the support of the nationalist right, which looked at him as a strongman. With the outbreak of the *fasci* crisis in Sicily, political opinion soon swung in his direction; he was summoned back to power and allowed to form a new government.

Despite the fact that Crispi was virtually summoned by the right, the left in Sicily was delighted as well. Crispi was the left's historic leader; besides, over the passage of years, many of his colleagues had become as monarchist as Crispi himself. Crispi was a Sicilian, moreover, one who had had firsthand experience with peasant unrest in 1848–49. Crispi, it was supposed, had a better grasp of the situation than any northern politician could have.

Indeed, Crispi regarded the *fasci* as part of a larger social question. Sicilian agriculture, he believed, was in urgent need of reform. He even went so far as to turn to Napoleone Colajanni. Though never a member of the Socialist Party, Colajanni was Sicily's leading political radical. He had take the *fasci* under his political protection, defending them in parliament and in the press. In late 1893, Crispi offered Colajanni the ministry of agriculture.[15]

Before reform, however, came the political threat. Crispi invited Colajanni to his office in Rome and, taking him by the arm, walked him to the window. He talked about French spies in the Vatican and about Russian warships off the coast of Sicily. He talked of an English vessel sailing toward a Sicilian port with a cargo of arms, of Italian anarchists massing in Tunis, ready for embarkation to Sicily. Foreign powers were behind the *fasci*, he said; these powers, frightened at the thought that Italy might become a great power with guns and ships and colonies overseas, were trying to destabilize Italy at any cost. It had been the young Crispi who had helped lay the plots for the 1848 rebellion in Sicily. It had been Crispi who had sneaked into Sicily in 1859 with false, blue-tinted glasses and a forged Argentinian passport. Now, as prime minister in 1893, the elderly Crispi seemed to have returned to the cloak-and-dagger world of his youth. Colajanni was invited to draw up his projects for agricultural reform; yet first, Crispi said, he needed time to deal with the political threat. Colajanni was aghast and hurriedly refused the offer of a ministry.[16]

On January 3, 1894, Crispi declared a state of siege in Sicily. The *fasci* were dissolved and the Italian army was sent to the island. As many had predicted, the troops inflamed the situation still further. With the emergency declaration of January, fresh rioting burst out. Troops moved in quickly, occasionally opening fire on the crowds. Within two weeks, order had been restored and the police were busy rounding up socialists and *fasci* leaders.

### The Condronchi Commissariat and the Return of the Right

Although the suppression of the *fasci* was criticized in the North, it was supported by the Sicilian middle class. In the months that followed, *fasci* leaders who were not in hiding or safely abroad were tried before a war tribunal in Palermo. Suppression even seemed to enjoy the support of the mafia. During these trials, one of the attorneys proclaimed:

Without the help of the mafia there can be no revolutions in Sicily. It is well known that the 1893 disorders in Sicily could not develop into a revolution because, as everyone knew, the mafia had refused to take part in them. Here we are referring to the *capi* without whom nothing can be organized. In a secret reunion at Piazza Aragonese [in Palermo] the socialist Bosco Garibaldi tried to induce several of the *capi* to unite with them. But the mafia had by now realized that the *fasci* were not strong enough to win; therefore they preferred to remain loyal to the government.[17]

This was pure fantasy. Against whom were the mafia *capi* supposed to be revolting? The suppression of the *fasci* had been ordered by Crispi and supported by the Crispian deputies from Sicily. These were men whom the mafia had put into office. Besides, the *cosche* could hardly have viewed the *fasci* with favor: from their perspective, the *fasci* were a disruptive new outfit out to encroach on their territory.

Still, the idea that without the mafia there could be no revolution in Sicily remained an unchallenged assumption in Sicilian politics.[18] The mafia was associated with revolution in the popular imagination, and it was necessary to invent a political "just-so story" to explain why the revolution had not taken place.

The right, however, had a special reason for taking satisfaction from Crispi's actions. By declaring a state of siege, Crispi was turning the clock back to the years before 1876. His government continued in power for another two years before toppling, in the early spring of 1896, when his dream of an African empire had perished with the Italian expeditionary forces on the plains of Adua. The defeat finished Crispi politically.

With the fall of Crispi, Rudinì was allowed to form his second government. One of his first acts was the institution of a "civil commissariat" for Sicily. The ostensible motive for this commissariat was to investigate the causes behind the *fasci*, as well as other financial and political scandals.[19] A barely less public object of investigation was muckraking. Any evidence of political graft and financial mismanagement that the investigations might discover was sure to reflect badly on the Crispian clienteles. As head of the commissariat Rudinì appointed Count Condronchi from Imola.

At first the Sicilian socialists rejected the idea of any cooperation with the commissariat; Rudinì's conservatives were, after all, their class enemies. Yet such a doctrinaire position chafed against their desire to justify themselves, to exonerate themselves publicly of the charge of plotting with foreign powers. The commissariat offered them a platform from which they might air their grievances and denounce their enemies. Since these denunciations often involved bringing forward voluminous evidence about the misdeeds of the Crispian clienteles, Condronchi had no objections.

Condronchi also ordered a scrutiny of the electoral lists. Alleging massive corruption, he soon cut the number of eligible voters in Palermo province by 49 percent and in Agrigento province by nearly two thirds.[20] The results were dramatic. In the 1895 elections, with Crispi still in power and able to use the prefects and police to support his followers, the left had won forty-one out of fifty-two seats (with seven going to the right and four to the far left). In 1897, with the right in power and new electoral rolls, out of fifty-nine seats contested, the left won just thirteen, while the right won thirty-three and the far left three. The election was, as Condronchi rather smugly remarked, "a true hecatomb of Crispians in Sicily."[21]

## The Notarbartolo Murder

For Rudinì events could hardly have taken a happier turn. He was already looking forward to a long investigation during which Condronchi would drag the reputations of Crispi and his allies through the mud. Now, lest anyone should accuse Rudinì and Condronchi of setting themselves up as judge and jury of their political adversaries, here were the socialists in Sicily offering to conduct this investigation for them.

The far left, however, saw the situation differently. Though only minority parties, socialists and radicals pictured themselves as the party of the future, the vanguard of the revolution destined to cleanse social inequality from the face of Sicily forever. Their ambitions were hardly limited to sandbagging Crispi for the benefit of Rudinì's conservatives. The far left wanted to show that the entire Italian state as well as both major political groups was corrupt and mafia-ridden from top to bottom. With the murder of Emanuele Notarbartolo, they thought they saw their chance.

A close friend and associate of Rudinì, Notarbartolo had served in Rudinì's municipal cabinet in the 1860s. Between 1874 and 1876 he had been mayor of Palermo. Appointed director of the Bank of Sicily just before the fall of the right, he remained at this post until he was removed by Crispi in 1890.[22] On February 1, 1893, he was murdered while returning home to the city from his estates near Caccamo, in the mountains southeast of Palermo.

The murder had been carefully planned. Notarbartolo made a habit of visiting his estates once or twice a month. Still, few outside his own family knew of his visit to the country on this occasion. He had told them that he would take the train back to Palermo on the evening of February 1, but he had made no specific plans. That afternoon, telegraphing his wife shortly before departing, he had boarded the train at the small station of Sciara near Caltanissetta.

Someone must have been following Notarbartolo's movements closely. Whoever it was relayed the exact time of Notarbartolo's departure to his murderers. They were probably already waiting in Termini Imeresi with two first-class tickets back to Palermo which they had purchased earlier that day.

According to the police reconstruction, Notarbartolo was murdered by two assailants who boarded the train at Termini.[23] The killing was the work of professionals; still, it was a messy business. Notarbartolo was stabbed twenty-three times with two different weapons. The upholstery was slashed, and there was blood everywhere, staining the furniture and smearing the mirrors and window glass of the first-class compartment.

Shortly after leaving Termini, the train had need to pass through a long tunnel. The noise reverberating from the stone walls as the train moved through would have been sufficient to drown out the victim's screams and cries for help. The darkness eliminated the possibility that the struggle might be observed by an onlooker watching the train go by.

Having accomplished their work in the tunnel, the killers needed to dispose of the body. It was unthinkable to fling it out just anywhere along this busy stretch of track, so they waited for the train to cross a deep ravine at the Ponte Curreri before opening the compartment door and pushing the body out. It was here that it was later discovered.

Notarbartolo was traveling in an old-fashioned first-class carriage, with independent compartments and no corridors. He was the only passenger in his compartment, ensuring the killers that there would be neither witnesses nor interruptions. Still, if the police reconstruction is correct, the killers had to wait for the train to make two stops before they were able to get rid of the body. The pool of blood on the compartment floor seemed to confirm that they had indeed waited with Notarbartolo's body for some time.

The north coast between Termini and Palermo was a crowded section of countryside filled with market gardens and small towns through which the train moved slowly, stopping at one suburban station after another. It would be strange if neither the conductor, the guards, the brakeman, the station masters, nor any of the other railway employees and passengers or simple bystanders had failed to notice that something was amiss.

In fact, people had noticed. The conductor remembered that two men with mustaches, aged about forty, had gotten into Notarbartolo's compartment at Termini. The story was confirmed by the station guard at Termini, who remembered two strangers with one-way, first-class tickets to Palermo. The assistant stationmaster, who happened to standing on the platform as the train pulled out, remembered seeing a man with "a hard face and grim and malicious eye" staring out at him through the window of Notarbartolo's compartment.[24]

The brakeman also remembered two men in cloaks, one of whom carried a package under his arm, disappearing from view behind the last carriage after the train had pulled into Altavilla. The police got a tip-off that the murderers had stopped at a farmhouse near Altavilla and changed their blood-soaked clothes. When the house was searched, the police discovered a pair of breeches covered in blood.

Beyond questioning witnesses and possible witnesses, police investigations moved in two directions. Palermo was teeming with rumors, and the police spent months evaluating over fifty anonymous letters and tip-offs they received (some from Palermo's insane asylum). With the help of the victim's family, they also compiled a list of Notarbartolo's principal political enemies.

As director of the Bank of Sicily, Notarbartolo had enjoyed a reputation for probity and severity. For this reason he was frequently in conflict with the bank's general council, whose membership included many who wanted the director to take a more indulgent view of their financial dealings.

Notarbartolo had thus not lacked enemies. Yet by the end of the 1880s, the bank's general council had begun to gain the upper hand in its struggle with the bank's severe director; the council members brought pressure on Crispi, who forced Notarbartolo to resign in 1890, replacing him with a more accommodating figure. This was three years before his murder, and by 1893, Notarbartolo was no longer in a position to hamper anyone's financial dealings. It was said, however, that in 1892, Notarbartolo had begun to assemble a dossier showing how certain of the council's members had been involved in stock frauds and had guaranteed loans to themselves. This would have provided a plausible motive. Unfortunately, no evidence concerning this dossier was ever uncovered.[25]

As the police continued to make no headway, their investigations were overshadowed by the *fasci* crisis at the end of the year. From the end of 1893 to the middle of 1895, when the case was officially closed, no effective action was taken. In 1896, however, the Condronchi commissariat decided to reopen the investigations.

Condronchi had been solicited by the Notarbartolo family, who were closely connected to the Sicilian aristocracy. Through the initiative of Emanuele's son Leopoldo, friends of the family brought the matter up before King Umberto, who, as early as 1892, began to show interest in the case. The court continued to express its hopes that Notarbartolo's murderers would be brought to justice, and, as the commissariat took office in 1896, Rudinì was asked by the Notarbartolo family and their friends to request Condronchi to reopen the investigations.

Condronchi needed little prompting. His sympathies lay with the family, and besides, he hoped that investigations into the activities of Notarbartolo's enemies while he was the director of the Bank of Sicily would bring to light evidence that would further discredit the Crispian bloc. He told Rudinì he thought that justice was being blocked by some "big shot" (*pezzo grosso*), some *"friend of Crispi's."*[26] There was a certain basis for these hopes: in 1888–89, during his first government, though officially neutral, Crispi had supported the council members in their struggle against Notarbartolo, and had been quick to dismiss Notarbartolo when this struggle became an open rupture.[27] Condronchi had the police investigate the connections between the Crispian deputies and the Palermo mafia, but these investigations went nowhere. Although the police could supply information about the *mafia* clientele of the Crispian bloc, there was no evidence linking either to the Notarbartolo murder. Had the matter been entirely in his hands, Condronchi would surely have dropped it at this point.

## Giuseppe Fontana and the Villabate *Cosca*

Of the various rumors circulating in Palermo about the possible involvement of the mafia in the Notarbartolo murder, some of the earliest and most persistent concerned Giuseppe Fontana and the Villabate *cosca*.

Fontana had been charged with armed robbery four times, though he was never convicted. He was reputed to be ruthless, and the rumors concerning his involvement in Notarbartolo's murder were strengthened when the police turned up a witness who had seen Fontana in Altavilla, near Termini Imeresi, a day before the crime. When a friend waved to him, Fontana had run up to tell the friend that he must, on no account, reveal to anyone that he had been seen in Altavilla.

Fontana is listed in the Sangiorgi report on the Sicilian mafia as one of the thirty-five members of the Villabate *cosca*.[28] The mafia in Villabate was organized in a Fratellanza similar to that of the Stoppaglieri of Monreale. Its local nickname was the "Zubbio."[29] The Villabate Fratellanza was also the center of a local political party which won the municipal elections in 1891. It was in power only a few months, however, before the police dissolved the town council, arresting members of the local *giunta* on the charge of being members of a criminal association. The town was placed under the administration of a commissariat appointed by the minister of the interior. In April 1893, two months after Notarbartolo's murder, the former police delegate of Villabate reported rumors that the Villabate mafia had organized the murder of Notarbartolo and that the principal assassin had been Giuseppe Fontana.[30]

The Fratellanza of Villabate was under the political protection of the man who was later to be charged with Notarbartolo's murder, the deputy Raffaele Palizzolo. Sangiorgi mentions that after the murder of Notarbartolo, the Fratellanza of Villabate held a banquet in honor of Palizzolo, who had persuaded the government to lift the sanctions against the Villabate communal council. Although Villabate was not in his parliamentary constituency, he was the town's representative on the provincial council and a close friend of the pro-Fratellanza mayor, Pitarresi. Palizzolo also had lands in the Villabate region, employing as his guardian the Villabate mafioso Matteo Filippello. The police wondered whether Filippello might be the connecting link between Palizzolo and the Villabate *cosca*. In June 1896, Filippello was the victim of a mafia ambush. Sangiorgi reports that, "according to rumor, the association [the Fratellanza of Villabate] had condemned Filippello because he had converted entirely to his own profit the reward paid to him by the instigator of the murder of Comm. Emanuele Notarbartolo without giving a part to his fellow members as specified by the rules of the congregation."[31] Filippello was only wounded in the ambush, but the man who told the police the reason for the attack, Loreto Lo Monaco, was found murdered shortly thereafter.

The police, as we saw earlier, had identified the villa Gentile near Monreale as a center of crime and as a staging area for livestock theft.[32] The Villabate *cosca* was involved in this activity as well. Sangiorgi writes that the estate was under the guardianship of Nicolò Trapani, whom he identified as an important *capomafia*. The police suspected that Palizzolo had commissioned Trapani to arrange the killing of Francesco Miceli, the son of Turi Miceli. Their case was plausible, yet, as usual, they were unable to turn suppositions and rumors into witnesses who would testify in open court. In 1893 Miceli's widow withdrew her accusations against Palizzolo, forcing the police to suspend their investigations.

Although the police had nothing that would hold up in court, the information they had implicating Fontana and the Villabate *cosca* in the Notarbartolo killing at least constituted a promising lead. Unfortunately, this line of inquiry soon received a serious setback: Fontana had a good alibi.

When questioned, Fontana claimed that he had left Sicily for Tunisia in the autumn of 1892 and had not returned until after the murder. The first inquiries seemed to confirm his story. When, under pressure from the Notarbartolo family, the police arrested Fontana in April 1894, he produced proof that he had indeed been in Tunisia at time of the murder. He showed his account books from Hammamet in Tunisia and copies of letters and telegrams sent to Palermo during the period. Some of these letters lacked a postmark, but their dates were confirmed by their recipients. There was finally a postal order sent from Palermo on the fourth of February and cashed by Fontana in Hammamet five days after the murder.

The Palermo police seem to have kept the Notarbartolo family informed about the progress of their investigations. This may have been irregular, though it is certainly understandable and, indeed, serves as another indication that they were not involved in a vast cover-up operation. The proofs Fontana displayed that he had been in Tunisia seemed genuine, however, and so, in 1894, the police felt that they had no alternative but to drop him from their list of suspects. Leopoldo Notarbartolo was not convinced. The account books could have been faked; the recipients of the letters could have been lying about their dates. Sangiorgi lists nine mafiosi with the surname Fontana, all of whom were related.[33] There was also a tenth Fontana, a first cousin of Giuseppe Fontana, also named Giuseppe. The police had heard that at the time of the Notarbartolo murder, this second Giuseppe Fontana was also in Tunisia.

In 1895, Leopoldo Notarbartolo and a police agent made a trip to Tunisia. They discovered that the first Giuseppe Fontana had indeed been in Hammamet, at least on the morning of the murder. On this particular morning, however, he had sailed from Hammamet southward in the direction of Sousse. Notarbartolo went to Sousse and discovered that Fontana's boat had not arrived there until five days after it had sailed from Hammamet. This left a gap during which it was conceivable that Fontana might have sailed to Trapani, leaving the second Giuseppe Fontana behind to conduct business in his name. From Trapani, Fontana could have boarded a train which would have taken him to Termini Imeresi in time to murder Emanuele Notarbartolo. After the murder, he could have gone back to Sousse in the original boat. Leopoldo Notarbartolo was convinced that this was precisely how Giuseppe Fontana had murdered his father.

The police and public prosecutor in Palermo were more skeptical. These were interesting speculations, but they hardly constituted positive proof. It was hypothetically possible that the first Giuseppe Fontana had traveled from Hammamet to Termini Imeresi, and it was hypothetically possible that the man who cashed the postal order had been the second, not the first, Giuseppe Fontana. Certainly the first Giuseppe Fontana had taken considerable care to construct an alibi establishing his presence in Tunisia at the time of the murder. Yet hypotheses were not proof. Besides, the hypothesis still did not explain why Fontana was seen in Altavilla on the day before the murder.

There was one further possibility of a positive identification. The police had made little use of the assistant stationmaster—the official who happened to be standing on the Termini platform as Notarbartolo's train pulled out, and who saw the man with "a hard face and grim and malicious eye" staring at him through the window of Notarbartolo's compartment. In 1897 the police had the official observe Fontana through a spy hole. The witness was shaken; indeed, he told the police, this was the man. Yet he also told them that he would deny everything if they forced him to testify in open court.

## Palizzolo

According to Napoleone Colajanni, public opinion in Palermo "immediately" focused on the deputy Raffaele Palizzolo as the figure most likely to have commissioned the crime.[34] This is not true, for Palizzolo's name does not appear in any of the early police reports.[35] It was on the list of enemies that the Notarbartolo family drew up; nevertheless, several more years were to pass before suspicions were concentrated upon him. Even in 1896, Condronchi did not regard Palizzolo as compromised; indeed, he consulted him privately, relying on his extensive knowledge of Palermo society.[36]

In different circumstances, Condronchi could not have made a better choice. Palizzolo was a member of both the Palermo provincial and municipal councils. He was on the administrative boards of a number of civic committees and charities. A deputy since 1882, he was also a leading member of the Bank of Sicily's general council.[37] In addition to these qualifications, Palizzolo had an impressively wide range of criminal connections. He had been associated with the brigand Antonino Leone in the 1870s, and the prefect Malsuardi had threatened to bring judicial sanctions against him if he did not withdraw his candidacy in the 1876 parliamentary elections. Palizzolo testified for the defense in the trial of the Amoroso brothers. According to Nicotri, Palizzolo had

close connections with four *cosche* (including that of Villabate) in the various parts of Palermo province where he owned or rented lands.

These lands were often acquired through using his relatives or acquaintances as go-betweens, as in the case of the lease of the Gentile alla Rocca estate. This particular estate had been placed under court administration after the Palermo tribunal had annulled a former contract between its previous administrator and a certain Diliberto and Bonanno. This estate was indicated by the police as the center of smuggling by groups operating in Mezzo Monreale with the complicity of the caretaker, Nicolò Trapani, considered a powerful mafioso.[38]

The "previous administrator" was Francesco Miceli. In July 1892, Miceli was murdered in an ambush. At first, the murder remained a mystery, until Miceli's widow told the police that, in his last hours, her husband had told her that he believed that Palizzolo had ordered his execution.

Palizzolo was later to claim that it was all a frame-up. Even were this so, the incident still shows that the Palermo police were not afraid of investigating Palizzolo. Palizzolo certainly had friends in the Palermo police; yet if these friends had covered up evidence and protected Palizzolo in the Notarbartolo murder, why had they failed to do so in the Miceli murder?

Palizzolo's career in parliament was extremely undistinguished; he is almost never reported as having spoken in debates, and in all probability spent most of his time in Palermo looking after his affairs and those of his clients. When he did sit in parliament, he usually sat with the right.[39] Yet he was no friend of Rudinì; Rudinì later told Condronchi that Palizzolo was a *canaglia*, a rogue, and that, should circumstances warrant it, Condronchi should not hesitate in ordering his arrest.[40]

Although Palizzolo sat with the right during the 1880s and again after 1896, in the 1890 and 1892 elections he presented himself as a Crispian. The temporary change of political affiliation was probably motivated by the fact that Palizzolo was deeply involved in stock transactions involving the Florio shipping company in Palermo, and Vincenzo Florio and Crispi were allies. Despite this connection, Palizzolo was never accepted by the left in Palermo. In 1890, Crispi had canvassed his supporters there to see whether they would back Palizzolo to stand against a follower of his rival Giolitti. They told him flatly that they would not, and Crispi's friend, Girolamo De Luca Aprile, the director of a pro-Crispian newspaper in Palermo, threatened to publish articles describing Palizzolo's unsavory past. As a result, Crispi dropped Palizzolo's candidacy. It was just as well that he did: had he insisted on backing Palizzolo, the friends of Rudinì, Giolitti, and Colajanni would certainly have begun to hear "rumors" linking Crispi to the Notarbartolo murder. Even though shunned by Crispi's official supporters, Palizzolo still tried to pass himself off as a Crispian in the early 1890s. He went so far as to invent a specious Garibaldino past for himself, and to declare that attacks on him were attacks on Sicily's glorious revolutionary tradition.

In reality, Palizzolo started his career neither with the right nor with the left but with Palermo's old Autonomist Party. This was a natural choice: the Autonomists included some of Sicily's richest and most powerful aristocrats, and by joining the Autonomists in the 1860s, Palizzolo gained contacts that facilitated his later financial dealings and property speculation. In 1873 he administered the public dole in Palermo, a useful way of acquiring clients. Later that year the Autonomists lost the municipal elections and were replaced by a *giunta* of the right, in which Notarbartolo later served as mayor. Notarbartolo discovered that Palizzolo had embezzled a large sum over the purchase of flour, and demanded that he pay back the missing money personally. This was the beginning of a history of enmity between the Notarbartolo family and Palizzolo.[41]

It was not until 1882 that Palizzolo was able to stand for, and be elected to, parliament. Shortly before this election, Emanuele Notarbartolo was kidnapped on his estates near Sciara by the band of Matteo Barone and the three Piraino brothers. He was released only after the payment of a considerable ransom, a sum raised when the brigands thought that the Notarbartolo family had met their first demands too easily. After receiving the ransom money and releasing their captive, the brigands had retired to hide in a farmhouse near Villabate, next to a property owned by Palizzolo.[42] What happened after that is somewhat obscure, but it seems that the police heard rumors of their presence, and that the prefect summoned Palizzolo, telling him to find out more information for them. Palizzolo had friends in the Villabate *cosca* who knew exactly where the brigands were. They told Palizzolo; he passed the knowledge along to his friends in the Palermo police. With this information, the police were able to capture all but one of the members of the band.[43]

This reconstruction of the 1882 kidnapping and the eventual capture of the kidnappers follows the account later given by Leopoldo Notarbartolo.[44] Since Palizzolo's assistance was more a gesture of good faith toward the prefect than a gesture of friendship for Notarbartolo, the Notarbartolo family felt no gratitude toward him. Indeed, the demonstration of Palizzolo's influence over the powerful Villabate *cosca*, whose livestock stealing operations extended not only to Ficarazzi and Misilmeri but also into Caltanissetta province, where the family held their lands, was profoundly unsettling. It was this rather than Palizzolo's role on the general council of the Bank of Sicily from 1888 to 1890 that seems to have first aroused Leopoldo Notarbartolo's suspicions that Palizzolo had been behind the murder of his father.

## The "Cover-up"

The Notarbartolo murder was never solved: the police could not break Fontana's alibi, nor were they able to uncover any material evidence against Palizzolo. Investigations never revealed the names of the killers or why they committed their crime. Certainly someone knew the answers. There was a network of complicity stretching from Caltanissetta province to the towns in the eastern and southern suburbs of Palermo. Had investigations penetrated this network, we would know a great deal about mafia power in the 1890s. Since they did not, the story of the Notarbartolo murder is less a story about a mafia murder than about a political scandal.

When he reopened the investigations, we saw that Condronchi nurtured hopes of landing some fat friend of Crispi's and frying him slowly in public. When these hopes proved illusory, his interest in the matter cooled. As his interest cooled, so did his willingness to tolerate the far left. For its part, the far left had no reason to seek to pin the blame for Notarbartolo's murder on the Crispians in particular; they wished instead to level their charges against the police and magistracy. These, they claimed, had brutally suppressed the *fasci* and imprisoned their leaders on trumped-up charges. Now they were protecting Palizzolo and covering up evidence about the Notarbartolo murder, evidence which, they said, demonstrated the involvement of both the state and the mafia. Condronchi had little sympathy for a campaign aimed at discrediting the state. Yet by now the scandal had its own momentum.

According to the far left, it was "immediately clear" that Notarbartolo's murder was the work of the mafia.[45] Throughout 1893, Palermo was indeed rife with rumors and speculation about the *alta mafia* and its involvement in the deed; yet the police had no concrete leads.[46] Although the charge of "covering up" important evidence was continually repeated, no one could say what this important evidence might be.[47]

There was nothing, in fact, to connect the Notarbartolo murder with the mafia. It was not a typical mafia assassination. Even the weapons were uncharacteristic. Knives were the classic weapon for the *crime passionelle*. The mafia, by contrast, favored the shotgun.[48] Even though on more than one occasion the victims of mafia executions were murdered or disfigured by a knife,[49] Notarbartolo was a highly respected and important figure in Palermo society, the last person one could imagine as the victim of such a mafia execution. The only thing that should have been immediately clear was that the killers had not been chosen in a round of *tocco*; they were not *cagnolazzi*; they were professional assassins.

The far left denounced the Palermo police and state prosecutor's office, saying that their failure to reveal the hidden evidence in the Notarbartolo case only confirmed the charges of corruption and wrongdoing that had earlier been laid before the Condronchi commissariat. There was a logical connection between the scandalous state of public finances in Sicily and the Notarbartolo murder. It was a scandal in which the state, the police, the Sicilian ruling class, and the mafia were all implicated. Had these accusations been limited to the far left press, the government would have ignored them. By now, however, Leopoldo Notarbartolo and much of the northern press were repeating them too. By 1897, the police were under intense pressure to do something.

The police had always suspected that the conductor and the brakeman had helped the assassins by ensuring that no one entered or looked into Notarbartolo's compartment after the train had left Termini Imeresi. There was a good deal to implicate these two. Why had the conductor failed to report the blood and signs of a struggle when he checked the train after it had arrived in Palermo? Why had he not checked the tickets of the passengers who had boarded at Termini Imeresi when he had checked the tickets of all the other passengers?

The brakeman's account was no better. One of the train's passengers on the evening of the murder was a fourteen-year-old boy. He frequently made the journey to Palermo, and liked to remain outside on the balcony. On the evening of the murder, the brakeman told him to remain inside.[50]

The conductor had a bad reputation: his former superior testified that he had been involved in smuggling between Termini and Palermo. He was said to have mafia friends. Both railwaymen lived in Bagheria, and in late 1893 the local police heard a rumor that the brakeman was terrified that the conductor wanted to "eliminate" him.[51]

Lacking a better alternative, the police decided to indict the conductor and the brakeman. It seemed clear enough that these two were somehow involved in the murder. It was even possible that the second assassin was the conductor himself, and that the brakeman's story of *two* mysterious strangers in cloaks was invented to mislead the police. Yet where was the first assassin? Who and what had induced the two railwaymen to take part in a murder? What, above all, was the motive? Although the state prosecutor believed that he could prove their complicity, a trial of the two railway-men alone was bound to appear inconclusive.

The trial took place in Milan at the end of 1899. Although new evidence against the railwaymen emerged, little was proved. The prosecution had prepared its case in a hurry: its summary of preceding investigations was confused and contradictory; the case itself amounted to a mere five pages. This was unfortunate, for the shoddy work of the prosecutor seemed to indicate shoddy work on the part of the police. The prosecutor had originally considered including Giuseppe Fontana among the accused, but at the last minute had changed his mind. Fontana was not even called to testify. Nor, of course, was Palizzolo. In terms of forensic evidence, the prosecutor was justified, for there was really no case against either of them. Yet the prosecution's failure to provide any background or possible motive for the crime, as well as its failure to identify the principal assassin, made its case look threadbare and unconvincing. These were serious defects in a trial that was intended, in large part, as a public confidence-building exercise.

On November 17, 1899, Leopoldo Notarbartolo took the stand. The Notarbartolo family had declared themselves an interested party, and this, under Italian law, gave them the right to testify under oath. It also gave their attorneys the right to participate in the trial. By now openly critical of the police, Notarbartolo chose three lawyers, two of whom, Carlo Alto-belli and Giuseppe Marchesano, were tied to the Palermo Socialist Party. Leopoldo Notarbartolo began his testimony by describing the conflicts between his family and Palizzolo from the 1882 kidnapping to his father's forced resignation from the Bank of Sicily. He noted that Palizzolo was suspected of being behind the murder of Francesco Miceli, adding that Miceli's widow had been frightened by the mafia into withdrawing her accusations. He identified Giuseppe Fontana as the principal assassin of his father, claiming that Fontana's alibi was false. At the end of his statement, one of his attorneys asked him why he thought the prosecutors had not summoned Palizzolo as either a defendant or a witness. This was the question that Notarbartolo had been waiting for; he replied simply, "Because they were afraid."[52]

These were explosive words, and the northern press was inclined to credit them. The socialists, already alerted, were giving the trial ample coverage. In the weeks that followed, the Sicilian socialist press published more articles enlarging on Notarbartolo's charges, discussing Palizzolo, the mafia, and the complicity and protection that both enjoyed from the police and the government.[53]

Rudinì was furious. He was no friend of Palizzolo's, he said, but Leopoldo Notarbartolo was determined to turn a trial that was supposed to restore public confidence in the state into a public circus.[54] Still, though he deplored Notarbartolo's methods and his alliance with the socialists, Rudinì confided to Condronchi that many of his criticisms were justified. The failure to pursue the case against Fontana demonstrated that there was "rot" in the prosecutor's office. And was not the chief of police a fine figure of public humbug: he had been friendly with Palizzolo for years; now here he was righteously thundering against him and saying that the magistrates were afraid to proceed. The police chief's sudden change of heart had also been noted by the prefect, Cesare de Seta, who remarked more prosaically that it was simply a matter of calculation: "It seemed to him advantageous to display himself as violently hostile to Palizzolo, even though in former times he was his friend."[55]

This was just a foretaste; Notarbartolo's accusations set off a chain reaction. It was now clear that the government was about to turn its back on Palizzolo, and his former friends and associates had to scramble for cover.

Rudinì was in a genuine quandary. He had served as one of Italy's leading conservative politicians for forty years. He had been the unchallenged leader of the right in Sicily since the birth of the Italian state. Every political nerve in his body must have been telling him not to support an initiative that could only discredit the Italian state, its institutions, and the men who served it. Yet his moral outrage was no less genuine and his sympathy for the Notarbartolo family was no less real. He had already defined Palizzolo as a *canaglia*, and if it turned out that he had been behind the Notarbartolo assassination Rudinì would have wanted to see him punished.

But was Palizzolo guilty? Rudinì simply had not decided. So long as he remained undecided, the police would do nothing. It was Rudinì's hesitations and not a police plot that was effectively shielding Palizzolo.

By 1897, this shield was beginning to crack. Rudinì had never actively protected or defended Palizzolo, but he had never urged the police and state prosecutors to investigate him either. But now such an investigation could only be a matter of time. Many of Palizzolo's political friends began to distance themselves while they still could, claiming that they had long harbored suspicions about him but that their warnings had gone unheeded. These statements, coming from officials most compromised by their past friendship with Palizzolo, naturally evoked pointed rejoinders from other officials to the effect that certainly *they* had not been the ones who had been protecting Palizzolo all these years. With Notarbartolo's statements in the

1899 trial, the climate of distrust between the police and the magistracy, and within the police itself, created a frenzy of accusation and counteraccusation. Nineteen hundred was to be a year of wrecked careers.

Faced with public outrage, and with official morale in Palermo visibly crumbling, the Italian government was forced to act with uncharacteristic rapidity. On December 11, 1899, the prime minister, Luigi Pelloux, suspended telegraph communication between Rome and Palermo while he obtained parliamentary permission to proceed against Palizzolo. Palizzolo was arrested in Palermo and charged with commissioning the murder of Notarbartolo. Later the charge of commissioning the murder of Francesco Miceli was added for good measure.

A warrant for the arrest of Giuseppe Fontana was also issued, but he proved more difficult to trace. Fontana was employed as an overseer on the estates of Prince Mirto in the Villabate region. Relations between Fontana and the Mirto family were extremely cordial. Several years before, when Fontana was arrested and imprisoned in Venice as part of the Siino's clan counterfeiting operation, the Mirto family had expressed its concern, offering him money and assistance.[56] In December 1899 the police knew that Fontana was hiding somewhere on one of the many Mirto properties. Prince Mirto, however, was not being cooperative, telling the prefect that he did not know where his overseer happened to be. Pelloux, in Rome, was having none of it, and instructed de Seta to tell Mirto that if he did not produce Fontana immediately, he would be arrested for shielding a fugitive from justice. Mirto asked for five days' grace. Before the end of the five days, with Fontana riding beside him in his private carriage, Mirto arrived to deliver the suspect not at the police station but at Chief of Police Sangiorgi's own house. Even Rudinì thought this excessive, remarking that Mirto was dealing with the Italian state as if he were a foreign power. The northern newspapers were even more scandalized. De Seta, however, was once again inclined to shrug off the incident. "It is not considered improper," he wrote Pelloux, "for an honest individual property owner to hire as custodians for his property, and to protect himself through them, persons belonging to the mafia."[57]

This time there would be no slip-ups. The prosecution drew up its case with care. Palizzolo and Fontana were tried in Bologna in proceedings starting in 1901 and lasting into early 1902. The Palizzolo-Fontana trial played to a packed house: journalists came from all over Italy to cover it, and there were correspondents from other European countries and from America as well. In the end, the jury convicted Palizzolo of organizing the murders of both Francesco Miceli and Emanuele Notarbartolo. Fontana was convicted as the material executor of the Notarbartolo murder. They were both sentenced to thirty years' hard labor.

## Socialists and Scandals

The socialists were triumphant. In 1895, when the party was still outlawed and many of the *fasci* leaders were in hiding, the Sicilian socialists had decided to cooperate with the Condronchi commissariat. It was a decision that implied an acceptance of the state as the proper instrument with which to pursue their struggle. The 1902 trial and guilty verdict seemed to vindicate that decision, and seemed as well to confirm the socialists' own status as a legitimate force in Italian politics.[58] Even better, the socialists were now riding on the crest of a wave of popular indignation. The northern press was echoing socialist themes, speaking of the need for radical reform in Sicily in order to root out backwardness, corruption, political clientelism, and, not least, the mafia. The republican Alfredo Oriani described Sicily as "a canker on the foot of Italy."[59] Even the London *Times* called the Bologna verdict "a mighty event in the history of a nation."[60] From Milan, the socialist deputy Leonido Bissolati greeted the Bologna verdict as "only an indication of the need for wider, profounder, and more thoroughly cleansing acts of justice." He called for a program of reform, a "transformation and valorization of that social terrain whereupon the evil weed of the mafia now draws its sustenance."[61]

Already in 1899, feeling that they now occupied the high moral ground, the socialists had begun to organize rallies and public demonstrations. In December 1899, Tasca di Cutò, the head of the Palermo federation, asked Sangiorgi's permission as chief of police for the socialists to carry their banners and distribute their propaganda during a commemoration ceremony in honor of Notarbartolo. Sangiorgi pulled him up short, telling him brusquely that they could do no such thing.[62] The socialists' hope that the government would now treat them as a legitimate political force was a miscalculation.

In Sicily it took awhile for the significance of the Bologna trial to sink in. Emanuele Notarbartolo had been a much-respected public figure; Sicilians had been horrified by his murder and had wished to see the culprits brought to justice. But what was taking place in Bologna did not appear to them to be a trial of Notarbartolo's murderers so much as a trial of Sicily itself. During the trial, Palizzolo's only support came from the pro-

Crispian press in Sicily, Naples, and Rome. Even an article by Gaetano Mosca in the Milanese *Corriere della Sera*, which, although it described Palizzolo as a "vain and irresponsible intriguer," also expressed doubts as to whether he was truly capable of murder, appeared accompanied by an editorial disclaimer.[63] As the trial drew to its close, Sicilians became increasingly appalled. With the announcement of the Bologna verdict, a "Pro-Sicily Committee" was formed. Its leader was the ethnographer Giuseppe Pitrè; its first members were conservatives, professionals and politicians, as well as the associates of the industrialist Vincenzo Florio.

From Palermo the prefect, de Seta, gave the committee his discreet support. From the first he had been doubtful about Palizzolo's guilt, and now he was inclined to regard the Bologna trial as an unfortunate opportunity for the socialist press to attack the state and its institutions. Choosing his terms carefully, he wrote to Prime Minister Giolitti that the leading members of the committee were "all political adversaries of Palizzolo," citizens whose only desire was "to give a certain satisfaction to their juridical consciences which had been offended by the contrived atmosphere in Bologna and, in this way, contribute to the maintenance of public order."[64] Even Giolitti's chief lieutenant in Sicily, Vittorio Emanuele Orlando, described them as men of "perfectly good faith" with "no odor of *mafiosità*" about them.[65]

Palizzolo and Fontana appealed their convictions. Their appeal was granted, and a new trial took place in Florence in 1903. By now the press had lost interest. Without the glare of publicity, the prosecution's lack of evidence became apparent. Both men were quickly acquitted. Palizzolo returned to a hero's welcome in Palermo.

### "We are the ones who are supposed to die"

In the end, who had won? The Sicilian historian Francesco Renda has no doubts. He has written that the acquittal of Palizzolo in 1904 was a victory for the mafia.[66] This has been the opinion of almost all writers; the acquittal of Palizzolo represented a defeat for reform and a victory for the mafia. Yet it is a strange conclusion, for neither reform nor the mafia was on trial, but Raffaele Palizzolo. Certainly Palizzolo emerges as an unattractive figure. He was connected with the Villabate *cosca*, and it is possible that the Villabate *cosca*, was connected to the murder of Notarbartolo. Yet Palizzolo stood accused of a murder, an accusation backed by nothing more than speculation and hypotheses. There was never a case against him. It is hard to see why his acquittal should count as a defeat for justice.

Nor is it easy to see what the mafia had actually gained. At the time of his brutal murder in 1891, Emanuele Notarbartolo was a retired civil servant. He was not an appropriate target for a mafia hit squad. It is likely that one of the actual assassins was connected to the mafia; it may even be that this assassin was Giuseppe Fortuna, who had been selected for the job by the Villabate *cosca*. Still there is a great deal of difference between claiming that someone had paid the mafia to murder Notarbartolo and claiming that the murder of Notarbartolo and the acquittal of Palizzolo represented a triumph for mafia interests in general. The Sicilian mafia was not in this or in any other period a unified force; it was neither a political nor a social movement; it had no general motive for killing Notarbartolo. The claim that Palizzolo's acquittal was a victory for the mafia really comes down to saying that it was a defeat for the far left. It had been the far left that had decided to use the Notarbartolo murder to demonstrate that the Italian state was rotten to the core and that the only alternative was that offered by revolutionary parties like the socialists.

What was the far left really proposing? In 1900, inspired by Leopoldo Notarbartolo's revelations in the Milan trial, Napoleone Colajanni wrote a mighty *j'accuse* directed at the magistracy, the police, and the government. The mafia, he wrote,—at least the mafia before 1860—had incarnated "the spirit of the individual reacting against the arrogance of power." During this period, "all the rebels, all who had suffered insults, all the victims" had supported the mafia, for this mafia was the "only means for the humble, the poor, for the workingmen to make themselves feared and respected." Yet the hopes of these victims for a new "kingdom of justice" had been betrayed by the state. The Italian government, he concluded, "has done *everything* to consolidate the mafia and render it omnipotent."[67]

There was still time, however; the "kingdom of the mafia" could still be overthrown. But it was imperative to act now:

To combat and destroy the kingdom of the mafia it is necessary—it is indispensable—that the government cease to be the *king of the mafia*! But the government has grown too accustomed to the pleasures of its illicit and dishonest authority; it has become insensible to the evils to which it is addicted. Have we reached the point where we can no longer hope for the cessation of the malfunction in any way other than through the destruction of the organ itself?[68]

The government, he said, needed to wipe the slate clean in Sicily, institute "a fair and practical administration, tightly controlled by the central

*Brigands arrested during the 1950s. Archivio Scafidi.*

government" and "strong police and magistracy."[69] Was this a call for a reimposition of martial law or for a new revolution? From the *carbonaro* uprising of 1820 onward, nineteenth-century Sicily had undergone an unceasing cycle of turmoil as revolutionary upheavals were succeeded by waves of fierce repression. Did Colajanni want to bring it all back again? Was Colajanni summoning Maniscalco and General Govone or the revolutionary *squadre* or both? Whatever was on his mind, it is clear that, first of all, he was calling for a crusade. Indeed, we saw that the 1902 Bologna verdict generated just such an atmosphere of reformist zeal. Yet it was very short-lived; by 1904, Palizzolo was back home in Palermo and the crusade was over.

One result of the Notarbartolo scandal was indeed a new campaign against the mafia. On the basis of the Sangiorgi report, the government indicted dozens of *cagnoli* and *cagnolazzi* as members of a criminal association. There were two large trials, in 1898 and 1901. Yet, as Diego Tajani and Carlo Morena had predicted in 1878, there was no point in indicting individuals as members of a criminal association when none of them could be indicted for specific crimes. Most of the men were acquitted for lack of proof; the few that were convicted received light sentences.

The trials proved an embarrassment to the state. They led to a fresh spat between the police and the magistracy, each accusing the other of protecting friends and clients in the mafia. The police were especially indignant when the attorneys for one of the *cosche* managed to have a police official indicted for abuse of power.[70] Seeing the futility of such trials, the government left the *cosche* in peace after 1901. The would-be revolutionaries would have to wait until the 1920s when the Fascist government would unleash a new, full-scale offensive against the mafia in Sicily.

The answer to the question of who had won is therefore that no one had. And the answer to the question of who had lost would be Sicily itself. Giuseppe Pitrè was appalled at the depth of northern hostility revealed at the Bologna trial. "Forty years ago—he wrote despairingly in 1902—who could have ever dreamt that things like this would be said about Sicily and Sicilians?"[71]

Pitrè's despair was echoed by the dramatist and columnist Scarfoglio in Naples in 1903. Now, he wrote, "our brothers" in the north have declared war upon us, sending down a "pack of socialists" with "with mouths filled with mud" and "with hearts bursting with murderous hate." Now "this state," "nourished" by the south's "best blood," tells us that "*we are the ones who are supposed to die.*"[72]

It was more than just a loss of self-esteem and prestige. A combination of circumstances—the rise and bloody suppression of the *fasci*, the Condronchi commissariat, and the Notarbartolo scandal—had all combined to wipe out Sicily's last indigenous political ruling group, the Crispian left. It was a ruling group whose demise hardly seems worth mourning. By the 1890s the transformation was complete: the revolutionary Peter Pans stood revealed as curmudgeonly old Captain Hooks. Their last political projects had been tariff wars and aggressive nationalism. It is not surprising that the Fascists later saluted them as their precursors.

What makes the history of Sicily in the last half of the nineteenth century a depressing tale is that the decline of the Crispian left reflects a larger pattern. During this same period, Sicily was declining economically and socially. Already by the 1880s, its rate of growth was slowing in respect to that of the North. Crispi's decision to turn Sicily into the granary of Italy disrupted the agrarian balance of the island by forcing a massive conversion to grain growing. It was also a decision that transformed the estates themselves; self-sufficient estates that had traditionally produced a variety of foodstuffs, giving employment to specialist workers and strips of land to share-cropping peasants, gave way to what Petrusiewicz calls "policed work camps," where armed guards oversaw the labors of an increasingly desperate rural proletariat.[73] These were the workers who called the strike during the harvest of 1893, the ones involved in riots later that year, the ones who confronted the troops sent in by Crispi the following January. It was these same men who, in their tens of thousands, began to emigrate overseas, fleeing a society that offered them no hope of a better life.

Nor were impoverished peasants the only emigrants. Sicily in these years produced three prime ministers: Crispi, Rudinì, and Vittorio Emanuele Orlando. It produced ministers, magistrates, professors, and public servants of note. Few, however, made their careers in Sicily itself. Like Gaetano Mosca in Milan or the great dramatist Luigi Pirandello in Rome, they wrote about Sicily, but they passed their working lives in the more dynamic cities of northern Italy.

In 1895, the northern Italian political scientist Guglielmo Ferrero wrote of Crispi and his generation, "Few generations of men have started their life's work so well yet finished it so badly." Crispi stood for Garibaldi and the Thousand, "a heroic and mad adventure, something half out of the Middle Ages and half from modern times." It was a brand of political adventurism that by now had outlived its usefulness: "we are tired of it all."[74]

Yet for all its faults, the Crispian left was autonomous and indigenous; its disappearance was tragic as it marked the final chapter in Sicily's long attempt to create its own ruling group. The 1848 parliament had been the high-water mark. This was a body that genuinely represented Sicily in all its diversity, a body that possessed the political legitimacy to tackle, had circumstances been in its favor, the island's numerous problems. That Sicily was never again able to produce a ruling group as well qualified and representative as the 1848 parliament was, in no small amount, the result of repression under both the Neapolitans and the successors of Cavour.

It was also, of course, the fault of Sicilians themselves. Gaetano Mosca believed political liberalism to be a system of rule by law whose prime virtue lay in its rationality and public utility. So great were the benefits of

such a society, that, as Mosca wrote, an enlightened individual had no difficulty in obeying its laws even when these thwarted his "natural propen-
sity to pursue his own vocations and interests, to satisfy his appetites, and
his own will to power and pleasure."[75] Sicily seemed to represent the complete inversion of all these enlightened values.

> There does not exist (Leopoldo Franchetti wrote) in the overwhelming
> majority [of Sicilians] the idea of a collective, social interest, superior to
> and different from the interest of individuals. . . . There is a lack in the
> generality of Sicilians of the idea of a law, superior to all, and for all
> equal. . . . They do not consider themselves to be a single social body
> uniformly subject to a single common law, inflexible and the same for
> everyone, but rather as so many groups of persons formed and main-
> tained by individual bonds.[76]

True enough perhaps, but it is worth entering a caveat. Ideas such as
public opinion, public utility, and a "collective, social interest" typically
evolve in societies of well-integrated, well-informed, and self-governing
citizens. They do not evolve in traditional societies, such as Sicily before
1848, or among the urban poor or an impoverished rural proletariat. They
are ideas, moreover, that, as Mosca argued in the case of Sicily,[77] need time
to grow. Had Sicilians been given the opportunity to develop solutions to
their problems from their own resources, instead of having reform imposed on them by the police, they might have achieved a better result.

With this, it is possible to return to the question with which we opened
this final chapter: why, after 1860, did Sicily's own ruling group make no
attempt to curb the growth of the mafia? The answer is complex in detail;
but it comes down to two major reasons. To begin with, Sicily's ruling
group stood in an ambiguous relation to the state from the very beginning.
After 1860 the newly unified Italian state had endeavoured to shut out the
revolution, excluding from power the *squadre* leaders, conspirators, and
followers of Mazzini. The excluded revolutionaries resisted by allying
themselves with an extralegal structure of power. We saw that, particularly
in Palermo province, these informal networks of power had existed for
centuries under the leadership of powerful baronial families. Decades of
revolutionary conspiracy had helped to transform these networks, formal-
izing them, articulating and extending them, and, above all, broadening
their bases.

Sicilian resistance to Piedmont in the 1860s and early 1870s seemed to
come from both the far left (the *rossi*) and the far right (the *neri*). Histori-

ans have sometimes been perplexed by this, especially as the two opposed forces, revolutionary and counterrevolutionary, had no difficulty in cooperating with each other. In reality, neither label has much meaning in this context: the revolutionaries of September 1866 had no program beyond that of setting off a revolution; whatever individuals may have feared or desired, there was never any possibility of a Bourbon restoration in Sicily, much less a reinstitution of feudalism (whatever that might mean). Instead, Sicilian resistance to Piedmont had a much more immediate goal: it was an attempt to prevent the disarticulation of a structure of submerged power which, although its roots were traditional, had arisen in the revolutionary struggle.

Both the revolutionaries and the emerging mafia were part of this submerged structure of power. The mafia, in the form that it was to take, not only emerged in and through the revolutionary struggle; this mafia also emerged as the political clients of the revolutionary party. Had the revolutionary party been allowed a share of power, it might have moved to clean out such clients.

The campaign eventually undertaken by Carlo Morena and Antonio Malsuardi in Sicily with the backing of Diego Tajani and Giovanni Nicotera in Rome in the late 1870s cleared the countryside of the brigand bands and brought order to towns convulsed in turf wars between rival Brotherhoods; yet it made no move against established political clients such as Antonino Giammona or the Nicolosi brothers of Lercara Friddi. The true character of such clients was a mystery to no one; yet by now they were too embedded in the left's network of power to be removed without causing damage to the network itself.

The second reason why Sicily's ruling group made no real attempt to confront the mafia is simpler: by the 1890s this group had its back to the wall, and it knew it. The fact that ideas such as public opinion and public utility had not really spread in Sicily meant that voting was largely opportunistic. Voters voted for the politicians who offered them the most. This meant that Sicilian voters tended to choose whoever seemed best connected to the government, for, it was assumed, the closer a politician got to the center of power, the more access he had to patronage. Whatever affection the Sicilian middle classes may have retained for the Crispian left, the 1895 elections showed that Sicilians voted out of perceived self-interest rather than out of sentiment: Sicilian voters did not usually elect men who could not do them favors.

The only issue that could really unite Sicily's political class was the demand for more government patronage to be directed to Sicily. Beyond this, it was every man for himself; every politician contended with his neighbor to see that the maximum share of government largesse was directed toward his constituents. Their mafia clients, by contrast, were under no such institutional constraints. The mafia's sources of power were extra-institutional; they stayed in office whether or not they won the elections. In the 1890s, this put the Sicilian ruling group in the miserable position of needing their mafia clients more than their mafia clients needed them. Throughout the entire Notarbartolo scandal, this ruling group was most notable for its silence, expressing only in the most perfunctory way the desire to see justice done and the good name of Sicily restored. These were men who desperately needed to retain the support of their mafia clients if they wished to be reelected.

The fall of the Crispian left had removed a class of intermediaries, one that had stood between Sicilian society and the Italian state. It was a class that had genuinely represented the island and had been able, on a number of issues, to stand united. The loss of this class rendered Sicily politically vulnerable; for its fall meant that a gap had opened up which there were only two forces left to fill. One was the mafia and the other was the Italian state.

Between 1900 and World War I, the mafia consolidated its position in Sicilian politics; yet it was still neither strong enough or sophisticated enough to make a direct bid for power. The mafiosi would need to wait until the end of World War II, when their American cousins returned to Sicily and broadened their horizons.

The real gainer from the fall of the Crispian left was the Italian state and, especially, Antonio Giolitti, the leader of the northern left and the predominant political figure throughout this period. It was Giolitti who was responsible for a political settlement in Sicily which endured until the consolidation of the Fascist regime, and which, in a modified form, was reintroduced after World War II. The government would not introduce martial law into Sicily; the government would not introduce new reforms; the government would not seek to suppress mafia *cosche* as long as they refrained from open warfare. The government would keep patronage to Sicily flowing; it would confirm Sicily's traditional dominance of patronage posts such as the ministries of public instruction, postal services, and public works. In exchange, the government expected absolute obedience form the Sicilian deputies; they were to follow the instructions of the prefects and support the government in all its acts. Napoleone Colajanni had been correct; the fall of Sicily's own ruling group meant that the Italian government became "king of the mafia."

# Conclusion

Toutes les révolutions entrent dans l'histoire, et l'histoire n'en engorge point.

——Guy Debord

In retrospect, Count Gualterio's 1865 report seems both prophetic and ironic. "Public spirit" in Palermo, he had written, was "gravely troubled" by "a deep and prolonged misunderstanding between the Country and Authority." Could the growth of the mafia all be just the result of a "misunderstanding," even a "deep and prolonged misunderstanding"?[1]

What sort of "misunderstanding" could it be then? Gualterio's report continues that the misunderstanding had not only made "it possible for the so-called *Maffia* or delinquent association to grow in audacity", but

what is more, the Government has found itself without the due moral authority to request the support of the numerous class of influential and authoritative citizens, while the preceding incidents impeded, perhaps from fatal necessity, the Chief of Police's office from drawing upon impartial sources and, therefore, during the recent outbreak of crime and unrest (which has many links with the various parties) it found itself unable to reassure the populace concerning the efficacy of its acts and bring to an end the unfortunate results that this outbreak of crime has produced.

It should no longer be necessary to specify what Gualterio meant by "preceding incidents" or to elucidate the "fatal necessity" that prevented the Palermo police chief, Felice Pinna, from "drawing upon impartial sources." It might, however, be useful to point out that what Gualterio is alluding to by the term "misunderstanding" is that alliance between the influential classes and the dangerous classes which, as we saw in the first chapter, is a recurrent theme in Sicilian history.

"Misunderstanding" is a diplomatic term. Gualterio was worried that the "influential and authoritative citizens" of Palermo were distancing themselves from a regime they felt was unresponsive to their needs. This worry was hardly pure fantasy. Sicily and Piedmont were two mismatched pieces of a political puzzle. When Piedmont tried to force Sicily into a political and institutional straightjacket, the influential and authoritative citizens of Palermo, seeing that their power and local autonomy was under threat, renewed their alliance with segments of the revolutionary and counterrevolutionary parties, as well as with the dangerous classes that both sides of the combat had tried to to recruit. Gualterio saw this clearly as well: "The liberals in 1848, the Bourbons during the Restoration, the *Garibaldini* in 1860 all found themselves under the same necessity and all soiled themselves with the same fault."

The 1867 parliamentary inquiry solicited the opinions of Sicily's senators. These were a group of Sicilian aristocrats and intellectuals nominated to the Italian Senate after 1860. We last encountered Romualdo Trigona, the prince of Sant'Elia, as the gruff leader of the "moderate" faction at the outset of the 1848 revolt. He was still active as a senator in 1867, and when the parliamentary inquiry asked him what, in his opinion, caused the 1866 uprising, he brusquely replied that it was a government that behaved like "a trigger-happy peace officer who destroyed local interests and offended many people's susceptibilities."[2] Other senators such as Vito d'Onde-Reggio or Emerico Amari may have used a more temperate language; yet the message was the same.

Approximately fifteen years later, a Neapolitan intellectual named Sebastiano Turiello restated the idea of a "misunderstanding" in a manner much less flattering to the influential citizens of Palermo. Sicily, Turiello wrote, remained a feudal society, though one with its own particular form.

In this society the clienteles represented "the natural guise in which a feudalism that has not exhausted its inner necessity reappears."[3] The reforms of the new, liberal state, he continued, had only "shorn off the outer branches of this feudalism." Despite the fact that the old feudal "organism" had been formally "dissolved," "the new one lacks sufficient vitality in the customs of society." Consequently, there had opened a "gap where anarchy reigns," and in this gap, "there is a multiplication of inferior organisms—similar to worms and mold—[which] flourish in the space made available by the lack of vitality in the superior organism and the failure of new organisms to be born."[4]

All these opinions point in the same direction. There was a rent in the political texture, a wound, gap, or disjuncture between the de jure political structure, represented by Piedmont and its Albertine Statute, and the de facto political organization of Sicily. It was a disjuncture that had to be bridged. The most natural class of mediators "between the Country and Authority" (as Gualterio put it) would seem to have been, on the one hand, Sicily's traditional ruling élite and, on the other, the leaders of the revolution. Unfortunately, as we have seen, the class of "influential and authoritative citizens" turned out to be smaller in number and less influential than Piedmont might have hoped. A large proportion of the traditional ruling class had been marginalized by over a decade of revolutionary strife and police repression. Cooperation with the second group, the revolutionary leaders, was, by contrast, ruled out by Piedmont itself; it was considered politically inopportune by Cavour and his successors. This meant that the disjuncture could be bridged only by coercive force, through men like General Govone who, however well meaning they may have been, still played the part of trigger-happy peace officers intent on spreading civilization through violence (as Sant'Elia put it).

In the decades before 1860, the alliance between the influential and dangerous classes in Sicily had been a part of the revolutionary struggle. It was a struggle that depended upon the maintenance of a clandestine network of control. This was a network that, on the one hand, reflected patterns of kinship and deference through which Sicily's barons had traditionally exercised their influence, while, on the other, it represented a new structure created by the sectarians. It was a system of submerged power that might, after 1860, have been brought to the surface and used to mediate between Sicily and Piedmont. Instead, Piedmont attempted to suppress this network, driving it back into clandestinity. The result was a war of attrition which reinforced the network's most negative aspects—its subversiveness, its violence, and its capacity for crime.

The Sangiorgi report reveals that by the 1890s this structure of sub-merged power had become so embedded in the society of western Sicily as to appear almost normal. It was not, as the prefect de Seta blandly assured Prime minister Pelloux, "considered improper for an honest individual property owner to hire as custodians for his property, and to protect him-self through them, persons belonging to the mafia."[5] By now, however, their capacity for subversion had gone; by now the mafia was no more rev-olutionary than the Crispian left. Yet their capacity for violence and crime was unabated. After 1900, the tacit acceptance of this situation by Italian governments paved the way for a gradual criminalization of Sicilian society as a whole.

The quotation in French that stands at the opening of this conclusion is an oblique reference to a verse from *Ecclesiastes*: "All the rivers empty into the sea and yet the sea never fills up." Debord, however, changes the terms to read: "All the revolutions empty into history and yet history is never fulfilled." We have seen the mafia as a creature of the revolution. It is as if revolution were a long tunnel through which groups from the Conca d'Oro passed. They entered it as the "dangerous classes," but they emerged from the other side as the mafia. What kind of revolution has an effect like this? The answer is that it is the revolution that can never reach its own fulfillment.

Those authors who worry over the question of whether the mafia repre-sented a revolutionary or counterrevolutionary force are giving to the idea of revolution a particular historical meaning. In this, revolution is a politi-cal upheaval that serves to sweep away unjust, repressive, and socially backward regimes, to cast them into the dustbin of history, and to set up free and progressive polities in their stead. If one accepts such a notion, or perhaps ideal, of revolution, it is indeed hard to accommodate the mafia, to recognize in them revolution's legitimate children. Yet this is not the only possible idea of revolution. At its simplest, a rebellion is a refusal to recognize the sovereignty or legitimacy of authority, to obey its dictates, or those of its officials. In this, very basic, sense, a revolution is a gap—a sus-pension of legality and civility; and it is in this sense that we can most eas-ily see the connection between revolution and mafia. The mafia are the soldiers of the permanent revolution.

The phrase *carrières ouvertes aux talents* has its antecedents in the French Revolution. In that context it refers to an ideal of meritocracy, of a society in which success is bestowed as a reward for merit, application, or talent rather than for birth or connections. This is the ideal for the postrevolutionary society, the society that comes afterward. But what are the *carrières ouvertes aux talents* during the revolution itself? A revolution is not one long pitched battle. There were in fact few pitched battles in the Sicilian revolution; there were instead intrigues, plots, uprisings, lootings, sackings, kidnappings, murders, vendettas, thefts and robberies, ambushes, escapes, marches and countermarches, barricades, bombardments, and, through it all, repression. The most promising career paths during the time of revolution were, we saw, revolution, politics, and crime, three overlapping activities that seemed to blend into one another. This was the revolution that swells and feeds upon itself so that it can never be satisfied. This is permanent, endemic revolution; this is the mafia.

In reality, there is no reason to think that these two ideas of revolution are incompatible. Francesco Crispi, Rosolino Pilo, Francesco Bentivegna, Francesco Riso, and Turi Miceli were all, in their way, idealists, all believers in the revolution's promise. In 1820, the dangerous classes of Palermo and the Conca d'Oro fell upon the Neapolitan troops in part out of the spirit of vendetta, but equally because they wished to turn the Carboneria promise of equality and brotherhood into a reality. The same might be said of the sulfur miners in Agrigento province, who, according to the 1859 police report, wanted to take "the possessions of the well-off, who, they say, ought all to be put to death, removing all distinctions of class, and divide among themselves, brothers in equality, the booty."[6] The same might be said of the throng of rowdy Monrealesi that burst into Palermo in 1866. It would be wrong to deny the mafia their revolutionary antecedents and ideals. Yet it would be a far greater error to overlook the reality their revolution created. In 1897, Francesco de Luca offered this judgment about the Fratellanza of Favara:

> If the idea of continual wrongs and never-ending calamities, along with the idea of a possible future redemption, was always in the minds of the *buona gente*, then it is clear that the Statute of the Fratellanza, which is so full of such ideas, cannot represent the charter of a criminal association at all. Instead it constituted an eloquent page in the social history of a people—a people persecuted and tormented from century to century—who throughout their bitter and backbreaking struggle to stay alive never once lost the hazy vision of a social redemption that was to come. This was a redemption that was not to be obtained through civil participation, however, but rather grasped immediately with knife thrusts and rifle shots—the only means available to the brutal mob.[7]

In this way, Sicily's struggle for freedom transformed itself into a vendetta, an extended mafio-political turf war in which no Sicilian can long remain free.

Permanent revolution exists alongside permanent repression as well. In its century and a half of existence, the Italian state has yet to find a policy toward Sicily that goes beyond playing, by turn, the roles of King Stork and King Log. What is particularly curious about this oscillation is that all the campaigns of King Stork–like repression begin their existence as state-sponsored revolution, as the necessary prelude to grandiose reforms that would turn Sicily into a prosperous and civil meritocracy. The campaigns of repression initiated in 1862, 1894, 1927, and 1946 were all, without exception, presented as aspects of land reform. The arguments have always been the same as those of Maniscalco in the 1850s: reform in Sicily is necessary and must be imposed from above; to ensure the success of these reforms, legitimate authority must be in complete control; to ensure complete control, the police and military must be given exceptional powers and a free hand. Not only has this been a policy that has consistently failed to achieve its desired goals, it is a policy that has failed at a high cost to both Sicily and the Italian state. When the campaign of repression invariably falters and the government swings back toward a King Log–like apathy, it abandons its reforms and development projects like carcasses that

*Monument to the Fallen.*

the mafia and their political friends can feast upon. With this, a larger section of the Sicilian population becomes criminalized. And with this, reformers and state officials begin to brood like failed revolutionaries and experience their relations with Sicily as a vendetta.

Marks of this vendetta are not hard to find. In 1883 the municipality of Palermo erected a small monument next to the spot where the police of Maniscalco shot the thirteen unfortunate prisoners taken during Francesco Riso's short-lived uprising. The monument took the form of a funerary obelisk inscribed with the thirteen names. On the fiftieth anniversary of Riso's rebellion, the municipality thought to give the monument a greater prominence by placing it on a stone platform. Today, however, both the obelisk and the platform are dwarfed by a much larger, more recent monument. Three naked steel shafts soar into the air. Floodlights and a low fence designed to keep the public away accentuate the sense of starkness and menace. Only the charitable hand of juvenile spraypainters serves to mitigate it in its incivil brutality.

At its base, the monument proclaims that it is dedicated to the "Fallen in the Struggle against the Mafia." Yet it not a monument to the fallen at all. Rather it is a call to arms, a cry of defiance, a cry for vengeance and for permanent revolution. Until the revolution finally stops, Sicily's wounds can never be healed.

# Abbreviations

| | |
|---|---|
| ACS Min G&G | Archivio Central dello Stato, Ministero di Grazia e Giustizia (National Archives, Rome, Ministry of Justice). |
| ACS Min Int | Archivio Centrale dello Stato, Ministero dell'Interno (National Archives, Rome, Ministry of the Interior). |
| *AbRf* | *Archive historique de la Révolution française* (Paris, periodical). |
| Arch di Psichiatria . . . | *Archivio di psichiatria, scienze penali et antropologia criminale* (periodical). |
| *ArchSto-SO* | *Archivio Storico per la Sicilia orientale* (periodical). |
| ASA | Archivio dello Stato, Agrigento (National Archives, Agrigento). |
| ASP Gab Pref | Archivio dello Stato, Palermo, Gabinetto Prefettura (National Archives, Palermo, Prefectural Cabinet). |
| *ASS* | *Archivio della Storia di Sicilia* (Palermo, periodical). |
| *ATTI* | *Atti parliamentari* (summaries of Italian parliamentary debates). |
| *CdS* | *Corriere della Sera.* |
| *GdS* | *Giornale di Sicilia.* |
| 1875 Hearings | *Inchiesta parlementare sulle condizioni sociali ed economiche della Sicilia (1875)* (1875 parliamentary hearings into public security in Sicily, reprinted Bologna, 1968. These statements are sometimes referred to as the *Inchiesta Bonfaldini* after the name of the chairman). |
| Malfattori | Set of documents concerning public security in Sicily in 1877 and 1878, including letters exchanged between Prefect Malsuardi, State Procurator Morena, Minister of Justice Tajani, and Minister of the Interior Nicotera. Labeled SICILIA: Associazioni di malfattori, in ACS Min di G&G, Misc affari penali, 1877, b. 44, fasc. 558 |
| La Mantia *verbale* | Copy of the depostion (*verbale*) of Rosario La Mantia together with other police reports in ACS Min G&G, under the title Min di G&G dir gen.le aa pp, misc 1879, b. 55, fasc. 620, "Relazioni di Rosario La Mantia." |
| *Moti* | *I moti di Palermo del 1866: verbali della Commissione parlamentare di inchiesta* (Parliamentary inquiry into the 1866 uprising, reprinted with an introduction by Magda da Passano, *Camera dei Deputati*, Rome, 1981). |
| *NQ / M* | *Nuovi Quaderni del Meridione* (periodical). |
| Palizzolo | Collected police reports and documents concerning Raffaele Palizzolo lodged in ACS Min Int., under the title Min |

|  |  |
|---|---|
|  | dell Int, dir gen PS, aa gg rr anno 1893–1904, b. .1, fasc. 1/11, Palizzolo Raffale ed altri/assassinio del comm. E. Notarbartolo. Other files on the Notarbartolo assassination are located at ACS Min G&G, Misc affari penali, b. 126, fasc. 1131, Palermo reati: processo Raffaele Palizzolo vol II. |
| Sangiorgi | Report of the Palermo police chief, Armando Sangiorgi, to the minister of the interior in a series of confidential letters from 1898 and 1899, with a summary dated 1900 titled *La mafia dell'agro palermitano*. These reports are now in ACS Min Int., and are labeled Min dell'Interno, dir gen PS, aa. gg. e rr. atti speciali (1898–1940): 1898–1899, *allegati* from 1900, b. 1, fasc. 1. |
| Stoppaglieri trial | 1875 Stoppaglieri trial in Palermo, now in Archivio dello Stato, Palermo, under label Tribunale civile e penale di Palermo, Fascicoli di procedimenti di assize, anno 1875, b. 143, fasc. 1, 8, 9, 10. |

# Notes

## Introduction

1. ASP Gab Pref, b. 7, cat. 35; also in ACS Min Int Varie, b. 7, fasc. 4. See also Alatri 1954, pp. 92–102, and Brancato 1956, p. 36.
2. Cutrera 1900, p. 57.
3. Trevelyan 1907, p. 155.
4. De Seta and di Marco 1980, pp. 155–56.

## Chapter I. The Setting: Sicily before the Mafia

1. See di Matteo 1967 and Gaja 1974.
2. Gaja 1974, p. 4.
3. Falcone 1991, p. 143.
4. Pontieri 1949, pp. 10–14.
5. Mack Smith 1969, p. 309.
6. Ibid., p. 307.
7. Cited in G. Falzone 1965, p. 160.
8. Mack Smith 1969, p. 335.
9. Ibid., pp. 128–29.
10. Mirabella 1961.
11. Candeloro 1980, 2:67.
12. Mack Smith 1969, p. 95.
13. Giuntella 1950.
14. Quoted in Sewell 1987.
15. Godechot 1980d.
16. Mathiez 1928, pp. 551–73; also Godechot 1980b, Francovich 1952, Soanen 1928, and Valenti 1965.
17. Matteo Mazziotti cited in Leti 1925, p. 126.
18. Labate 1904, p. 24 and passim for Naples; see also Colletta 1849.
19. Ibid., see also Candeloro 1990, vol. 1, chap. 1.
20. Ventura, 1821; Anonymous [Amari] 1847 (introduction to Palmieri 1847); and Chiaramonte, 1901.
21. Paternò-Castello 1848, p. 114.
22. Labate 1904, p. 35.
23. Cortese 1951, pp. 29–30.
24. Renda 1968, pp. 55–58. Renda is paraphrasing the description in Palmieri 1847, p. 329.
25. Paternò-Castello 1848, pp. 126–31 and 138–39.

26. Cortese 1951, p. 249.

27. Paternò-Castello 1848, p. 141.

28. Lea 1908, pp. 15 and 29.


## Chapter 2. The 1848 Revolt

1. Guardione 1901.

2. Sansone 1889.

3. Letter of 1820 cited in Renda 1968, pp. 30–31.

4. Alongi 1977, p. 25.

5. All quotations cited in Pontieri 1943, p. 347.

6. In Pilo 1914.

7. Dated October 29, 1847, in Curato 1970, p. 137.

8. On conspiracies, see La Masa 1850, Gori 1897, Beltrami-Scalea 1908, vol. 1, and Raffaele 1883.

9. Fardella 1887; see also Pilo 1914 and Beltrami-Scalea 1908, 1:255–56.

10. Pilo 1914.

11. Ibid.

12. Calvi 1851, pp. 48–49. The meeting is mentioned by both Pilo 1914 and Beltrami-Scalea 1908.

13. La Farina 1850–51, p. 5.

14. Letter of January 18, 1848, in Curato 1970, pp. 322–24.

15. Beltrami-Scalea 1908, 2:18.

16. Iachello and Signorelli 1987, pp. 110–11, 121.

17. Romeo 1973 passim; also Petrusiewicz 1989.

18. See the description of the Valguanera uprising in Barnaba 1981.

19. Fiume 1982, pp. 74 and 109–10.

20. See account of Francesco Malvica in Fiume 1984a.

21. Calvi 1851, p. 132.

22. Fiume 1984a.

23. Fiume 1982, pp. 109–10.

24. Calvi 1851, p. 132.

25. Napier to Minto in Curato 1970, pp. 334–35.

26. See documents in Curato 1970, pp. 373–74.

27. Mack Smith 1969, p. 424.

28. Pilo 1914.


## Chapter 3. The 1860 Revolution

1. Trevelyan's estimate based on Neapolitan sources (1907 p. 246).

2. De Cesare 1969, p. 75.

3. Cited in Schirò 1931, pp. 199–211.

4. Mack Smith 1994, p. 60.

5. Ibid., p. 111.

6. Ibid., pp. 116–17.

7. Ibid., pp. 106–7; see also Candeloro, 1994, 4:220.

8. Orsini 1857.

9. On Orsini, see Gori 1897.

10. Trevelyan 1907, pp. 71–72.

11. Trevelyan 1907, p. 72. See also Mack Smith 1994, pp. 121–22.

12. Mack Smith 1994, p. 10.

13. Candeloro 1990, 4: 220–28.

14. Mack Smith 1994, p. 109.

15. Trevelyan 1907, p. 68.

16. Candeloro 1990, 4:244–73.

17. Rossi 1982, pp. 59–64.

18. Cited in Tranfaglia 1983b.

19. Trevelyan 1907, pp. 108–9.

20. Ibid., p. 115.

21. Viola 1984, pp. 223–47.

22. Sansone 1891, pp. 21–33.

23. Ibid. and Spiridone 1899.

24. Letter dated March 5, 1853, quoted in Viola 1984.

25. Sansone 1891, p. 76.

26. Paolucci 1904.

27. Campo 1884, pp. 42–43.

28. Sansone 1891, p. 99.

29. See Mirabella 1961.

30. De Cesare 1969, pp. 21, 23–25.

31. Casarrubea and Cipolla 1982, p. 101.

32. Spiridone 1899.

33. Cited in De Cesare 1969, p. 23.

34. Letter April 3, 1853, cited in Viola 1984.

35. Brancaccio di Carpino 1901, pp. 12–13; De Cesare 1969, pp. 693–94.

36. Campo 1884, pp. 36–37.

37. Trevelyan 1907, p. 152.

38. See Villari 1881, pp. 373–77. I am quoting from Trevelyan's translation, 1907, p. 151.

39. De Cesare 1969, pp. 700–703.

40. Paolucci 1904, p. 113.

41. De Cesare 1969, p. 702.

42. Paolucci 1904, p. 118. I quote the translation by Trevelyan, 1907, p. 153.

43. Ibid., p. 124.

44. Anonymous [N.N.] 1860.

45. Petta 1861.

46. Brancaccio di Carpino 1863; Trevelyan 1907, p. 160; *Cronaca* 1863 pp. 43–45.

47. In Trevelyan 1907, p. 189.

48. Bandi 1906.

49. Trevelyan 1907, pp. 224–44; Winnington-Ingram 1889.

50. Pecorini-Manzoni, 1876.

51. De Cesare 1969, pp. 752–53; Pecorini-Manzoni 1876, pp. 36–37; Trevelyan 1907, pp. 362–64.

52. Pecorini-Manzoni 1876.

53. De Cesare 1969, pp. 772 and 761; see also Cronaca 1863.

54. De Cesare 1969, p. 760.

55. *Times*, June 8, 1860.

56. Trevelyan 1907, p. 302.

57. Ibid., p. 303.

58. Mundy 1859–61, p. 291.

59. Ibid., see also *Morning Post*, June 26, 1860, p. 5, cited in Trevelyan 1907, p. 364, n. 1.

60. Trevelyan heard this from the great Sicilian ethnologist Giuseppe Pitrè, see Trevelyan 1907, p. 307, n. 1.

**Chapter 4. 1866: The *Sette Mezzo* Uprising and the Week's Republic in Palermo**

1. See Baviera Albanese 1961.

2. Paolucci 1904, p. 176.

3. Abba 1904, see also Romano 1986, p. 59.

4. Quoted in Paolucci 1904, p. 166.

5. Mack Smith 1954.

6. Baviera Albanese 1961.

7. Mack Smith 1954.

8. Baviera Albanese 1961.

9. The image is from Asor-Rosa 1975.

10. D'Ideville 1872, 1:181.

11. Sacerdote 1957.

12. Falzone 1971c, p. 172; see also Alatri 1954, pp. 71–6.

13. Alatri 1954, pp. 72–76; Falzone 1975b.

14. *Memoria riservata*, August 8, 1865, in ASP Gab Pref, b. 7, cat. 35. Cited in Brancato 1962, p. 70.

15. Cited in Falzone 1971C.

16. Ibid.

17. From a manuscript describing the adventures of Salvatore de Benedetto, written by his brother Raffaele, quoted ibid., pp. 137–84.

18. Pecorini-Manzoni 1876, pp. 82–84. Graziano 1915 gives a more sympathetic account.

19. Alatri 1954, p. 77. See also Molfese 1964.

20. *ATTI*, January 11 and 15, 1862, pp. 615–16, 674–82.

21. Alatri 1954, p. 76. See also Maurici 1915, p. 260, and Pantano 1933, chap 10.

22. Govone 1929, p. 134; see also Brancato 1964.

23. Govone 1929. pp. 139–40.

24. Letter to General Alessandro Della Rovere, December 1862, ibid., p. 130.

25. *Corriere Siciliano*, May 31–June 10, 1868.

26. Merenda 1931. Also see Trevelyan 1907, pp. 296–97.

27. On the Nicolosi family, see ASP Gab Pref, b. 2, f. *Lercara situazione politica*; b. 7, f. *Informazione riservate sui sindaci (1865)*; b. 11, f. *Informazioni riservate commando truppe* (March 1867). Most of the information is summarized in Mangiameli 1990. See also

ASP Gab Pref, b. 39, cat. 20, fasc. 50, 1877, not cited by Mangiameli, in which Giovanni Nicolosi is listed as a *mafioso di prima categoria* and true leader of the "mafia in yellow gloves." On Calcedonio Nicolosi, see ASP Gab Pref, b. 2, fasc. 8. 2a div.ne. (2nd division). See also Commandante dei Carabinieri to Luogotenente del Re, Palermo, June 26, 1861, in Scicchilone 1952, p. 77; and Mortillaro 1868, pp. 12–13.

28. See Mangiameli 1990, pp. 88, 99.

29. ASP Gab Pref, b. 2, Segretario generale del Dicastero to Luogotenente, Palermo, May 11, 1861. Cited in Mangiameli 1990, pp. 86–87.

30. I am drawing on the so-called *grande propalazione*, taken by the prosecuting attorney, Carlo Morena, on April 10, 1866, cited in Ajello 1868, pp. 65–101.

31. Hence his nickname "Peppino" (from Giuseppe) "il Lombardo" (the northerner).

32. On Giammona, see the discussion later in this chapter and Lupo 1988a; Alatri 1954, p. 136n.

33. ASP Gab Pref, b. 50, *Inchiesta sulla famiglia Guccione di Alia ed altre* (1878).

34. Ibid.

35. Alongi 1977, pp. 84–96. See also Turrisi-Colonna 1864.

36. Report, December 1840, cited in D'Alessandro 1959, p. 65.

37. Mangiameli 1990, p. 88.

38. On the arrest of Petta, see ASP Gab Pref, b. 7, fasc. *Arresto di Petta Antonino da Lercara*, September 15, 1864, and Ajello 1868, p. 281.

39. Ajello 1868, pp. 70–71.

40. On Valenza and D'Angelo, see Hess 1973, pp. 47–50, 55–57, 89–91, and 106–8; and ASP Gab Pref, b. 85, cat. 20, fasc. 133.

41. Ajello 1868, pp. 75–78; Mangiameli 1990, p. 93; Hess 1973, p. 99.

42. Ajello 1868, p. 81.

43. Mangiameli 1990, p. 96.

44. See Abba 1904.

45. *Il Percursore*, January 14–16, 1865, cited in Brancato 1953, p. 170; and Saverio Friscia letter of January 21, 1865, cited in Brancato 1962, p. 64.

46. Pagano 1867, pp. 44–5, cited in Brancato 1953, p. 168, note 1. See also Vito D'Ondes-Reggio and Emerico Amari in *Moti*, pp. 41–43, 48–50.

47. Pezzino 1990a, p. 94

48. Alatri 1954, p. 96, 1.

49. Scicchilone 1952, pp. 122–35. See also Alatri 1954, pp. 135–39 and notes.

50. See speech of Luigi La Porta in *ATTI*, July 8, 1875.

51. On Spadaro, see Alatri 1954, pp. 123–24, 127n., and 136n. See also 1867 hearings, ibid., pp. 126–29, 155–57.

52. Brancato 1953 commenting on prefect's report of March 27, 1873, on the organizers of the 1866 uprising; see p. 183n. Alatri 1954, p. 136, gives the same list but draws it from the Questura (police station) report of October 5, 1866, also cited in Scicchilone 1952, p. 199.

53. Mangiameli 1990.

54. *Quarterly Review* 1867, p. 102.

55. See letter from F. DiGiovanni to M. Amari, May 19, 1865 in Brancato 1953, p. 174n; ASP Gab Pref, b. b. 27, cat. 19, fasc. 5.

56. *Quarterly Review* 1867, p. 112.

57. *Moti*, pp. 122 and 126–29.

58. Ibid., pp. 346–48.

59. Ibid.

60. Letter of Michele Pasciuta, cited in Brancato 1953, p. 184.

61. *Quarterly Review* 1867, p. 117.

62. Maurici 1915, pp. 413–98 and 527. On Bonafede, see Brancato 1966.

63. Brancato 1966. See also ASP, Gabinetta. Questura, b. 1, cited in Alatri 1954, pp. 131–32.

64. *Moti*, pp. 41–43, 44–47, 57–58, and 77–78.

65. Maurici 1915; Brancato 1953, 1966.

66. *Quarterly Review* 1867, p. 121.

67. "Impiegati d'antico macino," which I have translated as "municipal employees" for short; cited in Brancato 1953.

68. Anonymous [Raffaele] 1866.

69. *Quarterly Review* 1867, p. 121.

70. "Che vi era e doveva essere la rivoluzione." Don Lucifero Benedettino di Monreale, *Moti*, p. 303.

71. The first figure is the estimate of the French consul, the second that of Michele Pasciuta. The population at the time was something under 200,000. Brancato 1953, pp. 184 and 187.

72. Ibid., p. 184, citing Pasciuta.

73. *Quarterly Review* 1867, p. 108.

74. Brancato 1977; see also Brancato 1953, p. 184.

75. Alatri 1954, pp. 136–37 and 109.

76. *Quarterly Review* 1867, p. 124.

77. Catalanotto 1982.

78. Mortillaro 1868, pp. 150–51.

79. Cf. Salamone-Marini 1899.

80. Maggiorani 1866, p. 2.

81. Brancato 1953, pp. 136–37.

82. Ibid.

83. Note of January 8, 1877, in ASP Gab. Pref., b. 38, cat. 16, fasc. 2, cited in Brancato 1983, p. 226.

## Chapter 5. *Cosche* and *Mafiusi*

1. *Moti*, p. 117.

2. Ibid.

3. Ibid., p. 118.

4. See p. 68.

5. *Moti*, p. 118.

6. Quoted in Ciuni 1978, p. 385.

7. Pitrè 1889, pp. 288–90. See also 1870–71, pp. 70–71.

8. Cutrera 1979 (orig. 1896), pp. 27–28.

9. The phrase "he did it *pri u currivu*" refers to seemingly senseless or even self-destructive acts of violence. See Mosca 1980, p. 169.

10. Pitrè 1870–71; Cutrera 1979.

11. Anonymous [De Menza] 1878.

12. Bonanno 1984, Fentress and Wickham 1992, chap. 5.

13. Fentress and Wickham, 1992, chap. 5.

14. *Racconti popolari* of 1840, by the dialect novelist, Vincenzo Linares. On the history of the Beati Paoli, see Castiglione 1987.

15. See Labate 1904.

16. Messina 1990, chap. 1.

17. Those that do derive from Arabic, moreover, are usually borrowed from Spanish rather than derived directly from Arabic.

18. It appears in the third edition (though not the earlier two) of Mortillaro's dictionary (1862), where it is glossed as "a Piedmontese term introduced into the rest of Italy which means *camorra* [underworld]."

19. Cammareri Scurti, cited in Costanza 1964, p. 54.

20. In the 1876 edition of Mortillaro's Italian-Sicilian dictionary (1862).

21. Maggiorani 1866.

22. 1875 Hearings, pp. 522–23.

23. Fazio 1901, p. 13.

24. Monnier 1863 and Umiltà 1878; see also Chapter 1.

25. For Naples, see Monnier 1863, and Colletta 1874, p. 229; see also Umiltà 1878, pp. 39–40, and Collison-Morley 1925, pp. 166–72.

26. Cammareri Scurti 1899; Mazzamuto 1970.

27. ASP Gab Pref, 1877, b. 38, cat. 16, fasc. 2.

28. Ibid.

29. Ibid.

30. ASA, fasc. 18, letter from police delegate of Bivona January 28, 1870.

31. Barnaba 1981, pp. 26–27.

32. See Mosca 1980, pp. 65–69.

33. 1875 Hearings, *documenti*, p. 988.

34. 1875 Hearings, p. 486.

35. See Hess 1973, pp. 109–15.

36. 1875 Hearings, p. 486.

37. Turrisi-Colonna 1864, p. 30.

38. Ibid.

39. *Moti*, pp. 130–32.

40. 1875 Hearings, pp. 152–54.

41. Blok 1974, p. 63.

42. Carlo Morena to Minister of Justice, October 17, 1877, contained in Malfattori.

43. Ibid.

44. Galati's memorial is appended to 1875 Hearings; subsequent quotations are from this source.

45. Franchetti and Sonnino 1974, pp. 20–22.

46. Morena to Minister of Justice, October 17, 1877 in Malfattori.

47. Cutrera 1900, p. 172.

48. Mangiameli 1990. See also the comments of Police Chief Rastrelli and the lawyer Francesco Gestivo, 1875 Hearings, pp. 405 and 462–63; also Alatri 1954, p. 136, n. 5.

49. 1875 Hearings, pp. 452–63.

50. Sangiorgi, p. 10.

51. Messina 1990, pp. 38–39. According to Alongi 1977, p. 103, the term *cosca* spread from the Monreale area.

52. For the *fratuzzi* of Bagheria, see Cutrera 1900, pp. 145–52. For the *cosca* at Villabate, see separate report in Sangiorgi.

53. There were nine Fontanas in a single *cosca*, of whom eight were brothers and one an uncle. Sangiorgi p. 57.

54. Lupo 1988a.

55. Sangiorgi, November 8, 1898.

56. Ibid.

57. Sangiorgi, December 12, 1898, pp. 217ff.

58. Ibid., December 2, 1898, p. 190.

59. Ibid., November 8, 1898, pp. 37–40.

60. Ibid., December 2, 1898, pp. 189–97.

61. Ibid., November 8, 1898, p. 38.

62. Ibid.

63. Ibid., November 20, 1898.

64. Ibid., November 8, 1898.

65. Ibid., p. 42.

66. For the murders of Angelo Tuttolimondo, Lo Porto, and Caruso, see ibid., November 11 and 20, 1898.

67. Ibid., November 11, 1898, pp. 40–47.

68. Ibid., pp. 335–36.

69. Ibid., p. 336.

## Chapter 6. Violent Brotherhoods: The Mafia from 1866 to the Stoppaglieri

1. In Recupero 1987, p. 69.

2. *Quarterly Review*, 1867, p. 104.

3. Colletta 1849, p. 38.

4. Alatri 1954, pp. 43–48; quotation p. 44. See also Scicchilone 1952.

5. Salvatore Schiavo in 1875 Hearings, p. 376. See also comments of Police Chief Rastrelli, p. 405.

6. Giacomo Pagano in 1875 Hearings.

7. 1875 Hearings, p. 300.

8. Ibid., p. 376.

9. Ibid., p. 477.

10. *Moti*, p. 143.

11. De Cesare 1969, pp. 697–98.

12. *ATTI*, June 11–12, 1875.

13. See Alatri 1954, pp. 366–81, and Merlino 1953, pp. 103–5.

14. See reconstruction in Alatri 1954.

15. ASP Gab Pref, b. 7, cat. 35.

16. *Quarterly Review* 1867, p. 100.

17. ASP Gab Pref, b. 7 cat. 35. Alatri 1954, pp. 221–22.

18. The expression "brigand corridor" comes from a speech by the minister of the

interior, Giovanni Nicotera, cited in Cavalieri 1925, pp. xiv and xv. On brigands, see Anonymous [De Menza] 1878.

19. *ATTI*, June 5, 1875.

20. Cutrera 1904, p. 56. Falzone 1979.

21. See Anonymous 1876.

22. ASP, Gab Pref, b. 19, cat. 20, fasc. 27, 1868.

23. Ibid.

24. See report from Albanese in ASP Gab Pref, b. 19, cat. 20, fasc. 27, 1868. Hess 1973, pp. 109–15; Foti 1875.

25. See letters from sub-prefect and mayor of Cefalù in ASP Gab Pref, b. 33, cat. 24, fasc. 45, 1875.

26. See Albanese to Medici, June 14, 1869, in ASP Gab Pref b. 18, cat. 20, fasc. 48, and letter of June 18 from Medici to Minister Lanza, ibid., fasc. 1. See also Alatri 1954, pp. 360–64.

27. Cited in Pagano 1875. The passage is also cited in the introduction to the 1875 Hearings, note. 8, but here the sentiments have been somewhat toned down.

28. *ATTI*, July 6, 1875.

29. *Moti*, p. 285.

30. Anonymous [N.N.] 1860.

31. De Cesare 1969, pp. 694 and 707.

32. Alatri 1954, pp. 313–15. Cf. the information about the Quattrocchi family of Termini Imeresi in ASP Gab Pref, b. 38, cat. 16, 1877.

33. ASP Gab Pref, b. 1, 1867.

34. Alatri 1954, p. 136.

35. Ibid., p. 177. There is a certain amount of duplication as well as discrepancies in the various lists.

36. Alatri 1954, p. 281.

37. Brancato 1975a.

38. Alatri 1954, pp. 313–15.

39. Ibid., pp. 330–33 and 407–8; ACS Min G & G, Misc affari penali, b. 45, fasc. 573, "Furto al Monte di Pietà di Palermo."

40. For Pasquale Quattrocchi, see ibid., n. 32. On these and others arrested, such as Giovanni Bivona and Francesco Burgo, see letter of September 7, 1874, from the *giudice istruttore* Chiaja to Prefect Rasponi, cited in Alatri 1954, p. 583.

41. La Mantia *verbale*.

42. Ibid.

43. Decoded telegram from Morena to minister of justice, February 18, 1879, ibid.

44. Ibid.

45. Nelli 1976, pp. 70–71.

46. Prosecutor, Palermo, to minister of justice, January 18, 1879, in La Mantia *verbale*.

47. See Morena's letters to Malsuardi of January 30 and March 3, 1877, in Malfattori.

48. Malsuardi, letter of January 30, 1877, ibid.

49. Morena to minister of justice, March 3, 1877; see also his letter of October 30, 1877, in Malfattori.

50. Morena may also have been aware of Pietro Calà Ulloa's 1838 report.

51. Morena, letter of March 3, 1877, in Malfattori.

52. Tajani referred to this in *ATTI*, June 11, 1875.

53. Cutrera 1900 gives the name as "Giovanni Minasola."

54. ASP Gab Pref, b. 8, cat. 2, fasc. 29, cited in Alatri 1954, p. 123.

55. ASP Gab Pref, b. 12, cat. 23, fasc. "Telegrammi," cited in Alatri 1954, p. 199.

56. ASP Gab Pref, b. 25, cat. 20, fasc. 53, cited in Alatri 1954, p. 365.

57. Merlino 1953, pp. 103–5.

58. Ibid.

59. Cutrera 1900, pp. 127–28.

60. Cutrera does not mention this last fact. See Morena's letter of March 3, 1877, in Malfattori.

61. Ibid.

62. Alatri 1954, pp. 541 and 543.

63. Report of the *sotto-procuratore* of Monreale, included in Morena's March 3, 1877, letter in Malfattori.

64. Cutrera 1900, p. 135.

65. See notes in Alatri 1954, pp. 177 and 314.

66. Cutrera 1900, pp. 133–35.

67. Loschiavo 1933.

68. See Fentress and Wickham 1992, chap. 5.

69. Vincenzo Calenda, *Relazione sull'amministrazione della giustizia nell'anno 1872*, reported Jan. 3, 1873 in *GdS*. See also Brancato 1973.

70. The remark by the minister of justice is contained in Morena's letter of March 3, 1877, in Malfattori.

71. Ibid.

72. See Stoppaglieri trial. This was all confessed by a prisoner several years later.

73. Lupo 1988a.

74. La Mantia *verbale*, letter from prosecutor, Palermo, to minister of justice, Rome, August 20, 1879.

75. We might add Cutrera to this "conspiracy of silence." See Genco 1991.

76. Note from prosecutor, Palermo, to minister of justice, January 18, 1879, and telegram, January 17, 1879, in La Mantia *verbale*.

77. Prosecutor, Palermo, to minister of justice, January 18, 1879, in La Mantia *verbale*.

78. La Mantia *verbale*, January 31, 1879.

79. Ibid.

80. Falzone 1971c.

81. De Cesare 1969, p. 707.

82. ASP Gab Pref, b. 16, cat. 16, fasc. 22, letter of chief of police to prefect, October 5, 1866, quoted in Scicchilone 1952, p. 199, and cited in Brancato 1953, p. 47, n. 1, and Alatri 1954, p. 138.

83. Nelli 1976, p. 43.

84. La Mantia *verbale*.

85. Cutrera 1900, pp. 152–60.

86. The Amoroso trial, from September 1883 to March 1884, received ample coverage in *GdS*.

87. Cutrera 1900, pp. 152–60.

88. Monreale prosecutor's report, quoted in Morena's letter of March 3, 1877, in Malfattori.

89. Loschiavo 1933. *Stuppa* meant "stopping." See also Fentress and Wickham 1992, pp. 192–95.

90. Nelli 1976, p. 43.

91. Cited in Brancato 1977, who, unfortunately, does not give the exact locality.

92. Ibid.

93. De Luca 1897; see also Lestingi 1884 and Colacino 1885.

94. Compare V. Macaluso 1872 and 1877, an account from nearby Canicattì.

95. Colacino 1885, pp. 178–79.

96. Ibid.

97. De Luca 1897, p. 435.

98. Ibid.

99. Lestingi 1884.

100. Ibid.

101. Colacino 1885, p. 182.

102. Falcone 1991, pp. 97–99.

103. Maas 1970, pp. 86–96; Demaris 1981, pp. 1–3, 19–22.

104. Caso 1908, pp. 9–10.

105. Colacino 1885, pp. 181–82.

106. Cutrera 1900, pp. 122–23.

107. In Lestingi 1884.

108. Morena, letter of March 3, 1877, in Malfattori.

109. Cutrera, 1900, p. 123.

110. Police report, 1859, cited in Viola 1984.

111. Colaccino 1885, pp. 184 and 180. Alongi 1977 gives other examples of a murderous frenzy.

112. Lestingi 1884.

113. Cf. Sangiorgi, pp. 376–78: "These are the characteristic banquets of the mafia in which blood *vendette* are ordered and planned and those already accomplished are celebrated."

114. De Luca 1897, p. 441.


### Chapter 7. Mafia and Politics: The *Caso* Notabartolo

1. The phrase comes from Cesareo 1907.

2. Marmo and Casarino 1988, p.

3. Ibid.

4. Iachello and Signorelli 1987, p. 126.

5. Ibid., p. 120.

6. Maggiore-Perni 1897, p. 27, cited in Iachello and Signorelli 1987.

7. See Barone 1987, passim, for the electoral figures; see also Maggiore-Perni 1897.

8. Giarrizzo 1975.

9. Ibid.

10. Brancato 1956, chap. 19, sec. 7.

11. Ragionieri 1976, p. 1804.

12. Barnaba 1981.

13. Cited in Ganci 1980, p. 31.

14. Romano, 1986, pp. 218–19.

15. Ganci 1964.

16. Manacorda 1975, pp. 67–69; S. Romano 1986, p. 234.

17. Cutrera 1900, p. 169, n. 1.

18. See, for example, Nicotri 1906.

19. Ganci 1958.

20. Recupero 1987, pp. 49–50.

21. Barone 1987, pp. 251–85, esp. pp. 280–81.

22. Alatri 1954, p. 535, n. 1; see also summary in Magri 1992.

23. Magri 1992 and Lupo 1988a. The early police reports are contained in Palizzolo.

24. Magri 1992, p. 28. Detailed reports of the crime and the subsequent trials are provided in *GdS*, *CdS*, and the socialist *Avanti*.

25. Lupo 1990 and Colajanni 1971.

26. Farini 1961, 2: 908.

27. Magri 1992, pp. 55–63.

28. Sangiorgi, letter of January 5, 1900.

29. Cutrera 1900, pp. 118–20.

30. Sangiorgi, report of December 27, 1899; Magri 1992, pp. 76–78.

31. Sangiorgi, report of December 27, 1899; see also the testimony of General Mirri during the Milan trial in *CdS*.

32. Sangiorgi, letter of April 14, 1899; see also Pezzino 1990a, pp. 163–64.

33. Sangiorgi, letter of November 8, 1898.

34. Colajanni 1971.

35. See Palizzolo, especially the letter from Colajanni dated February 25, 1893, and the reports of the subprefect of Termini Imeresi the following March in Min dell Int, dirgen PS.

36. Lupo 1990.

37. Notarbartolo 1977 p. 333; also Lupo 1990.

38. Nicotri 1906, p. 147.

39. He usually spoke only to advocate subsidies to the Florio shipping industries. According to Lupo 1990, however, he did rise once in 1896; it was to speak of his belief in homeopathic medicine.

40. Farini 1961, 2: 908.

41. See Pezzino 1990a, pp. 157–65; also Lupo 1990 and Magri 1992, pp. 55–57.

42. Pezzino 1990a, pp. 161–65 and Lupo 1990.

43. Lupo 1990.

44. Notarbartolo 1977; an undated rough draft for this exists in the archives in Palizzolo, ACS Min G&G, Misc affari penali. It is clear that the state took Leopolodo Notarbartolo's accusations very seriously. For a contrary view, see the letter of Cesare de Seta to the prime minister, Giuseppe Saracco, on October 24, 1900, which follows in the file.

45. Franchi 1904, p. 46. Colajanni 1971 makes the same claim.

46. See the evidence assembled in the Condronchi papers cited in Lupo 1990.

47. See March 1, 1893, letter from prefect to the minister of the interior concerning Colajanni's charges in Palizzolo, Min dell Int, dir gen PS.

48. Letter from Prosecutor Sighele to Minister of Justice, February 26, 1894, in Palizzolo, Min dell Int, dirgen PS.

49. In addition to the case in Favara, there was such an execution in Misilmeri; see reports concerning the Fontana nuova in Malffatori.

50. See Enzo Magri's account in Magri 1992, pp. 23–45.

51. Ibid., p. 94.

52. Ibid., pp. 147–49.

53. See *Avanti*, December 5 and 12, 1899.

54. Letter to Condronchi, October 5, 1899, in Lupo 1990.

55. Ibid. See also de Seta's memorandum of January 14, 1900, in Palizzolo, ACS Min G&G, Misc affari penali.

56. Magri 1992, pp. 120–25.

57. The attempt to capture Fontana can be followed in telegrams from December 9–18, 1899, de Seta's letter dates from December 13, 1899, in Palizzolo, Min dell Int, dir gen PS.

58. Lupo 1990 cites a number of socialist's comments on the Bologna verdict.

59. *Il Giorno*, January 8, 1900.

60. Cited in Poma 1976, p. 107.

61. *Avanti*, August 1, 1902.

62. Ciphered telegram from Sangiorgi to Pelloux, December 25, 1899, in Min dell Int. dir gen PS.

63. *Corriere della Sera*, August 18, 1902, reprinted in Mosca 1980, pp. 51–54.

64. Letter of November 16, 1902, in Palizzolo, Min dell Int, dir gen PS.

65. Renda 1973, p. 103.

66. Ibid.

67. Colajanni 1971, pp. 48 and 21.

68. Ibid., p. 110.

69. Ibid., p. 88.

70. Lupo 1990.

71. *GdS*, August 7–8, 1902.

72. Lupo 1990.

73. Petrusiewicz 1989, p. x.

74. Cited in Mangoni 1985, pp. 188–94.

75. Mosca 1923, p. 156.

76. Franchetti and Sonnino 1974, 1:129.

77. Mosca 1923, p. 123.


## Conclusion

1. See Introduction.

2. *Moti*, p. 78; the original reads "civilizatore violento, intempestivo, guastatore di molte interessi e offensore di molte suscettibilità."

3. Turrielo 1882, pp. 255–56.

4. Ibid.

5. See p. 243.

6. See p. 213–214.

7. De Luca 1897, p. 451.

# Bibliography

Abba, G. C. 1904. *La storia dei Mille*. Rome.

Accattati, Vincenzo. 1982. "La legislazione contra la mafia, alcuni dati fondamentali relative alle misure di prevenzione." Conferenza Magistratura Democratica, Palermo.

Agnetta, F. 1875. *La legge e l'arbitrio*. Rome.

———. 1892. "Breve osservazioni sulla pubblica sicurezza in Sicilia." Rome.

Ajello, A., 1868. *Angelo Pugliese ovvero don Peppino il Lombardo*. (Transcript of trial made by Ajello.) Palermo.

Alatri, P. 1954. *Lotte politiche in Sicilia sotto il governo della Destra*. Turin.

Alberti, Carmelo. 1977. *Il teatro dei pupi*. Milan.

Alongi, G. 1977. *La maffia* [1885; expanded ed. 1904]. Palermo.

Altamonte, A. 1979. *Mafia, briganti, Camorra, e letteratura*. Milan.

Amico, Giuseppe Gabriele. 1972. *Codice segreto della mafia*. Milan.

Angiolini, Alfredo, 1904a. Review of Di Blasio, *Costumi de'Camorristi*. *Scuola Positiva* 7, no. 4.

———. 1904b. Review of Nicefero, "Il gergo nei normali." *Scuola Positiva* 7, no. 4.

Anonymous [Michele Amari]. 1847. See Palmieri 1847.

Anonymous (N.N.), 1860. *Racconto dei fatti della rivoluzione del 1860 in Misilmeri*. Palermo.

Anonymous [G. Raffaele] 1866. "Lettere di un uomo politico ad un ministro." Palermo.

Anonymous. 1876a. "Oservazzioni sulla requisitorie del pubblico ministro contro il commendatore Giuseppe Albanese." Palermo.

Anonymous. 1876b. "Il brigantaggio in Sicilia: cause, rimedii." Palermo.

Anonymous [Giuseppe De Menza] 1878. "Profili e fotografie per collezione." Printed by *GdS*. Palermo.

*Anthropologie Criminelle* 1904. *Ve Congrès international d'anthropologie criminelle* [1901]. Amsterdam.

Arcoleo, G. 1897. *Palermo e la cultura in Sicilia*. Milan.

Asor-Rosa, Alberto. 1975. *La cultura*. In *La storia d'Italia*. Vol. 4. Turin.

Avarna di Gualtieri, G. 1928. *Ruggero Settimo nel Risorgimento siciliano*. Bari.

Aymard, Maurice, and Giuseppe Giarizzo. 1987. *La Sicilia*. In *La storia d'Italia: le regioni dall'Unità a oggi*. Turin.

Balletta, G. 1896. *Misilmeri nelle rivoluzioni siciliane del 1848–1860*. Palermo.

Bandi, Giuseppe. 1906. *I Mille*. Rome.

Barnaba, Enzo. 1981. *I fasci siciliani a Valguanera*. Milan.

Barone, G. 1987. "Egemonie urbane e potere locale (1882–1913)." In Aymard and Giarizzo 1987.

———. 1991. "Il tramonto dei Florio." In *Meridiana* 11–12, pp. 9–47.

Baviera Albanese, Adelaide. 1961. "Premessa per uno studio storicogiuridico sulla legislatura della Dittatura e della Prodittatura in Sicilia." In *La Sicilia e l'Unità d'Italia*. Milan.

Beltrami-Scalea, Martino. 1908. *Rivoluzioni di Sicilia (memorie storiche)*. 2 vols. Rome.

Bianco, Giuseppe. 1905. *La rivoluzione siciliana nel 1820*. Florence.

Blok, Anton. 1974. *The Mafia of a Sicilian Village, 1860–1960*. New York.

Bonanno, Joe (with Sergio Lalli). 1984. *Man of Honor*. New York.

Bonomo, Giuseppe. 1968. "Pitrè e la poesia popolare siciliana." In *Pitrè e Salamone-Marino* 1968.

Borghese, M. 1939. "La rivolta siciliana del 1866 in un diario del tempo." *Nuova Rivista Storica* 1–2, pp. 34–47.

Brancacccio di Carpino, Francesco. 1901. *Tre mesi nella Vicaria di Palermo: le barricate, Milazzo*. Naples.

Brancato, Francisco. 1953. "Origini e carattere della rivolta palermitana del settembre 1866." In *ArchSto-SO*, 3rd ser., pp. 139–205.

——. 1956. *La storia della Sicilia post-unificazione*. Vol.1 *Il primo ventennio*. Bologna.

——. 1958. "Mafia e brigantaggio." *Quaderni del Meridione* 1, nos. 3–4.

——. 1962. *Francesco Perroni Paladini*. Palermo.

——. 1964. "Genesi e psicologia della mafia." in *NQ/M* 2, no. 5, pp. 5–27.

——. 1966. " 'Il marchese di Rudinì e Francesco Bonafede e la rivolta del 1866." *NQ/M* 4, no. 16, pp. 460–91.

——. 1975a. "L'ultimo Mazzini e l'opposizione meridionale." *NQ/M* 12, no. 49 (January–March), pp. 13–40.

——. 1975b. "La Sicilia e l'inchiesta del Franchetti e Sonnino." *NQ/M* 13 (July–December), pp. 51–52.

——. 1975c. "La Sicilia e l'inchiesta del Franchetti e Sonnino nella stampa estera." *NQ/M* 13 (July–December), pp. 187–97.

——. 1977. "Le classi sociali in Sicilia alla vigilia della rivoluzione del 1860."*NQ/M* 15, no. 60, pp. 393–412.

——. 1978a. "La mafia nell'opinione publica e nelle inchieste dall'unità d'Italia al fascismo." In *Commissione parlamentare d'inchiesta sul fenomeno della mafia in Sicilia*. Rome.

——. 1978b. *Storia del parlamento italiano*. Vol. 7. Rome.

——. 1983. "Mafia e formazione dell stato unitario." *NQ/M* 21, no. 81, pp. 3–27.

Cafisi, Giuseppe. 1863. *Pubblica sicurezza in Sicilia*. Palermo.

Caizzi, Bruno. 1950. *Antologia della questione meridionale*. Milan.

Calcagno, A. 1927: *Cause ed effetti della rivoluzione siciliana del 1848*. Palermo.

"Calpurnio." 1908. *Dai ricordi del carcere del comm. Raffaele Palizzolo*. Palermo.

Calvi, Pasquale. 1851. *Memorie storiche e critiche della rivoluzione siciliana del 1848*. 2 vols. London.

Camillieri, Andrea. 1984. *La strage dimenticata*. Palermo.

Cammarata, Felice. 1969. *Pupi e mafia*. Palermo.

Cammareri Scurti, Sebastiano. 1899. *Il diritto della vita*. PSI Magazine. Trapani Province.

Campo, Marietta. 1884. *Vita politica della famiglia Campo*. Palermo.

Candeloro, Giorgio. 1990. *Storia dell'Italia moderna*, 2nd ed. [1956]. 9 vols. Milan.

Candida, Renato. 1956. *Questa mafia*. Caltanissetta.

Canosa, Romano. 1991. *Storia delle criminalità in Italia, 1845–1945.* Turin.

Capuana, Luigi. 1892. *La Sicilia e il brigantaggio.* Rome.

———. 1970. *Comparatico* [1876]. Trans. A. Alexander. Rome.

Casarrubea, Giuseppe. 1978. *I fasci contadini e le origini della sezioni socialisti della provicia di Palermo.* Palermo.

———. 1981. *Uomini e terra a Partinico.* Palermo.

———. and G. Cipolla. 1982. *Società e storia un territorio: il Partinicese.* Palermo.

Caso, Gemma. 1908. *Gianbattista Falcone e la setta dei Fratelli Pugnalatori.* Foggia.

Castiglione, Francesco Paolo. 1987. *Indagine sui Beati Paoli.* Palermo.

Catalanotto, Pina. 1982. "Dal carcere della Vicaria all'Ucciardone: una riforma europea nella Palermo borbonica." *NQ/M* 20, no. 79, pp. 383–413.

Cavalieri, Enea. 1925: "Introduzione alla seconda edizione." In Franchetti and Sonnino 1974. Florence.

*Cenno storico da Maggio 49 a Maggio 60.* 1883. (Documents published on the occasion of the dedication of the monument to the thirteen victims of April 14, 1860.) Palermo.

Cesareo, G. A. 1907. "Discorso." (Speech for funeral monument commemorating Abele Damiani.) Trapani.

Chiaramonte, S. 1901. "Il programma del '48 e i partiti politici in Sicilia." *ASS* 26.

Church, Frederick. 1899. *Brigantaggio e Società segrete nelle Puglie* [Translation of English publication]. Florence.

Ciotti, Giuseppe. 1866. *I casi di Palermo: cenni storici sugli Argomenti di Settembre 1866.* Palermo.

Cirese, Alberto Maria. 1968. "Giuseppe Pitrè tra storia locale e antropologia." In *Pitrè e Salamone-Marino* 1968.

Ciuni, Roberto. 1978. "Un secolo di Mafia." In *Storia di Sicilia.* Vol. 9. Società per la storia patria. Naples.

———. 1987. *Mafiosi.* Milan.

Cocchiara, Giuseppe. 1941. *Giuseppe Pitrè e le tradizioni popolari.* Palermo.

Colacino, Tommaso V. 1885. "La Fratellanza: associazione di Malafattori." *Rivista di Discipline Carcerarie*, pp. 177–89.

Colajanni, Napoleone. 1885. "La delinquenza in Sicilia e le sue cause." Palermo.

———. 1895. "Gli avvenimenti in Sicilia e le loro cause." Palermo.

———. 1950. "Settentrionale e Meridionale d'Italia" [1898] In Caizzi.

———. 1971. "Nel regno della mafia" [1901]. Palermo.

Colletta, Pietro. 1849. *Storia del reame di Napoli dal 1730 al 1825.* Florence.

Collison-Morley, Lacey. 1925. *Naples through the Centuries.* London.

[Le] *Condizioni del regno delle due Sicilie.* N.d. [1862]. Turin.

Cortese, Nino. 1934. *Il governo napoletano e la rivoluzione siciliana del 1820–21.* Naples.

———. 1951. *La prima rivoluzione separatista siciliana, 1820–1821.* Naples.

Costanza, Salvatore. 1964. "Un inchiesta poco nota sulla mafia." in *NQ/M* 2, no. 5.

———. 1966. "La rivolta contra i 'cutrara' a Casetellamare del Golfo (1862)." *NQ/M* 4, no. 16, pp. 419–38.

———. 1980. *I giorni di Gibillina.* Palermo.

———. 1989. *La patria armata.* Istituto per la Storia del Risorgimento italiano. Trapani Province.

Craven, the Hon. Keppel. 1984. *A Tour through the Southern Provinces of the Kingdom of Naplu* [1821] Excerpted in Desmond Seward, *Naples.* London.

Cressey, Donald R. 1969. *Theft of the Nation.* New York.

Croce, Benedetto. 1970. *History of the Kingdom of Naples.* Trans. Frances Frenaye. Chicago.

*Cronaca.* 1863. *Cronaca degli avvenimenti di Sicilia da Aprile 1860 a Marzo 1861.* Turin.

Cuidera, Leonardo. 1903. *Vivai criminali in Sicilia: Castellammare del Golfo Palermo.*

Curato, F., ed. 1970. *Gran Bretagna e Italian nei documenti della missione Minto.* 2 vols. Rome.

Cutrera, Antonio. 1900. *La mafia.* Palermo.

——. 1904. "Varsalona, il sui regno e le sue geste." From *Scuola Positiva.*

——. 1979. "I ricottari," [1896]. Palermo.

D'Alessandro, E. 1959. *Brigantaggio e mafia in Sicilia.* Florence.

De Benedetto, Luigi. 1867. *Sulle nostre condizionia danni e rimedii.* Palermo.

De Cesare, Raffaele. 1969. *La fine di un regno* [1909] Milan.

Delitti. 1983. *Delitti d'onore dell'800 tratti delle Assise di Palermo.* Naples.

De Luca, Francesco. 1894a. "Prigione e processi: una pagina di storia siciliana." Girgenti. Reprinted 1974, Agrigento.

——. 1894b. "I Fasci e la questione siciliana." Reprinted 1974, Agrigento.

——. 1897. "Favara," *Scuola Positiva* 7, no. 4.

Demaris, Ovid. 1981. *The Last Mafioso.* New York.

DeMayo, G. 1911. *Polizia d profezia di S. Maniscalco.* In *Memorie storiche militari.* Vol. 3. Rome.

De Menza, Giuseppe. 1877–78. *Le cronache d'Assise di Palermo.* 2 vols. Palermo.

De Seta, Cesare, and Leonardo Di Marco. 1980. *Palermo e la città della storia d'Italia.* Bari.

De Stefano, Francesco, and Francesco Luigi Oddo. 1963. *La storia della Sicilia, 1860–1910.* Bari.

D'Ideville, Henry. 1872. *Journal d'un diplomat en Italie.* Paris.

Di Matteo, S. 1967. *Anni roventi: la Sicilia dal 1943 al 1947.* Palermo

Di Mercurio, Gaspare. 1915. *La settimana dell'anarchia del 1866 a Palermo.* Palermo.

Documenti. 1910. *Documenti della rivoluzione siciliana.* Fiftieth anniversary commemorative edition. Palermo.

Duggan, Christopher. 1982. "Cesare Mori e il processo ai banditi delle Madonie." *NQ/M*, no. 79 (July–September).

——. 1989. *Mafia and Fascism.* New Haven.

Durkheim, Émile. 1932. *La division du travail social.* 6th ed. Paris.

Espinosa, Agostino degli. 1955. *Il regno del Sud.* Florence.

Falcionelli, Albert. 1936. *Les sociétés secrètes italiennes.* Paris.

Falcone, Giovanni. 1989. "La mafia tra criminalità e cultura." *Meridiana* 3, no. 1, pp. 199–211.

——. 1991. *Cose di Cosa Nostra.* In collaboration with Marcelle Padovani. Milan.

Falcone, Giuseppe. 1895. "Mafia e Omertà." (Conference held in 1895 at the Circolo calabrese in Naples.) Avellino.

Falzone, Gaetano. 1961. "Francesco Crispi e l'inserimento della rivoluzione siciliana nella rivoluzione italiana." In *La Sicilia e l'unità d'Italia.* Milan.

——. 1965. *La Sicilia tra il sette e l'ottocento.* Palermo.

——. 1971a. *Il Risorgimento a Palermo.* Palermo.

——. 1971b. "Le decapitazioni di Polizzi Generosa." In Falzone 1971a.

——. 1971c. "Gentiluomini di campagna con Garibaldi." In Falzone 1971a.

——. 1975a. *La storia della mafia*. Milan.

——. 1975b. "Il 'generale' Corrao." In *ArchSto-SO*, ser. 4, vol. 1, pp. 169–87.

——. 1979. "La strage degli ultimi briganti maurini in Sicilia" in *Rassegna Storica del Risorgimento* (July–September).

Fardella di Torrearsa, Vincenzo. 1887. *Riccordi sulla rivoluzione siciliana degli anni 1848 e 1849*. Palermo.

Farini, D. 1961. *Diario di fine secolo*. 2 vols. Rome.

Fazio, G. 1901. *Memorie giovanili*. La Spezia.

Fentress, James. 1982. "La nuova mafia e il non-governo del DC." *Rinascita*, no. 37, October 1.

——. 1984. "The Black Sheep." *Journal of the Anthropological Society of Oxford* (October)

——. 1996. "On the Good Use of Murder. *New Formations*, no. 30, pp. 106–21.

——. and Chris Wickham. 1992. *Social Memory*. Oxford

Fernandez, Dominique. 1966. *Les événements de Palerme*. Paris.

Fincati, [?]. 1881. *Un anno in Sicilia, 1877–78: riccordi di un bersaggliere*. Rome.

Fiore, Carlo. 1988. "Il controlo della criminalità organizzata nello stato liberale: strumenti legislativi e atteggiamenti della cultura giuridica." *Studi Storici* 29, no. 2 pp. 421–36.

Fiume, Giovanna. 1982. *La crisi sociale del 1848 in Sicilia*. Messina.

——. 1984a. "Mafia società e potere in Sicilia contemporanea." *Storia Contemporanea*, no. 5.

——. 1984b. *Le bande armate in Sicilia: violenza e orginazzione del potere (1819–1849)*. Palermo.

——. 1990. "Ci sono donne nella mafia." *Meridiana* 7–8, pp. 293–303.

Fortunato, Giustiano. 1926. *Il Mezzogiorno e lo stato italiano: discorsi politici*. Florence.

Foti, Domenico. 1875. *Sull'andamento di taluni pubblici servizi in Sicilia*. Palermo.

Franchetti, Leopoldo, and Sidney Sonnino. 1974. *Inchiesta in Sicilia* [1876]. 2 vols. Florence.

Franchi, Anna. 1904. *Mafia e giustizia (a proposito del processo Notarbartolo)*. Florence.

Francovich, Carlo. 1951. "Filippo Buonarroti e la Società dei Veri Italiani." In *Il Ponte*.

——. 1952. "Gli Illuminati di Weishaupt e l'idea egualitaria in alcune società segrete del Risorgimento." *Mondo Operaio*, no. 4, pp. 553–97.

Gaja, Fillipo. 1974. *L'esercito della lupara*. Milan.

Galante Garrone, Alessandro. 1972. *Filippo Buonarroti e i rivoluzionari dell'ottocento (1829–1837)*. Turin.

Galasso, Giuseppe, 1982. *L'altra Europa*. Milan.

Ganci, S. M. 1954. "Il movimento dei Fasci dei lavoratori nella provincia di Palermo." *Movimento Operaio* 6 (November–December), pp. 817–38. Reprinted 1977 in Ganci, *I Fasci dei lavoratori: saggi e documenti*. Caltanissetta/Rome.

——. 1958. *Il commissariato civile per la Sicilia del 1896*. Palermo/Florence.

——. 1964. "La mafia nel giudizio di Napoleone Colajanni." *NQ/M*, 2, pp. 59–71.

——. 1966. "La rivolta palermitana del settembre 1866." *NQ/M* 4, no. 16, pp. 381–419.

——. 1968a. *Cultura progressiva e tendenze conservatrici in Giuseppe Pitrè*. In *Pitrè e Salamone-Marino* 1968.

——. 1968b. *Italia anti-moderata*. Parma.

——. 1973. *Da Crispi a Rudinì*. Palermo.

——. 1975. "Giuseppe La Masa e il problema dell'insurrezione in Italia." *Il Risorgimento in Sicilia*, no. 1, pp. 183–92.

——. 1977. "Paolo Valera: follailo e mafiologo." *Archivio Storico Siciliano* 4, ser. 3.

——. 1979. "Lanza di Scalea: uno che disse 'no' al Duce." in *Giornale di Sicilia*, October 29.

——. 1980. "La Sicilia contemporanea." In *Storia di Napoli e della Sicilia*. Vol 9. Palermo.

Gattuso, L. 1972. *Mezzojuso: nel riccordo delle vestigie antiche*. Palermo.

Genco, Mario. 1991. *Il delegato*. Palermo.

Genovese, A. 1963. *Paceco: un comune agricola della Sicilia occidentale (1860–1923)*. Trapani.

Giarizzo, Giuseppe. 1970. "Sicilia politica: 1943–45." In *ArchSto-SO*.

——. 1975. "La Sicilia e la crisi agrari." In Giarizzo et al. 1975.

——. 1987. *Sicilia oggi*. In Aymard and Giarizzo 1987.

——. 1994. *Massoneria e illuminismo nell'Europa del settecento*. Milan.

——. et al. 1976. *I Fasci siciliani*. Vol 1. Bari.

Giordano, Nicola. 1970. *Storia e storiagrafia del moto palermitano del sette e mezzo*. Palermo.

Giuntella, V. E. 1950. "La Giacobina Repubblica Romana." In *Archivio della Società romena di Storia patria*. Vol. 73, 3rd ser., no. 4. Rome.

Godechot, Jacques. 1980a. *Regards sur l'époque révolutionnaire*. Toulouse.

——. 1980b. "P. J. Briot et la Carboneria dans le royaume de Naples." In Godechot 1980a, pp. 371–81.

——. 1980c. "Les français et l'unité italienne sous le Directoire" [1952]. In Godechot 1980a, pp. 303–27.

——. 1980d. "Le babouvisme et l'unité italienne (1796–1799)," [1938]. In Godechot 1980a, pp. 259–283.

——. 1980e. "Saliceti ministre du royaume de Naples sous Joseph Bonaparte et Murat." In Godechot 1980a, pp. 357–69.

Gori, Agostino. 1897. *Storia della Rivoluzione italiana durante il periodo delle riforme (1846—Marzo 1848)*. Florence.

Govone, Uberto. 1929. *Il Generale Govone: frammenti di memorie*. Turin.

Graziano, V. 1915. *La squadra di Santo Meli nel 1860 in Sicania*. Caltanissetta.

Greco D'Orioles, P. 1928. *La rivoluzione siciliana del 1848, nei suoi precedenti, nella sua azione, nelle sue conseguenze*. Genoa.

Gribaudi, Gabriella. 1990. "Mafia, cultura e gruppi sociali." *Meridiana* 7–8, pp. 359–77.

Grisanti, Cristoforo. 1981. *Folclore di Isnello* [1899; rev. ed. 1909] Palermo.

Guardione, Francesco. 1901. *Il domino dei Borboni in Sicilia, 1830–1847*. Palermo.

Guarino, Cresenzio. 1955. "Antologia della mafia." *Nord e Sud* 11, no. 12 (November).

Hess, Henner. 1973. *Mafia and Mafiosi: The Structure of Power* [1990]. Trans. Ewald Osers. Lexington, Mass.

Hobsbawm, E. J. 1959. *Primitive Rebels*. Manchester.

——. 1972. *Bandits*. Hemel Hempstead.

Iachello, E., and A. Signorelli. 1987. "Borghesia urbane dall'ottocento." In Aymard and Giarizzo 1987.

Labate, Valentino. 1904. *Un decennio di Carboneria in Sicilia (1821–1831)*. Rome/Milan.

La Bolina, Jack [Augusto Vecchi]. *La vita e le geste di Garibaldi*. Modena.

——. 1920. *Cronachetto del riso italiano*. Florence.

La Farina, Giuseppe. 1850–51. *Istoria documentata dell rivoluzione siciliana, 1848–1849.* 2 vols. Capolago.

La Masa, Giuseppe. 1850. *Documenti della rivoluzione siciliana del 1847–49 in rapporto all'Italia.* Turin.

Lazzari, Santi. 1892. *La mafia.* Messina.

Lea, Charles Henry, 1908. *The Inquisition in the Spanish Dependencies.* New York.

Leone, M. 1910. *Misilmeri nel 1860.* Palermo.

Lestingi, Giuseppe. 1884. "L'associazione della Fratellanza nella provincia di Girgenti." *Arch di Psichiatria . . .* 5, pp. 452–63.

Leti, Giuseppe. 1925. *Carboneria e Massoneria nel Risorgimento italiano.* Bologna.

Linares, Vincenzo. 1840. *Racconti popolari.* Palermo.

Loschiavo, Giuseppe Guido. 1933. *Il reato di associazione per delinquere nelle province siciliane.* Palermo.

Lupo, Salvo. 1984. "Nei giardini della Conca d'Oro." *Italia Contemporanea,* no. 156, pp. 43–53.

———. 1987. *L'utopia totalitaria del fascismo (1918–42).* In Aymard and Giarizzo 1987.

———. 1988a. "Tra centro e periferia. Sui modi dall'aggragazione politica nel Mezzogiorno contemporaneo." *Meridiana* 2, no. 2, pp. 13–51.

———. 1988b. " 'Il tenebroso.' sodalizio': un rapporto sulla mafia palermitana di fin ottocento." *Studi Storici,* no. 2, pp. 463–89.

———. 1990. "Tra banca e politica: il delitto Notarbartolo." *Meridiana* 7–8, pp. 119–57.

———, with R. Mangiameli. 1990. "Mafia di ieri, mafia di oggi." *Meridiana.*

Lyttelton, A. 1990. "Discutendo di mafia e camorra." *Meridiana* 7–8, pp. 337–47.

Maas, Peter. 1970. *La mela marcia* [Italian trans. of *The Valachi Papers.*] Milan.

Macaluso, E. 1971. *La mafia e lo stato.* Rome.

Macaluso, V. 1872. *Un primo saggio di esemplare punizione e prodezze del Prefetto Gen. Medici nell'Irlanda d'Italia.* Agrigento.

———. 1877. *Nuovi documenti della polizia politica in Sicilia.* Rome.

Mack Smith, Denis. 1950. "The Peasant Revolt in Sicily in 1860." In *Studi in onore di Gino Luzzati.* Milan.

———. 1954. *Cavour and Garibaldi.* Cambridge. [Reprinted 1985.]

———. 1959. *Italy.* Ann Arbor.

———. 1965. "The Latifondo in Modern Sicilian History." *Proceedings of the British Academy* 51.

———. ed. 1968. *The Making of Italy, 1796–1870.* New York.

———. 1969. *A History of Sicily.* 2 vols. London.

———. 1972. Introduction to *Giuseppe la Farina: scritti politici.* Palermo.

———. 1994. *Mazzini.* London.

Macry, P. 1988. *Ottocento famiglia: élites e patrimoni a Napoli.* Turin.

———. 1989. "Tra rendita e 'negozio' a proposito di borghesia urbane meridionale." *Meridiana* 3, no. 1, pp. 61–77.

Maggiorani, Vincenzo. 1866. *Il sollevamento della plebe di Palermo.* Palermo.

Maggiore-Perni, F. 1897. *Popolazione di Sicilia.* Palermo.

Magri, Enzo. 1992. *L'onorevole padrino.* Milan.

Malatesta, A. 1941. *Ministri, deputati, senatori dal 1848–1922.* Rome.

Manacorda, Gastone. 1972. "Crispi e la legge agraria." In Giarizzo et al. 1976.

———. 1975. "I Fasci e la classe dirigente liberale." In Giarizzo et al. 1975.

Manganaro, P. 1975. "La cultura e i Fasci." In Giarizzo et al. 1975.

Mangiameli, Rosario. 1981. "Le allegorie del buon governo: sui rapporti fra mafia e americani in Sicilia nel 1943." Facoltà di scienze politiche, Università di Catania.

——. 1987. *Le regione in guerra (1943–50).* In Aymard and Giarizzo 1987.

——. 1990. "Banditi e mafiosi dopo l'Unità." *Meridiana* pp. 7–8, 73–119.

Mangoni, Luisa. 1985. *Una crisi fine secolo.* Turin.

"Manifestazione." 1877. "Manifestazione della opinione pubblica nella provincia di Palermo." Palermo.

Maniscalco, C. 1936. *Influssi mazziniani Sicilia prima del '48.* In *Rassegna Storica del Risorgimento.* Rome.

Marini, G. 1864. *Il buco nell'acqua.* Sciacca.

Marino, G. C. 1964. *L'opposizione mafiosa.* Palermo.

——. 1972. *Socialismo del latifondo.* Palermo.

——. 1976a. *Partiti e lotta di classe in Sicilia.* Bari.

——. 1976b. "I fasci siciliani e la questione meridionale." *ArchSto-SQ* 72.

——. 1979. *Movimento contadino e blocco agrario nell Sicilia giolittian.* Palermo.

Marmo, Marcella. 1990. "Ordine e disordine: la camorra napoletana dell'ottocento." *Meridiana* 7–8, pp. 157–91.

——, and Olimpia Casarino. 1988. " 'Le invincibililoro relazioni': identificazione e controllo della camorra napoletana nell fonti postunitaria." *Studi Storici* 22, no. 29, pp. 384–419.

Martone, L. 1988. "Elezioni e brogli. Sui ricorsi al Consiglio di Stato in età liberale." *Meridiana* 2, no. 3, pp. 73–91.

Mathiez, Albert. 1928. "L'origine franc-comtoise de la Charbonnerie italienne." *AhRf,* no. 30 (November–December), pp. 551–73.

Maurici, Andrea. 1915. *Il regime despotico.* Palermo.

Mazzamuto, P. 1970. *La mafia nella litteratura.* Palermo.

——. 1975. "La Sicilia di Franchetti e Sonnino." *NQ/M,* nos. 51–52.

Mazzarella, Salvatore. 1986. *Polizzi o della rivoluzione.* Palermo.

*Memorie della Rivoluzione siciliana dall'anno MDCCCXLVIII.* N.d. Biblioteca G. Fortunato, Rome.

Mercadante-Carrala, T. 1911. *La delinquenza in Sicilia.* Palermo.

Merenda, Pietro. 1931. "I contingenti delle squadre siciliane d'insorti nei combattimenti di Palermo del 27, 28, 29, e 30 maggio 1860." *Rassegna Storica del Risorgimento,* suppl., pp. 180–202.

Merlino, F. S. 1953. *Questa é l'Italia.* Milan.

Messanan, Eugenio Napoleone. 1969. *Racalmuto nella storia di Sicilia.* Canicattì.

Messieno, P. 1866. *Le sette giornate di Palermo.* Palermo.

Messina, Giuseppe L. 1990. *L'etimologie di "mafia," "camòrra," e " 'ndranghetta."* Acireale.

Mirabella, Tomasso. 1961. "L'idea autonomistica in Sicilia dal 1848 al 1860." In *La Sicilia e l'Unità d'Italia.* Milan.

Miraglia, C. 1967. "1860 Palermo: gli avvenimenti del maggio e del giugno visti dall'amministratore di una casa nobile." *ASS* III, vol., pp. 309–77.

Missori, M. 1941. *Governi alte cariche dello stato e prefetti del regno d'Italia.* Rome.

Mistretta di Paola, Giuseppe. 1988. *La rivoluzione del 1848 nella Sicilia occidentale.* Alcamo.

Molfese, Franco. 1964. *Storia del brigantaggio dopo l'Unità.* Milan.

Monnier, Marc. 1863. *La camorra mystères: de Naples*. Paris.

Morelli, E. 1950. "Mazzianesimo siciliano." In *Gius Mazzini, saggi e ricerche*. Rome.

Mortillaro, Vincenzo (Marchese di Villarena). 1862. *Nuovo dizionario siciliano-italiano*. Palermo.

———. 1865. *Reminiscenze de 'miei tempi*. Palermo.

———. 1868. *I miei ultimi ricordi*. Palermo.

Morvillo, A. 1864. *Storia e processo della tortura del sordo-muto Antonio Cappello*. Palermo.

Mosca, Gaetano. 1923. *Elementi di scienza politica*. Turin.

———. 1939. *The Ruling Class*. Trans. Hannah D. Kahn. New York.

———. 1980. *Uomini e cose di Sicilia*. Sellerio. [Originally series of articles for *CdS* in 1905.]

[Il] Movimento Operaio Italiano. 1978. *Dizionario biografico*. Rome.

Mundy, Rear-Admiral Sir Rodney. 1859–61. *H.M.S. "Hannibal" at Naples and Palermo during the Italian Revolution*. London.

Natoli, Luigi. 1927. *Rivendicazioni attraverso le rivoluzioni siciliani del 1848–60*. Treviso.

Natoli–La Rosa, A. 1886. *La mafia in guanti gialli*. Messina.

Nelli, Humbert S. 1976. *The Business of Crime: Italians and Syndicated Crime in the U.S.* New York.

Nicastro, G. 1978. *Teatro e società in Sicilia (1860–1918)*. Rome.

Nicastro, S. 1913. *Dal quarantotto al sessanta*. Milan.

Niceforo, A. 1897. "La meccanica della migrazione e la criminalità." *Scuola Positiva* 7, no. 2.

———. 1977. *La delinquenza in Sardegna* [1897]. Cagliari.

Nicotri, G. 1902. "Mafia e brigantaggio in Sicilia." *Scuola Positiva della Giurisprudenza Penale* 10, p. 65.

———. 1906. *Rivoluzione e rivolte in Sicilia*. Palermo.

———. 1925. Il primato *della Sicilia nella libertà costituzionale*. Palermo.

Notarbartolo, Leopoldo. 1977. *Il caso Notarbartolo* [1897]. Palermo.

Novacco, Domenico, 1963. *L'inchiesta sulla mafia*. Milan.

———. 1967. *Storia del parlamento italiano*. Vol. 12. *1919–1925*. Palermo.

———. 1976. *La questione meridionale: ieri e oggi*. Turin.

Onufrio, E. 1877. "La mafia in Sicilia." *Nuovi Argomenti* 4, pp. 361ff.

Orsini, Felice. 1857. *Memorie politiche*. London. [Reprinted 1940, Milan.]

Pacifici, Vincenzo G. 1984. *Francesco Crispi (1861–1867): il problema del consenso allo stato liberale*. Rome.

Pagano, Giacomo. 1867. *Sette giorni d'insurrezione*. Palermo.

———. 1875. *Le presenti condizioni della Sicilia e i mezzi per migliorarle*. Florence.

———. 1877. *La Sicilia nel 1867–77*. Palermo.

Pagano, Luigi Antonio. 1925. "Gli arresti per le demonstrazioni del 2 e 3 luglio 1859 in Palermo." *ASS*, pp. 1445–55.

Palmieri, Niccolò. 1847. *Saggio storico e politico sulla Costituzione del regno di Sicilia infino al 1816 con un'appendice sulla rivoluzione del 1820*. With an introduction and notes by "Anonymous" [Michele Amari]. Lausanne.

Pantaleone, Michele. 1960. *Mafia e politica*. Turin.

Pantano, Edoardo. 1933. *Memorie, 1860–1870*. Bologna.

Paolucci, G. 1904. "Da Francesco Riso a Garibaldi: memorie e documenti sulla rivoluzione siciliana del 1860." ASS., pp. 103–93.

Paternò-Castello, Francesco. 1848. *Saggio storico-politico sulla Sicilia.* Catania.

Pecorini-Manzoni, C. 1876. *Storia del 15a divisione Türr nella campagna del 1860.* Florence.

Perez, Francesco. 1957. *La rivolta siciliana del 1848.* Palermo-Florence.

Petrusiewicz, Marta. 1989. *Il latifondo.* Venice.

Petta, Gioacchino. 1861. *Piana dei Greci nella rivoluzione siciliana del 1860.* Palermo.

Pezzino, Paolo. 1988. L'intendente e le scimmie: autonomia e accentramento nella Sicilia di primo ottocento." *Meridiana* 11, no. 3, pp. 25–55.

——. 1990a. *Una certa reciprocità di favori.* Milan.

——. 1990b. "La tradizione rivoluzionaria siciliana e l'invenzione della mafia." *Meridiana* 7–8, pp. 45–73.

——. 1992. *La congiura dei pugnalatori.* Milan.

Picone, G. 1937. *Memorie storiche agrigentine.* Agrigento.

Pieri, Piero. 1953–54. "La nazione armata in Carlo Pisacane." *Archivio Storico per le Province Napoletane* 34, pp. 371–407.

Pilo, Rosalino. 1914. "Esatta cronaca dei fatti avvenuti in Sicilia." [Letter from Pilo to La Masa, March, 25 1852.] *Il Risorgimento Italiano* 7, no. 1 (January–February) pp. 1–25.

Pitrè, Giuseppe. 1870–71. *Canti popolari siciliani.* Vol. 1. [Reprinted Palermo 1978.]

——. 1875. *Fiabe, novelle, e racconti popolari siciliani.* Palermo. [Reprinted Palermo 1978.]

——. 1882. "Il Vespro siciliano nelle tradizione popolare della Sicilia." Palermo. [Reprinted Palermo 1979.]

——. 1889. *La famiglia la casa la vita del popolo sicilano.* Palermo [Reprinted Palermo 1978.]

*Pitrè e Salamone-Marino.* 1968. *Il convegno di studi per il 50 anniversario della morte di Giuseppe Pitré e Salvatore Salamone-Marino.* Palermo.

Poma, R. 1976. *Onorevole alzatevi.* Florence.

Pontieri, Ernesto. 1943. *Il tramonto del baronaggio siciliano.* Florence.

——. 1949. *Il riformismo borbonico.* Florence.

*Quarterly Review.* 1867. "The Week's Republic in Palermo, 1866," article by "an English resident in Palermo." *Quarterly Review* (London) 122 (January–April), pp. 100–36.

Raffaele, Giovanni. 1883. *Rivelazioni storiche della rivoluzione del 1848 al 1860.* Palermo.

Ragionieri, Ernesto. 1976. *Dall'Unità a oggi.* In *Storia d'Italia.* Turin.

Rampolla, Giovanni Cirillo. 1986. *Suicidio per mafia.* Preface, Pasquale Marchese; introduction, Giovanna Fiume. Palermo.

Recupero, A. 1987. *La Sicilia all'Opposizione (1848–74).* In Ayamard and Giarizzo 1987.

Renda, A. 1900. *La questione meridionale.* Palermo.

——, and F. Squillace. 1901. "Follie criminelle en Calabre." In *Anthropologie Criminelle.*

Renda, Francesco. 1968. *Risorgimento e classi popolari in Sicilia.* Milan.

——. 1973. "Il processo Notarbartolo ovvero per una storia dell'idea di mafia." In *Socialisti e cattolici in Sicilia (1900–1904).* Palermo.

——. 1976. "Funzione e bassi sociali della mafia." In *La mafia quattro stadi.* Bologna.

——. 1977. *I Fasci siciliani.* Turin.

——. 1984–87. *Storia della Sicilia, 1860–1917.* 3 vols. Palermo.

——. 1987. *La "questione sociale" e i Fasci (1874–94).* In Aymard and Giarizzo 1987.

Riccobono, Francesca, 1976. "Movimenti politici in Sicilia dal 1863 al 1870." Part 1 and 2. *NQ/M* 14, nos. 55 and 56, pp. 262–94, 395–410.

Riggio, G. 1978. *Vita e cultura agrigentina del '900*. Caltanissetta.

Rizzoto, G. 1962. *I mafiusi di la Vicaria di Palermo* [1862]. Lo Schiavo.

"Romano Italiano, A." 1875. "Rimedii per vincere e punire il malandrinaggio." Rome.

Romano, F. 1960. *Misilmeri nel Risorgimento*. Palermo.

Romano, S. F. 1952. *Momenti del Risorgimento in Sicilia*. Messina.

——. 1958. *Storia della Sicilia post-unificazione*. Vol. 11. *Ultima ventenni del XX secolo*. Palermo.

——. 1959. *Storia dei Fasci siciliani*. Bari.

——. 1966. *Storia della mafia*. Verona.

Romano, Sergio, 1986. *Crispi*. Milan.

Romeo, Rosario. 1973. *Il risorgimento in Sicilia*. Bari.

Rossi, Luciano. 1982. *Carlo Pisacane*. Milan.

Russo, N., ed. 1964. *Antologia della mafia*. Palermo.

Sacerdote, Giuseppe. 1957. *Vita di Garibaldi*. Milan.

Saitta, Armando. 1986. *Ricerche storiografiche su Buonarroti e Babeuf*. Rome.

Salamone-Marini, S. 1899. *Costumi e usanze dei contadini di Sicilia*. Palermo. [Reprinted Palermo, 1968.]

Salemi, Leonardo. 1934. "Carboneria, carbonari, e Borbonici nei moti del 1820 in Sicilia." *La Cultura Moderna* 63, pp. 429–333.

Salvadori, Massimo. 1976. *Il mito del buongoverno*. Turin.

Salvo, Roberto. 1982. "Mosca, la mafia, e il caso Palizzolo." *NQ/M*, no. 77 (January).

Sansone, Alfonso, 1889. "La Sicilia nel trentesette." *ASS* 14, pp. 362–566.

——. 1891. *Cospirazioni e rivolte di Francesco Bentivenga e compagni*. Palermo.

Saporito, V. 1926. *Trenta anni di vita parlamentare*. Rome.

Scalici, Emanuele. 1883. *La mafia siciliana*. Palermo. [Reprinted Palermo, 1984.]

Sceusa, Francesco. 1877. *La mafia ufficiale*. Naples.

Schiro, Don Giuseppe. 1931. "Monreale nel centenario dell'Unità d'Italia." *ASS*, ser. 111, vol. 11, pp. 199–211.

Scicchilone, Giuseppe. 1952. *Documenti sulle condizioni della Sicilia dal 1860 al 1870*. Rome.

Sewell, Wm. H., Jr. 1987. "Beyond 1793. Babeuf, Louis Blanc, and the Genealogy of 'Social Revolution.'" In K. M. Baker, F. Furet, M. Ozouf, and C. Lucas, eds. *The French Revolution and the Creation of Modern Political Culture*. London.

"Siculo Modestino." 1877. "Il brigantaggio e il governo: rivelazioni." Florence.

Sighele, Scipio. 1894. *I delitti della superstizioni*. Milan.

——. 1895. *La folla delinquente*. Venice.

——. with G. Bianchi and G. Ferrero. 1893–95. *Il mondo criminale italiano*. Turin.

Soanen, H. 1928. "La Franc-Maçonnerie et l'armée pendant la Révolution et l'Empire." *AhRf*, no. 30 (November–December), pp. 530–40.

Spiridone, Franco. 1899. *Storia della rivolta del 1856 in Sicilia organizzata dal Barone Francesco Bentivegna in Mezzoiuso e da Salvatore Spinuzza in Cefalù*. Rome.

Titone, Virgilio, 1957. "Considerazioni sulla mafia." In *Scienze giuridiche, politiche e sociali*. Palermo.

——. 1964. *Storia: mafia e costume in Sicilia*. Palermo.

Tommasi-Crudeli, T. 1871. *La Sicilia in 1871*. Florence.

Traina, A. 1868: *Nuovo vocabolario Siciliano-Italiano*. Palermo.

Tranfaglia, Nicola. 1983a. "Ma il brigante é un'altra cosa." *La Repubblica*, February 21.

———. 1983b. "Si mi diranno pazzo." *La Repubblica*, March 22.

Trevelyan, G. M. 1907. *Garibaldi and the Defence of Rome.* London.

———. 1909. *Garibaldi and the Thousand.* London.

Turiello, Pasquale. 1882. *Governo e governanti in Italia.* Bologna.

Turrisi-Colonna, Nicola. 1864. *Cenni sullo stato attuale della sicurezza pubblica in Sicilia.* Palermo.

Uccello, Antonio. 1974. *Carcere e mafia nei canti popolari siciliani.* Bari.

Umiltà, Angelo. 1878. *Camorarra et mafia.* Neuchâtel.

Vaccaro, Angelo. 1899. "La mafia" *Rivista d'Italia* 2, vol. 3.

Vaina, Michele. 1911. *Popolarismo e Nasismo in Sicilia.* Florence.

Valenti, Angela. 1965. *Gioacchino Murat e l'Italia meridionale* [1941]. Turin. [Enlarged ed.]

Ventura, Francesco. 1821. *De'diritti della Sicilia per la sua nazionale indipendenza.* Palermo.

Villari, Pasquale. 1979. *Le lettere meridionali* [1875]. Naples.

Villari, Raffaele. 1881. *Cospirazione e rivolta.* Naples.

Villari, Rosario, ed. 1976. *Il sud nella storia d'Italia.* 2 vols. Bari.

Viola, Aldo Maria. 1984. "L'attività cospirativa in Sicilia nel decennio della restaurazione Borbonica (1849–1860)." *NQ/M* 22, no. 87–88, pp. 223–47.

Winnington-Ingram, H. F. 1889. *Hearts of Oak.* London.

# Index

La Mantia, Rosario, 197–98, 207–9
La Masa, Giuseppe, 44, 46–47, 50
  in 1848 rebellion, 51–52, 56–57, 62, 68
  in 1860, 94
  at Gibilirossa, 105–6
Landi, General Francesco, 95, 100
Lanza, General Ferdinando, 101, 111
  offers truce, 113–14
Lanza, Pietro (prince of Scordia), 58, 67
Lanza di Trabia, Ottavio, 90
La Porta, Luigi, 82, 92, 117
  responds to Fortuzzi, 192
Lercara Friddi, 129–31, 132–33, 174
Leone, Antonino, 236
Lestingi, Giuseppe, 218
*lettere di scrocco* [extortion letters], 131, 166,
  184
Licata, Salvatore, 184–85
Linguaglossa, prince of, 194
Lipari, Giuseppe, 205
livestock theft, 132–33, 174–75
Lo Coco, Don Angelo, 214
Lombroso, Cesare, 218
Lo Monaco, Lorenzo, 234
Loschiavo, Giuseppe Guido, 205
Lupo, Salvo, 174, 208

*macinato*, 61, 63
Mack Smith, Denis, 20
Madonna degli Stigmati, Convent of the,
  143
*maestranza*, 28, 30, 49–50
*Maffia. See* mafia
mafia
  and the 1867 inquiry, 148–49
  in 1880s, 224–25
  Giuseppe Albanese and, 186
  Amoroso family, 210–11
  and the *carbonaro*, 156–57
  Colajanni on, 246–47
  different notions of, 6–7
  etymology and legends of, 152–55
  in Favara, 214–16, 218–20
  Gualterio on, 2–3, 147, 188, 253–54
  and the influential classes, 155–56
  initiation rites of, 217–18
  involvement in Notarbartolo murder,
    239–40
  and the Italian government, 258–59
  of Malaspina, 166–72
  of Monreale, 197–99, 200–210
  Morena on, 199–201
  the police view of, 159–61
  and popular culture, 157–59
  and revolution, 228–29, 257
  and Sangiorgi, 172–80, 248

and the Sicilian ruling class, 151–52,
  224–25, 252
Villabate *cosca* of, 233–34, 236, 238–39
*mafiusu/mafiusa*, 152. *See also* mafia
*Mafiusi di la Vicaria, I,* 157–59
Magenta, battle of, 78
Maggiorani, Vincenzo, 155
Magione, Piazza, 89–90
Majo, General de, 53, 55, 57
Mala, the, 157
Malaspina, 166–72
Malsuardi, Prefect Antonio, 198–200
  and Palizzolo, 236
Manin, Daniel, 75
Maniscalco, Salvatore, 83–87, 91, 92, 101,
  111, 137
  and the *malavita*, 186–87, 199
  and the Sicilian ruling class, 150
Mano Fraterna. *See* Fratellanza
*manutengolo*, 148, 160–61
Maraviglia, Giuseppe, 198, 209–10, 213
Marchesano, Giuseppe, 241
Maria Carolina of Naples, 19
Marineo, in cholera riots, 38
Marino, Jessie White, 76
Marino, Salvatore, 196–98, 203, 207–9
Marmo, Marcella, 223
Marsala
  in 1820, 33
  Garibaldi and, 95
Marx, Karl, 36
Massa-Quarnero, 101
Matranga, Salvatore, 198, 209–10, 213
Maurigi, Judge Giovanni, 123, 162–63
Mazzini, Giuseppe, 43, 73–79
  and Garibaldi, 116
  and secret revolutionary committee in
    1860, 90
  attempted uprising in 1870, 195–96
Medici, General Giacomo, 94, 151, 195, 202
  capture of Badia by, 138
  capture of Pugliese by, 138–39, 185
  report on Partinico by, 189–90
Meli, Santo, 125–26
Messina, 22, 32
  during 1820 revolt, 32–33
Messina, Giuseppe L., 154
Metternich, 22
Mezzoiuso, 81–82
Mezzomonreale, 175
Micato, Gabriele. *See* Pugliese, Angelo
Miceli, Antonino, 134
Miceli, Davide, 207
Miceli, Francesco, 149, 207
  murder of, 234
  Nicotri on, 237